D0462546

Uncle John's BATHROOM READER.

TUNES INTO TV

By the
Bathroom Readers'
Institute

Bathroom Readers' Press
Ashland, Oregon

OUR "REGULAR" READERS RAVE!

"Please don't tell, but as a plumber, I get a lot of chances to read your books on the clock. Great stuff."
—Steve

"I love your books—every single one is a work of art. You all deserve medals for doing your duty to this country."
—Sam

"Upon retirement, I found myself spending more time on the throne, reading the newspaper and doing sudoku. But that only took up one visit, and now I have my *Bathroom Readers*."
—Thomas

"Love the books! Many a leg cramp has resulted from 'extended stays,' but all are worth it!"
—Pete

"I love your books, and so does my son, who is now 22 and has been reading them (often out loud to his friends) since he was a teenager."
—Kelli

"Keep on rolling with your long and useful compendiums of knowledge! They have become eagerly anticipated gifts for my husband. I can hear him cracking himself up right now..."
—Cree

"Just wanted to say I love your *Bathroom Readers*. So much great information. They are a joy to read."
—Lillian

"My 13-year-old son has been an avid *Bathroom Reader* reader for years. Our 9-year-old, at his brother's encouragement, started reading them, too. After one year, he has advanced three reading levels. Thank you, Uncle John!"
—Evelyn

UNCLE JOHN'S BATHROOM READER®
TUNES INTO TV

For information, write:
The Bathroom Readers' Institute, P.O. Box 1117,
Ashland, OR 97520
www.bathroomreader.com • 888-488-4642

Cover design by Michael Brunsfeld, San Rafael, CA
(*Brunsfeldo@comcast.net*)

ISBN-13: 978-1-60710-181-9 / ISBN-10: 1-60710-181-5

Library of Congress Cataloging-in-Publication Data
Uncle John's bathroom reader tunes into tv.
    p. cm.
Includes bibliographical references.
ISBN 978-1-60710-181-9 (pbk.)
1. Television programs—United States—Miscellanea.
2. Television broadcasting—United States—Anecdotes.
I. Bathroom Readers' Institute (Ashland, Or.)
PN1992.9.U53 2011
791.4502'07—dc22
                              2010046061

Printed in the United States of America
First Printing
1 2 3 4 5   15 14 13 12 11

THANK YOU!

The Bathroom Readers' Institute sincerely thanks the people whose advice and assistance made this book possible.

Gordon Javna	Mark McCracken
Brian Boone	Adam Bolivar
Amy Miller	Claudia Bauer
John Dollison	Claire Breen
Jay Newman	Scarab Media
Thom Little	JoAnn Padgett
Sharilyn Carroll	Melinda Allman
Michael Brunsfeld	Dan Mansfield
Angela Kern	Monica Maestas
Jack Mingo	Amy Ly
Jill Bellrose	Annie Lam
Megan Todd	Ginger Winters
Michael Kerr	Tom Mustard
William Dooling	Sydney Stanley
Brandon Hartley	David Calder
Malcolm Hillgartner	Karen Malchow
Jahnna Beecham	Media Masters
Eleanor Pierce	Publishers Group West
Elizabeth Harvey	Bloomsbury Books
Jessika Shannon	Raincoast Books
James Greene Jr.	Porter the Wonder Dog
Michael Conover	Thomas Crapper

CONTENTS

Because the BRI understands your reading needs, we've
divided the contents by length as well as subject.

Short—a quick read

Medium—2 to 3 pages

Long—for those extended visits, when something
a little more involved is required

* Extended—for those leg-numbing experiences

STAY TUNED...

S ince you can't haul your TV into the bathroom, we made this book so you could still get your fix on the throne: *Uncle John's Bathroom Reader Tunes into TV.* Why a whole book about television? Because it's our national pastime! Sorry, mom, but all that time spent in front of a glowing screen instead of playing outside was worth it, because TV has given us role models, life lessons, cautionary tales, history, and world events... not to mention characters, commercials, and catchphrases. Television is a world unto itself, and in this book, we've covered pretty much every aspect of it. You'll find:

• **The most-watched:** stories behind TV's biggest hits, from *Star Trek* to COPS.

• **The unwatched:** shows that never aired, shows so bad that no one watched, and shows so *good* that no one watched.

• **The stars:** the giants of the small screen, from Ed Sullivan to Bill Cosby, Lucy to Oprah, and even Philo T. Farnsworth.

• **The origins:** the big 4 networks, *The Golden Girls, Modern Family, The Monkees,* and the evening news.

• **The scandals:** stars getting fired, producers getting angry, and shows getting canceled.

All that, plus soap operas, game shows, kids' shows, television in other countries, how a TV works, and our attempt to explain what happened on *Lost.* (We've also included a handful of articles from the BRI archives because they were so good we just had to include them in our pursuit of the most all-encompassing TV book ever.)

On behalf of all of us at BRI headquarters—which is just north of the Ponderosa Ranch, just east of the 4077th, south of 77 Sunset Strip, 30 miles from 30 Rock, and forever Lost in Space—happy viewing, er, reading.

And as always,

Go With the Flow!

—Uncle John

TV FIRSTS

Everything started somewhere, although not on channel 1.

First TV show. The first small-scale "experimental" broadcast to the few research institutions, companies, and individuals in the U.S. who owned a TV set occurred on April 30, 1939. What was shown? The opening ceremony of the New York World's Fair.

First commercial TV stations. On July 1, 1941, the FCC approved two TV stations to broadcast TV signals: New York-based television affiliates of radio networks CBS (WCBW) and NBC (WNBT).

First TV commercial. An ad for Bulova watches aired on WNBT's first full day of programming on July 1, 1941. It ran during a baseball game between the Brooklyn Dodgers and the Philadelphia Phillies. Cost of the ad time: $4.

First Saturday morning kids' TV. At 7 a.m. on August 19, 1950, ABC premiered a one-hour block of TV made for children. The hour consisted of *Animal Clinic*, which featured live animals and interesting facts about them, and *Acrobat Ranch*, a circus-themed variety show hosted by two acrobats.

First prime-time cartoon. Collections of cartoons originally made for movie theaters (*Tom & Jerry, Bugs Bunny*) aired on TV throughout the 1940s and '50s, but the first made-for-TV cartoon to air at night was *The Flintstones*, premiering in 1960 on ABC.

First interracial kiss on American TV. Sammy Davis Jr. and Nancy Sinatra kissed—on the cheek—on Sinatra's 1967 variety show *Movin' with Nancy*. (The first interracial kiss between fictional characters: Captain Kirk kissed Uhura on *Star Trek*, 1968.)

First major dramatic TV role for a black actor. African Americans had appeared on TV since the late '40s, but always in minor

---

Studies show: TV is the third most talked-about subject, after "cost of living" and "family."

roles. The first black actor to headline a show was Bill Cosby on *I Spy* (1965–68).

First TV show broadcast on the Internet. *The Drew Carey Show* broadcast an episode online and on ABC simultaneously in 1996.

First gay character. A 1972–73 ABC sitcom called *The Corner Bar* featured a character named Peter Panama, played by Vincent Schiavelli. It was the first time a show had a regular character who was explicitly identified as a homosexual.

First full-color broadcast. On January 1, 1954, NBC made the first nationwide, all-color telecast with its coverage of the Tournament of Roses Parade from Pasadena, California.

First spin-off. The CBS Western series *Trackdown* begat the bounty hunter drama *Wanted: Dead or Alive* in 1958.

First belly button on display. Censors in the '60s were still nervous about showing something as provocative as a female navel, so they compromised with the producers of the 1965–66 beach sitcom *Gidget:* Bikini-clad extras could show their belly buttons, but lead actress Sally Field could not.

First condom commercial. In 1975 KNTV, a San Jose station, ran an ad for Trojan condoms despite a nationwide government ban on advertising contraceptives on TV. (It aired only once.)

First fall slate of programs to produce no hits. NBC's fall 1983 schedule included nine new programs: *Manimal, Jennifer Slept Here, Boone, Bay City Blues, We Got It Made, Mr. Smith, For Love and Honor, The Rousters,* and *The Yellow Rose.* For the first time ever, all were canceled before the spring.

First morning show. NBC's *Today* debuted on January 14, 1952. It was hosted by newsman David Garroway.

First toilet on TV. The very first episode of *Leave It to Beaver* in 1957 was shelved for a few weeks by network censors because it showed a toilet. (Wally and the Beav tried to keep a baby alligator in the toilet tank.)

In 1987 Ronald Reagan turned down a $1 million offer to guest star on *Dynasty*.

DRAWN FROM LIFE

*Where do cartoon characters come from? You might be
surprised at the inspirations behind some of these.*

ROSIE. Voiced by Jean Vander Pyl, the Jetsons' robot maid
was based on Shirley Booth's performance of a wisecracking maid on the 1960s sitcom *Hazel*. Hazel called her boss
"Mr. B.," so Rosie called George Jetson "Mr. J."

KRUSTY THE CLOWN. When *Simpsons* creator Matt Groening was a kid in Portland, Oregon, in the 1960s, he often watched
a gravelly voiced, world-weary TV clown named Rusty Nails. "He
was actually a very sweet clown," says Groening, "with an incredibly frightening name."

DEXTER'S LABORATORY. For an animation project at an art
institute in 1992, budding artist Genndy Tartakovsky drew a tall,
goofy-looking ballerina. Thinking she needed a nemesis, he drew a
nerdy little boy with big glasses. Tartakovsky decided the boy was
a genius scientist, just like his own older brother. But the mischievous ballerina, named Dee Dee, was modeled on Tartakovsky himself: When he was young, he would annoy his brother by messing
with all of his scientific equipment. Tartakovsky built *Dexter's Laboratory* around the duo, which premiered in 1995.

RUGRATS. In 1991 cartoon producer Arlene Klasky had one day
to come up with a new series for Nickelodeon. She and her writing partner, Paul Germain, had a few ideas, but nothing was working. Then Klasky looked at her baby and wrote a few things down
in her notebook. "Then I called Paul and just read him my notes:
'If babies could talk, what would they say?'" The next day, they
pitched the idea to Nickelodeon…and *Rugrats* was born.

BUTT-HEAD. When animator Mike Judge was in college, he
lived next door to a 12-year-old kid who called himself "Iron-Butt." Judge recalls, "Supposedly, you could kick him in the butt
as hard as you wanted, and it wouldn't hurt him." A troublemaker,
Iron-Butt used to sneak into Judge's house and once burned down
a tree. He became the inspiration for Beavis's friend, Butt-head.

"The great thing about animation is that you don't have to pay the actors squat." —Homer Simpson

SITCOM ZINGERS

Some of the best verbal put-downs in the history of TV.

Stuart: I take my coffee the way I take my women.
Stacy: Are you sure you want to pay $75 for a cup of coffee?
—*Spin City*

Frank: I didn't come here to be liked.
Radar: You certainly came to the right place.
—*M*A*S*H*

Louie: Do you know what the difference is between people like you and people like me?
Alex: Two million years of evolution.
—*Taxi*

Ralph: You have just made fun of something very big that's close to my heart.
Alice: The only thing big that's close to your heart is your stomach.
—*The Honeymooners*

Diane: Do you know the difference between you and a fat, braying ass?
Sam: No.
Diane: The fat, braying ass would.
—*Cheers*

Meg: Guess what? I made the Flag Girl squad!
Stewie: Yes, good for you. Now you can be somewhere else when the boys don't call.
—*Family Guy*

Jessie: Do you realize we haven't argued for 15 seconds?
Slater: It was 20. Shut up.
—*Saved by the Bell*

Rose: Can I ask a dumb question?
Dorothy: Better than anyone I know.
—*The Golden Girls*

Frasier: Niles, I would shave my head for you.
Niles: A gesture which becomes less significant with each passing year.
—*Frasier*

Dave: Have you ever heard the expression, "It's easier to catch flies with honey instead of vinegar"?
Bill: Have you ever heard the expression "Only a hillbilly sits around and tries to figure out the best way to catch flies"?
—*NewsRadio*

Mary Tyler Moore's first acting job: She played an elf in an appliance commercial.

WEIRD GAME SHOWS

Here are some of the strangest game shows ever to air on American television.

A**CROSS THE BOARD (1959)** Concept: Two contestants competed to see who could finish a crossword puzzle first. (Have you ever watched somebody else fill out a crossword puzzle? It's pretty boring.)

LUCKY PARTNERS (1958) Host Carl Cordell read part of the serial number on a dollar bill. Players in the studio—and viewers at home—won prizes if they had a dollar bill with matching numbers. Because of the large number of bills in circulation, there were rarely any winners on *Lucky Partners*.

CELEBRITY BOWLING (1971) That's pretty much it: Celebrities came on and bowled. Frequent guests included Telly Savalas, Roy Rogers, Bobby Darin, Carroll O'Connor, and Sammy Davis Jr. Amazingly, the show ran for seven years and inspired a similar show called *Celebrity Tennis* in 1974.

BALANCE YOUR BUDGET (1952) Between segments by financial experts who provided budgeting techniques and home economics tips, housewives who were in debt competed to win a treasure chest full of cash.

TRASHED (1994) Contestants tried to answer questions correctly. If they didn't, the opposing team got to smash the losing team's prized possessions with a sledgehammer.

THE GRUDGE MATCH (1991) Real people came on to settle a dispute or disagreement in a boxing ring, using "weapons" such as oversize boxing gloves, cream pies, and water balloons. At the end of the show, the studio audience voted on a winner.

E.S.P. (1958) Led by host Vincent Price, two contestants were placed in isolation booths, and experiments were conducted to see which person had stronger psychic abilities. After three weeks of shows in which no psychic powers were ever detected, it became a "news" show about E.S.P. (It lasted only a month.)

Incredible Hulk producers changed Bruce Banner's name to David. (Bruce was too "comic-booky.")

BENSON SAVED MY LIFE!

Kids learn a lot from TV. Sometimes they even learn good things.

• One summer day in 2010, a five-year-old boy named Andrew was playing at a New Jersey lake when he wandered into deeper water and began struggling. His mother tried to help, but lost her footing on the slippery rocks and started panicking. Then Andrew disappeared beneath the surface. Suddenly, a neighbor, 8-year-old Reese, ran to the water's edge and dove in. A few long seconds later, Reese surfaced, holding Andrew around his shoulders, and pulled him safely to shore. The save was textbook lifeguarding…a skill Reese had learned from a *SpongeBob SquarePants* episode in which SpongeBob becomes a lifeguard.

• Miriam, 12, from Long Beach, New York, was in music class in 2010 when her friend Allyson started choking on a piece of gum. Miriam administered the Heimlich maneuver and the gum popped out. She later said, "I saw in my head Squidward with his clarinet lodged in his throat, and then SpongeBob does the Heimlich and the clarinet comes flying out of his mouth!"

• In 1986 Tanya, 6, started choking on a piece of candy. Her friend Brent, 5, ran over and squeezed her from behind. Brent's mother screamed for him to stop, but thankfully he didn't listen—a moment later the candy popped out and Tanya started breathing again. Where'd he learn that maneuver? "Benson was choking," said Brent, who'd recently watched a rerun of *Benson*. "A guy squeezed him and lifted him up and saved Benson!"

• "The farther I got out, I could tell the ice was getting thinner, but I didn't think I was going to break through," said 13-year-old Joe…who broke through. With only his head and hands above the surface at a neighborhood pond in Shawnee, Kansas, Joe began to panic. But then he heard the calls of his older brother, Jacob: "Don't flop around! Remember *Man vs. Wild*? Stay calm!" Joe followed his instructions, and a few minutes later, firefighters rescued him. Had Joe not remained calm, said one of the rescuers, he'd most likely have drowned. The brothers credit the Discovery Channel show with saving Joe's life.

Billy Graham *never* watched TV on Sunday…except to see the Beatles on *Ed Sullivan* (1964).

HISTORICAL GOOFS

If a series takes place in the past, set designers and prop masters do their best to make sure that all the details are historically accurate. But sometimes they slip up.

Series: *Freaks and Geeks* (1999–2000)
Item: In one episode, Bill (Martin Starr) digs into a carton of I Can't Believe It's Not Butter! margarine. In another, Sam (John Francis Daley) squirts ketchup out of a plastic bottle.
Goof: The show takes place in 1980. I Can't Believe It's Not Butter! wasn't marketed until 1986; ketchup was sold only in glass bottles until 1983.

Series: *The Winds of War* (1983)
Item: In this world-spanning miniseries depicting the early years of World War II (1939–41), one scene set in Canada shows the red-and-white "maple leaf" Canadian flag.
Goof: That flag wasn't adopted until 1965.

Series: *Boardwalk Empire* (2010–present)
Item: One of the main characters is famed gangster Lucky Luciano (Vincent Piazza).
Goof: It's 1920 when the series begins. According to some sources, budding gangster Charlie Luciana didn't adopt the name "Lucky Luciano" until 1930.

Series: *That '70s Show* (1998–2006)
Item: The show is set between the years of 1976 and 1979, and lots of period consumer products and technology are used as props.
Goof: Many are anachronisms. A few examples: Cassette tapes made of clear plastic are shown, but those weren't in use until 1984—before then, they were a solid color. Snack Pack pudding cups are in plastic, but in the '70s the product was packaged in tin cans. And *Star Wars* fan Eric Foreman's (Topher Grace) green light saber wasn't produced until *Return of the Jedi* hit movie theaters in 1983.

Rob's phone # on *The Dick Van Dyke Show:* (914) 636-9970, same as creator Carl Reiner's.

Series: *Roots* (1977)
Item: Near the beginning of the miniseries, a slave doctor examines Kunta Kinte (LeVar Burton) in the year 1767. As he does so, he sings "Pop Goes the Weasel" to himself.
Goof: The song wouldn't exist for another 30 years. The music was written around 1800; English lyrics were published in 1850.

Series: *Band of Brothers* (2001)
Item: An on-screen graphic in this World War II drama indicates the date is April 11, 1945. After his troops enjoy a moment of peace listening to musicians, Captain Nixon (Ron Livingston) informs them of major news: Hitler has killed himself, and the war should be over soon.
Goof: Hitler committed suicide on April 30, 1945.

Series: *Deadwood* (2004–06)
Item: Sol Star (John Hawkes) tells town sheriff Seth Bullock (Timothy Olyphant), "Your fly is down."
Goof: *Deadwood* is set in 1876. The modern zipper didn't exist yet (it wasn't perfected until 1913). Star should have told Bullock his fly was "open."

Series: *Happy Days* (1974–84)
Item: On a 1975 episode, Richie (Ron Howard) gets involved with Adlai Stevenson's 1956 presidential campaign in order to impress a cute girl.
Goof: Richie is shown carrying around a 50-star American flag. The flag didn't sport that design until the 50th state, Hawaii, joined the union…in 1959.

Series: *Hogan's Heroes* (1965–71)
Item: In a scene in a German laboratory, a periodic table of the elements hangs on a wall, listing 103 chemicals.
Goof: It's a 1960s-era chart. During World War II, the timeframe of *Hogan's Heroes*, the mainstream scientific community had only confirmed 92 known elements. (Ironically, the 11 other elements were discovered during the development of nuclear science, many by the Manhattan Project during World War II.)

TV TREASURES

The good news: You can own a part of TV history—a famous prop or part of a set. The bad news: It's going to cost you.

Lost in Space: Anything associated with the 1965–68 cult sci-fi series commands out-of-this-world prices, but nothing more than a three-foot-tall model of the *Jupiter 2* space pod that helped the Robinsons return to Earth. It was destined for the junkyard after the show's cancellation, but someone saved the wood, steel, and aluminum prop...and sold it at auction in June 2010 for $85,000. (Penny Robinson's space suit, worn by actress Angela Cartwright in the first season, was a relative bargain at $20,000.)

I Dream of Jeannie: A dozen prop genie bottles, based on a 1964 Jim Beam special edition decanter, were made for the 1960s sitcom. Most of them are lost, but one turned up in 2010 that had been in the private collection of a former executive of Screen Gems, *Jeannie*'s production company. It sold at auction for $42,500.

Daniel Boone: Expected to fetch $12,000 at a 2009 auction, Fess Parker's coonskin cap from the 1964–70 frontier series took in more than twice that: $27,500. A collector bought the iconic headpiece from a man who had received it as a childhood gift back in the 1970s.

The Green Hornet: The show introduced Bruce Lee (as sidekick Kato) to American audiences, so anything worn by him on camera is highly sought after. Kato's chauffeur cap sold for $27,500 in 2010.

Battlestar Galactica: If you've ever wanted to dress up as a Cylon, one of the evil robots from the original 1978 series, you missed your chance—a costume went at auction in 2008 for $55,000. (One catch, though: It was designed for a 6'7" actor.)

Captain Kangaroo: The navy blue jacket and slacks with silver piping that Bob Keeshan wore "many hundreds of times" during the long-running kids' show nabbed $40,000 at auction in 2008.

SNL TRIVIA

Live from this page, it's Saturday Night Live *facts!*

• Why was *SNL* created in 1975? Johnny Carson told NBC to stop using the late-night Saturday time slot to air reruns of *The Tonight Show*. (Carson didn't like *SNL*. He once said the cast members "couldn't ad-lib a fart at a bean-eating contest.")

• Who has said "Live from New York, it's *Saturday Night!*" the most? Darrell Hammond (69 times).

• In 1973, two years before the show premiered, nine-year-old future cast member Mike Myers starred as future cast member Gilda Radner's son in a Canadian commercial for British Columbia Hydro. "I cried on the last day," said Myers, "because I had fallen so in love with her."

• In 1977 *SNL* ran a surreal sketch in which John Belushi, as an old man, surveys the graves of his former cast members, noting, "I'm the last one left." He would be the first *SNL* cast member to die.

• Jim Henson created special, adult-oriented Muppet characters for *SNL's* first season. They were later dropped due to technical difficulties and fan indifference (and are almost always cut out of reruns).

• Matt LeBlanc is the only *Friend* who's never hosted *SNL*.

• Bob Elliott, half of the comedy duo Bob and Ray, appeared on *SNL* in 1979; his son Chris joined the cast in 1994; his granddaughter Abby joined the cast in 2008.

• Minutes before a 1984 episode, the studio audience heard a profanity-laced tirade backstage by a writer whose skit was just cut. That writer was Larry David. He quit, then returned two days later as if nothing had happened. (He later wrote the incident into a *Seinfeld* episode.)

• What do Prince, R.E.M., Aerosmith, and System of a Down have in common? They used the F-word in an *SNL* music performance...and the censors didn't notice.

Most common first name of *SNL* cast members: Chris (Elliott, Farley, Guest, Kattan, Parnell).

A BUN IN THE OVEN

The facts of life: Even TV producers have to face them. When an actress gets pregnant, what do they do with her character? As these stories show, sometimes they have to get very creative.

SOMEBODY ELSE'S BABY

Friends co-star Lisa Kudrow's pregnancy in 1997 presented a problem for the show. Her character, Phoebe, was not in a relationship, nor did writers think she was at a point in her life where she'd get pregnant. And they didn't want to introduce a baby into a show about carefree twentysomethings. They also didn't think baggy clothes or hiding behind shopping bags would work, so they wrote the pregnancy into the show. Except it wasn't *her* baby—Phoebe agrees to be a surrogate carrier for her sister-in-law. This allowed Kudrow to go through her pregnancy on-camera and then conveniently give the "baby" away so that the show wouldn't have to deal with it postpartum. Later on, the show went in another direction and wrote in a pregnancy that was entirely faked—Jennifer Aniston's character, Rachel, became pregnant, even though Aniston wasn't.

NOT PREGNANT, JUST FAT

On *Frasier*, Niles (David Hyde Pierce) pines for his father's nurse Daphne (Jane Leeves) for years, and finally woos her away from her fiancé. Around the same time (2000), Leeves got pregnant. Writers felt it was too soon in the Niles/Daphne relationship for parenthood, so instead they had Daphne feeling so stressed out and guilty about leaving her fiancé that she starts binge eating and gaining weight. In short, Leeves was pregnant, but Daphne got fat. When Leeves took a few episodes off to give birth, her character "went to a fat farm." Niles comments that "she's doing so well at the spa. She's already lost 9 pounds, 12 ounces"—the weight of Leeves's real-life baby daughter.

A WINK AND A NUDGE

The Nanny actress Lauren Lane got pregnant in 1997. Her character, C.C. Babcock, was perpetually single and unlucky in love, and

---

During Lucille Ball's 1952 pregnancy, censors required her condition to be referred to as "expecting."

had an unrequited crush on her boss, so producers ruled out the possibility of writing the pregnancy into the series. The writers took the old sitcom approach of awkwardly masking Lane's growing belly with clothes and props, but they also included many jokes that let the audience know they didn't think they were fooling anyone. On one episode, C.C. remarks, "I was watching *Seinfeld*, and Elaine must have been, I don't know, 12 months pregnant, and they didn't even acknowledge it. They just kept hiding her behind these huge props." Lane delivers the line while holding a potted plant.

HOT DOG!
Alyson Hannigan of *How I Met Your Mother* announced that she was pregnant in 2008. The show is carefully plotted over many seasons, and her character, Lily, wasn't supposed to be pregnant yet, so writers turned the sight of an increasingly and obviously pregnant Hannigan into a running gag—she hides behind large, round objects like globes and basketballs. In one episode, Lily recalls the time she won a hot-dog-eating contest. Viewers see her flashback, and in her moment of victory, she lifts up her shirt to reveal her "very full stomach."

RECAST (AND PAY THE PRICE)
Hunter Tylo left the soap *The Bold and the Beautiful* for a more high-profile part on the prime-time *Melrose Place* in 1996. Just before she was to report to her new job, she told producers she was pregnant. Executive producer Aaron Spelling's method for hiding Tylo's pregnancy: fire her and recast the role (Lisa Rinna got the part). Tylo sued Spelling and his production company for pregnancy discrimination, wrongful termination, and breach of contract. Spelling's lawyers argued that Tylo had a clause in her contract that forbade her from changing her appearance in any way, and that it would have been impossible for her to play a sexy vixen while pregnant. The jury sided with Tylo and awarded her $5 million.

ALIEN ABDUCTION
What did *The X-Files* do when star Gillian Anderson's pregnancy couldn't be hidden by her character's signature trenchcoats or by chest-up filming? Her character was abducted by aliens, of course.

ONE-EPISODE WONDERS

*The longest-running prime-time show of all time is Gunsmoke, which aired
630 episodes over 20 years. It remained one of the top 30 most-watched
shows for that entire span and is regarded as one of the true classics of
TV. On the opposite end of the spectrum are these shows: ones that
were so poorly received and little-watched that they were
all canceled after only one episode.*

Quarterlife (2008)

TV producers Marshall Herskovitz and Edward Zwick
have produced some of the most critically acclaimed
shows of the past two decades, including *thirtysomething* and *My
So-Called Life*. *Thirtysomething* was about unhappy people in their
30s, *My So-Called Life* was about unhappy teenagers. Their 2007
series *Quarterlife* was about unhappy people in their 20s. Because
none of their previous shows attracted big audiences on network
TV, and because the target audience (people in their 20s) spend
more time online than they do watching TV, Herskovitz and
Zwick decided to broadcast *Quarterlife* over the Internet on the
social networking site MySpace. It was a huge hit—more than
nine million people watched the show online, or about double the
number that saw *My So-Called Life* on ABC. Thinking that those
nine million people would follow the show, NBC picked up *Quarterlife* and debuted it at 10 p.m. on February 26, 2008. The viewers
did *not* follow—it was one of the least-watched programs in NBC
history, with 3.1 million viewers, and its worst 10 p.m. performer
in 20 years. *Quarterlife* was immediately canceled (although you
can still find old episodes...on the Internet).

Rosie Live (2008)

Rosie Live was an attempt by NBC to revive the TV variety show,
a format not widely seen on television since the 1970s. Hosted by
comedian and talk-show host Rosie O'Donnell, the show featured
comedy, singing, and dancing, with appearances by Alanis Moris-
sette, Liza Minnelli, Gloria Estefan, Kathy Griffin, Conan
O'Brien, Rachael Ray, and Alec Baldwin. NBC heavily hyped
the first episode, which aired on the blockbuster TV night of

Thanksgiving. It looked like a sure-fire ratings bonanza, but *Rosie Live* pulled in only about five million viewers…and it wasn't the family-friendly entertainment promised. Jane Krakowski of *30 Rock* gave what *TV Guide* called a "career-low stripper-ish ode to product placement," and O'Donnell and singer Clay Aiken, both openly gay, performed a song about which one of them was "gayer." O'Donnell and NBC had plans to make the show into a regular series, airing new episodes on holidays. That idea was scrapped.

Secret Talents of the Stars (2008)

In the spring of 2008, CBS debuted this modern-day follow-up to such '70s celebrity spectacles as *Battle of the Network Stars* and *Circus of the Stars*. The premise: Minor or fading celebrities would show off their unknown or little-known talents. In the first episode, *Star Trek*'s George Takei sang country music, country singer Clint Black performed standup comedy, former child star Danny Bonaduce rode a unicycle, wrestler Ric Flair salsa danced, boxer Joe Frazier sang soul, boxer Roy Jones Jr. rapped, model Cindy Margolis did some magic tricks, drummer Sheila E. juggled, and game-show host and political pundit Ben Stein danced the jitterbug. Then a panel of judges (singer Brian McKnight, actress Debbie Reynolds, and talent agent Gavin Polone) and viewer votes determined winners of each episode, who would then face off against each other in a championship episode. Five more preliminary rounds and the final episode were never even produced… because CBS canceled the show after its first airing.

Emily's Reasons Why Not (2006)

This show seemed like such a sure-fire hit that ABC executives put it on the air without having seen a single finished episode. It revolved around a book publisher (played by movie star Heather Graham) trying to put her life back together after the messy end of a relationship. ABC called the show the "linchpin" of its post-*Monday Night Football* lineup and poured millions into an advertising campaign. *Emily's Reasons Why Not* debuted on January 9, 2006. The plot dealt with a man who didn't want to sleep with Emily, so she assumed he was gay, when in fact he was a Mormon practicing abstinence until marriage. The episode was roundly criticized by both Mormon and gay-rights groups. The next day, ABC president Steve McPherson canceled the show.

Melba (1986)

Melba Moore was a Broadway star in the '60s and '70s, appearing in the original cast of *Hair* and winning a Tony Award for her performance in *Purlie*. Then she shifted to a career as an R&B singer with a string of hits on the soul chart like "You Stepped into My Life," "Falling," and "Love's Comin' at Ya." She was a popular entertainer in the African-American community, so in 1985 CBS developed *Melba*, a sitcom about an upper-middle-class black family very similar to NBC's *The Cosby Show*. CBS planned to debut the show on January 28, 1986…which happened to be the same day that the *Challenger* space shuttle exploded, killing everyone on board. Result: *Melba* still aired on CBS, opposite news coverage on the other networks. Not surprisingly, shell-shocked viewers tuned into the news coverage of the tragedy. Ratings for *Melba* were so low that CBS canceled the show the next day. Recognizing that *Melba* might work under better circumstances, the network gave it another chance in August 1986, airing a repeat of the first episode. That showing did *even worse*: At the time, it was the least-watched show in CBS history.

The Hasselhoffs (2010)

In 2010 former *Baywatch* and *Knight Rider* star David Hasselhoff was back in the public eye—he was a judge on *America's Got Talent*, took a turn on *Dancing with the Stars*, and was thoroughly embarrassed when his daughter leaked to the Internet a video of him lying on his floor, shirtless and extremely drunk, eating a cheeseburger. Unable to resist, cable channel A&E signed up Hasselhoff—and his family—for a reality show in the vein of its successful celebrity-at-home show *Gene Simmons: Family Jewels*. A&E produced eight weeks' worth of shows, and with much publicity debuted *The Hasselhoffs* in December 2010. Despite promises that the show would address "the cheeseburger incident," it brought in just 718,000 viewers, a low number even for cable. After only one broadcast, A&E canceled *The Hasselhoffs*, pulling future episodes off the schedule and even abandoning planned encore airings of the premiere.

GILLIGAN'S DEADLY SINS

According to some fans, Gilligan's Island isn't the silly, meaningless froth it appears to be; it's a religious allegory about sin and human frailty. Is it true?

GET THEE BEHIND ME, LITTLE BUDDY!
The theory goes something like this: Producer Sherwood Schwartz aimed to put something deeply meaningful on TV, and in 1964 came up with *Gilligan's Island*, a comedy about seven people trapped on an island. Schwartz's supposed deep meaning: The island represents hell, and the seven people are trapped there because each of them personifies one of the seven deadly sins.

• **Ginger represents LUST:** She's a foxy "movie star" who dresses in sexy, skin-tight outfits.

• **Mary Ann represents ENVY:** A girl-next-door type, she's jealous of Ginger's beauty (and of how Ginger was included in the theme song, while Mary Ann was initially referred to as "and the rest").

• **The Professor represents PRIDE:** Because of his superior intellect (with which he can make anything out of a coconut), he acts like he's superior to the other castaways.

• **Mr. Howell represents GREED:** He's "the millionaire."

• **Mrs. Howell represents SLOTH:** A work-averse "millionaire's wife," she never helps in any tedious island activity, like cleaning or cooking.

• **The Skipper represents GLUTTONY and ANGER:** He's a fat guy who always wants more to eat. And in almost every episode, he gets mad at Gilligan for messing up an escape plan and smacks him with his captain's hat.

• **Gilligan:** He is lazy and could represent sloth, with the self-serving Mrs. Howell taking gluttony from the Skipper. Or he could represent Satan. (It's *his* island, after all.) The proof: He always bungles their plans for escape...because there is no escape from hell. And he always wears red.

THE TRUTH: Schwartz has been asked about this theory many times and comments, "A lot of people have written to me saying they understand *Gilligan's Island* is the seven deadly sins. That was never in my mind."

THE RATINGS GAME

How do those Nielsen people figure out what you're watching? Science.

W**HERE EVERYBODY KNOWS HIS NAME**
In 1936 the 39-year-old owner of a Chicago-based marketing company attended a convention in New York, where he saw a new device called an Audiometer. Attached to the tuning mechanism on a radio, it would make a record of when the radio was turned on and what station it was tuned to. (The device had a stylus that physically marked a roll of waxed-paper tape.) In other words, it tracked radio listening. The man bought the patent rights, as well as every Audiometer that had been manufactured. His name: Arthur C. Nielsen.

In the early 1940s, Nielsen started talking people into letting his company install Audiometers in their homes. From the results, he extrapolated information to determine what radio listeners in a given region were listening to. Loosely speaking, if 10 percent of his Chicago test audience, for example, listened to *The Adventures of Sam Spade*, it stood to reason then that ten percent of *all* Chicago's radio listeners had tuned in to the show. The man then offered that information to advertisers, who could use it to better target their marketing. They were wary at first, but the numbers proved accurate again and again, and by 1950 the Audiometer was the most successful radio marketing service in the country.

When TV caught on as a broadcast medium, Nielsen adjusted for the times, modified the Audiometer, gathered new sample audiences, and grew his company into the most influential and well-known TV ratings company in the world. He called it Nielsen Media Research.

HOW IT WORKS
Arthur Nielsen died in 1980, but the Nielsen company lives on. His national ratings system has been revamped several times over the years, and today about 5,000 homes in the U.S., carefully selected as a statistical cross-section of TV viewers (based on age, race, income, and other factors), take part in it via electronic boxes called People Meters that plug into their TVs and record

Lex Luthor never appeared on *Adventures of Superman.*

what shows they watch. (Another 20,000 or so people take part in local program ratings, recording what they watch in Nielsen TV Ratings Diaries, which they send in to the company once a week.)

BY THE NUMBERS

The most commonly cited Nielsen figures are given as two numbers. For example, let's say that an episode of the CBS comedy *Two and a Half Men* got a Nielsen rating of 8.5/13.

Points: The first number, the "points" (8.5, in our example), refers to the percentage of the 115 million American homes with televisions estimated to have watched the show. In this case, it's 8.5 percent, or about 9.78 million homes.

Share: The second number, the "share," refers to the percentage of homes that are actually watching television at that time that are watching that particular program. In this example, 13 percent of viewers caught *Two and a Half Men*.

Total viewers: The number of viewers can be much higher, as the system only counts homes. Based on the size of an average American household (just under two people), Nielsen would calculate that 14.3 million people watched that episode of *Two and a Half Men*.

Demographics: Nielsen tells advertisers the viewing habits of certain portions of the population, based on criteria like age, gender, and income level. Generally, the younger-adult demographic, the 18–49 age group, is regarded as the most valuable to advertisers. Younger viewers are less likely to have established brand loyalties, and are more likely to have disposable income to spend on consumer goods.

If a show does well in the 18–49 demographic, its network can charge advertisers more money for ad time. For example, in the 2009–10 season, NBC's *The Office* was viewed by an average of 7.79 million people each week, making it the 59th-most-watched show on TV. But in the 18–49 category, it scored a 4.0 average, meaning 4 percent of all people in that age group watching television at the time watched *The Office*. In that demographic, *The Office* was the 17th-most-watched show on TV. As such, an ad during *The Office* cost about $220,000—more than the $150,000 for CBS's *NCIS*, which is the #1 scripted show in total viewers, but scored lower in the all-important 18-49 demographic.

NO ACTOR REQUIRED

*Some of the best-remembered characters in TV history
never actually appeared on-screen.*

SHOW: *Cheers*
CHARACTER: Vera Peterson
DESCRIPTION: Norm (George Wendt) was always at the bar, so viewers frequently heard about his wife Vera, but never saw her...until one 1986 episode in which Vera appears, sort of: It's Thanksgiving, she arrives late, and the other characters are in the middle of a food fight. Just before she comes on-screen, she gets hit in the face with a pie, which completely obscures her face.

SHOW: *Frasier*
CHARACTER: Maris Crane
DESCRIPTION: Producers intended for Maris, the first wife of Niles (David Hyde Pierce), to appear at some point, but decided against it when they realized that over the years, they had described a woman who couldn't physically exist, and so would be impossible to cast. What we're told about Maris: She is extremely thin (one character says she resembles a whippet; another says she is unable to leave footprints in snow), has webbed fingers, is an albino, and can't stretch her legs more than a few inches due to "extraordinarily tight quadriceps."

SHOW: *The Mary Tyler Moore Show*
CHARACTER: Lars Lindstrom, Phyllis's husband
DESCRIPTION: Mary's neighbor Phyllis (Cloris Leachman) frequently bragged about her husband, Lars—he was a talented, handsome, adventurous doctor. And even though he lived with Phyllis, next door to Mary, he never appeared on camera. And when Phyllis was spun off into the 1975 series *Phyllis*, Lars was killed off.

SHOW: *Will & Grace*
CHARACTER: Stan Walker

DESCRIPTION: Stan was the anti-Lars. The third husband of boozy, pill-popping Karen (Megan Mullally), he was said to be a morbidly obese and unethical businessman. How obese and unethical? He goes to prison for tax evasion, and when he's released, Pizza Hut congratulates him with a full-page newspaper ad. (And like Lars, Stan dies off camera, having never been shown.)

SHOW: *My So-Called Life*
CHARACTER: Tino
DESCRIPTION: The show's high-school characters often talked about a party "Tino" was throwing the upcoming weekend, or a party he'd thrown the previous weekend. He was also the lead singer of a band called the Frozen Embryos. The show's writers had intended for Tino to be so cool that he couldn't possibly exist.

SHOW: *Diff'rent Strokes*
CHARACTER: The Gooch
DESCRIPTION: This scary character is a school bully who terrorizes Arnold (Gary Coleman) and his friends. His real name is never given—he's known only as "the Gooch." He's mentioned in a dozen or so episodes when Arnold comes home from school and complains about him, but viewers never see him in action...or find out what "the Gooch" means.

SHOW: *Twin Peaks*
CHARACTER: Diane
DESCRIPTION: While investigating the murder of Laura Palmer, FBI agent Cooper (Kyle MacLachlan) routinely tapes messages for Diane, his secretary back home. But since Diane was never seen, or even depicted receiving the messages, her very existence could be called into question (as was true with everything else on *Twin Peaks*).

HEARD...BUT NOT SEEN:
- Charlie (John Forsyth) on *Charlie's Angels*
- Carlton the doorman (Lorenzo Music) on *Rhoda*
- Orson (Ralph James) on *Mork and Mindy*.

What time did the sitcom *Wednesday 9:30 (8:30 Central)* air? Guess.

TV Q&A

Watching a TV, it turns out, is a lot easier than understanding how it works. Here's a very simplified look at the complex science behind how an electrical signal is sent through the air and into your house, and then transformed into an image.

How is a TV signal broadcast over the air?

Today many U.S. homes get their TV programming from cable or satellite services, but TV signals are still broadcast over the air, and your TV can still receive them through its antenna. Since June 2009, all over-the-air television stations in the U.S. have been required to broadcast their signals in binary, or digital, form, which means they convert both the visual and the audio components of the television signal into sequences of ones and zeros, known as *bits*, before transmitting them over the air to your TV. A digital converter inside your TV then converts all those ones and zeros back into pictures and sound. Digital TV signals are similar to those broadcast by AM radio: The strength (or *amplitude*) of the TV signal is varied (*modulated*) to create the ones and zeros— that's why it's called *amplitude modulation*, or AM for short.

Why is TV broadcast on different channels?

For the same reason radio stations have different frequencies: to prevent different stations from interfering with each other. All broadcast signals are made up of radio waves that are classified according to their *frequency*, or the number of waves that are transmitted per second. All radio waves travel at the same speed: the speed of light. Because of this, shorter radio waves—those with a shorter *wavelength*—have a higher frequency: In a given amount of time, more short waves can pass a point in space than can longer radio waves. These frequencies are measured in cycles per second, or *hertz*. They range from 30 kilohertz (30,000 hertz) to 300 gigahertz (300 billion hertz). Only 30,000 of the 30 kHz waves will pass a given point every second, versus 300 billion of the 300 GHz radio waves.

Over-the-air TV stations are assigned specific bands of radio frequencies. Your local Channel 7 station, for example, is assigned the band of frequencies from 174 million hertz (mega-hertz, or MHz) to 180 MHz. (The *bandwidth* is said to be 6 MHz wide, from 174 MHz to 180Mhz.) Restricting channel 7 to this band prevents it from interfering with local channel 12, which is assigned the 204–210 MHz band, or with local channel 4, which is assigned the 66–72 MHz band, or with any other local TV station. Your TV is designed to receive only one band at a time. When you select channel 7, for example, you are telling the TV to ignore all of the signals except those in the 174–180 MHz band.

What's the difference between analog and digital television?

In the good old days of analog television broadcasting, the TV camera at the TV studio converted visual images into an electron-ic signal. In fact, analog TVs worked because they functioned, mechanically speaking, as TV cameras in reverse: At the TV sta-tion, light, in the form of a visual image, entered the TV camera and into the front end of a specialized cathode-ray tube called a *vidicon*. The vidicon converted the images into an electronic sig-nal that the TV station broadcast (along with the audio signal) over the air to your TV. Inside your television, the process was reversed: The video signal was fed into the back end of a cathode-ray tube that was very similar to a vidicon. The cathode-ray tube then converted the electronic signal back into the visual image and displayed it on the front surface of the tube—the TV screen. Digital TV signals are not an exact, electronically represented image because they are bits of computerized code; at their most basic, they are a "1" or a "0." A digital converter in a modern tele-vision, put simply (well, not *that* simply), takes those bits of digital code and converts them into the images and sound that they were programmed to carry. One advantage of digital TV is that digital signals take up much less bandwidth than analog signals did. The bandwidth that is freed up can be used to provide high-definition wide-screen pictures, digital stereo sound, or even multiple chan-nels where before there was only room for one.

What's the difference between VHF and UHF?

Very high frequency, or VHF, is a designation given to radio frequencies from 30 to 300 MHz. Channels 2 through 13 are all broadcast in the VHF band. When TV licenses were first granted to commercial broadcasters in 1941, all the frequencies were in the VHF range. TVs had channels 2 through 13, and that was it. By the late 1940s, the number of TV stations around the country had grown to the point that the Federal Communications Commission, which regulates radio and TV broadcasting, realized that more television frequencies were needed. That's when *ultra high frequency*, or UHF, television came into being. UHF frequencies are those between 300 MHz and 3 GHz. Frequencies within this range correspond to channels 14 through 83. (Not all of the available channels were used—many cities had just a few UHF broadcasters. And many channels, including channels 52 to 83, have since been reallocated for other, non-TV purposes.) The first UHF TV station: KC2XAK, channel 24, in Bridgeport, Connecticut, which went on the air in 1949.

Why is there no channel 1?
There used to be, but there hasn't been since the late 1940s, when the frequency band assigned to channel 1, 44–50 MHz, was reassigned to public safety communications, such as police radios.

Why is it necessary to turn to channel 3 or 4 when watching an external device like a VCR or DVD player?
Because there is rarely a channel 3 *and* a channel 4 in the same geographical region. Viewers pick the channel that doesn't broadcast in their area so they won't get interference from local TV stations.

* * *

SATURDAY NIGHT LIGHTS

The Dukes of Hazzard was a massive hit when it debuted in 1979. It was most popular in the South, but that created a problem. Since *Dukes* aired on Friday night at 9:00 p.m., so many people in Mississippi stayed home to watch the show that high-school football game attendance dropped dramatically. School districts responded by rescheduling football games for Saturday night.

FIRST LINES QUIZ #1

Lots of people know the first lines of classic novels—"Call me Ishmael," for example. But the first lines of classic television shows? See how many series you can identify based on their opening bits of dialogue. (Answers are on page 498.)

1. "Are you finished with this juice, Peter?"

2. "School days, school days, teacher's golden aw....dammit! My brother is trying to follow me to school again!"

3. "Captain's Log, Stardate 41153.7. Our destination is Planet Deneb IV, beyond which lies the great unexplored mass of the galaxy."

4. "Stay away from the gas! Stay there!"

5. "Space. It seems to go on and on forever. Then you get to the end, and a monkey starts throwing barrels at you."

6. "Bert! Bert! Come here, quick! Look out there. There's millions of people out there watching us on TV."

7. "Once upon a time, there were three little girls who went to the police academy, and they were assigned very hazardous duties."

8. "Gloria, I hurried back."

9. "We tripped along the sidewalks of New York. [Answers phone.] Hello? Why are you sending him home? Does Alan have a temperature? Oh, that's not much."

10. "This is the way it began on that extraordinary night. The night he came."

11. "Gone fishin'."

12. "Since I was a kid, I've been able to sleep through anything—storms, sirens, you name it. Last night, I didn't sleep."

13. "Come on, it's getting late. You stop dancing around with that food and start eating it."

The 1973 *Mannix* episode "Little Girl Lost" was solved 20 years later on *Diagnosis Murder*.

TV MYTHS AND LEGENDS

Our friend's brother's nephew's cousin's friend's brother saw
Charles Manson at the Monkees audition, so it must be true,
right? Just like these other TV-related urban legends.

Myth: Bill Cosby hated *Amos 'n' Andy*'s stereotypical
depiction of African Americans as lazy buffoons so much
that he bought the rights to the show...so he could pull
it from circulation.

Truth: When the hit radio show *Amos 'n' Andy* moved to TV in
1951, it was heavily criticized by the NAACP for its demeaning
portrayal of blacks. The organization urged CBS to cancel the
show, but it ran until 1953, at which point reruns were syndicated
well into the 1960s. The NAACP and many prominent figures,
including Bill Cosby, continued to speak out. While Cosby didn't
buy the show to make it disappear, his clout, popularity, and public opposition led CBS to permanently pull *Amos 'n' Andy* from
syndication in 1966.

Myth: The kid who played the nerdy Paul Pfeiffer on *The Wonder*
Years (1988–93) became shock rocker Marilyn Manson.

Truth: Josh Saviano portrayed Paul on the ABC dramedy *The*
Wonder Years. After the show ended, he retired from acting, went
to Yale, and became a lawyer. "Marilyn Manson," meanwhile, is
the stage name of Florida rock musician Brian Warner. While the
two men bear a resemblance, Warner is seven years older than
Saviano and was already performing as Marilyn Manson while
The Wonder Years was on the air. The rumor probably spread
because Marilyn Manson found mainstream popularity just as
Saviano disappeared from the public eye.

Myth: Charles Manson auditioned for *The Monkees*.

Truth: Before he became a murderer, Manson was an unsuccessful
rock musician. (Music producer Terry Melcher declined to sign
him, and Manson may have had actress Sharon Tate killed
because he was looking for Melcher—Tate was renting a house
that Melcher had once lived in.) Public knowledge about Man-

Three versions of the *Davy Crockett* (1955) theme song hit the top 10, almost simultaneously.

son's rock connections (he was also acquainted with Beach Boy Dennis Wilson) led to the urban legend that he'd auditioned for the Monkees—the show and the band—in 1965. But he couldn't have—in 1965, he was serving a jail sentence for forgery. (However, among the future famous musicians who did try out for the Monkees: Stephen Stills, Harry Nilsson, and Paul Williams.)

Myth: Longtime TV star Sandy Duncan (*Funny Face, The Sandy Duncan Show, The Hogan Family*) has a glass eye.
Truth: Shortly after *Funny Face* debuted in 1971, Duncan's doctor discovered a noncancerous tumor behind her left eye. An operation removed the lump, but it left Duncan blind in that eye. So while it appears "glassy," the eye is real.

Myth: *Joanie Loves Chachi* was a massive hit in South Korea. The reason: *chachi* is the Korean word for "penis."
Truth: It's been widely reported that the 1982 *Happy Days* spinoff *Joanie Loves Chachi* was the most popular American TV show ever broadcast in South Korea, and scores of curious viewers tuned in because the title translated as *Joanie Loves Penis*. None of it's true. "Chachi" has no meaning in Korean, and *Joanie Loves Chachi* never even aired on South Korean broadcast television. The whole thing started as a joke that creator Garry Marshall told in interviews while promoting the show.

* * *

AW, NUTS

In March 2001, Nick at Nite aired the 1983 *Three's Company* episode "The Charming Stranger," as it had done dozens of times before. This time, an eagle-eyed viewer called the network to alert them to something that nobody had noticed before: Star John Ritter's private parts were visible—for about a second—through the bottom of a pair of boxer shorts. Ever since, the episode has aired with the offending footage deleted. When Ritter heard about the incident, he quipped to the *New York Observer*, "I've requested they air both versions, edited and unedited, because sometimes you feel like a nut, and sometimes you don't."

BANNED ADS

In the world of TV advertising, there's a fine line between attention-grabbing...and unacceptable. Here are a few ads that were banned, pulled, rejected, legislated against, or otherwise taken off television.

Company: *Expressen*, a national Swedish newspaper (2004)
Commercial: Two shirtless men sit next to each other in a sauna. One has his eyes closed. The second man keeps peeking over at the first man's lap, secretively at first, then more blatantly. Finally, the first man opens his eyes just as the other man leans in to get a closer look. After an awkward pause he gives a look and a nod, inviting him to go for it. The "peeker" reaches over, picks up an *Expressen* newspaper from the other man's lap, and begins reading.
Banned! Swedish censors found it too suggestive, even though the camera zooms out to show that both men are wearing towels.

Organization: People for the Ethical Treatment of Animals (PETA) (2008)
Commercial: In a spot titled "Sex Talk," two parents tell their teenage daughter, "We need to have a talk about sex. We think you should be having a lot of it, sweetie." The daughter expresses concern about getting pregnant, to which the parents respond, "Pop out all the kids you want! We can leave them at the shelter, or dump them in the street." It ends with the tagline, "Parents shouldn't act this way. Neither should people with dogs and cats."
Banned! Citing sensitivity for the city's massive homeless population in the wake of Hurricane Katrina (especially over the line "dump them in the streets"), stations in New Orleans said no to the ad.

Company: Pepsi (2001)
Commercial: Dressed as Goldilocks, *Sex and the City* star Kim Cattrall wanders into a football locker room and finds a bunch of chilled cans of soda. After tasting them all, she decides that Pepsi One is "just right." The camera cuts to the football players returning, at which point Cattrall is in the team's hot tub.

Banned! Did Pepsi remove the ad from circulation because of the implied nudity or sexual innuendo? Nope. The NFL threatened to sue because the players' jerseys looked too much like those of the Chicago Bears.

Organization: Physicians Committee for Responsible Medicine (2010)
Commercial: This Washington, D.C.-based health advocacy group produced a public service announcement that depicted an obese man, dead on a table in a morgue, holding a hamburger. A woman cries over the body as McDonald's iconic "golden arches" logo appears, along with the tagline, "I was lovin' it." (It referred to McDonald's slogan, "I'm lovin' it.")
Banned! The commercial, meant to agitate for healthier options on fast-food menus, aired twice in the D.C. area. When PCRM tried to air it in West Palm Beach, Florida, no station would touch it—they didn't want to get sued by McDonald's.

Organization: Sweden Democrats Party (2010)
Commercial: The anti-immigration SDP paid for this election ad, which depicted a retired woman with a walker slowly inching her way up to vote. In front of her are two levers: one labeled "Pensions," the other labeled "Immigrants." Viewers don't see which lever gets pulled...because the woman is overtaken by a mob of burka-wearing Muslim women.
Banned! Swedish network TV4 refused to air it, calling it "hate speech."

Organization: Mancrunch.com, a gay dating website (2010)
Commercial: Two men in football jerseys sit next to each other on a couch watching a game. They reach for a potato chip at the same time. Their hands touch. They stop, look longingly at each other, and then kiss passionately while the screen fades to the tagline, "Mancrunch.com. Where many many many men come out and play."
Banned! Mancrunch.com submitted the commercial to air during the 2010 Super Bowl. CBS "decided not to accept this particular spot" and offered no further explanation.

FROM TV...TO RADIO?

Many popular radio shows successfully jumped over to TV: The Lone Ranger, The Jack Benny Program, and Amos 'n' Andy, to name a few. But even well into the 1950s, some producers thought TV was a passing fad, so they created radio versions of TV shows.

Series: *I Love Lucy*
From TV: The Lucille Ball sitcom was the #1 show on television for four years in the 1950s. It was so popular that it drove many people to buy their first television.
To radio: Producers thought a radio version would be an easy—and cheap—way to gain a larger audience. So they took the audio from a *Lucy* episode in 1952 and called it a pilot for a radio series. Ultimately CBS Radio decided against airing the show. (Trivia fact: *I Love Lucy* was itself inspired by a radio comedy called *My Favorite Husband*, starring Lucille Ball.)

Series: *Have Gun–Will Travel*
From TV: Richard Boone starred as Paladin, a gentleman gunfighter for hire in this popular CBS Western, which ran for a total of 225 episodes from 1957 to 1963.
To radio: A year after its TV debut, the series successfully made the backward leap to radio, and CBS Radio aired more than 100 episodes from 1958 to 1960. Original episodes were written and produced solely for radio, and John Dehner was the voice of Paladin. *Have Gun–Will Travel* was one of CBS's last radio dramas.

Series: *Tom Corbett, Space Cadet*
From TV: This 1950–55 science-fiction series about a rookie astronaut (Frankie Thomas Jr.) and his adventures in space aired variously on CBS, NBC, ABC, and DuMont.
To radio: Unlike *I Love Lucy*'s recycled audio track, and unlike *Have Gun*'s new-for-radio cast, Thomas and the rest of the *Tom Corbett* TV cast starred in new episodes written especially for the radio version of their show, which ran for six months in 1952.

In 1953 Art Linkletter hosted a record five prime-time shows at the same time.

CHANNEL SURFING INTERNATIONAL

What do we in America have in common with the rest of the world?
We all seem to enjoy really weird escapist television.

Show: *Les Guignols de l'Info* (France)
Title in English: *The News Puppets*
Details: This puppet-based sketch comedy show debuted on state-run channel Canal+ in 1988. It then leaped to the top of the ratings during the first Gulf War in 1990, when the comedy turned from innocuous to lampooning French and world politicians. The satire is sharp and irreverent, and the puppets themselves are brilliantly carved caricatures of well-known political figures. In 2002 the show was absorbed into *Le Grand Journal*, a *60 Minutes*-style news magazine show. The news puppets are the most-watched segment.

Show: *Shoten* (Japan)
Title in English: *Jokes for Points*
Details: A Sunday-night TV staple in Japan since 1969, this game show pits six kimono-clad comedians against one another in a contest to see who can think up the best joke on a subject delivered by the host. (It's sort of like *Whose Line Is It Anyway?*) The prize for the best joke in each round is a cushion called a *zabuton*, and the ultimate winner is the first comedian to earn 10 cushions. It's an ongoing hit. In 2010 only the Winter Olympics drew more Japanese viewers.

Show: *Yeh Rishta Kya Kehlata Hai* (India)
Title in English: *What Is This Relationship Called?*
Details: This soap opera follows the different experiences of two modern young Indian women, one hoping to marry for love, the other discovering the love of her life within her traditional arranged marriage. In every episode, the independent woman experiences heartbreak while the woman in the arranged marriage lives happily.

Show: *Xian Jiàn Qí Xiá Zhuàn* (China)
Title in English: *Chinese Paladin 3*
Details: The swords-and-sorcery video game *The Legend of Sword and Fairy* is very popular in China—so popular that TV producers there turned it into this soap opera (likely a TV first). Set in ancient China, the show combines midair sword fights, lush costumes, epic camera work, and a plot line in which a mysterious cult tries to destroy the world. Every time a new sequel in the video game series comes out, the title of the show is updated too (hence the "3").

Show: *El Notifiero con Brozo* (Mexico)
Title in English: *The News with Brozo*
Details: It's Mexico's take on *The Daily Show*...if it were hosted by a clown in a green wig. Brozo (actor Victor Trujillo) started out in 1988 as the host of a kids' show called *The Caravan* but morphed into a political satirist. Brozo is so revered in Mexico that he demands, and gets, absolutely no state censorship of his program. The result is that he can lampoon any person or issue he cares to, and get away with it. Meanwhile, politicians and personalities go to great lengths to get on the show, knowing that the media exposure is worth any potshots they're liable to receive from Brozo.

Show: *Geugeos Neomu Jaemissda* (North Korea)
Title in English: *It's So Funny!*
Details: North Korea is one of the most isolated countries on Earth—its strict totalitarian government allows almost no outside news or pop culture. It's not surprising, then, that a North Korean comedy show produced by the state propaganda division isn't quite what Americans would call funny. Broadcast periodically since 1970, the show consists entirely of sketches in which two uniformed soldiers, one of each gender, converse. A 2010 installment was about the greatness of beans: The male soldier tells the female soldier that he feels good and looks handsome because he eats a lot of beans. "If we farm in the way the general tells us, we will become happy!" the woman responds. End of sketch.

Winner of a 2004 British poll to select the "most respected mother": Marge Simpson.

THE SOPRANOS, STARRING RAY LIOTTA

Some actors are so closely associated with a specific role or TV series that it's hard to imagine he or she wasn't the first choice. But it happens all the time.

SEINFELD, STARRING PAUL SHAFFER
Co-creator Larry David based the character of George Costanza on himself. However, David didn't want to play the part, so the show's other creator, Jerry Seinfeld, offered the role to *Late Night with David Letterman* bandleader Paul Shaffer via a message on Shaffer's answering machine. Shaffer was so busy with his musical duties on *Late Night with David Letterman* that by the time he heard the message, it was too late—Jason Alexander had been cast instead.

MONK, STARRING MICHAEL RICHARDS

A few weeks before *Seinfeld* aired its final episode in 1998, one of the show's stars, Richards, was looking for his next job and read the script for *Monk*, a comic police drama about a detective with obsessive-compulsive disorder. ABC wanted the show, especially because Richards was interested. But the actor didn't think the script was funny enough. He passed, and then so did ABC. The USA cable network picked it up, and *Monk* became the network's most-watched show ever, winning three Emmy Awards for Outstanding Actor in a Comedy Series for star Tony Shalhoub.

THE OFFICE, STARRING PAUL GIAMATTI

When NBC began work on an American version of the hit British comedy *The Office*, executives told the show's producers they had one person, and one person only, in mind for the lead role of clueless office manager Michael Scott: film star Paul Giamatti (*Sideways, American Splendor*). Giamatti preferred making movies and turned down the role, so it was offered to Steve Carell, best known at the time for the film *Bruce Almighty*.

In 1998 Americans watched 25 hours of TV a week. In 2008: 26 hours.

30 ROCK, STARRING RACHEL DRATCH

30 Rock star and creator Tina Fey wrote the role of self-obsessed actress Jenna Maroney for Rachel Dratch, Fey's longtime collaborator on *Saturday Night Live* and in the Chicago improv comedy scene before that. A pilot episode was filmed with Dratch, but NBC felt that she wasn't attractive enough for the part and forced Fey to fire her friend. *Ally McBeal* veteran Jane Krakowski ended up playing Jenna; Dratch has played several bit parts on *30 Rock* throughout the show's run.

MAD ABOUT YOU, STARRING BONNIE HUNT

Comedian and talk-show host Bonnie Hunt starred in several TV series; all of them were short-lived. The one she turned down lasted for seven years. She was *Mad About You* producers' first choice for the lead role of Jamie Buchman, ultimately played by Helen Hunt, who won four Emmy Awards for it. (The actresses aren't related.)

BATMAN, STARRING LYLE WAGGONER

When casting the campy 1960s TV series, producers narrowed down the choices for the lead roles of Batman and Robin to two sets of actors: Lyle Waggoner and Peter R.J. Deyell, and Adam West and Burt Ward. West and Ward won out. Also almost cast: Spencer Tracy, who was offered the role of the Penguin. He said he'd take the role if he could "kill Batman" (request denied).

THE SOPRANOS, STARRING RAY LIOTTA

Show creator David Chase's pick for the role of Tony Soprano: James Gandolfini. Only problem: Gandolfini was completely unknown. HBO executives aggressively pursued Ray Liotta, who had appeared in many mob-themed movies, including *Goodfellas*. Chase ultimately got his way, and got Gandolfini.

GREY'S ANATOMY, STARRING ROB LOWE

The original choice to play the lead role of Dr. Derek "McDreamy" Shepherd was 1980s teen heartthrob Rob Lowe. But he wasn't quite right, so producers went with another 1980s teen idol: Patrick Dempsey, who was having so much trouble finding work that he was considering leaving acting for good. (He'd also just been rejected for the lead role on *House*.)

NETWORK ORIGINS: NBC

*The broadcast TV networks no longer monopolize the
airwaves, but they still wield tremendous influence.
And the grandfather of them all is NBC.*

RADIO DAYS
For radio producer American Marconi Wireless (AMW),
selling radios during World War I was easy. Most radios at
the time were two-way and direct, and were used by people to
converse with each other. Interest was confined to two groups: the
military, and shipping companies. But a 25-year-old executive at
AMW named David Sarnoff knew that for the company to survive after the war, it would need to find new markets.

In 1916, shortly after AMW was bought out and renamed
Radio Corporation of America (RCA), Sarnoff wrote a letter to
his fellow RCA executives. In it, he spoke of the future of radio:
He pictured a "radio music box" that, he said, would one day be in
every home. To those homes, mass transmitters would broadcast
signals—instead of direct, two-way messages, the network would
relay music and entertainment, one way, to millions of listeners.
Sarnoff's bosses weren't interested. The war was still on, and
radios were selling fine. There was no reason to shift the whole
notion of radio to what Sarnoff called "broadcasting."

FIGHT NIGHT
By 1921 World War I had been over for more than two years.
And Sarnoff had been right—as the military market disappeared
and the shipping market became saturated, sales of RCA radios
plummeted. Sarnoff wrote another memo to RCA brass about
the entertainment potential of radio. It was already taking off,
with amateur hobbyists building their own crude transmitters,
some forming them into actual radio "stations," and more people
were investing in radios for their homes. Still, RCA management
was skeptical.

But Sarnoff didn't let it drop. In July 1921, he hired an
announcer to broadcast over the nascent airwaves a heavyweight
boxing match between Jack Dempsey and Georges Carpentier.

The fight took place in New Jersey, but the audio feed was sent by telegraph wire to KDKA in Pittsburgh, one of the very first radio stations, which then broadcast it to the general public. The announcer asked listeners to send letters to RCA, telling them what they thought of the fight. Based on the volume of mail received in the next few weeks, RCA execs concluded that 300,000 people had listened in. They were finally convinced: Commercial radio was the future.

A NETWORK IS BORN

RCA couldn't market their expensive, hand-constructed cabinet radios unless there was something for people to listen to. So, after a few false starts, in 1926 RCA launched its own radio network: the National Broadcasting Company (NBC). "National" was a bit of an overstatement, as the network consisted of just two stations: one in New York City, and one 10 miles away in Newark, New Jersey. Head of the new broadcasting division: David Sarnoff.

But NBC rapidly expanded across the country, signing up local radio stations to be affiliates. That got the attention of national advertisers, who liked the idea of buying a single ad that would appear simultaneously across broad swaths of the country. It also got the attention of the entertainment world, which saw radio as a medium to promote movies and musicians.

BANDWIDTH ON THE RUN

In 1927, in an attempt to crowd out competitors from taking footholds, NBC split into two networks: NBC Red and NBC Blue Networks. Red consisted of pure entertainment; Blue was news, cultural shows, and some fledgling entertainment shows that were still looking for sponsors.

As NBC entered the western time zones, the three-hour time difference proved a problem, so they spun off two more networks: NBC Orange (which carried Red network programming) and NBC Gold (which carried the Blue network shows). Headquartered in San Francisco, Orange and Gold had a facility made up of five studios and staffed with a news bureau and its own orchestra, which re-created the original broadcasts from NBC Blue and NBC Red. (When "time shifting"—recording on vinyl—became more economically feasible in 1936, Orange and Gold were absorbed back into Blue and Red.)

With NBC dividing up the radio dial with its own spin-off divisions, the Federal Communications Commission demanded that they divest themselves of one of their networks. In 1943 NBC sold off the less profitable Blue network to Life Savers magnate Edward Noble, who turned it into ABC (see page 303).

LIVE WITH PICTURES

NBC dominated radio throughout the '30s, '40s, and '50s with long-running shows such as *Fibber McGee and Molly*, *The Great Gildersleeve*, and *Death Valley Days*, while serving as the base for comedy and music shows hosted by Bob Hope, Fred Allen, and others. But by the mid-'40s, television was clearly the future.

RCA approached the TV industry the way they had approached radio—they made shows that people wanted to watch so they would buy the television sets RCA manufactured. In 1947 RCA stimulated TV sales by having NBC cover the World Series. And in 1951, coaxial cable linked stations in the east and then spread west, resulting in the first transcontinental broadcast.

NBC became the first major TV broadcaster, partly because it had a large bank of popular radio performers, like George Burns and Bob Hope, who readily stepped in as hosts of their own TV shows. But NBC realized that TV was more than just sound—it was visual—so the network began recruiting stars from the dying vaudeville circuit. That's where NBC found its first big star: Milton Berle of *Texaco Star Theater*, which would go on to be NBC's first hit, ranking as the #1 show on television (what there was of it) in the 1950–51 season. Historians belive that Berle was so popular that it led many Americans to buy a TV set. By 1952, more than 1.4 million American homes had bought one...a large portion of them manufactured by RCA.

*　　*　　*

THE POTSIE MANEUVER

Amazing fact: Anson Williams (Potsie on *Happy Days*) is the cousin of Dr. Henry Heimlich, creator of the Heimlich Maneuver.

CURSED?

*Some TV series have had multiple cast members suffer career setbacks,
or even die, under bizarre circumstances or in rapid succession.
Is it just a coincidence…or is it some kind of curse?*

THE SUPERMAN CURSE

Adventures of Superman (1952–58) made former movie bit player George Reeves a star, but his contract with the show forbade him from taking other roles while shooting for the series. He began to resent the role, and often called his Superman costume a "monkey suit" on set. His resentment may have been justified—he was ultimately typecast, and found it hard to fit in work outside the show's production schedule.

With *Superman* coming to an end in 1958, Reeves was looking forward to the future, professionally and personally. He ended his affair with a married showgirl and became engaged to socialite Leonore Lemmon. But on June 16, 1959, three days before the wedding, Reeves was found dead in his bedroom of a gunshot wound to the head. His death was ruled a suicide, but no powder residue was found on his hands, and a private investigator hired by Reeves's mother found a second bullet hole at the scene, suggesting that a second gunshot was fired…an unlikely occurrence in a suicide.

Reeves's death gave rise to the legend of a "Superman curse"— the theory that actors who played the Man of Steel would be beset by bad luck and doomed to relative obscurity…or an untimely death.

Others supposedly affected by the Superman curse:

• **Christopher Reeve:** An equestrian accident in 1995 left Reeve, the star of four Superman movies from 1978 to 1987, paralyzed from the neck down. He died in 2004 at age 52.

• **Brandon Routh:** A relatively unknown actor with just a few bit TV roles to his name, 26-year-old Brandon Routh was cast to play Superman in the 2006 movie franchise reboot *Superman Returns*. The movie performed below expectations (it made "only" $200 million at the box office) and was critically drubbed. Another

Superman movie, *The Man of Steel*, is in the works, but Routh's contract was not renewed and he won't be returning to the role. His only major credit since *Superman Returns* is a handful of episodes of the action show *Chuck*.

THE *NIGHT COURT* BAILIFF CURSE

After only a single season on the sitcom *Night Court* (1984–92), actress Selma Diamond, who played court bailiff Selma Hacker, died from lung cancer at the age of 64. Her replacement, Florence Halop, died from lung cancer at the age of 63, also after just one season. Producers decided not to take any more chances and hired a much younger actress, 32-year-old Marsha Warfield, to replace Halop. She stayed on *Night Court* until the show was canceled. (And as of 2011, she's still alive.)

THE *DIFF'RENT STROKES* CURSE

Diff'rent Strokes (1978–86) was about two orphaned African-American boys (Gary Coleman and Todd Bridges) who were adopted into a white family consisting of a wealthy businessman (Conrad Bain) and his teenage daughter (Dana Plato). While it's common for former child stars to struggle as adults, the three *Diff'rent Strokes* kids had particularly difficult setbacks.

• **Dana Plato:** The actress became pregnant in 1984 at the age of 20 and was written out of the show. She quit acting, moved to Las Vegas, and began working at a dry cleaner. She posed nude for *Playboy* in 1989 and things went downhill from there—she robbed a video store at gunpoint in 1991, and was arrested a short time later for forging a Valium prescription. After a 30-day stint in jail, she entered rehab and tried to restart her career, but the only work she could get was in soft-core porn. In May 1999, she appeared on Howard Stern's radio show and was subjected to a slew of insults from callers. The following day, she committed suicide by taking an overdose of pain pills.

• **Todd Bridges:** After *Diff'rent Strokes* ended, he became addicted to crack and spent time in jail for attempted murder. He was eventually acquitted of trying to kill his drug dealer, but was arrested again in 1993 for stabbing a man in the chest. Bridges dodged another bullet when prosecutors concluded that he had acted in self-defense. He finally kicked drugs in the late 1990s.

- **Gary Coleman:** Coleman, one of the most famous and recognizable child stars of all time, never grew taller than 4'8" due to a congenital kidney ailment. He required daily dialysis and had many other health problems, including heart trouble and seizures. During *Strokes*, Coleman was the highest-paid actor on TV, earning $100,000 per episode. By 1989, however, he was nearly broke, and sued his adoptive parents for "misappropriation of funds"—in other words, for stealing his money. He won the suit, but legal fees ate up the financial award, leaving him just as broke as when he'd started.

In the late 1990s and early 2000s, he attempted suicide twice, filed for bankruptcy, and was arrested for punching a female fan and for domestic violence. In 2008 Coleman ran over a photographer outside a bar, and the matter was settled in a civil suit. In January 2010, he was arrested for attacking his wife again. Four months later, Coleman died after falling down the stairs in his home and suffering a head injury.

THE REALITY SHOW COUPLES CURSE
Perhaps Uncle John should turn down ABC's offer to star in the next season of *The Bachelor* (and not just because he's happily married). Why? Reality show couples, whether they were together before a show began or met because of it, have little chance of living happily ever after:

- **Jessica Simpson** and **Nick Lachey** showcased their new married life on MTV's *Newlyweds* (2003–05)…and then split up.

- **Travis Barker** and **Shanna Moakler** of *Meet the Barkers* (2005–06): Split!

- **Hulk** and **Linda Hogan** of *Hogan Knows Best* (2005–07): Split!

- **The Gosslins** of *Jon & Kate Plus 8* (2007–09): Split!

- **Carmen Electra** and **Dave Navarro** of *Til Death Do Us Part—Carmen & Dave* (2004): Split!

- In 15 cycles of *The Bachelor* (2002–present) and six cycles of *The Bachelorette* (2003–present), only one couple has gotten and stayed married.

- **Happy exception:** Ozzy and Sharon Osbourne of *The Osbournes* (2002–05).

Redundant: the "n" in NCIS: *Navy* stands for "navy."

TOILET TALK

We'd be flushed with embarrassment if we didn't drop in at least a few bathroom quotes from TV land.

"Welcome. I am honored to accept your waste."

—Japanese toilet, *The Simpsons*

Charles: You serve our food *and* build latrines?
Igor: Don't worry, sir, I washed my hands before I built the latrine.

—*M*A*S*H*

Elizabeth: That's it, Mark. I'm not staying here anymore. Every faucet leaks. Your toilet actually *rocks*.
Mark: I kind of like that.

—*ER*

"This toilet comes with a lifetime guarantee! So we'll never have to worry about buying another one. And when I die, Kyle will inherit the throne. It'll be like Shakespeare!"

—Jim, *According to Jim*

"How many of you kids want to wake up in a public bathroom lying in a pool of what you hope is your own filth?"

—Jerri, *Strangers with Candy*

Janitor: You've been stealing pudding cups and toilet paper?
J.D.: No! I hate pudding and I don't use toilet paper. I have one of those French things that shoots water up your butt.
Janitor: Bidet?
J.D.: Bidet to you, sir!

—*Scrubs*

"Listen, you, I'll use these facilities when I'm damn well ready! Until then you shall continue to sanitize my crevice and be damn grateful for the opportunity! Starting right…hmmp…hmmp, well then, not now, but soon!"

—Baby Stewie, *Family Guy*

"The toilets of today aren't worthy of the name. They come in designer colors and they're too low. When you flush them, they make this weak, almost apologetic sound. Not the Ferguson! When you flush, BA-WOOSH! A Ferguson says, 'I'm a toilet! Sit down and give me your best shot!'"

—Al, *Married… with Children*

STREET SMART

Were you one of the millions of kids who grew up watching Sesame Street?
If so, these facts are for you, brought to you by the letters "U.J."

• In 1966 Carnegie Foundation president Lloyd Morrisett noticed that his three-year-old daughter was mesmerized by a TV test pattern. He wondered aloud at a dinner party if TV might be used for educational purposes for toddlers, since they were already so clearly interested in it. TV producer Joan Ganz Cooney hosted that party; a year later, Morrisett and Cooney formed the Children's Television Workshop, the company that would soon produce *Sesame Street.*

• The first episode aired on PBS on November 10, 1969.

• The show initially had an annual budget of $8 million, unheard of for a kids' show at the time. Half of the money came from the federal government; most of the rest came from the Carnegie Foundation.

• In 1970 the Mississippi State Educational Television Commission banned *Sesame Street* because it depicted racial inte-

gration. The decision was reversed 22 days later.

• In the mid-1970s, about 130 episodes of *Sesame Street* were produced each year. In 2010, due to public television budget cuts, only 26 were made.

• As of this writing, 4,212 episodes have aired—nearly five times as many as *Mister Rogers' Neighborhood.*

• Grover was originally green, not blue.

• Muppet game-show host Guy Smiley's "real" name is Bernie Liederkrantz.

• Cookie Monster's real name is Sid.

• First major female Muppet character on *Sesame Street*: Zoe, introduced in 1992.

• Big Bird is an 8' 2" Golden Condor and has 6,000 feathers (real turkey feathers, dyed yellow).

• Most frequent "sponsor": the letter B (210 episodes).

First deaf character on television: Linda on *Sesame Street.*

- Largest number of the day: 40. Lowest: 0.

- The Count, born on October 9, 1,830,653 B.C., is roughly two million years old.

- Ernie's song "Rubber Duckie" (performed by Jim Henson) reached #16 on the pop chart in 1970.

- The show has been aired—either in reruns of the original U.S. episodes or in locally produced versions—in 180 countries. Today it's regularly aired in 16 countries, including Mexico (*Plaza Sésamo*) and South Africa (*Takalani Sesame*).

- Four of the six main puppeteers of *Avenue Q*, the 2003 Broadway musical that parodies *Sesame Street*, were former *Sesame Street* puppeteers.

- ATV, the company that owned the rights to the Beatles' songs, once sued *Sesame Street* for $5.5 million because of a song parody used on the show: "Letter B," based on the Beatles' "Let It Be," performed by a Muppet rock band called the Beetles. After Michael Jackson bought the rights to the Beatles' song catalog in 1985, the case was dropped.

- To encourage kids to eat healthier, Cookie Monster is now shown voraciously eating a variety of foods, not just cookies. His classic song "C Is for Cookie" has given way to a new tune called "Cookies Are a Sometimes Food." In 2007 this inspired an urban legend that Cookie Monster was being replaced with Veggie Monster.

- Another *Sesame* myth: Bert and Ernie are homosexual partners. In 1993 rumors surfaced that the two were getting married—or were about to be killed off due to network pressure. Children's Television Workshop released a statement saying that Bert and Ernie are not gay because "they are puppets."

- Characters *are* revamped, though. Telly debuted in 1979 as Television Monster, sort of like Cookie Monster, but crazy for TV instead of cookies. He even had an antenna on top of his head and his eyes would spin around whenever he turned on a television. A year later, the antenna was removed and he was reintroduced as an excessive worrier.

- The most marketed character since his official 1985 debut: Elmo. But he'd been a part of the show for years before becoming a superstar—as a nameless, non-speaking extra nicknamed "Baby Monster."

TECHNICAL FLOPS

Who doesn't want the latest gadget that makes TV better? Some caught on—remote controls, full color, big screens. These didn't.

Color overlay: Color TV was widely available by the late 1960s but was prohibitively expensive. Enter the TV Color Screen—a colored plastic sheet placed over the TV screen to simulate color. The $1 overlay was separated into four bands: The top was blue-tinted, the next orange, then yellow, then red. The strips were supposed to blend together to create the illusion of color, but all they did was make faces look orange and grass look red.

Picture-in-picture: Problem—there are two shows you want to watch on at the same time. Solution, in the 1980s—picture-in-picture, a feature on TV sets that put two channels on the screen, one in a small window in the corner. The option had its drawbacks (you couldn't *listen* to both shows at the same time) and had nearly disappeared by 2000, made obsolete by DVRs, which can record a show while you watch another one.

Bed glasses: Ever find it too much trouble to sit up to watch TV? Try Bed Glasses, mirrored shades outfitted with prisms that allow you to see your favorite show while lying flat on your back. Initially marketed to the general public, these weren't a big seller, so the manufacturer reconceived the glasses as a quasi-medical device for the bedridden.

Pocket TV: Today you can buy a $100 pocket-size digital TV, but tiny TVs weren't always so cheap. Sinclair Electronics debuted a black-and-white model with a two-inch screen in 1977, but the machinery required it to be the size of a dictionary (and it cost $400—or $1,200 in today's dollars). Only a few hundred sold. In 1984 the first true pocket-size color TV arrived: Casio's TV-10 weighed 12 ounces and measured 5"x 3" x 1". The battery-powered device couldn't generate a very bright image, though, making watching anything on it difficult. And it cost $300—almost as much as a full-size TV at the time. Few sold, but Casio kept offering them into the 1990s.

TROUBLE ON THE SET

On-screen, everybody got along. Off-screen?
They were at each other's throats.

ETHEL DOES NOT LOVE FRED

Besides Lucille Ball and Desi Arnaz, the only regular cast members on CBS's *I Love Lucy* (1951–57) were William Frawley and Vivian Vance, who portrayed the Ricardos' neighbors, Fred and Ethel Mertz. Their characters would often insult each other's physical flaws (he was bald, she was slightly overweight). Offscreen, Frawley and Vance were even nastier to each other. Vance almost didn't take the part because of the 22-year age difference between herself, 42 at the time of the show's debut, and Frawley, 64. She complained constantly that he was old enough to be her father. Frawley began to resent Vance's snide comments and fired back. He once remarked to a reporter that Vance was "one of the finest gals to come out of Kansas, but I often wish she'd go back there." When Frawley died in 1966, Vance exclaimed (on the set of *The Lucy Show*), "Champagne for everyone!"

NUDE FEUD

Kirk Cameron was the breakout star of ABC's *Growing Pains* (1985–92)—and a teen idol. His popularity meant that he had more power over the show than most of the producers did. In 1988 he converted to evangelical Christianity and started forcing script and even cast changes if he felt the content was too racy. For instance, when his character, Mike Seaver, was scripted to marry Julie, the family's live-in nanny, in a 1989 episode, Cameron insisted that the wedding be called off and that Julie McCullough, the actress who played Julie, be fired. Why? McCullough had previously appeared nude in *Playboy*. She showed up for work one day thinking her character would be getting married—but instead, the script change called for her to stand up Mike at the altar. Once a regular cast member, McCullough disappeared from the series. By 1991 the producers were fed up with Cameron's constant demands and quit en masse. *Growing Pains* was canceled the following year.

BE COS HE SAID SO

Most of the child cast members of *The Cosby Show* followed star and producer Bill Cosby's rules: Show up on time and be respectful of adults (he insisted they call him "Mr. Cosby"). But Lisa Bonet, who portrayed daughter Denise, frequently showed up late, if she showed up at all. Bonet was massively popular with teen viewers, so Cosby put up with it…until Bonet made the movie *Angel Heart* in 1987: In shocking contrast to her character on the squeaky-clean family sitcom, Bonet played the underage love interest of Mickey Rourke's character, and the movie featured graphic sex scenes. That was too much for Cosby, so he took Bonet off *Cosby* in a way that benefited him, too: He produced a spin-off, *A Different World*, depicting Denise at college. A year into the run of that show, however, Bonet got pregnant (she was married to rock star Lenny Kravitz at the time). Cosby fired her. She eventually returned to *The Cosby Show*, but again began showing up late for rehearsals. Cosby fired her for good this time and didn't invite her back for the series finale in 1992.

DON'T CALL ME SHIRLEY

Although *Laverne & Shirley* episodes opened with the lead characters skipping down the street arm in arm, the actresses who played the brewery-working roommates had a contentious relationship offscreen. Penny Marshall (Laverne) and Cindy Williams (Shirley) often clashed over minor things—such as which actress had more lines in an episode or the most square footage in her dressing room. As the series continued its seven-year run (1976–83), Williams became increasingly resentful of the power she felt Marshall wielded. Penny's brother, Garry Marshall, had created the series, and Marshall's father and sister worked on the show as producers. Williams began to refer to her co-star derisively as "management." Williams finally walked off the set in 1982, claiming that producers were using her real-life pregnancy to force her out. She filed a $20 million lawsuit that was later settled out of court. That also meant that the final season of *Laverne & Shirley* didn't have Shirley in it—Laverne (and Lenny, Squiggy, and the rest) moved to Los Angeles without her—but the show couldn't withstand such a seismic shift and was canceled in 1983.

Inscribed on Jackie Gleason's headstone is his catchphrase, "And Away We Go!"

TV INDUSTRY TERMS

Every profession has its own lingo. Here's some terminology that may come in handy the next time you're visiting a TV studio or sitting in on a production meeting. (More on page 341.)

Sweeps week: The periods throughout the year during which people across the country fill out "ratings diaries," recording what TV shows they watch, for the Nielsen Company. During sweeps periods—in November, February, May, and July—networks release new series, special episodes, etc.—because getting good ratings during a Sweeps Week means you can charge more for advertising. In the first Sweeps Week in 1954, the ratings diaries were collected in a "sweep" of the country from east to west—that's where the name comes from. These days, the sweeps actually last about a month.

Overscanning: When a broadcaster sends out a television signal, the image is designed to be a little larger than a TV screen, so it fills the entire screen. On some older TVs, as much as 10 percent of the image couldn't be seen.

Zapping: Changing channels when a commercial comes on.

Zipping: Fast-forwarding through commercials while viewing a prerecorded show.

Aspect ratio: The shape of a TV as a ratio of width to height. The National Television Standards Committee set the standard of 4:3 in 1941. That means that if the width of your television screen is 40 inches, the height will be 30 inches—a ratio of 4:3. Widescreen TVs have a higher width-to-height ratio: 16:9. Since most new TVs are now manufactured with this ratio, most TV shows are now shot in 16:9, too.

Cold open: When a TV show goes right into the program before the title or opening credits appear, then runs the title and credits a few minutes later (or has no opening sequence at all). It's a device used to get viewers interested in the show before they have a chance to change the channel. Some examples of shows that begin with a cold open: *Star Trek*, *Saturday Night Live*, *Seinfeld*, *The Office*, and *Law & Order*.

THE DAILY SHOW

*A look at the evolution of "the most
important television program ever."*

• *The Daily Show* premiered on July 21, 1996, hosted by ex-college
basketball player and ESPN *SportsCenter* anchor Craig Kilborn.
One of Comedy Central's first original programs, it was conceived
as a parody of news shows, like *Saturday Night Live's* "Weekend
Update" or HBO's *Not Necessarily the News*, but with a news-
magazine approach, complete with interviews and remote segments, similar to a sleepy local news program.

• Early features included "5 Questions," random questions for
celebrity guests ("What's better, the screaming of 10,000 fans, or a
hug from your mom?"); "Out at the Movies," movie reviews by gay
film critic Frank DeCaro; "This Day in Hasselhoff History"; and
"Last Weekend's Top-Grossing Films, Converted into Lira," delivered in Italian.

• In an interview with *Esquire* in 1997, Kilborn said about co-
creator and head writer Lizz Winstead, "Lizz does find me very
attractive. If I wanted her to **** me, she would." Winstead and
the rest of the show's producers suspended Kilborn for a week.
Winstead left the show not long after the incident.

• Jon Stewart took over in 1999 (Kilborn left to host *The Late,
Late Show* on CBS) and, with a new writing staff, developed *The
Daily Show* into a satire of cable news and politics.

• Prominent former *Daily Show* "correspondents" include Stephen
Colbert, now the host of the spin-off *The Colbert Report*; Steve
Carell (*The Office*); Rob Corddry (*Hot Tub Time Machine*); Ed
Helms (*The Office*); and comedians Lewis Black, Demetri Martin,
and Mo Rocca.

• The "Moment of Zen" at the end of each episode, usually a clip
from the show humorously taken out of context, has been on the
show since day one. The first "Moment": film footage of a yak
giving birth.

- Under Stewart's reign, *The Daily Show* has won seven straight Emmy Awards for Best Comedy/Variety Series, two Peabody Awards, a GLAAD Media Award, and a Teen Choice Award.

- The three most-watched *Daily* episodes: One with presidential nominee Barack Obama as a guest in October 2008 (3.6 million viewers), one with guest Michelle Obama in September 2008 (3 million), and one with President Barack Obama in October 2010 (2.9 million).

- The show's theme song was written by Bob Mould of the influential post-punk band Hüsker Dü and performed by They Might Be Giants.

- In the summer of 2010, a story on the women's interest website Jezebel.com accused *The Daily Show* of being "a boy's club where women's contributions are often ignored or dismissed," after the show hired a sexy new female correspondent (Olivia Munn). The story contained quotes from several former staffers. The show responded with a letter on its own website, signed by more than 30 female staffers, addressed, "Dear People Who Don't Work Here." The letter continued, "We must admit it is entertaining to be the subjects of such a vivid and dramatic narrative. However, while rampant sexism at a well-respected show makes for a great story, we want to make something very clear: The place you may have read about is not our office."

- In a 2010 *Time* magazine poll, Stewart, even though he hosts what is really a comedy show, was named "America's most trusted newsman," with 44 percent of the vote. (NBC's Brian Williams came in second.)

- As of November 2010, in the 18-to-49-year-old demographic most sought by advertisers, the most-watched late night show was not one hosted by Jay Leno, David Letterman, or Conan O'Brien. It was *The Daily Show*.

*　　*　　*

"People will pay more to be entertained than educated."
—Johnny Carson

DÉJÀ VIEW

With careers spanning dozens or even hundreds of projects, it's no surprise that TV actors and writers like to throw in the occasional nod to one of their earlier works.

David McCallum: He achieved TV stardom in the 1960s as Russian spy Illya Kuryakin on *The Man From U.N.C.L.E.* Forty years later, he played Ducky, the medical examiner on *NCIS*. In a 2008 episode, Gibbs (Mark Harmon) is asked what Ducky looked like as a young man. Gibbs replies, "Illya Kuryakin."

Kelsey Grammer: In a 2004 *Frasier* episode, Nannette (Laurie Metcalf) is lamenting her longtime role as a nanny on a kids' TV show. She asks Frasier, whose first TV appearance was on a 1984 *Cheers* episode, "Do you have any idea what it's like to play the same character for 20 years?" Frasier gives her a knowing look.

Peter Boyle: The veteran actor played Frank on *Everybody Loves Raymond*. In one episode, Frank gives his son the same speech about morality (minus the curse words) that Boyle gave to Robert De Niro in 1976's *Taxi Driver*. In another episode, Frank dresses up for Halloween as the Frankenstein monster, the role he played in 1974's *Young Frankenstein*.

Katey Sagal: On a 2000 episode of *Futurama*, Sagal, who voices the cyclops Leela, meets another cyclops named Alkazar, falls in love, and marries him. All is well until he says, "Call me Al"— before she knows it, the dignified Leela is acting like Sagal's breakout character Peg, Al Bundy's loveless wife on *Married...with Children*. Leela sports Peg's bouffant hairdo, whines like her, and watches Alkazar sit on the couch with his hand down his pants, the way Al did.

Bob Newhart: On *Newhart*, Mike (Peter Scolari) mentions Newhart's old show, *The Bob Newhart Show*, to innkeeper Dick Loudon (Newhart). Mike calls it "the one with the shrink who stutters." Dick replies, "He didn't stutter, he...he...he stammered."

George Reeves (*Adventures of Superman*) was buried in his Clark Kent suit.

Peter Scolari: Scolari starred as the father in the TV version of *Honey, I Shrunk the Kids.* A running joke throughout the 1997–2000 series is that no one can remember the name of the "other guy" from the 1980s Tom Hanks sitcom *Bosom Buddies.* That other guy: Peter Scolari.

Tony Hale: On *Arrested Development,* Hale's character, Buster, dances to Styx's "Mr. Roboto" while sitting in a truck. Hale was re-creating a Volkswagen commercial from 1999 in which he did the same robotic dance moves to the Styx song in a VW Golf.

Courteney Cox: On *Cougar Town,* Travis (Dan Byrd) is looking through his mother's (Cox) yearbook, sees a photo, and remarks, "Is that you dancing onstage with Bruce Springsteen?" In 1984, when Cox was 20 years old, she played a concertgoer who gets pulled onstage to dance with the Boss in his "Dancing in the Dark" video.

John Lithgow: Dick Solomon (Lithgow), an alien on *3rd Rock from the Sun,* meets the "Big Giant Head" alien (William Shatner) at an airport. BGH tells Dick that while he was on the plane he saw a gremlin on the wing. Dick responds, "The same thing happened to me!" Shatner was referencing his role from the 1963 *Twilight Zone* episode "Nightmare at 20,000 Feet," which Lithgow reprised in 1983's *Twilight Zone: The Movie.* (In another episode, Dick gives the same speech about the evils of rock 'n' roll that Lithgow's character gave in the 1984 movie *Footloose.*)

John Schneider: On the Superman drama *Smallville,* Jonathan Kent (Schneider) drives his pickup truck while listening to the "Good Ol' Boys" theme song from Schneider's breakout 1970s show, *The Dukes of Hazzard.* In another episode, his *Hazzard* co-star Tom Wopat shows up in the Dukes' familiar-looking orange Dodge Charger.

*   *   *

Random fact: TV personality Ed McMahon was a decorated colonel in the Korean War, flying 85 combat missions.

DOG SHOWS

One thing that you don't see much on TV anymore are sitcoms or dramas that revolve around animals—shows like Lassie, Mister Ed, and Gentle Ben had their heyday in the 1950s, '60s, and '70s. But with the hits came the misses. Here are some of the more forgettable "dog shows"—which, in this case, means both a "show about dogs" and "a show that turned out to be a dog."

Show: *Run, Joe, Run*
Duration: 26 episodes (1974–76)
Bad dog! *The Fugitive* was a high-stakes drama: After being falsely accused of murdering his wife, a man goes on the run, both to avoid the cops and to find the real murderer. In 1974 *The Fugitive* was remade…for kids. In this version, Joe, a German Shepherd in the army's K-9 corps, is wrongly accused of attacking his master, and goes on the run to avoid being put down. The end product was both less and more dramatic than *The Fugitive:* With no mysterious-killer element, it wasn't as exciting. And because it was about a friendly dog that people wanted to kill, *Run, Joe, Run* traumatized its audience of children.

Show: *Dad's a Dog*
Duration: One pilot episode in 1989
Bad dog! By 1989 actor Peter Bonerz, best known as Jerry the orthodontist on *The Bob Newhart Show*, was struggling to find acting work, so he agreed to star in this failed sitcom pilot…in which he played a struggling actor who can only find work on a bad sitcom…also called *Dad's a Dog*. The premise of the show-within-a-show: A man dies but his soul and voice live on in the body of his family's dog. The show-biz work scenes are juxtaposed against the actor's equally bizarre off-set life, where his family makes fun of him because he's on a show called *Dad's a Dog*.

Show: *K-9000*
Duration: A 1991 two-hour TV movie that served as an unsuccessful pilot episode

---

Bad dog! A Los Angeles cop (Chris Mulkey) volunteers to take part in a K-9 (police dog) program. But he doesn't get just any highly trained German Shepherd—he's partnered with a half-dog/half-robot cyborg. What's more, the human cop and the dog-robot cop can communicate telepathically via a microchip implanted in the (human) cop's brain.

Show: *McGurk: A Dog's Life*
Duration: One pilot episode in 1979
Bad dog! Norman Lear dominated TV comedy in the '70s, producing hit shows like *All in the Family* and *Maude*, in which characters would openly and passionately discuss politics and social issues. Lear had an idea that the best way to discuss the absurdities of human behavior (particularly racism) might be for "outsiders" to do it. So he came up with *McGurk*, in which human actors wore dog costumes and makeup. The main character was world-weary and distrusting of anything new, particularly a new puppy in the neighborhood. In other words, he was a canine version of Archie Bunker from *All in the Family*.

Show: *Family Dog*
Duration: 10 episodes (1993)
Bad dog! *Amazing Stories* was a mid-'80s NBC anthology series, and its most-watched episode was 1987's "Family Dog," a lavishly animated but darkly comic story about a neglected, nameless dog and his unhappy family. *Amazing Stories* producers discussed a *Family Dog* stand-alone series, but no network thought a cartoon would work on prime-time TV. The huge success of Fox's *The Simpsons* in 1990 completely disproved that theory, and so *Amazing Stories'* executive producer Steven Spielberg, along with film director Tim Burton, approached CBS again. This time the network agreed, but production delays kept *Family Dog* off the air until 1993, six years after "Family Dog" had first aired. It also lacked the feature-film-quality animation of the original *Amazing Stories* segment, and the edgy tone of the show had been lightened up considerably. *Family Dog* aired for 10 episodes before CBS put it to sleep.

INTERACTIVE TV

*Since the earliest days of television, producers have tried to get viewers
more actively involved with the medium—with mixed results. Here
are some notable attempts at getting the viewer "into" TV.*

Winky Dink and You (1953–57)

This was the first attempt at an interactive television
show. It premiered on CBS on Saturday mornings and
was hosted by Jack Barry (later the host of *The Joker's Wild*). Barry
instructed kids watching the show to get out their Winky Dink
kits (available via mail order for 50 cents), which included
crayons and a "Magic Window." Kids were told to put these clear
plastic sheets on their TV screens (they stuck via static electricity). Barry would then introduce a wild-haired cartoon boy named
Winky Dink and his dog, Woofer, who would go on an adventure.
At some point, the TV audience would be encouraged to draw
something on the Magic Window to help Winky and Woofer get
out of trouble—a bridge over a river, a cage to trap a lion, or an ax
to cut down a tree. Whatever the kids drew on the sheet would
seem like it was part of the show—making the kids feel involved.
Winky Dink and You was a huge success, with more than two million kits selling over a four-year run. Concerns about the effects of
"television radiation"—and parents' complaints about kids drawing directly on TV screens—led to the show's demise in 1957.

Sing Along with Mitch (1961–64)

This show, which aired every night on NBC, featured goateed and
mustachioed American recording star Mitch Miller inviting viewers not just to watch the show but to sing along with him and his
guests. They sang nostalgic hits like "Five Foot Two, Eyes of Blue,"
"Silver Threads Among the Gold," and "Won't You Come Home,
Bill Bailey." To help, captions of song lyrics appeared on the bottom of the screen, with a bouncing ball to follow (making it a pre-
cursor to that other great interactive medium, karaoke). *Sing
Along with Mitch* was successful for a while, but ratings dwindled as
musical tastes veered away from Miller's old-fashioned songs. The
show was canceled in 1964.

Most DVR'd TV episode ever: the 2010 *Hawaii Five-O* premiere (3.4 million recordings).

Smellovision (1965)

In April 1965, BBC Television in the U.K. interviewed a professor from London University who announced that he had perfected a technology that allowed odors to be transmitted along with television broadcasts. To demonstrate it, he put ground-up coffee and onions in the "Smellovision" transmitter...and told viewers, "For best results, stand six feet away from your set and sniff," and to report to the network if they had smelled anything. It was, of course, a hoax...but several people called in to the network to report that they had smelled the odors in their homes. Some even said that the smell of the onions had made their eyes water—proving that interactive television sometimes only relies on an overactive imagination.

Talkback to Showtime (1981)

This was one of the first shows to allow viewers to call in and vote on a given subject—in real time. It debuted in September 1981, and allowed viewers of the cable network Showtime to call a 900 number—for a 50-cent charge—and vote on questions asked by the hosts, Renny Temple and Caren Kaye. Example: One of the first shows asked viewers if the Showtime program *Bizarre*, a Canadian sketch comedy show, had A) too much nudity and rough language, B) not enough nudity and rough language, or C) just the right amount of nudity and rough language. (Winner: B—by a lot.) *Talkback* didn't last, but the call-in feature did. It's now used on a number of shows, including *American Idol* and *Dancing with the Stars*, where viewers can call in (using toll-free numbers) and vote for their favorite performers.

The Box (1985)

This music channel, originally dubbed the Video Jukebox Network, first went on the air in 1985 in Miami as an experimental music video channel. It ran edgier material than its big competitor, MTV, including a lot of hard-core rap. The channel became extremely popular, and went national in 1990 as "The Box." And it became interactive, too: Viewers could call a 900 number (for a charge) and enter a code to request a particular video. By 1992 the Box had 16 million regular viewers in the U.S. and the U.K. In 1999 it was bought by MTV; in 2001 it became MTV2, with less music and more reality shows, but still with occasional viewer interactivity.

Vidéoway (1989–2006)
This service was first offered by Canadian cable giant Videotron in Montreal in 1989, and quickly spread around the country and to the U.K. Subscribers received a remote they could use like a regular remote, but with extra buttons for interactive functions. They could play video games, choose which camera angle they wanted while watching a sporting event, and take part in local question-and-answer shows. There were even dramas and comedies made in Montreal in which viewers could vote on plot directions as the show progressed. Vidéoway was very popular, with millions of subscribers, and lasted all the way until 2006, when it was replaced by the digital television service Illico.

Full Service Network (1994–97)
In December 1994, Time Warner launched this network on an 18-month test run to 4,000 homes in Orlando, Florida, as the "most futuristic network introduced so far." Viewers could order TV shows, movies, and sporting events; view a local entertainment guide; order and play video games; and, with nothing but their remotes, order pizzas and drinks from Pizza Hut. Plagued by technical problems, cost overruns, and the fact that Time Warner had become more interested in the new kid on the interactive block—the Internet—the Full Service Network was shut down in 1997.

TiVo (1999–present)
TiVo is the first and most recognizable brand name of digital video recorder (DVR), which records TV shows digitally and stores them on a hard drive. It's much more interactive than a VCR, allowing users to record two shows at once and pause live television. More than four million TiVo boxes have been sold in the U.S., and millions more off-brand DVRs have been issued by cable companies. While the interactivity is revolutionary (when a show is scheduled to air is no longer relevant), it has had a negative effect on the TV industry—so many people are recording shows and fast-forwarding through the commercials that advertisers have begun to look for other ways to make an impression on viewers, such as more prominent product placement.

ANTIQUES ROADSHOW: THE TOP FINDS

Since 1997 millions have tuned in weekly to the PBS series Antiques Roadshow *to see what treasures lie hidden in America's attics. Here are some of the most valuable items discovered to date.*

ANCIENT CHINESE STATUE
The owner of this marble lion statue inherited it from her grandparents, who bought it in a curio shop on a vacation in China in the 1920s. It turned out to be, as Sotheby's appraiser Lark Mason said in a 2002 episode, "one of the finest examples of Tang dynasty art that's appeared in recent years." It was carved sometime between A.D. 618 and 907 and is worth about $250,000.

GOLD CEREMONIAL SWORD
Before the Medal of Honor was first awarded in 1862, the highest honor an American officer could receive was a dress, or ceremonial, sword made of solid gold. In 1848 General William O. Butler was awarded such a sword for his service in the Mexican-American War—Butler fought in the Battle of Monterrey and injured his leg. It was passed down through the generations to the man who took it to an *Antiques Roadshow* taping in Charlotte, North Carolina, in 2002...where it was appraised for $200,000.

SEYMOUR CARD TABLE
The owner of this mahogany table bought it at a garage sale for $25. While cleaning it, she noticed its delicate inlay work and became curious, so she brought it to the *Antiques Roadshow* in 1997. Appraisers Leigh and Leslie Keno were dumbfounded to find a label on the back identifying it as the work of father-and-son master cabinetmakers John and Thomas Seymour, English émigrés to Boston in the late 18th century. Estimated at $300,000, the circa-1797 table later sold at auction for $500,000.

ART DECO JEWELRY
In 1998 a Virginia woman brought in a collection of gaudy rings,

bracelets, and pendants dating to the Jazz Age of the 1920s. Her friends told her it was just costume jewelry, but she wasn't convinced. She was right: The large "fake" gems were not only real rubies (2.5–3 carats each) but rare Burmese ones...and diamonds. Total worth: $257,000.

19TH-CENTURY NAVAJO BLANKET
Lots of people have that blanket that they drape over the back of a chair—maybe it's even an old, handmade blanket that's been in the family for generations. A man walked into a 2001 *Antiques Roadshow* taping in Tucson, Arizona, with his family's old blanket, a handwoven one with stripes of black, brown, blue, and white. He brought it in because family legend held that it had originally been a gift from the famed frontier scout Kit Carson. As it turns out, it's a national treasure—a Navajo blanket from the 1850s that was specially made for a chief. It dates from the Navajo blanket trade; less than 50 still exist. "When you walked in with this," appraiser Donald Ellis told the owner, "I just about died." The blanket now hangs in the Detroit Institute of Arts. Estimated worth: about $400,000.

PEANUTS COMIC COLLECTION
When Charles Schulz drew his *Peanuts* comic strip, he'd make a copy of the drawing and send it to the newspaper syndicate that managed the series. The originals he just gave away. In a 2009 taping in Phoenix, Arizona, a woman brought in a collection of Schulz's original *Peanuts* "masters" from the 1950s—she'd started collecting them because she and her son were big fans. Total worth: $450,000.

CHINESE JADE COLLECTION
At a 2009 taping in Raleigh, North Carolina, a woman brought in two bowls and two sculptures made from carved jade and celadon, a type of Chinese pottery, that her father had bought while stationed in China in the 1940s. It turns out they were crafted in the 18th century for Emperor Qianlong (ruler during the Qing dynasty). "I would doubt if he paid more than a hundred dollars for any one of these," appraiser James Callahan said. "It's the best thing I have ever seen on the *Roadshow*." The collection's worth: $1.07 million, the first and (so far) only million-dollar estimate on *Antiques Roadshow*.

I LOST ON *JEOPARDY!*

*Recently, one of our writers auditioned for and made it on
to the TV game show* Jeopardy! *Here's his report of how
a game show is made, what it's really like, and why
he couldn't tell us if he won. (He didn't.)*

• **Getting an audition is fairly difficult.** Each January, *Jeopardy!*
offers an online contestant test: 50 general-knowledge questions
in 10 minutes. If you pass (reportedly, you have to get at least 48
correct), a contestant coordinator sends you an e-mail a few
weeks later and invites you to one of the auditions, held in hotel
ballrooms in several major cities around the country.

• **The audition is a grueling test of you, your smarts, and your
personality.** It's a three-hour ordeal that gauges about 20 potential contestants' knowledge, personality, and ability to play the
game. Part one: another 50-question quiz. Part two: auditioners
participate in a mock game of *Jeopardy!* with a computerized game
board and buzzers. Scores aren't kept—it's a test to see if you
speak clearly, phrase your responses in the form of a question, and
keep the game moving along briskly. Part three: a personality
interview. Three contestant coordinators simply ask you about
yourself and what you would do with all that prize money. If you
passed the written test and impressed the panel with your
sparkling personality, several months later the coordinator calls
with congratulations and a show taping date.

• **Multiple shows are taped in one day.** Most game shows, *Jeopardy!* included, film five episodes—a week's worth of shows—in
one day. Taping occurs on Tuesday and Wednesday. Because of
this, contestants are told to bring three outfits with them in case
they win a game and come back as the next episode's "returning
champion." The different clothes create the illusion for home
viewers watching the next day that it's the next day.

• **There are no "fabulous parting gifts."** That may have been a
game show standard in the 1960s and '70s, but it's no longer true.
Gone are the cases of Turtle Wax, Rice-a-Roni, and the board-
game version. Contestants receive a *Jeopardy!* tote bag and a silver

picture frame with *Jeopardy!* written on it. (It's for the photograph they get of themselves with host Alex Trebek.)

- **...but you do get money...** The player who comes in first gets to keep whatever money they win. Second- and third-place contestants get a flat fee: $2,000 for second place, $1,000 for third.

- **...which covers your expenses.** *Jeopardy!* tapes in Culver City, California. You have to pay for your own travel and hotel. However, if you are a returning champion and win enough to return for the next week's taping, *Jeopardy!* pays your airfare.

- **It's a long day.** Each day's contestants (about 15 people) stay at the same hotel (which offers a special contestant discount), and at 7:00 a.m. they all gather in the lobby to board the *Jeopardy!* Bus, a shuttle that takes them to the Sony Pictures Studio. *Jeopardy!* is one of the many productions filmed there—*Wheel of Fortune* is made on the set next door to *Jeopardy!* Once they reach the studio, contestants are ushered into a "green room" with couches and bottled water, where they get an orientation ("speak clearly, don't be nervous, phrase your answers in the form of a question").

- **You have to rehearse.** After a mic fitting and a few minutes in the makeup chair, the contestants get to check out the *Jeopardy!* set. Each player gets to test the "clicker," or "answering device," and play a rehearsal game for a few minutes. At about 10:00 a.m., the studio audience is let in and the contestants head back to the green room. The order of who gets to play in each of the five episodes is chosen at random—names are placed on notecards, facedown on a table. Until their names are picked, contestants may watch from the studio audience.

- **Alex Trebek is kept far, far away.** Since the 1950s quiz-show cheating scandals, FCC rules prohibit the host from interacting with contestants, as he may have prior knowledge of the day's questions. So contestants do not meet or even see Trebek until the taping begins and he saunters out on stage.

- **It's shot in real time.** The commercial breaks on TV last about two minutes, and they do in taping as well. If Trebek flubbed a question (or "answer") during the game, he rerecords it during the break. The time can also be used for the judges (an independent accountant and one of the show's writers) to deliberate on any disputed answers. If there are no problems to fix, Trebek takes questions from the studio audience. Most commonly asked question: "How many of the answers do you know?" Trebek's standard response: "All of them, because I have them in front of me."

• **You have to wait.** There's a three-month lead time between filming and airing. A show shot in January, for example, won't air until April, although at the time of taping, they tell you exactly what day it will air so you can tell your family and set your TiVo. You also have to wait for your prize money. Whether it's first-place winnings or a runner-up prize, the check comes three months after the episode airs.

• **You can't tell anyone how you did.** They want to keep the element of surprise, both to discourage betting and for good TV. Producers begrudgingly allow contestants to tell their family how they did, but they'd prefer you didn't.

*   *   *

SAX MANIACS

Over the past 20 years, the saxophone has been the instrument that girls most want to play in school bands. Why? According to the *New York Times*, it's because Lisa Simpson plays it on *The Simpsons*. The *Times* reported on the phenomenon in 1996, citing band teachers who say they have way too many saxophone players, or who have to convince girls to play something *besides* the saxophone…otherwise they'd have a band "made up entirely of saxophones." But Tim Timmons, a music dean at the University of Missouri, theorized that the sax boom may have been caused by other influences—for instance, around the same time that the fad began, Jay Leno debuted as host of the *Tonight Show* with saxophonist Branford Marsalis as his bandleader. And then there was one of the most memorable and replayed moments of the 1992 presidential campaign: Bill Clinton's saxophone performance of "Heartbreak Hotel" on *The Arsenio Hall Show*.

EMMY TRIVIA

Interesting facts about the biggest award in TV.

• First Emmy winner: a Los Angeles ventriloquist named Shirley Dinsdale, who, in 1949 won for Most Outstanding Personality. (Ironically, the first Emmy ceremony wasn't televised.)

• "Emmy" comes from "Immy," the nickname for the image orthicon tube, a component of early TV cameras.

• ABC canceled *Barney Miller* in May 1982. Four months later, it won the Emmy for Outstanding Comedy Series.

• Most total wins by a prime time show: *Frasier*, which won 37 over its 1993–2004 run. Among those were five straight wins for Outstanding Comedy Series, a record.

• Most wins for Outstanding Drama: a three-way tie between four-time winners *Hill Street Blues*, *L.A. Law*, and *The West Wing*.

• Most Emmys won in a single season: HBO's *John Adams* miniseries, with 13 (2008).

• Most nominations in one year: *Roots*, with 37 (1977).

• Comedian Bill Maher has racked up 26 nominations for performing, writing, and acting on his shows *Politically Incorrect* and *Real Time*. He's never won.

• Most-nominated drama: *ER*, with 124 nominations (and 22 wins). Most-nominated comedy: *Cheers*, with 117 (28 wins). Most-nominated show overall: *Saturday Night Live*, with 126 nominations (28 wins).

• There's an Emmy Award for TV specials called "Best Special Class Program." The Academy Awards telecast has won it, but the Emmy Awards telecast cannot win that Emmy Award—it's ineligible.

• Candice Bergen (for *Murphy Brown*) won the Emmy for Lead Actress in a Comedy Series five times in seven years. She probably could have won more, but after she won her fifth in 1995, she took her name out of consideration.

• Angela Lansbury has been nominated for her performances 18 times...with no wins. She never won for *Murder, She Wrote*, although she was nominated every year for all 12 years of that series' run.

• Low-rated shows that had their runs extended after a Best Series Emmy in their first season: *Cheers, Arrested Development, 30 Rock,* and *Hill Street Blues.*

• In 1994 *Star Trek: The Next Generation* became the first non-network series nominated for Outstanding Drama Series. First cable series to be nominated: *The Sopranos* (1999).

• 29 sitcoms have won the Best Comedy Series award at the Emmys. Fifteen of them took place in or around New York City, four in the Los Angeles area, two each in Washington, D.C., and Boston, two in military camps, and one each in Minneapolis, Miami, Seattle, and Scranton, Pennsylvania.

• The most-nominated prime-time series never to win an Emmy: *Newhart* (1982–90). It was nominated for 25 awards—including Outstanding Comedy series

twice. A lot of those were for Julia Duffy, nominated seven consecutive years for Supporting Actress in a Comedy Series.

• *Tonight Show* hosts connection: Steve Allen hosted the ceremony in 1955 and 1980; Johnny Carson, from 1971 to '74; Jay Leno in 1990; Conan O'Brien in 2002, 2003, and 2006.

• Regional Emmys (mostly awarded in news categories) are given out annually in 20 areas around the country.

• In 2000 two shows produced (and largely written) by David E. Kelley won the Outstanding Comedy *and* Outstanding Drama awards: *Ally McBeal* and *The Practice.* It's the only time someone has won both top awards in one night.

• Roxana Zal is the youngest prime-time Emmy winner, earning the award for Supporting Actress in a Special in 1984 at age 14 for *Something About Amelia.* The youngest-ever nominee was Keshia Knight Pulliam of *The Cosby Show,* nominated for Supporting Actress in a Comedy Series in 1986 at age six.

In its 9-year run, *The Facts of Life* received only 1 Emmy nomination: for hairstyling. (It lost.)

DEAD AIR

As if television didn't already feature plenty of fake death and mayhem, sometimes a real tragedy occurs live on the air.

DECEASED: Tommy Cooper
WHAT HAPPENED: Cooper was a popular British comedian and magician well known for performances that would often go intentionally awry. Unfortunately, during an April 1984 appearance on the variety show *Live from Her Majesty's*, he collapsed onstage as millions of British viewers watched at home. Everyone in the theater that night, including his onstage magician's assistant, thought it was a gag (he'd done that bit before). The live audience continued laughing, completely oblivious to what was going on—Cooper, 63, was having a massive heart attack as he keeled over backward behind the red stage curtain. On the other side, his manager struggled to pull him backstage while the show's director frantically cut to a commercial. Cooper was pronounced dead shortly afterward.

DECEASED: Robert "Budd" Dwyer
WHAT HAPPENED: While serving as the treasurer of Pennsylvania, Dwyer was brought up on charges for allegedly accepting a bribe from a California accounting firm. Dwyer repeatedly claimed he was innocent, even after a jury found him guilty. On January 22, 1987, the day before he was scheduled to be sentenced, Dwyer called a press conference. As the event was broadcast throughout Pennsylvania, Dwyer once more professed his innocence...then pulled a .357 Magnum out of a manila envelope. As several reporters rushed the stage to disarm him, Dwyer pointed the gun at his head and pulled the trigger. He died instantly.

DECEASED: The Crew of the Space Shuttle *Challenger*
WHAT HAPPENED: The launch of the space shuttle *Challenger* was a major news and cultural event in January 1986. It was the first spaceflight with civilians onboard, including Christa McAuliffe, a schoolteacher. Because of that, thousands of schools across the country canceled classes so students could watch the blastoff

of the *Challenger* from Florida's Kennedy Space Center. Just 73 seconds after liftoff, the spacecraft exploded over the Atlantic Ocean, killing its seven-member crew. Investigations later revealed that a seal on a rocket booster had failed. The accident brought the shuttle program to a standstill for nearly three years.

DECEASED: Christine Chubbuck
WHAT HAPPENED: TV journalist Chubbuck fought depression and suicidal tendencies throughout most of her adult life. In 1974 while she was working as a news anchor at WXLT, a St. Petersburg, Florida, station, she grew increasingly despondent after learning that a station employee whom she had a crush on had begun dating a sports reporter. A few months later, in July 1974, while hosting the morning talk-show *Suncoast Digest*, Chubbuck said, "In keeping with Channel 40's policy of bringing you the latest in blood and guts, and in living color, you are going to see another first—attempted suicide." Chubbuck pulled out a revolver and killed herself. The station quickly cut to a black screen, a standard public service announcement, and then a movie. Chubbuck's ashes were scattered into the Gulf of Mexico during a ceremony attended by 120 family members, friends, and co-workers. She was 30 years old.

*   *   *

MAKE ROOM FOR MURDER

In 1953 Danny Thomas's family sitcom *Make Room for Daddy* debuted on ABC. Thomas was ordered, against his wishes, to cast film star Jean Hagen (*Singin' in the Rain*) as his wife Margaret. On-screen, Hagen was beloved and received three Emmy nominations. But off-screen, Thomas couldn't stand her attitude or what he thought was her slovenly appearance. "For God's sake, Jean," he once yelled during a rehearsal, "Put on high heels, put on a little lipstick!" After the third season, Hagen decided to quit the show, but by then, she was too popular to recast the role. Thomas was so incensed that he made sure Hagen could never return even if she wanted to. When the fourth season of *Make Room for Daddy* premiered in 1956, viewers were shocked to learn that Margaret was dead. She was the first main character ever killed off on a family sitcom.

THE RURAL PURGE

*In the early 1970s, CBS undertook a massive programming overhaul
and canceled more than a dozen shows. But it wasn't a random
housecleaning. As actor Pat Buttram of Green Acres said,
"They killed anything with a tree in it." Here's why.*

THESE KIDS TODAY

In 1969 CBS programming chief Fred Silverman noticed a
growing trend in television: Shows about young, hip,
professional city dwellers were getting all of the attention, the high
ratings, and the advertising dollars. Research from Nielsen Media
backed up his observation. Audiences between the ages of 18 and
50 were attracted to programs like *Laugh-In, The Mod Squad,* and
Julia, which were about young people of various races and were
often set in cities. Advertisers began to notice the trend, too, and
they urged Silverman to pursue this audience. Younger viewers,
particularly urbanites, have the least-ingrained brand loyalties and
the highest disposable incomes, making them very attractive to
marketers. (They're what drove CBS to develop *The Smothers
Brothers Comedy Hour* a couple years earlier—see page 444.)

COUNTRY BROADCASTING SYSTEM

Silverman looked at the programs CBS was offering, and found
that almost every one on the prime-time schedule was the exact
opposite of what advertisers wanted: Most were shows with rural
settings, aimed at older viewers. CBS's roster clearly wasn't sophisticated, multicultural, or urban—it had a bunch of corny comedies
like *Petticoat Junction* and *Mayberry R.F.D.,* and variety programs
like *The Ed Sullivan Show* and *The Red Skelton Show.*

It wasn't as if these shows were falling behind in the ratings—
CBS was the most-watched network overall, and many of the rural
and older-skewing shows were still top-30 hits. But the people
watching them didn't fall into the prime marketing demographic.
Silverman had a bold idea: Go for the young, urban crowd by
completely overhauling the CBS lineup. All of the shows that had
been on the air for more than a decade would be canceled, as
would series that didn't appeal to young adults and those that

were set in the country. It didn't matter how popular they were—
if they didn't fit Silverman's plan for a new era in television, they
were out. TV insiders nicknamed it the "Rural Purge."

CULTURAL REVOLUTION

Silverman tested his concept with a single cancellation, *Petticoat
Junction*, in the spring of 1970. It was a good candidate—it was
the most "country" show in the lineup, and the lowest-rated one.
Replacing it in its time slot: *The Mary Tyler Moore Show*, about a
single professional woman working at a big-city TV station.
Canned a few months later was *The Red Skelton Show*, which had
been on the air for 20 years and finished the season at #7.

Midway through the 1970–71 season, CBS debuted *All in the
Family*, a controversial comedy about a Queens bigot trying to
make sense of a rapidly changing world. Both it and *Mary Tyler
Moore* were hits. More importantly, they were shows relevant to
their era, and they brought in young viewers. In short, they were
the complete opposite of *Petticoat Junction* and *Red Skelton*.

CLEANING HOUSE

At the end of the 1970–71 season, it was a bloodbath at CBS.
Among the canceled shows: *Mayberry R.F.D.* (the #15 show on
TV), *Hee Haw* (#16), *The Jim Nabors Hour* (#29), *Green Acres*,
The Beverly Hillbillies, *Hogan's Heroes*, *Lassie*, and *The Ed Sullivan
Show*, which, after 24 seasons, attracted few viewers under 40.

After the 1972 season, Silverman cut *The Glen Campbell
Goodtime Hour* and the 12-year-old *My Three Sons*. The only long-
running shows kept: *Here's Lucy* and *Gunsmoke*...which were canceled in 1974 and 1975, respectively, after Silverman left CBS.

YOU'RE GONNA MAKE IT AFTER ALL

It was a risky move to cancel long-running hits, but it paid off.
CBS successfully courted young, urban viewers with young, urban
shows—and created a new era in television. CBS's new shows
defined the 1970s, none more so than the shows of Norman Lear,
who created *All in the Family* and other comedies that explored
social issues, such as *Maude* and *Good Times*. And more edgy shows
rounded out CBS's new lineup between 1971 and 1975: *The Bob
Newhart Show*, *M*A*S*H*, *One Day at a Time*, and *The Jeffersons*.

The f-word and its various forms were used 2,980 times during the three-year run of *Deadwood.*

LET'S GET *LOST*, PART I

We've never done this kind of thing before—lay out a TV series and tell you the entire plot. But then, there's never been a show as complicated, ambitious, weird, or wacky as ABC's Lost (2004–10). If you're a fan, you'll probably enjoy revisiting the island. If you've never seen the show, you'll probably end up...lost.

MYSTERIOUS ISLAND

Jack Shephard wakes up in a jungle and hears screams. He runs onto a beach to find the burning wreckage of Oceanic Airlines Flight 815. Jack was on that plane when it took off on September 22, 2004, from Sydney, Australia, bound for Los Angeles. Then it crashed on this deserted island. There are 47 other survivors, and on that first night they hear strange noises coming from the jungle: metallic clanking and trees snapping in half.

The next day, a smaller group of the "Lostaways" (a fan nickname for the Oceanic survivors) encounters a polar bear in the jungle. Later, they're attacked by a monster made out of smoke, and it kills the plane's pilot. Then they pick up a radio signal recorded in 1988 by a Frenchwoman. It says, "If anyone can hear this, please help us. They are dead. It killed them all."

What the hell is going on? It's going to take a full six seasons to explain these mysteries and many others. Starting with: Who are these people?

MAN OF SCIENCE, MAN OF FAITH

The Lostaways are strangers to each other...or are they? Flashbacks reveal that many have eerie connections, and they all may have crossed paths before. In addition, they're all deeply broken people—usually because of family problems. Jack (Matthew Fox), a surgeon, was in Australia picking up the body of his dead father, Dr. Christian Shephard (that name is no accident, as we'll find out later). Christian was never impressed with Jack, leading Jack to became a perfectionist. Jack ultimately rats out Christian for operating while drunk.

Then there's John Locke (portrayed by Emmy winner Terry

O'Quinn). He's messed up because his absentee father, whose kidneys were failing, tracked him down, talked him into giving him a kidney, and then threw him out a window, paralyzing him. Locke was in Australia for a soul-searching "walkabout" (it's not a coincidence that John Locke shares his name with a famous philosopher), but wasn't able to—because he couldn't walk. Oh, except now that he's on this weird island, he *can* walk, which makes Locke think that he's been brought there for some special purpose. What special purpose? He asks the island. And then suddenly a bright light shines out from a metal hatch in the middle of the jungle.

THE NUMBERS

Hugo "Hurley" Reyes (Jorge Garcia) also has a secret: He's a multimillionaire. Severely depressed, he spent time in a mental hospital, where he met a patient named Leonard who kept repeating the numbers "4, 8, 15, 16, 23, 42." After Hurley was released, he played the numbers in the lottery and won $156 million.

But Hurley believes the numbers cursed him. Shortly after winning the lottery, his grandfather died and his fast-food chicken franchise was destroyed by a meteorite. Desperate to learn what the numbers mean, Hurley flew to Australia to find the man who gave them to Leonard, but found only the man's widow. She said the numbers drove her dead husband crazy. Hurley is convinced that his bad luck caused Flight 815 to crash (after all, 8 and 15 are two of the numbers). He also believes the crash freed him of the curse…until he visits Locke's hatch and finds the same numbers chiseled into the metal.

AND THE REST…

Other major characters (the first season listed 16 regular cast members in the opening credits, a prime-time record) include:
• Kate (Evangeline Lilly), a fugitive who killed her abusive stepfather.
• Sawyer (Josh Holloway), a Southern con man and Jack's rival for both island leadership and Kate's heart.
• Sayid (Naveen Andrews) an Iraqi ex-torturer so wracked with guilt that he can be easily manipulated.
• Walt (Malcom David Kelley), a 12-year-old who was on the flight with his father, Michael (Harold Parrineau), whom he had just met.

Lawrence Welk's vanity license plate: A1 AND A2.

• Sun and Jin (Yunjin Kim and Daniel Dae-Kim), a South Korean couple whose marriage is on the fritz until Sun, formerly sterile, gets pregnant on the island.

BLACK AND WHITE AND GOOD AND EVIL

Jack finds his father's coffin in the wreckage, but the body is gone. Jack does eventually find Christian (John Terry), though...walking through the jungle. He leads Jack to a cave occupied by two skeletons, one of which holds a black stone; the other, a white stone. Jack names the skeletons Adam and Eve.

But what really spooks the group is when they find out that Ethan (William Mapother), who has been living in their camp as a survivor, wasn't actually on Flight 815—he's lived on the island for years, and he implies that he's not alone. Ethan then kidnaps pregnant Australian survivor Claire (Emilie de Ravin), and a flashback reveals that her father is also Christian Shephard, and her baby's father is her lame artist ex-boyfriend who doesn't really love her. But fellow crash survivor Charlie (Dominick Monaghan) does. Charlie, a rock star and heroin addict, heads into the jungle to get Claire back, but Ethan gets to him first and tries to kill him. Some of the Lostaways rescue Charlie and find Claire. Charlie kills Ethan, and Kate delivers Claire's baby, whom Claire names Aaron.

COME SAIL AWAY

Sayid then finds a map that belongs to a woman named Danielle Rousseau, who, as it turns out, is the Frenchwoman who broadcast the cryptic radio signal. Sayid discovers that she came to the island with a science expedition in 1988. What happened to the rest of her team? The Smoke Monster got them.

Toward the end of Lost's first season, Michael and Walt build a raft and, along with Sawyer and Jin, attempt to sail back to civilization. Then Ethan's people—whom the Lostaways call "the Others"—intercept them and kidnap young Walt. The rest remain adrift at sea (and don't hit land until season 2). Locke finds and decides to open that mysterious hatch with some dynamite he salvages from a wrecked ship he finds on the island. Locke, Jack, and Kate peer into the hatch and...the first season ends.

Turn to page 312 to get even more Lost.

For Charlie's heroin-snorting scenes on *Lost*, actor Dominic Monaghan snorted brown sugar.

A SHOW IS BORN

A look at how some favorite shows took shape.

SEINFELD (NBC, 1989–98)
When stand-up comic Jerry Seinfeld pitched a pilot to NBC in 1989 called *The Seinfeld Chronicles*, based on his quirky observational humor, he and co-creator Larry David famously called it "a show about nothing." After a disastrous test screening (viewers said it was "too Jewish" and that "George is a loser"), the network decided to pass. Fox almost picked it up, but NBC executive Rick Ludwin saw potential in the show and offered to take it into his division—late night and special events—and air a few episodes as specials during weeks when *Saturday Night Live* wasn't scheduled to run. David and Seinfeld overhauled the show: They changed the theme music to the now-familiar bass-popping riff; they got rid of the waitress character who was going to be Jerry's comic foil and brought in Julia Louis-Dreyfus to play Elaine, his ex-girlfriend; and they changed Kessler's name to Kramer. (George, based on David, remained a loser.) The name of the show was shortened to *Seinfeld*, in part because ABC's *The Marshall Chronicles* had flopped badly. A summer test run did well enough to earn *Seinfeld* a spot in the fall 1989 lineup on Thursday nights after *Cheers*, but it struggled for three seasons before it finally cracked the top 30, the beginning of an enormously successful nine-year run.

LAW & ORDER (NBC, 1990–2010)
Dick Wolf (who honed his skills writing for *Hill Street Blues* and *Miami Vice*) wanted to create a gritty, "ripped from the headlines" New York crime drama that gave equal focus to the detectives and the prosecutors. "In 1988," he told *TV Guide*, "you could not give away hour-long shows in syndication [for nightly, pre-prime-time reruns]; you could only sell half-hour shows. So the original thinking was to try to make an hour-long show that could be split in half and sold as two half-hour shows." Wolf toyed with several vague concepts, including "Night & Day," "Life & Death"…and "Law & Order." He quickly came up with a concept: One half of

---

the show would focus on police detectives tracking down a criminal; the other would show the criminal being prosecuted. Wolf shopped it to Fox, who didn't think it fit their "edgy" programming, and CBS turned it down because it didn't have any big-name stars. NBC liked the pilot but was afraid that it couldn't maintain the same intensity every week. Wolf assured them it could...and *Law & Order* did so for 20 years. Ironically, even in its hour-long format, it's one of the most successful shows ever in syndicated reruns.

LAW & ORDER: SVU (NBC, 1999–present)

In 1998 Dick Wolf produced a TV movie featuring Chris Noth's *Law & Order* character, who'd been fired from the precinct (and the show) three years earlier. The title was simply *Exiled*, but NBC marketed it as *Exiled: A Law & Order Movie*. Result: It was the highest-rated TV movie of the year. Wolf realized he could use the "Law & Order" name to create a franchise of cop shows, each with a different premise. The first of those, Wolf thought, should be about the special victims unit, also known as the sex-crimes division. Wolf's original title for the series, which debuted in 1999, was *Law & Order: Sex Crimes*, but the network nixed it in favor of *Special Victims Unit*.

LEAVE IT TO BEAVER (CBS/ABC, 1957–63)

In 1956 the prolific radio and TV writing team of Joe Connelly and Bob Mosher (with 1,200 episode credits to their names) set out to create a family sitcom that looked at life from the point of view of the kids, unlike the parent-based *Father Knows Best* or *The Donna Reed Show*. They drew from stories of Connelly's sons and wrote a pilot called "It's a Small World." It aired in April 1957 on CBS's anthology show, *Heinz Studio '57*. Series regulars Jerry Mathers (the Beaver) and Barbara Billingsley (June Cleaver) starred, but different actors played brother Wally and father Ward. (Wise-guy neighbor Eddie Haskell was played by future Spinal Tap member and *Simpsons* voice actor Harry Shearer.) When CBS picked up the show, they named it *Wally and the Beaver*, until sponsors required a change to *Leave It to Beaver* because they feared viewers might think it was a nature program.

FUNNY NAMES

*A sitcom is only 22 minutes long, so everything
is an opportunity for writers to throw in a
gag or a pun—even character names.*

Scrubs: When Dr. Reid (Sarah Chalke) begins dating a new
intern named Keith, she has second thoughts when she finds
out that his last name is Dudemeister. He points out that it's
German, but that it does in fact mean "master of dudes."

Murphy Brown: Reporter Corky Sherwood (Faith Ford) dates a
writer named Will Forest. On the eve of their wedding, she
freaks out when she realizes that her married name will be Corky
Sherwood-Forest.

Glee: On a 2010 episode, the Glee Club wants to perform music
by Britney Spears. Club member Brittany is against it. "Britney
Spears has made my life hell," she claims. The reason: Her full
name is Brittany S. Pierce.

30 Rock: Liz Lemon's many ex-boyfriends have almost all had
funny names. They include Floyd DeBarber (a reference to Floyd
the barber from *The Andy Griffith Show*), Carol O'Conner, and an
uptight British man named Wesley Snipes.

Cheers: When her mother is on her deathbed, Carla (Rhea Perl-
man) promises to continue the family tradition of naming a son
after her father and the mother's maiden name. The resulting
name: Benito Mussolini. (Carla later changes her mind.)

Arrested Development: This one is an elaborate joke. The Bluth
family adopts a Korean teenager who they think is named Annyong, because that's what he says whenever they say hello to him.
But they're mistaken: *annyong* is the Korean word for "hello." In
the last episode of the series, the boy reveals that his name is a
Korean word meaning "one day." His grandfather gave him the
name and sent him to the U.S. to exact revenge on the Bluths
"one day" for stealing a business idea from him. The word for "one
day" in Korean, and the boy's name: Hel-Loh.

FOOD STYLING SECRETS

*Ever drooled over a juicy cheeseburger or a frosty milkshake on a
TV commercial? Here's some bad news: You probably wouldn't
want to eat them. Why? Because they've been pumped up,
glued, and painted to look tasty by a "food stylist."*

FAKE SOUP'S ON!
Food doesn't look good for long. Right after it hits
the plate, it starts to melt, cool, deflate, dry out, wilt,
perspire, or brown. And the degeneration begins even faster
under hot TV lights. That's why commercial producers and
cooking shows hire food stylists, people who know how to work
around these challenges and make food appear delicious and
perfect. As stylist Lisa Golden Schroeder says, "Taste is of little
concern, but looks are everything." Here are some of the tools
of the trade:

• **Brown shoe polish** is painted onto steaks and burgers to make
them look like they're perfectly cooked, just out of the oven or off
the grill.

• **Blowtorches** are used to quickly brown and sear the surfaces
and edges of raw meats, to brown chicken skin, and to "fire roast"
vegetables.

• **Scissors** are used to cut a triangle out of the unseen back of a
burger patty. The meat is then spread apart to give the illusion of a
very large patty.

• **White glue** glistens under hot studio lights and produces a
glossy, buttery look. It's also used as a substitute for milk in cereal
commercials, and for mayonnaise on sandwiches because it stays
thick and creamy.

• **Hair spray** prevents lettuce and vegetables from wilting, and
can also temporarily revive dry-looking foods—particularly breads
and cakes.

• **Spray deodorant** is how stylists get the look of tiny, frosty ice

---

Dick Van Dyke reached the height of 6'1" when he was just 11 years old.

crystals on the outside of an ice cream container. It also makes delicate fruits—particularly grapes—shine.

• **Motor oil** is probably what you're seeing if the commercial features maple syrup. Its color and consistency mimic those of the edible stuff.

• **Spray-on fabric softener** keeps foods from blending together, or from soaking into each other. Cold pancakes are sprayed with this before the stage syrup is applied.

• **Syringes** are used to pump water or air into foods to make them look full and plentiful. Water is used to inflate chicken skins; air is injected into mashed potatoes for fluffiness.

• **Cardboard squares** keep food from sinking or falling. They're placed between a bun, burger patty, and condiments to make the hamburger look taller. They also soak up excess liquid.

• **Glycerin** is painted on "food" to provide the perfect amount of shine and desired wetness. (It works especially well with seafood.)

• **Tampons** are dunked in water and then heated in a microwave for a few seconds. Then they're placed behind a plate of food to give the appetizing appearance of heat and steam.

• **Needle-nose dropper bottles** place air bubbles where they are needed, and where they will stay. For example, a few on top of a strawberry milkshake (which is really shortening, red dye, and maybe some strawberries) can make it look freshly blended for hours.

• **Marbles** are placed just below the surface of chunky stews and thick soups to make them look more "hearty."

• **Dishwashing detergent** is used to remove fat from raw and cooked meat to make sure the pieces look clean and appetizing.

• **Waterproofing spray,** typically used to protect shoes and winter coats, is misted on buns, breads, and cakes—it prevents sagging under hot studio lights and protects the breads from the moisture of other foods (a burger patty, for example).

Dana Plato was an Olympic figure skating hopeful until she was cast on *Diff'rent Strokes.*

DANGER ON THE SET!

Even in the unreal world of TV, sometimes things get a little too real.

EXIT, STAGE HOSPITAL
In the closing moments of a 1961 episode of *The Charlie Drake Show*, the British slapstick comic was supposed to be thrown through a door made of very light balsa wood. Unfortunately, a stagehand didn't know the plan and, thinking the door looked flimsy, reinforced it with heavier wood before showtime. Drake hit it headfirst, was knocked unconscious, and lay in a coma for four days. (He recovered.)

NOT SUCH A SPOOF
In 1995 comedian Tracey Conway had just finished a sketch on the Seattle comedy show *Almost Live!* when she fell to the floor and started convulsing. The live audience cracked up—until they realized she was having a heart attack. Then her heart stopped. A police officer in the audience performed CPR for several minutes until paramedics arrived; they promptly pronounced her dead. They were wrong, fortunately, and Conway made a full recovery. She is now a motivational speaker on the subject of health care. Ironically, the skit Conway had just finished was called "ERR," a spoof of *ER*.

HARD-HITTING COMEDY
In September 2009, Conan O'Brien was having a footrace with actress Teri Hatcher on the set of *The Tonight Show* when he slipped, fell backward, and hit his head on the floor. Slightly dazed, he went to a commercial, walked to his dressing room, changed clothes, and came back out to continue the taping—but realized he couldn't read his cue cards. "It was like a menu for an Egyptian restaurant," he said later. He tried to continue, but producers finally stopped the Friday-night taping and sent him to the hospital, where he was diagnosed with a concussion. "I promise," he told the crowd on the following Monday's show, "if you're a good audience, I'll do it again!"

FATHER OF THE YEAR?

Samuel Koch, a 23-year-old German daredevil, was a contestant on the German game show *Wetten Dass?* ("Wanna Bet That...?") in 2010. He performed a stunt that involved donning spring-powered stilts and jumping over five speeding cars as they drove at him in succession. As he jumped the fourth car—which was being driven by his father—one of the stilts clipped the top of the car, and Koch was slammed face-first onto the pavement. A TV audience of 10 million saw the accident before the cameras cut away from Koch's motionless body. He suffered numerous broken bones (including neck vertebrae), was paralyzed, and went into a coma. He later awoke, but doctors say he may be paralyzed for the rest of his life.

MORE CRINGEWORTHY MOMENTS

• In 1979 Erik Estrada was riding a motorcycle in a scene for the show *CHiPs* when he lost control of it. The 900-pound bike flew into the air and landed on top of Estrada. He fractured several ribs, broke both wrists, and was in the hospital for 10 days.

• The sci-fi drama *The Powers of Matthew Star* was slated to begin airing in 1981, but while filming an episode, star Peter Barton fell onto a pyrotechnic flare, igniting it. Co-star Lou Gossett Jr., who was tied to a chair, then fell on top of Barton. Gossett was only mildly injured, but Barton suffered third-degree burns to a quarter of his body and remained hospitalized for months. Barton recovered fully; the show hit the air a year after its intended debut. It lasted for one season.

• In a different kind of on-set accident, *Glee* star Chris Colfer found himself in need of a toilet in the middle of filming, so he rushed into the nearest bathroom he could find and relieved himself. "I had, like, 27 Diet Cokes and I had to use the restroom really bad," he said later. "I noticed the toilet wouldn't flush, and the sink wasn't working either. I looked up and realized there was no ceiling." It was a prop bathroom for *Monk*, the series shooting next door on the lot, and had no actual plumbing.

THE SHOW MUST GO ON!

*Not quite a spin-off, not quite a retooling, a "continuation" is a series
that keeps going despite the absence of one or more main characters.
But it's risky business to mess with a beloved show...*

THE GOLDEN GIRLS

Old show: At the beginning of the seventh season of *The
Golden Girls* in 1991, Bea Arthur let producers know that
she would be leaving the show at the end of the season. She was
ready to move on to other things—and so was NBC, which soon
announced that the show would wrap up in May 1992. In the final
episode, Arthur's character, Dorothy, marries her boyfriend (Leslie
Nielsen) and moves out of the Miami house she shares with her
friends.

Continued: The rest of the cast had no interest in leaving what
was still a top-30 show, and rival network CBS thought there was
some life left in the series. It bought the rights and came up with a
new concept called *The Golden Palace*: The three remaining ladies
buy and run a Miami hotel (and clash with the hotel's chef Chuy,
portrayed by Cheech Marin). Running on Friday night, *The Gold-
en Palace* floundered in the ratings, finishing the year at #57. CBS
canceled it in early 1993.

THREE'S COMPANY

Old show: In its 1983–84 season, *Three's Company* fell out of the
top 10 for the first time since its beginning in 1977, tumbling to
#35. Producers decided to make massive changes, so at the end of
the season, Terri (Priscilla Barnes) moves to Hawaii, Janet (Joyce
DeWitt) gets married, and Jack (John Ritter) falls in love with a
girl named Vicky (Mary Cadorette) and proposes.

Continued: Terri and Janet were written out, and the show
became about Jack, Vicky, and their new landlord, Vicky's disap-
proving, meddlesome father (Robert Mandan). The show came
back in the 1984–85 season, retitled *Three's a Crowd*. The changes
didn't right the sinking ship—it finished #57 in the ratings for the
year and was canceled by ABC.

Keep up: O.J. Simpson's 1994 Bronco chase started at the Kardashians' house.

SANFORD AND SON

Old show: *Sanford and Son* was a vehicle for comedian Redd Foxx, but he left the comedy after six seasons in 1977, while it was still a top-30 hit for NBC. Why? ABC had offered him more money to do a variety show, *The Redd Foxx Comedy Hour*.

Continued: With Sanford gone, NBC planned to continue with the son, portrayed by Demond Wilson. Then a salary dispute led to *his* departure, leaving NBC with a *Sanford and Son*...without either. Producers quickly revamped the show, introducing a new character named Phil (Theodore Wilson), an old military buddy of Sanford never before mentioned, who is tasked with running the Sanford Arms, a boardinghouse Sanford buys in one of the last episodes of *Sanford and Son*. NBC canceled the new incarnation after four barely watched episodes. (*The Redd Foxx Comedy Hour* lasted a little bit longer, until January 1978.)

COLUMBO

Old show: *Columbo*, starring Peter Falk as the wily police detective, aired for seven seasons as part of *The NBC Mystery Movie*, a "wheel" series in which it alternated with other detective shows, such as *McCloud* and *McMillan and Wife*. *Columbo* was by far the most popular segment, and by 1977 Falk was commanding $250,000 an episode...but he wanted to make only four episodes a year. Unable to justify the expense, NBC canceled the *Mystery Movie*—and *Columbo*—in 1977.

Continued: By 1978 the network had a change of heart and decided it wanted to continue *Columbo*. Neither Falk nor any of the original *Columbo* producers were interested, so NBC went ahead with *Mrs. Columbo*, based around Columbo's wife, an amateur sleuth. (Mrs. Columbo had never been seen on *Columbo*, or mentioned by her first name.) When *Mrs. Columbo* debuted, she was given the name Kate (and was portrayed by Kate Mulgrew). After five episodes in spring 1979, all tenuous *Columbo* connections were dropped—Kate had divorced Mr. Columbo (never seen on *Mrs. Columbo*) and re-adopted her maiden name of Callahan, and the show was retitled *Kate Loves a Mystery*. That version lasted eight episodes.

Laugh-In's catchphrase "look that up in your Funk and Wagnalls" increased dictionary sales by 20%.

CARNAC

In a recurring Tonight Show bit, Johnny Carson donned a cape and feathered turban and became "Carnac the Magnificent." Ed McMahon handed him a sealed envelope, which Carnac would hold up to his forehead. Then he'd say an "answer," open the envelope, and read the "question"— a groaningly bad, punny punchline. A few examples.

A: "Gatorade."
Q: "What does an alligator get on welfare?"

A: "Milk and honey."
Q: "What do you get from a bee that has an udder?"

A: "An unmarried woman."
Q: "What was Elizabeth Taylor between 3 and 5 p.m. on June 1, 1952?"

A: "Camelot."
Q: "Where do Arabs park their camels?"

A: "Rub-a-dub-dub."
Q: "What does a masseuse do to your dub-dub?"

A: "Supervisor."
Q: "What does Clark Kent use to keep the sun out of his eyes?"

A: "Head and shoulders."
Q: "What do you see if you open the trunk of the Godfather's car?"

A: "E-I-E-I-Owwwww!"
Q: "What did Old MacDonald say when he got a vasectomy?"

A: "Shareholder."
Q: "What did Sonny Bono used to be?"

A: "Disjoint."
Q: "What was dat hippie smoking?"

A: "Rose Bowl."
Q: "What do you say when it's Rose's turn at the bowling alley?"

A: "Follow the yellow brick road."
Q: "What are the directions to a urologist's office?"

A: "Three Dog Night."
Q: "What's a bad night for a tree?"

A: "Igloo."
Q: "What do you use to keep your ig from falling off?"

PRIME-TIME PROVERBS

Reflections on life from some of TV's most popular shows.

ON LOVE
"My love for you is like this scar: ugly, but permanent."
—Grace, *Will & Grace*

Emily: Bob, do you love me?
Bob: Sure.
Emily: Why?
Bob: Why not?
—*The Bob Newhart Show*

ON SPECULATION
"If frogs could fly...well, we'd still be in this mess, but wouldn't it be neat?"
—Drew,
The Drew Carey Show

ON EDUCATION
"If you couldn't read, you couldn't look up what's on television."
—Beaver, *Leave It to Beaver*

ON MONEY
"There are two things I won't do for money. I won't kill for it and I won't marry for it. Other than that, I'm open to about anything."
—Jim Rockford,
The Rockford Files

ON CHILDBIRTH
"Home delivery is for newspapers, not babies."
—Oscar, *The Odd Couple*

ON WINNING
"There's nothing to winning, really. That is, if you happen to be blessed with a keen eye, an agile mind, and no scruples whatsoever."
—Alfred Hitchcock,
Alfred Hitchcock Presents

ON DIVORCE
"Alimony is like keeping up payments on a car with four flats."
—*Laugh-In*

ON FIGHTING
"As we prize peace and quiet above victory, there is a simple and preferred method to deal with force—we run away."
—Teacher, *Kung Fu*

Farrah: A swordsman does not fear death if he dies with honor.
The Doctor: Then he's an idiot.
—*Doctor Who*

Case in point: There are exactly nine spikes on Bart Simpson's head.

THE BIRTH OF NETWORK NEWS

Even for those of us old enough to remember, it's easy to forget what life was like when TV viewers had just four or five channels to choose from, and network news anchors were among some of the most trusted and influential people in America.

LAST STOP

In 1947 NBC hired an announcer named John Cameron Swayze to host its nightly 15-minute national radio newscast. He didn't stay there long—after a couple of months, Swayze's bosses decided his animated style wasn't appropriate for the news. They offered him two choices: 1) get lost, or 2) transfer to their brand-new television news, where, because so few people would see him, it wouldn't matter if he was any good or not.

In those very early days, television was largely an experimental medium. Only about 170,000 U.S. households owned TV sets, all of them in and around 19 cities in the Northeast. It wasn't yet clear if "radio with pictures" would ever catch on. Swayze agreed to take the demotion and move over to television, but it was a humiliating blow to his ego and career.

CAMEL WALK

The next year, NBC decided that its TV news division would cover the Democratic and Republican National Conventions. Swayze, as the only NBC journalist assigned full-time to television, hosted both broadcasts. He performed well enough that the network assigned him to host its first national TV news program, to be launched in February 1949.

Sponsored by Camel cigarettes, the show, called *Camel News Caravan*, was only 15 minutes long. Swayze sat at a desk, read stories into the camera, and presented film clips, just like news anchors do today. But that's about all that *Camel News Caravan* had in common with modern network news broadcasts.

FIGHT NIGHT, EVERY NIGHT

Camel believed that compelling images sold more cigarettes than hard news did, so it required the show to emphasize visual appeal over news value. Have you ever heard the local news cliché "If it bleeds, it leads"? At *Camel News Caravan*, the rule of thumb was, as one employee put it, "Talking heads, bad; cracking heads, good."

NBC had film exchange agreements with European newsreel companies and the BBC, and each day *Caravan* writers pored over the incoming footage, looking for scenes of people fighting, rioting, or being beaten to a pulp. If they found anything, it went in the broadcast. If there was no story to go with the pictures, the writers would find a similar story in the news and "match" it to the film.

Once, for example, the writers found some footage of Syrian police beating citizens in Damascus, but there was no information about it. Not a problem. As NBC News writer Gerald Green recounted in Jeff Kisseloff's book *The Box: An Oral History of Television*, "You'd concoct a lead. You'd find something in the Associated Press wire that said, 'Israel rejects Syrian claim to border villages,' and you'd say, 'Israel today firmly rejected any Syrian protests about...,' et cetera, 'as a consequence of which there was rioting,' and up would come these guys getting banged on the head."

NO "NO SMOKING"

Today, news divisions operate with little interference from sponsors and network brass. But as long as Camel was paying the bills for *Camel News Caravan*, they levied strict controls to protect their business interests—selling as many cigarettes as possible. Public figures and celebrities who died from cancer were never described on *Caravan* as having died from the disease; they died "after a long illness." Shots containing "No Smoking" signs were banned, and so was footage of real-life camels—executives believed the appearance of the beasts clashed with the sophisticated image of Camel cigarettes.

And no one could even be shown smoking a cigar: Camel sold *cigarettes*. That created problems whenever Winston Churchill was in the news, because the British prime minister was rarely seen without one. *Caravan* news writer Rueven Frank lobbied for an exception to the rule and got one. "I could show Churchill with a cigar," he recounted in his book *Out of Thin Air*, "but I got no more than a specific waiver; the rule still held. No one else. Not even Groucho Marx." When gangster Lucky Luciano made headlines, *Caravan* referred to him as *Charles* Luciano to avoid calling attention to Lucky Strike cigarettes, made by a rival company.

Each broadcast ended with a live shot of a single Camel cigarette burning in an ashtray next to Swayze, sometimes with a carton of Camels sitting beside it. There were never any butts in the ashtray—not ever—and cleaning the ashtray before the broadcast was one of the most important duties of the studio crew. On *Camel News Caravan*, smoking was a clean habit, not a dirty one.

STAY AWHILE

It didn't really matter what NBC put on the air in 1949, because the TV viewing audience was so small and no one took the medium seriously yet. Even those few people who did own TV sets still got their news from newspapers and radio. But as time passed and it became clear that television was here to stay, the journalists at *Camel News Caravan* pushed for higher standards, and the program began to improve.

When NBC initially made John Cameron Swayze the host of *Camel News Caravan*, they saw him as a benchwarmer, someone who could keep the show going until TV took off, at which point they could replace him with someone better. But Swayze clicked with TV viewers, and *Camel News Caravan*, with Swayze as its host, was the #1 national TV news broadcast well into the 1950s.

Part II of the story is on page 228.

Part II of the story is on page 228.

*   *   *

"Television won't be able to hold on to any market it captures after the first six months. People will soon get tired of staring at a plywood box every night."

—Darryl F. Zanuck, head of 20th Century Fox, 1946

...replace literature. From 1985 to 1992, he hosted a TV series called *Ray Bradbury Theater.*

THE REAL "REALITY"

Since 2000, scripted drama has taken a back seat to reality TV. But those "reality" shows are actually a lot more scripted than you might think.

GET REAL

In 2010 a reality-show producer—who wished to remain anonymous—told *Esquire* magazine what really goes into making unscripted television. Among the revelations: "Everything you see has been mapped out," "The contestants are edited into one-dimensional characters," and "You can make a big storyline from the littlest thing." Here are some other examples of "unreality" that we uncovered.

THE BACHELOR (ABC, 2002–present)
Reality TV: The women who swoon over the bachelor are high-strung drama queens who yell at each other and cry all the time.
Reality: They're drunk. According to former contestants, if the fists aren't flying, the cameras stop, and the ladies are given several glasses of wine. Once they're a bit more animated, the cameras are turned back on.

CASH CAB (Discovery Channel, 2005–present)
Reality TV: A taxi driver roams New York City, picks up random people, and informs them that they're on *Cash Cab*. If they get enough questions right, the cabbie gives them a wad of cash.
Reality: According to an Associated Press profile of the show, about half of the contestants on *Cash Cab* are handpicked in advance; many are up-and-coming actors and comedians. And the cash they're awarded is fake—they get a check later.

CHEATERS (syndicated, 2000–present)
Reality TV: When one member of a couple suspects the other of having an affair, they contact the show and the accused is put under surveillance. Every episode ends with a dramatic confrontation in which the cheater is caught, an obscenity-laden physical altercation results, and host Joey Greco chastizes the cheater.

Reality: One former participant told *Inside Edition* that she was paid $500 to pretend to be having an affair. There was even an episode in which Greco got stabbed by a confronted cheater—and the participants from the episode later came clean and said it was all staged.

HELL'S KITCHEN (Fox, 2005–present)

Reality TV: Each season's winner is awarded the position of executive chef at one of host Gordon Ramsay's prestigious restaurants.

Reality: Only one out of the eight winners so far actually ended up with that position. (Ramsay has only so many restaurants, and so many positions to give out to reality-show winners.) Most other winners were given assistant-chef or even entry-level positions.

A SHOT AT LOVE WITH TILA TEQUILA (MTV, 2007–08)

Reality TV: In what was billed as the first-ever "bisexual reality show," 16 male and 16 female contestants competed to win a relationship with model and Internet celebrity Tila Tequila.

Reality: After Bobby Banhart won, he learned that Tequila already had a boyfriend. "They wouldn't even give me her phone number," Banhart complained. Tequila's response: "People move on with their lives." She also said that the show was even more fake than Banhart knew—she later came out as a lesbian and admitted that she'd wanted to pick Dani Campbell, a female contestant, but producers made her choose Banhart.

THE HILLS (MTV, 2006–10)

Reality TV: On one episode of this series in which young, beautiful, and rich Angelenos fall in and out of love and talk about it over lunch, Spencer Pratt and Heidi Montag get married. Later, Pratt phones co-star Lauren Conrad to apologize for releasing her sex tape.

Reality: The wedding wasn't legal—it was a "symbolic" ceremony. And Conrad admits, "I wasn't on the other end of that call." In the show's final episode, a backdrop is removed, revealing a soundstage and camera crew. So was *The Hills* fake all along? Sort of yes, sort of no. The people played themselves, but the plots were loosely orchestrated. With the big reveal, producers tried to create a shocking finale that would get people talking.

SVAMPBOB FYRKANT!

*American phrases can lose something in translation. And when
American TV shows get exported to other countries,
their titles often lose something, too.*

Married...with Children. The droll title works in English
but is hard to translate, so when the show was exported,
new sarcastic titles were devised. In Estonia, the show is
called *Tuvikesed*, literally "Lovebirds," and in Denmark, it's *Vore
værste år*, "Our Worst Years." The Czech Republic named it *Ženatý
se závazky*, or "Married with Liabilities," while Poland watches
Świat według Bundych, "The World According to Bundys." The
French came close to the original, with *Mariés, deux enfants*, or
"Married, Two Children." (Instead of renaming it, many countries
around the world made their own versions of *Married...with
Children*—see page 140.)

Chip 'n' Dale Rescue Rangers. Thomas Chippendale's furniture
apparently never made it overseas, or at least not enough for the
pun of Chip 'n' Dale, Disney's animated chipmunks, to translate.
So when the 1980s cartoon show *Chip 'n' Dale Rescue Rangers* was
exported to Portugal, the characters were renamed *Tico e Teco*,
which, so far as we can tell (our Portuguese is rusty), has no second meaning in Portuguese. In Germany, they're *Chip und Chap*.
Sweden knows them as *Piff och Puff*, although when they first
appeared in a Swedish comic book, the duo was referred to only as
"the two rats."

Knight Rider. In Latin America, where "Knight" is neither a sur-
name nor a mounted soldier, David Hasselhoff's action series was
known as *El Auto Fantástico* ("The Fantastic Car").

Hill Street Blues. The Israeli version attempted to play up the
double meaning of the title (they're cops, and they get stressed
out) with a name that translates awkwardly to "Blues for the Men
in Blue Uniform."

Six Feet Under. Also in Israel, *Six Feet Under*'s translation,
"Deep in the Ground," steers clear of the American idiom (and
the American nonmetric measurement system).

Scooby Doo's Freddy was named after CBS executive Fred Silverman.

ER. In Spain, ER becomes redundant with the local title *ER Emergencias*—literally, "Emergency Emergency Room."

Diff'rent Strokes. The Spanish title of the white-man-adopts-black-children sitcom cuts right to the chase: *Blanco y Negro*, or "Black and White." Elsewhere, the show is known as "Little Boy Arnold Is Popular" (Japan) and "My Family Is a Mess" (Brazil).

Bob the Builder. In Finland, this kids' show isn't about a guy named Bob, and he isn't a builder. He's known there as *Puuha-Pete*, or "Potter Pete."

Growing Pains. This show was a family sitcom starring Alan Thicke as a psychiatrist and dad. In France, it was titled *Quoi de neuf docteur?*: "What's Up, Doc?" In Sweden, it was titled *Pappa vet bäst*: "Dad Knows Best."

Murder, She Wrote. In Germany, it's known as *Mord ist ihr Hobby*, or "Murder Is Her Hobby" (which explains all those murders in that tiny Maine town).

SpongeBob SquarePants. Many translators shorten the name of this cartoon. Sweden's *SvampBob Fyrkant* translates to "Sponge-Bob Square"; in France, it's *Bob L'éponge* ("Bob the Sponge"); in Italy, it's simply *Spongebob*; and the Icelandic translation is *Sveinn Svampur* ("Sponge Boy").

One Life to Live. The daytime soap is popular around the world, but titles vary. In Italy, *One Life to Live* gets a literal translation: *Una vita da vivere*. In Israel, the show is titled *Likhiot Et Hakhayim*, or "Living the Life," and in Spain, it's known as *Solo se vive una vez*, roughly "You Only Live Once."

*   *   *

HI, I'M TROY McCLURE!

A partial list of the films made by *The Simpsons'* washed-up actor:

"P" is for Psycho	*Make-Out King of Montana*
The President's Neck Is Missing!	*David vs. Super-Goliath*
The Greatest Story Ever Hulaed	*Three Men And A Nuke*
Give My Remains to Broadway	*The Unbearable Moistness*
The Verdict Was Mail Fraud	*of Sweating*

The Partridge Family house was firebombed during the filming of **Lethal Weapon** (1987).

UNUSUAL TV PETS QUIZ

Try to match up each pet name with the pet type and the show it was on. (Answers are on page 498.)

1. Marcel	a) Lion	aa) *Miami Vice*
2. Nibbler	b) Moose	bb) *Futurama*
3. Gary	c) Rooster	cc) *Saved by the Bell*
4. Rowdy	d) Furry alien	dd) *Green Acres*
5. Elvis	e) Three-eyed alien	ee) *Scrubs*
6. Fred	f) Duck	ff) *Seinfeld*
7. Kitty Cat	g) Human	gg) *Grizzly Adams*
8. Arnold	h) Robot	hh) *American Dad*
9. Speedy	i) Cockatoo	ii) *The Drew Carey Show*
10. Jub-Jub	j) Snail	jj) *Baretta*
11. Bruce	k) Ocelot	kk) *Northern Exposure*
12. Sigmund	l) Bat	ll) *The Jetsons (1980s)*
13. Ben	m) Stuffed dog	mm) *The Addams Family*
14. Morty	n) Talking goldfish	nn) *Honey West*
15. Little Jerry	o) Alligator	oo) *SpongeBob SquarePants*
16. Kevin	p) Wheelchair-bound dog	pp) *Friends*
17. Mr. Ugh	q) Capuchin monkey	qq) *The Munsters*
18. Orbitty	r) Iguana	rr) *Dinosaurs*
19. Klaus	s) Bear	ss) *The Simpsons*
20. Igor	t) Pig	tt) *General Hospital*

First time the word "vampire" was used on the vampire show *Dark Shadows*: 410th episode.

ARTIFICIALLY SWEETENED

What if the studio audience isn't laughing at what's supposed to be funny? What if there isn't a studio audience at all? There's always "sweetening"—tweaking a program's audio with a laugh track or some other canned response. This is the story of "canned laughter."

SILENCE IS DEADLY

Laughter is contagious. That's why radio comedies in the 1930s often employed studio audiences—their laughter showed listeners at home which lines were supposed to be funny, and make them think the show itself was well liked by many people. Television continued that tradition. The problem: Sometimes nobody in the live audience laughed, or they laughed at the wrong parts, or too hard, or for too long.

LAUGHING ON THE INSIDE

In the late 1940s, CBS sound engineer Charley Douglass came up with a solution for the problem of underwhelming audience responses: artificial laughter. Making fake laughter was fairly simple: create tape loops of ideal audience responses, then insert them whenever they were needed.

Douglass started collecting audiotapes of shows from the CBS archive. He listened carefully to them, analyzing why one laugh worked and another didn't. Douglass soon noticed that laughter came in many varieties: An audience could titter slightly, chuckle, or roar. And then there was the timing: the instant laugh, the surprised laugh, the delayed one, and, with a particularly intelligent or obscure joke, the rolling laugh as members of the audience got the joke at different times. Douglass realized that dozens of taped laughs would be required.

Ideally, Douglass thought, the canned laughter should be hearty but not too loud, enthusiastic but not disruptive, and just long enough to not throw off the performers' delivery. He aimed to make it consistent and reproducible, and realistic enough to augment or even replace an actual audience.

THE MYSTERY MACHINE

Douglass compiled his tape loops and programmed them into a device called the Laff Box. And that's all that's really known about it: He was so protective of his invention that he wouldn't even let his clients see it. From the accounts of those who caught a brief glimpse, it's likely that Douglass was inspired by the Mellotron, an electronic instrument that looks like a keyboard, with each key playing a recorded sound stored on magnetic tape. (The Mellotron later became a favorite instrument of bands like King Crimson and Electric Light Orchestra.)

Similarly, the Laff Box was probably a keyboard with a different kind of laugh attached to each key, and Douglass "played" it to match the right laugh to the joke or situation. The first show to employ Douglass and his mysterious machine: a short-lived 1950 NBC sitcom called *The Hank McCune Show*.

MAN IN THE BOX

Here's how Douglass worked: He'd arrive at a TV studio pulling a dolly that carried his machine in a padlocked box. The session would start with Douglass in an editing room watching the finished recording of the show, and a producer would dictate when to insert a laugh while Douglass took notes. After the meeting, Douglass would head into a room that could be locked from the inside. There, he would add the laughter. Nobody else was allowed to be present or watch him work.

Extensive analysis of the laughs Douglass added to shows indicates that each of his Laff Box's keys could offer 10 different variations of the same kind of laugh, and all of his recorded laughs were sped up slightly to pack in more laughter. Douglass could adjust the volume with a foot pedal so the response could begin with a burst, or with a rising wave, a split second after the joke and drop off in time for the next piece of dialogue.

Some shows required relatively subtle additions; others would add a laugh after nearly every line. *Hogan's Heroes* was notorious for its overwhelming laugh track; *The Andy Griffith Show*, on the other hand, had a barely audible one. Douglass also added subtle audience noise—"uh-ohs," whoops and hollers, and wild applause greeting a star's first entrance. It took him a full workday to "sweeten" a half-hour sitcom, for which he charged $100 ($800 in today's money).

COLLECTING LAUGHS

When Douglass was no longer allowed access to the CBS archive in 1955, he expanded his own collection, trying to get "clean" laughs that didn't overlap with dialogue. One good source: a performance from mime Marcel Marceau's 1956 American tour. He also relied on shows with nonverbal comedy sequences (tapes of which he got from the TV studios and production companies that made them), such as the mime-heavy *The Red Skelton Show* and the extended physical sight-gag sequences of *I Love Lucy*.

Over the years, Douglass accumulated hundreds of laughs, freshening them every so often with new ones and reintroducing old ones that he'd retired years earlier. Aficionados of his work claim to be able to tell what year a TV episode was produced solely by the laugh track.

HOW SWEET IT IS

In the 1970s, Douglass's monopoly was broken. One of his protégés, Carroll Pratt, split off and formed his own company, Sound One, with new laughs that sounded more natural to some producers' ears. Douglass retired in 1980, and in 1992 he was honored with a lifetime-achievement Emmy Award. He died in 2003 at age 93. Douglass's work is carried on by his son, Bob, but not with his dad's Laff Box: Using what could be more accurately called the Laff Laptop, which contains hundreds of laughs accessible only through proprietary software, Bob does electronically what his father did with hand-cut recording tape.

The responsiveness of the new technology is such that sweetening is now routinely added in real time during the seven-second delay on live awards shows, including the Emmys and the Academy Awards. Even live sports presentations are sweetened now, with augmented boos, gasps, and cheers from the crowd. As the saying goes, you can't believe everything you hear.

*   *   *

Milestone: On February 3, 2008, The CW's news magazine *CW Now* was watched by about 349,000 people—making it the least-watched prime-time show in network television history.

TV OF THE 1940s

*When national broadcasting began in the late 1940s, TV was
such a novelty that nearly anything could get on the air.
Weird shows can be found on cable access today…
but back then these were prime-time viewing.*

Author Meets the Critics (NBC)
Yes, they actually used to talk
about books on TV! On this
show, one critic would praise a
new book and another critic
would trash it. The author
would then defend himself.

Teenage Book Club (ABC)
Not even in 1948 did
teenagers want to stay home
on Friday nights and discuss
books. The show lasted just
two months.

Let's Rhumba! (NBC)
A 15-minute show of people
dancing the rhumba.

Monodrama Theater (Dumont)
One actor performs an entire
play—by himself—in front of
a curtain. No sets, no props.

Gay Nineties Revue (ABC)
Vaudeville was already dead
by 1948…except on this
program, a showcase for old
vaudeville acts. Today there
are few TV hosts over 40, but
this show was hosted by 81-
year-old Joe Howard, a vaudeville veteran of the 1890s.

You Are an Artist (NBC)
This popular show featured an
artist named Jon Gnagy, who
drew a picture while he talked
about how he did it.

Tales of the Red Caboose
(ABC) This show consisted
of film of model trains running on tracks, over which a
narrator told railroad stories.
It was sponsored by Lionel
Trains.

Birthday Party (Dumont)
Broadcasts of real kids' birthday parties.

The Amazing Polgar (CBS)
Dr. Franz Polgar hypnotized
selected members of the studio
audience.

Cash and Carry (Dumont)
A game show held in a super-
market in which everything on
the shelf was a Libby product
(the show's sponsor). One
segment had viewers phone in
and guess what was hidden
under a barrel. Bonus: There
was a mime performance on
every show.

TV MUSTACHE HALL OF FAME

From handlebars to soup catchers, here's a look at the tube's finest facial fuzz.

Honoree: Tom Selleck, for bringing the macho 1970s "porn-star" mustache to living rooms all over the world in his 1981–88 hit TV show *Magnum, P.I.*

Mustache moments: Tom Selleck's mustache is so famous that in 2009 a "Tom Selleck's Mustache" page was started on Facebook. It has more than 6,000 fans. The American Mustache Institute has ranked Selleck's at number 10 in their "Mustaches That Changed History" category. Selleck is well aware of how iconic his mustache is. He shaved it off in 2001, and then, on *Late Night with Conan O'Brien*, participated in a skit in which he comforted his former mustache as it lay dying in a tiny hospital bed.

Honoree: Geraldo Rivera, for conducting a (mostly) serious career in television journalism for more than four decades while sporting an extraordinarily bushy 'stache.

Mustache moment: During the 2005 Michael Jackson child-molestation trial, Rivera was so sure that Jackson was being framed that he publicly vowed to shave his mustache if Jackson was found guilty. Jackson was acquitted; Rivera's mustache lived on. Rivera has had the 'stache since his professional career began in the early 1970s, causing him to once remark, "My mustache is older than my wife."

Honoree: Gene Shalit, for maintaining what is arguably the most recognizable (or at least most face-obscuring) mustache in the history of TV.

Mustache moment: When Shalit announced in November 2010 that he was leaving *The Today Show* after 40 years as their film, theater, and book critic, dozens of newspapers and websites broke the story with some variation of the headline "Gene Shalit and His Mustache Leaving *Today*." Someone on Twitter remarked that they'd "miss Gene Shalit's mustache more than Gene Shalit."

First TV-inspired fashion fad: all-black clothes, inspired by Hopalong Cassidy (1950).

Honoree: David Suchet, as ace detective Hercule Poirot on the British/PBS series *Agatha Christie's Poirot* (1989–present), for making a fake, black, meticulously waxed, curled, too-short mustache look real.

Mustache moment: Over the course of the more than 20 years he has played the suave Belgian detective, Suchet always puts the mustache on last when getting into his costume and character. "I don't know what it is, but psychologically it enables me to come back to him," he says. And he takes the mustache off at lunch every day—so he doesn't damage it.

Honoree: John Astin, for getting a job in a classic TV series *because* of his mustache.

Mustache moment: Astin secured the role of Gomez Addams on *The Addams Family* (1964–66) because he was the only interested actor who agreed to grow a mustache for the part. Astin, now in his 80s, is still acting—and still sports that mustache. It's now completely white. "I learned to sneeze through my mouth so I don't mess up my mustache," he said.

Honoree: Cesar Romero, for refusing to shave off his signature pencil mustache.

Mustache moment: When Romero was offered the role of the Joker in the *Batman* series in 1966, producers wanted him to shave his mustache. He refused. "He said, 'I want to keep my mustache,' which we found odd," Adam West (Batman) said many years later. "But when you think about it, throughout his long career he is always seen with a mustache. So we said, 'Okay, we'll just plaster the white makeup over it.'" That's what they did—though Romero's mustache is still quite visible under the Joker's face paint.

Honorable mentions:
- Groucho Marx (*You Bet Your Life*)
- Wilford Brimley (*Our House*, Quaker Oats commercials)
- Ned Flanders (*The Simpsons*)
- Jason Lee (*My Name Is Earl*)
- Alex Trebek (*Jeopardy!*...prior to 2001)

KOOKIE TALK

In 1959 Edd Byrnes was a major teen idol—he played Kookie, a hipster valet (and later detective) on 77 Sunset Strip (1958–64). When Kookie wasn't fixing his hair (Byrnes had a hit song called "Kookie, Kookie, Lend Me Your Comb"), he was delivering his own brand of beatnik-inspired slang, like this.

Yuks; yaks; yolks: Laughs

Monster: Telephone

Come on big: Fall in love

Pitch the volume: Tell a story

Struggle: Dance

The beam comes: Getting the hang of something

Wrapping: Clothes

Jambake: Party

Stacked off: Angry

Ticky: Stale, corny

Mill: Car motor

Jug: Carburetor

Give skin: Shake hands

Dawn rise route: Getting up early

Splash: Bath

Wheeling: Driving

Joyville: Happiness

Light up the tilt sign: Tell a lie

Washington: Dollar

Stony: Broke

Mushroom people: Night owls

Stow the vitamins: Eat a lot

In orbit: The best

Smoked in: Arrived

Crazy bit: Something funny

Detroit iron: Muscle car

Bomb: Sports car

Accordion: Beat-up car

Flip: Odd person

Fold a fender: Park a car

Race your wheels: Get excited

Luggage: Bags under the eyes

Shock frock: Strapless dress

Q: What was the brand name of the first television set? A: The Philco Predicta.

THEME SONG SINGERS

A lot of shows have instrumental theme songs, or no song at all. But many have used theme songs by well-known singers. Can you match the show to the singer of its song? (Answers on page 498.)

1. *The Love Boat*

2. *Moonlighting*

3. *Pee-wee's Playhouse*

4. *The Dukes of Hazzard*

5. *Gilmore Girls*

6. *The Wonder Years*

7. *Married...with Children*

8. *Growing Pains*

9. *The Big Bang Theory*

10. *A Different World*

11. *Mr. Belvedere*

12. *The Hogan Family*

13. *Designing Women*

14. *Family Ties*

15. *Maude*

16. *Love, American Style*

17. *That '70s Show*

18. *Freaks and Geeks*

19. *Rawhide*

20. *The Beverly Hillbillies*

a) Frank Sinatra

b) Johnny Mathis

c) Aretha Franklin

d) Joan Jett

e) B.J. Thomas

f) Leon Redbone

g) The Cowsills

h) Jack Jones

i) Carole King

j) Barenaked Ladies

k) Frankie Laine

l) Waylon Jennings

m) Al Jarreau

n) Cyndi Lauper

o) Ray Charles

p) Cheap Trick

q) Roberta Flack

r) Joe Cocker

s) Donny Hathaway

t) Flatt & Scruggs

TV theme song composer Mike Post (*Hill Street Blues*) began his career in Kenny Rogers's band.

ON TV

Pithy quotes about TV, from people who know it best.

"I have never seen a bad television program. God gave me a mind, and a wrist that turns things off."
—Jack Paar

"Seeing a murder on television can help work off one's antagonisms. And if you haven't any antagonisms, the commercials will give you some."
—Alfred Hitchcock

"Television is the first culture available to everybody and entirely governed by what the people want. The most terrifying thing is what people *do* want."
—Clive Barnes

"It is difficult to produce a television documentary that is both incisive and probing when every twelve minutes one is interrupted by twelve dancing rabbits singing about toilet paper."
—Rod Serling

"Television has proved that people will look at anything rather than each other."
—Ann Landers

"They say that ninety percent of TV is junk. But ninety percent of everything is junk."
—Gene Roddenberry

"So long as there's a jingle in your head, television isn't free."
—Jason Love

"Your cable television is experiencing difficulties. Please do not panic. Resist the temptation to read or talk to loved ones."
—Announcer, *The Simpsons*

"I hate television. I hate it as much as peanuts. But I can't stop eating peanuts."
—Orson Welles

"Just because your voice reaches halfway around the world doesn't mean you are wiser than when it reached only to the end of the bar."
—Edward R. Murrow

"It's an invention that permits you to be entertained in your living room by people you wouldn't have in your home."
—David Frost

65% of Americans consider TV a "necessity."

THE REMOTE CONTROL

Once upon a time, you had to get up off the sofa and physically change the channel on a TV. But then the folks at Zenith came to the rescue of couch potatoes everywhere. Here's a history of the magical device we call the remote control.

IN THE BEGINNING

The first idea for a remote control didn't have anything to do with changing channels—it was all about blocking ads. Eugene MacDonald Jr., president of Zenith Radio, hated TV commercials and figured that other Americans did, too. So in 1950, he told his researchers to create a system that would mute all ads by "remote control." Zenith wasn't the only company working on this idea—other television manufacturers also saw a potentially huge market for such a device. But the idea was ahead of its time, technologically, and Zenith never came up with a working prototype.

ACTION AT A DISTANCE

Scientifically speaking, for one thing to influence or control another, there must be something that moves between them—air, touch, or the transfer of electrons, for example. Modern television remotes send beams of infrared light to tell the TV what to do, but it took engineers many years to come up with that. Earlier methods included:

• **Wires.** The first commercially available remote-control device was Zenith's Lazy Bones system (1950). While Lazy Bones did allow users to flip through channels without leaving the couch, it had a bulky cord that attached to the TV set, which people kept tripping over.

• **Visible light.** Zenith also tried to market a system called the Flashmatic (1955), which used four light-sensitive cells mounted in the corners of the TV cabinet. By shining a flashlight into it, one cell raised the volume, another lowered it, and the other two changed the channel. But the cells couldn't distinguish between a flashlight and other light sources—like lamps or sunlight—so channels would often change without warning. Also, users had trouble remembering which cell controlled which function.

- **Radio waves.** Several companies tried to develop systems that detected specific radio-wave frequencies. But radio waves are not obstructed by walls and can travel long distances. Customers didn't want to install a system that could be interfered with by a neighbor's remote control.

CLICK IT

Zenith's first successful system used pressurized air and high-frequency sound waves. The device was pretty simple: The user pressed a button, which activated a tiny spring-loaded hammer inside the unit, which struck an aluminum rod, which sent out a sound wave, which made the TV react. (When the button was pushed, the remote made an audible "clicking" sound, which is why some people still call remotes "clickers.")

Space-Commander 200, as it was called, hit stores in 1956. Price, with TV included: $650 ($5,000 in today's money). The hefty price tag hindered sales, as did the fact that any noise produced by any piece of metal near the remote (jingling keys, a dog's collar) also made the TV react, unpredictably changing channels and turning the set off and on. By 1962 Zenith engineers had worked out the kinks, and this remained the technology for most remote controls for two more decades.

FINALLY IN CONTROL

Modern remotes operate by broadcasting waves of infrared light. When viewers push a button on their remote, it releases a specific digital pattern (or code) of infrared waves, which the television interprets as an instruction. They're called "infrared" waves because they have a slightly lower frequency than red light, the lowest frequency of visible light. But they have a higher frequency than radio waves, so they can't penetrate walls. Infrared remote controls also use cheap and readily available transistor technology, and since they don't have mechanical components, they are small and thin.

In 1980 electrical engineer Paul Hrivnak formed Viewstar to manufacture the first infrared remotes. They cost about $100 ($250 today), but in five years, Viewstar had sold a million of them. By 1990 infrared technology dominated the remote market. The devices are now considered a household necessity and come free with TV sets (and stereos, and DVD players...).

TV CHARACTERS, REAL MEDICINE

Here are some psychiatric disorders commonly seen in TV land, and how they manifest in real life. (In other words, don't believe what you see on TV.)

AMNESIA

On TV: Amnesia is one of the most common psychiatric disorders on television. Usually caused by a head trauma, it can cause characters to forget weeks, months, or years of their lives, or—often—their entire identities.

Example: On *ALF*, ALF gets bonked on the head and thinks he's an international spy, and not, in fact, a space alien in hiding.

In reality: Amnesia is a real condition, but it's quite different from the way it's depicted on-screen. It is caused by head trauma, but memory loss is usually limited to a few moments before or after the accident; normal memory function returns in a few hours or a few days. Cases of people permanently forgetting whole sections of their lives—let alone their personality—are few and far between.

ASPERGER'S SYNDROME

On TV: Characters stated or implied to have this mild form of autism are generally portrayed as antisocial, obsessive, and coldly rational. They usually speak in a rapid monotone and possess a wide variety of physical tics.

Examples: Lawyer Jerry Espenson (Christian Clemenson) on *Boston Legal* is explicitly described as having the condition, and he never removes his hands from his lap, even while walking. Sheldon Cooper (Jim Parsons) on *The Big Bang Theory* is a physics genius, but socially awkward to the point that he alienates even other physics geniuses. Dr. Temperence Brennan (Emily Deschanel) on *Bones* is so wrapped up in anthropology that she doesn't understand slang, sarcasm, or pop-culture references.

In reality: Asperger's syndrome is characterized by problems with social interaction, not necessarily overtly antisocial behavior. A patient may want to establish relationships with other people but be unable to do so because of an inability to understand basic rules of human interaction. Those with Asperger's syndrome display a lack of empathy because they have a hard time imagining what's going on inside another person's head. And while TV characters are often high-functioning, even geniuses, in reality, improved mental abilities don't characterize Asperger's as much as an obsession with a single, narrowly defined field of interest. For example, a patient might memorize the average rainfall in various countries, but display no interest in learning about meteorology.

NIGHT TERRORS

On TV: Night terrors are vivid nightmares, akin to hallucinations, that cause the sufferer to physically act out—thrashing around, shouting, or fighting.

Example: On one episode of *The Simpsons*, Homer visits Bart in his school classroom, dozes off, and falls victim to his night terrors, which cause him to writhe around on the ground, screaming, "Cobras! Cobras!"

In reality: Night terrors are very different from nightmares, which occur while the patient is asleep. The patient's brain is technically, though not completely, awake during a night terror. This means that, as far as the brain is concerned, the events of the dream (or nightmare) are actually occurring. When experiencing a night terror, the patient usually appears conscious, though extremely afraid. Still, they are not fully conscious and cannot respond to the real world.

MULTIPLE PERSONALITY DISORDER

On TV: Probably the most dramatic psychiatric disorder on television, this condition causes characters to suddenly change personalities. They have no control over the switch, and they won't remember what they did when one of their alternate personalities took over.

Example: On *The Untied States of Tara*, the title character (Toni

Collete) has four different personalities, one of which is a 15-year-old; another is a male trucker.

In reality: It's listed in the *Diagnostic and Statistical Manual of Mental Disorders*, but many psychiatrists question whether or not this condition really exists at all.

REPRESSED MEMORIES

On TV: Like amnesia, repressed memories stop characters from remembering trauma: perhaps childhood abuse, or the reason behind a deep-seated fear, or the night their mother was murdered in front of them. Their repressed memories seem to center around events that happened in childhood, and require several episodes worth of work to uncover and overcome, usually with the help of psychotherapy or hypnosis.

Examples: On *The Simpsons*, a therapist helps Marge Simpson realize that she is afraid of flying because she has repressed the memory that her father was a flight attendant. It takes Dexter (Michael C. Hall) on *Dexter* a full season to figure out that his first memory—as a toddler covered in blood—is from the night his mother was murdered in front of him.

In reality: Repressed memories are not completely accepted by the mainstream psychiatric community. While repressed memories often involve childhood abuse, these cases are so rare—and each one is so unique—that it makes it hard to define the condition. And most psychiatrists deal with the opposite problem: Helping a patient overcome traumatic memories that persistently intrude into their daily life.

TOURETTE'S SYNDROME

On TV: Characters with Tourette's syndrome yell out obscenities or awkward phrases at completely inappropriate times.

Example: A new student on *South Park* suffers from the condition. (Eric Cartman then pretends to have Tourette's in order to get away with swearing in school.)

In reality: Tourette's very rarely involves *coprolalia*, the scientific term for involuntary swearing. Usually, Tourette's involves only minor motor or vocal tics (such as making uncontrollable sounds or hand gestures). Those who have Tourette's can usually lead perfectly normal lives. Some don't even realize they have it.

WEIRD TV TOYS

Many kid-friendly TV shows spawn popular action figures and play sets. But a few shows that aren't so kid-friendly offer toys, too—toys that few children would want. Like these.

Show: *Night Court*
Toy: Bull Shannon puppet
Details: Richard Moll played the simpleminded, whimsical bailiff Bull Shannon on the 1980s sitcom *Night Court*. Bald and nearly seven feet tall, Moll made Bull the show's most recognizable character. *Night Court* was definitely not a kids' show—it aired at 9:30 and took place in a courtroom where the majority of the defendants were prostitutes—but that didn't stop the marketing of a Bull Shannon hand puppet. With a round head and hinged mouth, it resembled a Muppet. *Night Court* even plugged it with an appearance on a 1986 episode—Bull tried ventriloquism, and the puppet was his dummy.

Show: *Doctor Who*
Toy: The TARDIS "play set"
Details: The 1970s version of the long-running *Doctor Who* was intellectually dense, dialogue driven (in thick British accents), and low budget, with very few special effects. In other words, it was not very appealing to American kids. Nevertheless, *Doctor Who* toys were produced in 1975, and most inexplicable was the TARDIS, Doctor Who's time machine. On the show, it was the size of a phone booth on the outside, but defied physics to be a huge room on the inside. That can't be done with a cheap plastic toy, of course, so kids who got a TARDIS set got a toy phone booth—with none of the cool time machinery on the inside—large enough to hold a single plastic Doctor Who doll.

Show: *Laverne & Shirley*
Toy: Secretary play set
Details: This toy was for little girls and boys who wanted to play "office"—it included miniature plastic imitations of a calculator, stapler, bookshelf, notepad, and adding machine. While that

---

Which of the *My Two Dads* was the real dad? It was never divulged.

doesn't sound terribly exciting, it also didn't make any sense—neither Laverne nor Shirley ever worked as a secretary. They worked on the assembly line in the Shotz Brewery until the final season, when Cindy Williams (Shirley) left the show and Laverne got a job in an aerospace testing plant. (It's also not historically accurate: *Laverne & Shirley* took place in the late 1950s and early 1960s, about a decade before calculators became commercially available.)

Show: *All in the Family*
Toy: Archie Bunker's Grandson doll
Details: It was a TV event in 1975 when Gloria (Sally Struthers) gave birth to her and Meathead's (Rob Reiner) first child, Joey, on *All in the Family*. A Joey doll, marketed as "Archie Bunker's Grandson," was released by Ideal Toys in 1976, and it became almost as controversial as *All in the Family* itself. That's because Joey was the first doll that was, as the box said, "a physically correct male." Joey had a functional penis—it was a "drink and wet" doll. America wasn't ready for a functioning, anatomically correct male doll, so Joey was pulled from store shelves after just a few months.

Show: *Here's Lucy*
Toy: View-Master reels
Details: Three-dimensional View-Master slides have been made for hundreds of movies, TV shows, and attractions, including *Superman*, *Star Wars*, and Disneyland. Apparently, someone thought kids would want to visit, in 3-D, a 1971 episode of Lucille Ball's sitcom *Here's Lucy* called "Lucy and the Astronauts," in which Lucy and Uncle Harry (Gale Gordon) assist in an astronaut splashdown and go through decontamination procedures.

Show: *Dark Shadows* (ABC, 1966–71)
Toy: Barnabas Collins *Dark Shadows* Game
Details: This soap opera about vampires was popular with children, despite its graphic bloodletting. So in 1969, Milton Bradley released this *Shadows* board game "for ages 6 and up." Object: Spin the wheel to collect bones and be the first player to assemble a skeleton. (It included glow-in-the-dark vampire teeth.)

Mr. T's legal name: Mr. T. (His name at birth: Laurence Tureaud.)

UNCLE JOHN'S PAGE OF LISTS

Some random bits from the BRI's bottomless trivia files.

4 SONS FROM MY THREE SONS
1. Mike
2. Robbie
3. Chip
4. Ernie (adopted)

6 ACTORS IN TITLE ROLES WHO SANG THE THEME SONG
1. Will Smith, *Fresh Prince of Bel-Air*
2. Linda Lavin, *Alice*
3. Kelsey Grammer, *Frasier*
4. Chuck Norris, *Walker, Texas Ranger*
5. & 6. Scott Baio and Erin Moran, *Joanie Loves Chachi*

5 MOST FREQUENT SNL MUSICAL GUESTS
Paul Simon (8)
Tom Petty (8)
Randy Newman (6)
James Taylor (6)
Beck (6)

7 OBSCURE CABLE TV NETWORKS
1. Water Channel (water sports)
2. Wine TV
3. Tennis Channel
4. Volksmusik (German folk music)
5. Wealth TV (shows for the rich)
6. Retirement Living TV
7. The Karaoke Channel

4 TONY DANZA CHARACTERS
1. Tony, *Taxi*
2. Tony, *Who's the Boss?*
3. Tony, *Hudson Street*
4. Joe, *Family Law*

6 TV CARTOON BABY SPIN-OFFS
1. *Tiny Toon Adventures*
2. *Popeye and Son*
3. *Flintstone Kids*
4. *Muppet Babies*
5. *A Pup Named Scooby-Doo*
6. *Tom and Jerry Kids*

7 OF ENDORA'S MISNOMERS FOR DARRIN ON BEWITCHED
1. Dobbin
2. Durwood
3. Delmore
4. Darryl
5. Darwin
6. Dirndl
7. Delwood

8 CELEBS WHO TURNED DOWN DANCING WITH THE STARS
1. Cindy McCain
2. Condoleeza Rice
3. Todd Palin
4. Sylvester Stallone
5. Rachael Ray
6. Betty White
7. Ann Coulter
8. Erin Brockovich

3 TV-INSPIRED FASHION FADS
1. Coonskin caps (*Davy Crockett*)
2. Headscarves (*Rhoda*)
3. Feathered hair (*Charlie's Angels*)

First pop song turned into a TV series: *Harper Valley PTA* (1967).

HITLER'S TV NATION

If you think the first Nazis on television were on Hogan's Heroes, *think again. Long before TVs invaded living rooms of American households, the Third Reich was well on its way to becoming the world's first "TV nation."*

EMPIRE STATE
On January 31, 1935, a minor British government panel made a routine announcement that sent the government of Germany into a panic. After six months of inquiry and debate, the Television Committee issued a report finding that the BBC was ready to initiate regular television broadcasting.

The German government, by then under the control of the Nazi Party, didn't particularly care about television technology as such, but it did care about propaganda. So a television race was on, with Germany's radio-based Reichs-Rundfunk-Gesellschaft (Empire Broadcasting Company), or RRG, suddenly under pressure to transmit television before the British did. The goal: to prove Germany's superiority.

FIRST IS FIRST
While the British took their time to create a usable system (the visual BBC debuted in 1936), German scientists who had been working on experimental TV rushed to finish their research first. On March 22, 1935, less than two months after the Television Committee announcement, RRG demonstrated what it called the "first television program service on Earth." The program consisted of RRG executive director Eugen Hadamovsky announcing that no matter how quickly the U.K. or the U.S. developed television broadcasting, the Germans would still be first, because it had been invented in 1884 by German Paul Nipkow, who had patented a theoretical device called an "electrical telescope."

This wasn't completely untrue. Nipkow had come up with a mechanical scanning wheel—a rapidly rotating disk with a spiral of holes in it that scanned an image. But American inventor Philo Farnsworth had proven it obsolete and impractical in the 1920s when he introduced his own workable TV system (see page 484).

In the RRG presentation, an elderly, senile Nipkow posed in front of nonworking TV sets and recited a scripted story about how he had invented TV as a lonely teenager on Christmas Eve. His aim, he said, had been to invent a way for people like him to see their families from afar.

A SCANNER, DARKLY

However, there were problems with RRG's "first broadcast." For one, it used Nipkow's spinning disk technology, which yielded a muddy image with few details. In comparison, the system that Philo Farnsworth had already developed in the U.S. produced a much better-quality picture. Furthermore, RRG's "regular broadcasts" over the next year were just the same test broadcasts of old feature films and newsreels that researchers had already been sending every day to a few experimental TV sets.

Because Nipkow's disk scanner required huge amounts of light in a small space, the device presented a fire hazard. Just six months later, in July 1935, the German TV facility caught fire, destroying most of the equipment and suspending broadcasts for six months. That allowed the facility to replace the Nipkow disk cameras with more modern ones. As a consolation to Nipkow, the newly upgraded broadcasting unit was named Paul Nipkow Fernsehsender ("TV station").

GERMANY'S GOT TALENT

In summer 1936, when Berlin hosted the Olympics, the idea of covering the Games on television seemed like a great propaganda opportunity. Because Germany was a very poor country at the time, almost no one owned a TV set. So the RRG set up 27 public viewing rooms, each big enough for 40 people, in Berlin and Hamburg. As a result, more than 160,000 Germans could watch the events on television.

After the Olympics, the viewing rooms remained extremely popular as the RRG continued to broadcast carefully selected programs: upbeat films, traditional German music and dance presentations, and, as World War II progressed, softball interviews and glowing portraits of Nazi Party officials. But so few people were able to watch—the viewing rooms accommodated only 0.2 percent of the population—that propaganda chief Joseph Goebbels didn't bother arranging for much TV content. He preferred radio as the mass medium for party news.

OFF THE HERR

The Nazis' broadcast service began unraveling, along with their war effort, in late 1943. On November 23, Allied bombers targeted the Germans' main transmitter, destroying it and knocking it off the air permanently. Since the viewing rooms were attached by cables, programming was able to continue with small local broadcasts until October 1944, when Germany was under pressure on two war fronts and so many TV employees had been drafted into the army that maintaining the service became too difficult. On May 2, 1945, the Russian army shut down the TV studios and "the world's first broadcasting service" was history.

*   *   *

TONIGHT SHOW FACTS

• On the first episode of the *Tonight Show* in 1954, host Steve Allen announced to the audience, "I want to give you the bad news first: This program is going to go on forever. You think you're tired now? Wait until you see one o'clock roll around!" He was right—it's the longest-running entertainment show in world history.

• No host has ever been injured by one of the many exotic animals brought onto the show, but in 1999 guest Elizabeth Hurley was bitten on the ear by a chimpanzee.

• Since Conan O'Brien was fired from *Tonight* in 2010, NBC removed all mentions, photos, and video of him from its website.

• In 1957 *The Tonight Show* producers decided to change the show's format to a news program. (A few months later, they switched it back.)

• On his first broadcast of *The Late Show* after Johnny Carson died in 2005, David Letterman delivered his monologue as usual, and then announced that all of the jokes had been written by Johnny Carson. He'd been sending Letterman jokes, once or twice a week, since his retirement in 1992.

First Japanese cartoon to air in the U.S.: *Astro Boy* (1963).

IT'S IN MY CONTRACT

*If you're a big star and a show wants you badly enough,
you can ask for just about anything...and get it.*

FRED MACMURRAY

In 1960 TV producers approached film star MacMurray with a concept for *My Three Sons*—a sitcom about a widower and his three sons. MacMurray liked the script and the concept, but he didn't want to give up his successful movie career, and he figured that if he were on a weekly TV series, which shot around 30 episodes a year, he'd have no time left for films. Amazingly, the producers were willing to work around his schedule. During the 1960–72 run of the show, each season's episodes were written all at once, over the summer. Each fall, MacMurray would film all of his scenes for the entire year over a 65-day period. He was then free to make movies, which included *The Apartment*, *The Absent-Minded Professor*, its sequel *Son of Flubber*, and *The Happiest Millionaire*.

DEAN MARTIN

In 1964 singer/actor Martin had an unexpected comeback with his #1 hit "Everybody Loves Somebody." Attractive movie and recording offers flowed in, and NBC offered him a weekly variety series, *The Dean Martin Show*. The $20,000-a-week salary ($140,000 in today's money) was too good to turn down, so Martin jokingly told NBC executives that he'd do the show on the condition that he would only have to show up for the weekly tapings—in other words, about two hours each Sunday afternoon. Martin thought NBC would refuse, but to his surprise, they agreed, and the arrangement stood for nine years. (One of the show's trademarks was an onstage door, through which a celebrity would enter for a cameo. The reason Martin always looked so surprised was that he genuinely was—he never attended a rehearsal.)

DREW CAREY

The Drew Carey Show was a big hit, ranking in or just below the top 20 from 1996 to 2001. In 2001 ABC was suffering a huge ratings decline and didn't have many hits, so it signed Carey to a lucrative multiyear contract through a ninth season in 2004. Carey got $750,000 per episode, or about $60 million in total. Unfortunately for ABC, the show's ratings began to drop immediately after the ink on the contract had dried. The show finished the 2001–02 season at #57, and in 2002–03 was #119—the least-watched network show. ABC tried to cancel *The Drew Carey Show*…but according to Carey's contract, a ninth season would have to happen—at a cost of $3 million per episode. The contract didn't actually specify that ABC had to *air* the negotiated 26 episodes, so Carey and the producers took the opportunity to experiment on ABC's dime—a laugh track was abandoned and so was a studio audience, in favor of building fourth walls to sets and filming with handheld cameras. ABC did finally air the episodes over the summer of 2004, where they fared poorly against NBC's coverage of the Summer Olympics.

BILL COSBY

In 1996 CBS signed superstar Bill Cosby to return to television for the first time since the end of *The Cosby Show* in 1992. That show had been such a hit—#1 for five of its eight years—and Cosby was so beloved that CBS offered unprecedented concessions: Cosby could make whatever show he wanted, with casting approval and a guaranteed two-year run. But Cosby didn't choose a broad-appeal family sitcom like the network had hoped. Instead, he decided to make *Cosby*, an American adaptation of the British show *One Foot in the Grave*, a dark comedy about a bored retiree who feels useless. Ultimately, CBS paid Cosby $44 million for *Cosby*. The results: middling. The moody, abrasive show premiered with 24 million viewers, but ultimately averaged only about seven million over its four-year run. In its last year, 1999–2000, *Cosby* finished 82nd in the ratings.

*   *   *

TV Superstition: Lucille Ball considered the letters "ar" to be lucky, probably because her career skyrocketed after she married Desi Arnaz. All of her TV character names included those letters: Lucy Ricardo (*I Love Lucy*), Lucy Carmichael (*The Lucy Show*), Lucy Carter (*Here's Lucy*), and Lucy Barker (*Life With Lucy*).

Mike Wallace's (*60 Minutes*) first TV job: pitchman for the 1949 kids' show *Super Circus*.

CONTROVERSIAL KIDS' SHOWS

Sometimes kids' shows aren't for kids.

Rude Dog and the Dweebs

Surf-inspired sportswear was a fad in the 1980s, and one of the biggest brands was Sun Sportswear. Sun's clothes featured an angular white dog named Rude Dog, with "rude" being Jamaican and ska music slang for "juvenile delinquent." Rude Dog clothes were such a hit that the company spun off the mascot into a Saturday morning cartoon show for CBS in 1989 called *Rude Dog and the Dweebs*. Talking with a sarcastic Brooklyn accent, Rude Dog drove a pink Cadillac through Beverly Hills, trying to avoid a dogcatcher and getting into trouble with other dogs. Parent groups objected to the show, claiming that it encouraged antisocial behavior, and that Rude Dog looked like Spuds McKenzie, Budweiser's pit bull mascot. CBS got so many complaints—including ones that accused *Rude Dog* of encouraging children to drink—that it canceled the show after one season.

Garbage Pail Kids

Garbage Pail Kids cards, a spoof of Cabbage Patch Kids dolls, were *the* collectible item for grade-schoolers in the 1980s. The cards featured pictures of grotesque, mutant, and disgusting children, smeared with boogers, bugs, and gore, who had names like Peeled Paul (a skinless boy) and Brady Back Ribs (a baby eating his own flesh). The cards were banned in hundreds of schools, and parents hated them, but they were so popular with kids that CBS planned an animated series in 1987 featuring the freakish kids as characters. The network heavily hyped the show in the weeks leading up to its premiere, prompting protests from organizations like the American Family Association and Action for Children's Television. CBS got spooked and canceled the show before it ever aired. The 13 produced episodes were eventually released on DVD in 2006.

Mighty Mouse: The New Adventures

In 1987 CBS met with animator Ralph Bakshi to hear his pitches for Saturday morning cartoons and hired him to produce a new series of Mighty Mouse cartoons—despite the fact that Bakshi was best known for his X-rated 1972 film *Fritz the Cat*. When *Mighty Mouse: The New Adventures* debuted that fall, it wasn't quite as kid-friendly as CBS had hoped. One episode showed male characters showering together, for example. And in another, "The Littlest Tramp," Mighty Mouse finds the remains of a crushed flower and inhales it in order to trigger memories of the friend who gave it to him. CBS censors ordered the scene cut, claiming that it was a drug reference, but the show's staff protested and were allowed to restore it. It aired without complaint in October 1987. Eight months later, Donald Wildmon of the American Family Association saw the episode and publicly accused CBS of "hiring a pornographer to do a cartoon for children, and then allowed him to show the hero sniffing cocaine." Bakshi denied it, saying he'd be "crazy" to do such a thing, and compared the accusations to McCarthyism. In the end, CBS cut the scene from reruns; it canceled the show outright four months later.

Lunch with Soupy Sales

This show ran locally in Detroit beginning in 1953, and then went national in 1959. The format was loose, with Sales clowning around and often getting hit in the face with a pie (his trademark), along with comedy sketches, guest appearances, and lively music. It was largely ad-libbed, which became a problem on the New Year's Day 1965 episode. Annoyed that he had to work on a holiday, Sales told the kids watching at home to "go into [their] parents' bedrooms" and remove "the funny green pieces of paper with pictures of U.S. presidents" from their wallets, put them in an envelope, and "send them to old Soupy." Many children actually did it—Sales received hundreds of envelopes in the mail. The show's production company, Screen Gems, was livid and suspended Sales for two weeks. Sales continued hosting the show for more than a decade (but he kept the money).

Dustin Hoffman's and Michael Jackson's guest roles on *The Simpsons* were uncredited.

"MERRY CHRISTMAS, CHARLIE BROWN!"

Bwaa bwaa, bwaa bwaa, fa la la la la, la la la la.
(Translation: Here's the story of one of America's all-time
favorite holiday specials, A Charlie Brown Christmas.)

STRIKING OUT

In 1964 television producer Lee Mendelsen made a documentary about Willie Mays that garnered good reviews and good ratings. Looking for a new subject, he thought, "I've done the world's greatest baseball player; now I should do the world's worst baseball player." The player he wanted: Charlie Brown.

So Mendelsen approached *Peanuts* creator Charles Schulz with the idea of producing a documentary about Schulz's comic strip. The two went to work on *Charlie Brown & Charles Schulz.* When Mendelsen was finishing this project, the promotions department of Coca-Cola called him and asked him to also create a *Peanuts* Christmas special for CBS (to be sponsored by Coke). Mendelsen immediately accepted, and phoned Schulz. They wrote the script in one day.

THE TRUE MEANING OF CHRISTMAS

With the story worked out, Mendelsen and Schulz went in search of someone to bring the kids to life. Schulz suggested the animator that Ford Motors had hired to do its *Peanuts* commercials, Bill Meléndez (*Bambi, Fantasia,* and Bugs Bunny cartoons).

Getting *A Charlie Brown Christmas* on the air proved difficult. CBS wanted to hire adult actors for the voices, demanded a laugh track, and wanted to drop a Bible verse recited by Linus. But Schulz, who had started the popular strip in 1950, was powerful enough to get what he wanted, and he wanted actual children's voices with no laugh track. He held firm about the biblical verse, too, because the special was supposed to be about "the true meaning of Christmas." After some negotiation, the network relented.

Result: Shulz and his associates made exactly the kind of low-

---

Not where you'd think: *Dallas* took place in Braddock, Texas.

key special they'd envisioned (complete with a jazz score by Vince Guaraldi, which CBS had also initially blocked).

The plot: Charlie Brown directs a Christmas play in order to understand the true meaning of the holiday in spite of all the commercialism surrounding it. He finds a wilting tree, and he and his friends decorate it. It shines magically as they all sing "Hark! The Herald Angels Sing." CBS execs didn't get it and expected the special to flop.

A HOLIDAY SECURITY BLANKET

Instead, from its first airing on December 9, 1965 (in *Gilligan's Island's* regular time slot), *A Charlie Brown Christmas* became an instant TV classic. Critics lauded its message of anticommercialism (even though it *was* sponsored by Coca-Cola), and it won both an Emmy and a Peabody Award.

Still, Schulz, Mendelsen, and Meléndez cringed at the rougher aspects of *A Charlie Brown Christmas*, such as the choppy animation (all their budget would allow) and the kids' static speaking style (for example, Sally was voiced by a little girl too young to read, so she had to be fed her lines phonetically). Viewers didn't seem to care—it was the special's sincerity that stood out. "The original ideas we tried for," Schulz later said, "keeping to the true meaning of Christmas, using young children's voices, Guaraldi's cool, spare jazz, and aiming for a grown-up *and* family audience, have stood the test of time."

WORKING FOR PEANUTS

More shows followed, including two perennially aired specials: *It's the Great Pumpkin, Charlie Brown* (1966) and *A Charlie Brown Thanksgiving* (1973), and the feature film *A Boy Named Charlie Brown* (1969). In all, the team of Schulz, Mendelsen, and Meléndez produced more than 40 prime-time specials and projects over the next three decades.

But the most beloved *Peanuts* TV show is still the Christmas special. Beware, however, that if you want to watch the *entire* show, you'll have to watch it on video. Networks now routinely make cuts—you may miss Sally writing a letter to Santa, or Linus complaining about the commercialism of Christmas, for example—in order to fit in...more commercials. Good grief!

CHUCK CUNNINGHAM SYNDROME

*Sometimes, TV characters disappear suddenly with
no explanation. What happened to them? A bad
case of Chuck Cunningham Syndrome.*

CHUCK CUNNINGHAM, HAPPY DAYS
Coined online, the term "Chuck Cunningham Syndrome" describes when a TV character vanishes from the show. The term comes from *Happy Days*. In the show's first season (1974), the Cunningham family had three children: young Joanie (Erin Moran), teenage Richie (Ron Howard), and college student Chuck (Gavan O'Herlihy). Chuck was conceived by creator Garry Marshall as a mentor to Richie, but when Fonzie (Henry Winkler) became the breakout character as well as an older idol for Richie, there was no need for Chuck, who only appeared occasionally anyway. On a 1975 episode, Chuck (then played by Randolph Roberts) walked up the stairs of the Cunningham home holding a basketball…and never came back down. He was never mentioned again. Even in an episode a few years later, Howard Cunningham (Tom Bosley) only refers to his "lovely daughter and loudmouth son." What about Chuck?

CARL DIXON, GOOD TIMES
When actress Esther Rolle wanted to quit *Good Times* in 1977, her character, Florida, married a man named Carl Dixon (Moses Gunn), who was diagnosed with cancer, prompting the couple to move to Arizona for him to convalesce. But a year later, Rolle returned to the show. Where was Carl? It was never explicitly stated whether he'd recovered or had died. He was simply never spoken of again.

JUDY WINSLOW, FAMILY MATTERS
Family Matters began in 1989 as a standard family sitcom about a working-class African-American family named the Winslows. But that changed when the nerdy next-door neighbor Steve Urkel

(Jaleel White) became a cultural phenomenon in 1991. *Family Matters* producers responded by devoting as much screen time as possible to Urkel. This meant that some other character would get shut out, and it turned out to be Judy (Jaimee Foxworth), the youngest Winslow daughter. As of the fourth season premiere in 1993, Judy was gone without a mention. (Foxworth had such a hard time getting work that she eventually resorted to adult film work under the stage name "Crave.")

MANDY HAMPTON, *THE WEST WING*
Mandy (Moira Kelly) was a major character in the first season (1999–2000) of *The West Wing*, serving as a media consultant to President Bartlett (Martin Sheen), a job that, according to flashbacks, she'd held during his presidential campaign. But in fall 2000, Mandy ceased to exist. This was especially strange because the first season ended with a cliffhanger in which the president was shot, and Mandy was there. When the next season picked up at the exact moment it had left off, Mandy was gone. Creator Aaron Sorkin later revealed that the character "wasn't working," and so she, and the actress who portrayed her, were dismissed.

ROSS GELLAR'S OTHER FAMILY, *FRIENDS*
The birth of Ross' (David Schwimmer) son Ben was a major plot point in the first season of *Friends*, and the kid made occasional appearances, usually with his primary parents, Carol and Susan, Ross' ex-wife and her partner. *Friends* ran for 10 years, but in its seventh season, Ross and Rachel (Jennifer Aniston) had a child named Emma together, and Ben was seen only one more time and thereafter forgotten. Susan, meanwhile, hadn't been seen since the sixth season; Carol disappeared after the seventh.

SPEARCHUCKER JONES, M*A*S*H
The African-American doctor was a major character in the book, movie, and first few episodes of the TV series version of M*A*S*H, until writers learned that during the real Korean War, there were no black army surgeons. So Spearchucker (Timothy Brown) was surgically removed halfway through the first season with no explanation—he was in one episode and not in the next.

EDITED FOR TV

*When big-screen films are aired on TV, networks are often forced to
dub in new words to mask foul and profane language.
And sometimes they do it in pretty ridiculous fashion.*

THE EXORCIST (1973)
In the film: The possessed Regan MacNeil (Linda Blair)
says some very nasty things about Father Karras's (Jason
Miller) mother.
On TV: "Your mother sews socks that smell, Karras!"

REPO MAN (1984)
In the film: Car repossessor Bud (Harry Dean Stanton) uses a
certain epithet, also involving a mother, a lot.
On TV: He says "melon farmer" a lot.

DIE HARD 2 (1990)
In the film: At the end, just before he throws his lighter into the
stream of fuel and blows up the jet to kill the bad guys, Lieutenant
John McClane (Bruce Willis) says, "Yippee kai-yay, [expletive]!"
On TV: "Yippee kai-yay, Mr. Falcon!" (There's nobody named Mr.
Falcon in *Die Hard 2*.)

THE BIG LEBOWSKI (1998)
In the film: As he's smashing a Corvette with a tire iron, Walter
(John Goodman) yells to the presumed owner, "See what happens
when you **** a stranger in the ***?"
On TV: "See what happens when you find a stranger in the
Alps?"

SNAKES ON A PLANE (2006)
In the film: The most famous line from this over-the-top action
movie is FBI agent Neville Flynn (Samuel L. Jackson) screaming,
"I've had it with these [expletive] snakes on this [expletive] plane!"
On TV: "I've had it with these monkey-fighting snakes on this
Monday to Friday plane!"

40% of Americans believe police shows are "fairly accurate." Only 14% of real police agree.

NATIONAL LAMPOON'S VACATION (1983)

In the film: After getting his family lost late at night in a danger-ous-looking neighborhood, Clark (Chevy Chase) asks a stranger for directions. The guy rudely responds, "**** your mama!"
On TV: The guy replies, "Who do I look like, Christopher Columbo?"

KILL BILL, VOL. 1 (2003)

In the film: The Bride (Uma Thurman) wakes up from a coma just in time—she is about to be assaulted by a guy who announces, "My name is Buck, and I like to ****."
On TV: "My name is Buck, and I like to party."

THE USUAL SUSPECTS (1995)

In the film: In the police lineup scene early in the film, all five stars (Kevin Spacey, Gabriel Byrne, Stephen Baldwin, Kevin Pollak, and Benicio del Toro) are each made to read ta line heard by a witness, "Hand me the keys, you ******* **********!"
On TV: "Hand me the keys, you fairy godmother!"

NOVOCAINE (2001)

In the film: A criminal named Duane (Scott Caan) threatens a dentist (Steve Martin) to stay away from Duane's sister (Helena Bonham Carter). In a moment of anger and frustration, Duane screams "Jesus Christ!"
On TV: "Cheese and spice!"

*   *   *

NOT JUST COOKIES

When cookies aren't around, *Sesame Street's* Cookie Monster will eat pretty much anything. So far, he's devoured a cookbook, half of a Volkswagen Beetle, the moon, a 1973 Ford F-250 truck, a brick wall, Rosebud from *Citizen Kane*, a hot-dog stand, a Christmas tree, a mailbox, a manhole cover, studio lights, a vacuum cleaner, a chunk of the *TV Guide* logo, Stephen Colbert's Peabody Award, a yo-yo, and Hooper's Store.

Before *Candid Camera*, Alan Funt hosted a radio show called *Candid Microphone.*

TV STUDIES

TV has become such a large part of most people's lives that scientists who want to study the phenomenon have plenty of research material. Here are some of their findings.

TV AND TEEN PREGNANCY

Study: In 2008 the Rand Corporation monitored the TV viewing habits of more than two thousand 12-to-17-year-olds, specifically those who watched shows with sexual content, including graphic depictions of characters having sex.

Findings: After controlling for socioeconomic status and other factors that influence pregnancy rates, the researchers found that the odds of the subjects becoming pregnant or causing a pregnancy increased with the amount of sexual content they watched on TV. Those who watched the most sexual content were twice as likely to become involved in a pregnancy than those who watched the least. Researchers speculated that the frequent portrayal of sex on TV as risk free may encourage kids to have unprotected sex, since few characters ever contract STDs or have an unwanted pregnancy.

BORN TO WATCH

Study: In 1991 Penn State University researchers studied 226 adoptive families to see whether the adopted children's TV-watching habits matched those of their new family or those of their biological parents.

Findings: Adopted children and their biological parents frequently had more similar taste in programming, particularly for cartoons and sitcoms. This was true even in cases where the biological parents and children had never met.

FOOD FOR THOUGHT

Study: As reported in the journal *Pediatric Research* in 2007, researchers fed cheese pizza to boys ages 9 to 14. One group ate while watching TV—two episodes of *The Simpsons*—and the second group ate without TV. Some boys in each group were fed a small snack (glucose dissolved in water) before being served the pizza.

Finding: The TV watchers ate more, regardless of whether they

---

Original working title of *Grey's Anatomy: Complications.*

had the snack beforehand. Those who had the snack and didn't watch TV ate the least. Conclusion: For boys in this age group, watching TV leads to overeating.

TV AND THERAPY
Study: In 2008 Iowa State University psychologists surveyed 369 college students on both their TV viewing habits and their attitudes toward psychological counseling. The researchers were looking for a correlation between portrayals of therapists on TV—Dr. Frasier Crane on the sitcom *Frasier*, Dr. Jennifer Melfi on *The Sopranos*, etc.—and the students' feelings about the profession.
Findings: The more the students watched shows with fictional therapists, the more they associated a stigma with seeking psychological treatment, and the less willing they were to consider ever seeking professional help for themselves. The researchers speculated that the viewers were turned off by unfavorable portrayals of mental-health professionals on TV.

TV AND RETENTION
Study: In 2002 University of Iowa researchers divided 324 adults ages 18 to 54 into three groups and had them watch 45 minutes of TV: One group watched violent content, one watched sexual content, and one watched neutral content. Each group was shown the same nine commercials for laundry detergent, soft drinks, and cereal, and then tested to see how well they remembered the ads.
Findings: The groups that watched the violent and sexual shows remembered 67% fewer commercials than the third group. Difficulty remembering the commercials was most pronounced among those ages 18 to 25, the demographic most prized by advertisers. "The simplest explanation is that people who watch a sexual program are thinking about sex. People who watch a violent program are thinking about violence, not laundry detergent," said one researcher.

*   *   *

Toasted: On Ryan Murphy's 1999–2001 teen comedy *Popular*, the characters eat at a restaurant called Croutons. On Murphy's current teen comedy *Glee*, the characters eat at Breadsticks.

NETWORK ORIGINS: CBS

CBS trailed NBC through most of its radio years but zoomed ahead—and stayed there—when the TV era began. Here's the story of the "Eye Network."

ARTHUR'S THEME

In the 1920s, talent agency Columbia Concerts Corporation (CCC) dominated the music industry. Under founder Arthur Judson, CCC managed and booked more than 100 conductors, musicians, and singers for concert and radio performances. Basically, if any of the big radio networks wanted top-shelf musicians to appear on their shows, they had to consult with Judson.

That's what NBC chief David Sarnoff did in 1927—he needed a lot of performers for programs on his new radio network. Judson thought he could demand any price because Sarnoff needed the talent so badly, but Sarnoff wouldn't play ball, and walked away from Judson and CCC.

Judson was outraged but also frustrated that he himself had botched the negotiations. Then he had an idea: If Sarnoff wouldn't hire his acts, he'd start his *own* radio network...and stock it with his own clients!

LET'S PUT ON A SHOW

Judson felt sure that his performers could outshine any musicians found by NBC. Based on that promise, he and his business partners convinced 16 radio stations in the Northeast to join his network, which Judson wanted to call the United Independent Broadcasters Company (UIB).

One problem: Judson didn't have the money to run a radio network. So he used his contacts in the music industry and convinced Columbia Phonograph Company that exposure on radio would sell records—if they provided access to their artists and recorded music, UIB would promote Columbia. Judson was so hell-bent on getting Columbia on board that he renamed the network the Columbia Phonograph Broadcasting System (CPBS).

Judson then bought a Brooklyn radio station, WABC, outright, mainly so the network could have a studio from which to

---

All of the gross foods eaten on *Fear Factor* had to be approved by the FDA.

broadcast. WABC became the CPBS headquarters and "flagship" station when the network went on the air on September 18, 1927.

HAVE A CIGAR

Before long, CPBS started running out of money; potential advertisers weren't interested in doing business with a small, struggling operation. This forced Judson in 1928 to sell CPBS and WABC to a partnership led by William Paley, the 27-year-old son of Samuel Paley, head of La Palina cigar company. Paley immediately went after the biggest advertiser he knew—his father. It was a good match—when La Palina advertised on CPBS's Philadelphia affiliate, their cigar sales skyrocketed.

In January 1929, William Paley bought out his partners. For $400,000 (about $5 million today), Paley got what had grown to be a network of 22 affiliates and a payroll of 16 employees. He then changed the name of the company to the Columbia Broadcasting System, or CBS. By December he had extended the network to the West Coast and made mutually beneficial ad revenue sharing agreements with 70 stations, tripling the size of the CBS network and turning its finances around in under a year.

Unlike NBC, which aired programs to get listeners to buy RCA-made radios, and to get radio stations to buy RCA-made signal transmitters, CBS's business model under Paley was to make money by selling advertising on shows that attracted listeners. Paley and the other CBS brass scouted out promising new stars, such as Kate Smith, Bing Crosby, Al Jolson, and the comedy team of George Burns and Gracie Allen. Unfortunately, he couldn't pay them as much as NBC could, so once they became popular, the stars fled to NBC. But by 1932, CBS had more affiliates than NBC.

WHAT'S THE NEWS?

With the Great Depression in full swing and the clouds of war hanging over Europe in the mid-'30s, Paley predicted that Americans would soon want quality news. Turning down an offer from the Associated Press to license its news, Paley decided to build his own news bureau from scratch.

One of the bureau's first reporters in 1938: Edward R. Murrow. His live coverage of Nazi bombs falling on London, broadcast at great personal risk from the roof of a building, sealed CBS's reputation as the network with on-the-spot news during World War II. Murrow and news director William L. Shirer put together a team that would define news well into the television era, including such future TV regulars as Howard K. Smith and Eric Sevareid.

THE EYE OF THE STORM

After World War II, CBS still couldn't offer stars more money than NBC, but it figured out a loophole. CBS offered lower salaries, along with payments for the "right to broadcast" the stars' shows. Under the tax code, such a rights payment was considered a capital gain, which was taxed at a much lower rate than regular income tax (25 percent of capital gains versus 82 percent of income above $400,000). This started a stampede of stars to CBS, including Jack Benny, Burns and Allen (returning), and Edgar Bergen—just in time for the television era.

CBS began experimental TV broadcasts in New York in 1939. They lasted for about an hour a day and reached the few hundred people in the area who had TV sets. The network definitely had to play catch-up with NBC, which had the scientific advantage of being run by RCA, a technological and electronics firm. Paley purchased a research-and-development firm called Hytron Laboratories and set out not only to get programs on the air but to do what NBC hadn't thought about yet: offering them in color.

Ultimately, NBC and CBS both went on the air in New York in July 1941, both in black-and-white. NBC won the color battle, though. The system that its parent company, RCA, developed earned FCC approval because, when adopted, the signal required to transmit color was also compatible with black-and-white sets. The system developed by CBS's Hytron Labs was not. So CBS was forced to adopt RCA/NBC's technology. Well into the 1970s, whenever CBS broadcast a show in color—which was all of them by then—it had to pay a licensing fee to RCA...the parent company of its competitor.

*   *   *

Black gold: By the end of *The Beverly Hillbillies'* run in 1971, Jed Clampett's oil fortune was said to be $95 million. In today's money, that's $498 million worth of "Texas tea."

The CBS "eye" logo made its television debut on October 20, 1951.

GOSH, BATMAN...

The 1960s Batman TV series is well known for its campiness. But we've always liked the lessons on civics and citizenship Batman/Bruce Wayne gave to his ward, Robin/Dick Grayson. Here's some of Batman's choicest advice.

Robin: You can't get away from Batman that easy!
Batman: *Easily.*
Robin: *Easily.*
Batman: Good grammar is essential, Robin.

Batman: Better put five cents in the meter.
Robin: No policeman's going to give the Batmobile a ticket.
Batman: This money goes to building better roads. We all must do our part.

Dick: Gosh, economics is sure a dull subject.
Bruce: Oh, you must be jesting, Dick. Economics dull? The glamour, the romance of commerce. It's the very lifeblood of our society.

Dick: What's the use of learning French, anyway?
Bruce: Language is the key to world peace. If we all spoke each other's tongues, perhaps the scourge of war would be ended forever.
Dick: Gosh, Bruce, yes. I'll get these darn verbs if they kill me!

Batman: When you get a little older, you'll see how easy it is to become lured by the female of the species.
Robin: I guess you can never trust a woman.
Batman: You've made a hasty generalization, Robin. It's a bad habit to get into.

Robin: Gosh, Batman, those look like honest eyes.
Batman: Never trust the old chestnut, "Crooks have beady little eyes." It's false.

Bruce: Most Americans don't realize what we owe to the ancient Incas. Very few appreciate they gave us the white potato and many varieties of Indian corn.
Dick: Now whenever I eat mashed potatoes, I for one will think of the Incas.

Robin: We'd better hurry, Batman.
Batman: Not too fast, Robin. In good bat-climbing as in good driving, one must never sacrifice safety for speed.
Robin: Right again, Batman!

In 1966 *Batman* was honored by the National Safety Council for promoting seat belt use.

THE HEIDI BOWL

*Today, pro football is the single most popular thing on NBC, and
games always run in their entirety. But in 1968, the sport was still
trying to gain a foothold in television. Here's the story of the game that
made TV networks realize football was serious business.*

SWISS CHEESE

One of the most dramatic games in football history took
place on November 17, 1968. Late in the game, with a play-
off spot hanging in the balance, the Oakland Raiders trailed the
New York Jets. Amazingly, with just over a minute left to play, the
Raiders scored two touchdowns and won, 43–32. Fans in the
stands said it was the most incredible football game they'd ever
seen. And the millions of people watching it on TV? They didn't
get to see the thrilling end of the game. Instead, they saw the
beginning of a made-for-TV movie called *Heidi*.

PROGRAMMING AS USUAL

In the late '60s, pro football games usually lasted about two and a
half hours. So NBC had scheduled the broadcast of the Raiders-
Jets game at 4 p.m. Eastern time, which seemed to leave plenty of
time for a much-hyped adaptation of the 1880 Swiss children's
novel *Heidi* to air promptly at 7 p.m. The beloved classic hadn't
been made into a movie since Shirley Temple played the title
character in 1937. NBC spent millions on its version and cast
movie stars Jean Simmons, Michael Redgrave, and Maximillian
Schell.

But before *Heidi*, there was the game: a thriller with lots of
penalties and lead changes. Near the end of the fourth quarter, the
Joe Namath-led Jets kicked a field goal and pulled ahead of the
Raiders, the defending conference champions. With 65 seconds
left to play, the Jets were ahead 32–29. NBC broadcast operations
supervisor Dick Cline had a decision to make. It was now 7
p.m.—time for *Heidi* to start—but the game wasn't over. The
movie's sole sponsor, Timex, had a contract with NBC that
Heidi would start on time, and network brass had specifically
ordered Cline to cut away from the game if necessary.

Private eye Mike Hammer's safe combination was 36-24-36.

At that same moment, NBC executives decided that they *should* air the game's final moments and pay a penalty to Timex. They attempted to reach Cline to tell him...but they couldn't get through. The network phone lines, as well as the phone lines of many affiliates, were all jammed with football fans begging the network not to cut away, and *Heidi* fans wondering if the movie would start on time.

Cline never got the call, so at 7 p.m., *Heidi* aired as scheduled.

LET'S GO TO THE VIDEOTAPE

As *Heidi* began, the game got even more exciting. The Jets incurred a penalty and turned over the ball to Oakland. The Raiders' Charlie Smith caught a 20-yard pass and ran it 43 yards for a touchdown, putting Oakland ahead, 36–32, with 42 seconds to play.

When that news scrolled across the bottom of screens just a few seconds into the movie's opening credits, the calls of protest erupted into an avalanche, swarming the switchboards of NBC and its East Coast affiliates. NBC president Julian Goodman finally got through to Cline and demanded the game be returned to the air. Cline couldn't do it—the video feed had been dropped, and by the time they got it back online, the game would be over.

Meanwhile, on the field, the Jets' Earl Christy fumbled the ball on a punt return on the 10-yard line. Preston Ridlehuber of the Raiders recovered it and took it in for another touchdown. Final score: Oakland 43, New York 32.

OFF-FIELD FUMBLE

When the score scrolled across TV screens, thousands of enraged football fans tried to call NBC headquarters in New York City. When they couldn't get through, many of them began dialing every other New York institution they could think of, from the police and fire departments to the *New York Times*.

Within hours, Goodman released a statement, characterizing the decision to cut away from the game as "a forgivable error committed by humans who were concerned about children expecting to see *Heidi* at 7:00 p.m." In a bid for sympathy, he added, "I missed the end of the game as much as anyone else."

Inspired by the breast cancer death of a character on *The L Word*...

MONDAY MORNING QUARTERBACKING
Overnight, network heads decided that NBC would have to make things right somehow. The plan: show film of the unseen 65 seconds of the football game on *Today* in the morning, and then again on *The Huntley-Brinkley Report* in the evening. There was only one problem: The tape didn't have play-by-play commentary—it was just raw footage of on-field action. NBC aired it anyway, and brought in sportscaster Curt Gowdy to re-create the audio from the night before.

The debacle resulted in some permanent changes to the way sports were presented on television. NBC changed its policy of cutting away from sports competitions that ran long, and ordered that from then on, programming would be shifted for as many minutes as necessary. Furthermore, the network installed a separate phone line between its headquarters and its control room, independent of its switchboard. (The special phone, still in use, is nicknamed "the Heidi Phone.")

FOR YOUR CONSIDERATION
NBC did find a little humor in the incident. When the Emmy nominations began in 1969, the network ran full-page ads in entertainment trade papers promoting *Heidi* for awards consideration. Among the review excerpts raving about the movie was a quote from the Jets' Joe Namath: "I didn't get a chance to see it, but I heard it was great."

*　　*　　*

THE 13 MOST-WATCHED DRAMA SERIES FINALES

1. *Magnum, P.I.* (1988)
2. *Dallas* (1991)
3. *Gunsmoke* (1975)
4. *The Fugitive* (1967)
5. *Star Trek: The Next Generation* (1994)
6. *St. Elsewhere* (1988)
7. *MacGyver* (1992)
8. *Miami Vice* (1989)
9. *L.A. Law* (1994)
10. *Quantum Leap* (1993)
11. *Knots Landing* (1993)
12. *Bonanza* (1973)
13. *Matlock* (1995)

HILFE, MEINE FAMILIE SPINNT

Married...with Children (Fox, 1987–97) was often criticized for being crass and lowbrow. It was so offensive...that it became one of the most remade American shows in the world.

Germany. Dubbed and subtitled episodes of *Married...with Children* were so popular in Germany that TV producers there decided to make a German-language version in 1993 to compete with the American show, still on the air. Title: *Hilfe, Meine Familie Spinnt* ("Help, My Family Is Nuts"). The show was a carbon copy of the original: It involved an unhappy shoe salesman, his sex-hungry wife, his ditzy blond daughter, his smart but shallow son, an annoying neighbor couple, and even a wise-cracking dog—and the episodes were word-for-word translations of the original show's first year. (Except the family's name was "Strunk" instead of "Bundy.") Ratings were decent but not good enough for prime time, and *Hilfe, Meine Familie Spinnt* was canceled after one season—clobbered in the ratings by the original *Married...with Children.*

Brazil. First airing in 1999, the Brazilian-made version was called *A Guerra dos Pintos*—"The War of the Pintos"—the family name being Pinto rather than Bundy (*pinto* is Brazilian slang for "penis"). Again, even though it was based on scripts from the original series, it couldn't beat the American version in the ratings and was canceled after two seasons.

Colombia, Chile, and Argentina. Each of these Spanish-speaking countries produced its own local *Married...*, each of them titled *Casados con Hijos*, a direct translation of "Married with Children." The first, in Colombia, used replicas of the original's sets, and lasted for 26 episodes in 2004. The Chilean *Casados con Hijos* was the most successful—but after remaking all 259 episodes of *Married* from 2006 to 2008, it went off the air because producers ran out of source material. (The Bundys in this show were the Larraíns, the actual last name of Fernando Larraín, the Chilean actor in the Al

Bundy role.) In the Argentine version, 215 episodes were made in just a year and a half (2005–06), and it won a prestigious Martín Fierro Award, the "Argentine Emmy."

Hungary. In 2006 Hungary aired its most expensive sitcom: *Egy Rém Rendes Csalad Budapesten*, or "A Gruesomely Decent Family in Budapest"—its take on *Married...with Children*. Unlike the other remakes, this show was technically a spin-off. Premise: The Hungarian Bardis family inherits a country house from their American cousins, the Bundys (even though the Bundys were far from wealthy enough to own a second home, even in Hungary). Despite the involvement of some of the original show's producers, this series lasted just 26 episodes, getting crushed in the ratings by reruns of *ER*.

Russia. The Russian version, debuting in 2006, was called *Schastlivy vmeste*, or "Happy Together." In this version, Al and Peg Bundy became Gena and Dasha Bukin. The seemingly all-American show turned into Russia's most popular sitcom of all time, and by 2008, nearly all of the original show's episodes had been remade. In 2010 brand-new episodes began airing. There are more than 300 Russian episodes now—making it more successful than the American version, which, with 259 episodes, is one of the longest-running U.S. sitcoms. Where do Russian producers get ideas for new episodes? They hired writers from the original *Married...* and also accept fan submissions.

*　　*　　*

THE HOLY GRAIL

After the first season of *Monty Python's Flying Circus* aired on the BBC in 1969, the network planned to record over the master tapes. Why? They didn't believe the show had any future value. And besides—videotape was very expensive. *Python* cast member Terry Gilliam found out about the plan and made a deal with the BBC: If they gave him the master tapes for the shows as they were produced, he would pay for new blank video cassettes. The network agreed, and Gilliam got the tapes, saving the classic comedy series' first season from being lost forever.

WHY DOES DARRIN LOOK DIFFERENT?

Viewers count on the actors in favorite shows to be there each week. So it's a little unsettling when "old reliables" are suddenly, inexplicably...replaced.

Series: *Bewitched* (ABC, 1964–72)
Old actor: Dick York
New actor: Dick Sargent
Details: Dick York played Darrin Stephens, the befuddled mortal husband of witch Samantha. Throughout his time on the series, York was in constant pain due to a back injury sustained during the filming of the 1959 Western *They Came to Cordura*. During the fifth season, he could barely move, and episodes had to be written around his inability to stand for sustained periods. After he collapsed on the set and was rushed to a hospital in 1969, York quit the show for good. Rather than write Darrin out of the show, *Bewitched* producers decided to bring in a new actor to portray him. They went with Dick Sargent, who had actually been the original choice for the part in 1964 (he had been unavailable to do the series then). Darrin's new appearance was never explained (not even as "magic"), and Sargent stayed with *Bewitched* until it ended production.

Series: *The Partridge Family* (ABC, 1970–74)
Old actor: Jeremy Gelbwaks
New actor: Brian Forster
Details: Nine-year-old Jeremy Gelbwaks landed his first-ever acting role when he was cast as Chris Partridge, the drummer in the family band. But after one season, Jeremy had to quit because his father's job required the family to move to Virginia. Another actor, Brian Forster, was quickly cast, and stayed on the show until its end. ABC reportedly didn't receive a single letter or call about the switch. Bonus: Teen idol David Cassidy quit *The Partridge Family* at the end of the fourth season in 1974. Producers lined up

Australian pop star Rick Springfield to replace him...but then the network canceled the show.

Series: Various revivals of *The Brady Bunch* (1977, 1988, 1990)
Old actresses: Eve Plumb, Susan Olsen, Maureen McCormick
New actresses: Geri Reischl, Jennifer Runyon, Leah Ayers
Details: *The Brady Bunch* never cracked the Top 20 in its initial run (1969–74), but was so popular in reruns that it spawned several follow-up specials and series. Eve Plumb, who played middle daughter Jan, was eager to move on and opted out of the 1977 *The Brady Bunch Variety Hour*, a glitzy variety show hosted by the *Brady* actors in character. Plumb was replaced by bubbly Geri Reischl. (*The Simpsons* parodied this in 1997—serious-minded Lisa refuses to participate in a spin-off called *The Simpsons Smile Time Variety Hour*, and the new "Lisa" is a vivacious teenage blonde.)

Plumb did return for the 1988 TV movie *A Very Brady Christmas*, in which the grown-up Brady kids head home for the holidays with their spouses and kids. Susan Olsen (Cindy) couldn't make it, however, because she was on her honeymoon, so Jennifer Runyon stepped in.

Ratings for the movie were so good that CBS turned it into a regular hour-long drama series called *The Bradys*. In this reworking, the adult Brady kids faced problems like divorce and infertility...and it was one of the biggest bombs in TV history. The original Marcia, Maureen McCormick, missed the whole affair because she was pregnant; Leah Ayers played her character instead.

Series: *The Fresh Prince of Bel-Air* (NBC, 1990–96)
Old actress: Janet Hubert-Whitten
New actress: Daphne Maxwell Reid
Details: Outspoken college professor Vivian Banks (or Aunt Viv, to Will Smith's title character) was initially portrayed by Janet Hubert-Whitten, a veteran of TV and film. But the show was built as a starring vehicle for rapper Will Smith. Hubert and Smith had many run-ins (she claims that he and producers "made sure no one outshone him"). After Hubert-Whitten complained

one too many times, she was fired from the show—a contract clause that didn't allow her to get pregnant was cited, even though her pregnancy had been written into the show. In 1993 Daphne Maxwell Reid took over the Vivian role.

Series: *The Munsters* (CBS, 1964–66)
Old actress: Beverley Owen
New actress: Pat Priest
Details: Owen was a 27-year-old actress under contract with Universal Studios when she was cast in the company's spooky sitcom in 1964. Owen considered herself a serious actress, and hated playing the role of Marilyn, the "ugly" girl in the family (she was pretty, blond, and normal-looking; everyone else was a monster). Halfway through *The Munsters'* first season, Owen got married and asked to be let out of her contract. Rather than write out the character, which was essentially a running joke, *Munsters* producers replaced her with Priest, a 28-year-old actress who had done mostly stage and commercial work.

Series: *Roseanne* (ABC, 1988–97)
Old actress: Lecy Goranson
New actress: Sarah Chalke
Details: Lots of sitcoms have switched actors; *Roseanne* used two actresses interchangeably for the same role over the years. Lecy Goranson portrayed eldest daughter Becky Conner until 1993, when Goranson started college. Canadian actress Sarah Chalke (later a regular on *Scrubs*) was cast as the new Becky and stayed until Goranson wanted to come back in 1995. In 1996 Goranson left *Roseanne* again, and producers once more brought in Chalke, who stayed for the remainder of the show's run.

    Roseanne's writers were smart enough to acknowledge these switcheroos. On Chalke's first episode as Becky (the first time around), Roseanne (Roseanne Arnold) comments that she's "been gone so long, I barely recognize her." Later in the episode, the whole family is watching *Bewitched* and debating the merits of the two different Darrins. Becky says she "likes the second Darrin much better."

A "KING" DETHRONED

Nat "King" Cole was one of America's favorite entertainers in the 1950s, so NBC built a variety show around him. Although the show was popular, it was canceled. Why? Simple: In that era, advertisers didn't want to invest in a show headlined by an African American.

BLACK AND WHITE
Television began broadcasting in color in 1954, but at that time, American TV stars came in one color only: white. Jim Crow laws mandating racial segregation were still in effect. But after Jackie Robinson broke Major League Baseball's color barrier and the civil-rights movement started picking up steam, change was in the air.

Before the rock 'n' roll era, Nat "King" Cole was one of America's most successful singers and pianists, with seventeen Top 10 hits, including "Mona Lisa," "Orange Colored Sky," and "The Christmas Song." Jack Benny said Cole was "the best friend a song ever had." Cole's gentle baritone led millions to buy his records and inspired NBC to do something new in TV: build a musical variety show around a black entertainer. The network knew that if any star could lead the way toward racially integrated programming, it was Cole.

ON THE AIR
The Nat "King" Cole Show debuted at 7:30 p.m. on November 5, 1956, as a 15-minute program. Cole's clout and popularity helped line up top performers, including Ella Fitzgerald, Peggy Lee, Count Basie, and Tony Bennett. Critics praised the show, and it competed well against ABC's hit travelogue, *Bold Journey*.

Cole often performed with his arm draped over a fellow singer's shoulders. But, anticipating negative, racist responses—especially in the South—he had to be extremely careful not to appear too friendly with white performers on camera—particularly women. Simply touching a white woman's arm during a musical number could have been enough to cause a riot in some areas. Cole and NBC were careful not to depict any "untoward" contact, and they received no complaints from viewers.

Longest-running spin-off series: *The Simpsons,* spun off of *The Tracey Ullman Show* in 1989.

MAD AD MEN

The real problem facing *The Nat "King" Cole Show* was with advertisers. The custom at the time was for one company or product to sponsor a program, paying for its production costs. Advertisers were secured for Cole's show, but they backed out, leaving NBC to scramble to find local advertisers and piece together the financing. Cole and most of his guests even worked for industry scale—Hollywood's minimum wage—to help keep the show in production.

Despite the shoestring budget and lack of a national sponsor, NBC kept the faith, expanding the show to 30 minutes in 1957 and renewing it for the fall season. Then, in December, Cole quit, unwilling to fight for sponsors any longer. The 57th and final episode of *The Nat "King" Cole Show* aired on December 17, 1957. When asked by reporters why the show ended, Cole joked, "Madison Avenue is afraid of the dark."

LEGACY

Cole remained as popular as ever, and he toured and recorded several more hit records before his death from lung cancer in 1965 at age 45. He was posthumously inducted into the Jazz Hall of Fame (1993) and the Hit Parade Hall of Fame (2007), and honored with a Grammy Lifetime Achievement Award (1990).

For its part, NBC continued its efforts to break through TV's color barrier. In 1965 it debuted *I Spy* with Bill Cosby. In 1968 it cast Diahann Carroll as a young African-American widow and mother in the Top 10 hit sitcom *Julia*. But it wasn't until 1970 that the network (or any network) would have a successful, fully sponsored variety series hosted by an African American: *The Flip Wilson Show*.

*　　*　　*

HIGH TIMES

In August 2010 Sacramento station KTXL broadcast a 30-second ad showing people delivering testimonials about a wonderful new product that helped ease symptoms like joint pain, nausea, and anxiety. It was the first ever TV ad for marijuana in history.

Makes sense: The first Charmin commercial was filmed in Flushing, New York.

LOST TV PILOTS

If you thought Gilligan's Island *or* Alf *were goofy ideas for TV shows (which they were), you should see the stuff that doesn't make it onto the air. Someone actually filmed pilot episodes of the following shows.*

Baffled! (1973)
A race-car driver (Leonard Nimoy) gets injured in a crash and suddenly begins seeing visions of murders that haven't occurred yet. He solves the crimes before they happen with the help of a female student of psychic phenomena.

Clone Master (1978)
A government scientist (Art Hindle) makes a bunch of clones of himself (all played by Hindle), then sends them out into the world to fight crime and catch evildoers. Each episode would have focused on a different clone's adventures.

The Tribe (1974)
Set 40,000 years ago at the end of the Ice Age, this series chronicled a Cro-Magnon family's struggles to survive harsh living conditions and skirmishes with a rival tribe of primitive Neanderthals.

The Mysterious Two (1979)
A man must stop two popular televangelists...because they're actually evil aliens who are brainwashing humanity in order to take over the planet.

Judge Dee (1974)
Lots of shows in the 1970s were about sensitive people traveling around, generously helping others with their personal problems for free (*Kung Fu* and *The Incredible Hulk* are two examples). In *Judge Dee*, a judge wanders his rural district helping people and resolving disputes. The twist: *Judge Dee* is set in 7th-century China. It's not to be confused with *High Risk*, in which six former circus performers hit the road and help people solve their problems...for money.

Danger Team (1991)

A ball of space goop crash-lands in a sculptor's studio. Naturally, he molds the goop into three figurines. The figurines come to life, but only the artist can see them. The artist and the goop men team up to fight crime.

Steel Justice (1992)

A little boy idolizes his policeman father and likes to secretly tail him when he goes out on drug busts and stakeouts at night. One night, the kid gets killed. Dad is distraught...until he meets his new crime-fighting partner—a fire-breathing, 100-foot-tall robot dinosaur that's possessed by the spirit of his dead son.

Wurlitzer (1985)

A man inherits a decaying diner and its antique Wurlitzer juke-box. The plot: In each episode, the man selects a song on the jukebox and is then transported back in time to the year that song came out. Why? To help people with their problems. In the pilot episode, he listens to a Jefferson Airplane song, goes to 1968 San Francisco, and helps a hippie quit drugs.

America 2100 (1979)

Two stand-up comedians are accidentally put into suspended animation. They awake at the dawn of the 22nd century to find the world run by a supercomputer with the voice and old jokes of fellow comedian Sid Caesar.

Danny and the Mermaid (1978)

Danny is an oceanography student failing all of his classes. Then he meets a mermaid who, along with her talking dolphin friend, helps Danny get better grades by escorting him all over the ocean and tutoring him on sea life.

Ethel Is an Elephant (1980)

A New York photographer fights with his landlord to keep his unusual pet in his apartment—an elephant (named Ethel) that was abandoned by the circus. Most of the comedy revolves around unsuccessful attempts to hide Ethel behind furniture.

On *That '70's Show*, Fes's name was an acronym for Foreign Exchange Student.

THE *ST. ELSEWHERE* HYPOTHESIS

*Fun fact: Almost all of television takes place inside
the mind of an autistic child. At least, that's what some
fans of a 1980s hospital drama still think.*

A GLOBAL CONCERN

As the action wraps up on the final episode of the NBC medical drama *St. Elsewhere* (1982–88), St. Eligius Hospital is seen under a light snowfall. The scene then cuts to Tommy Westphall (Chad Allen), the autistic 10-year-old son of hospital administrator Dr. Donald Westphall (Ed Flanders). Dr. Westphall walks in, but he's not a doctor—he's dressed as a construction worker. His colleague Dr. Auschlander (Norman Lloyd) is there, too, only now he's Tommy's grandfather and Westphall's father. Westphall comments to Auschlander, "I don't understand this autism thing, Pop. He sits there, all day long, in his own world, staring at that toy." The toy? A snow globe.

As the three leave the room to go have dinner, Westphall takes the globe from Tommy and places it on the mantel. The camera zooms in: Inside is a tiny replica of St. Eligius Hospital, with snow coming down. The implication: During the entire run of the show, every episode and every character of *St. Elsewhere* had existed only in Tommy's mind. With this twist ending, the writers rendered not only their own show a fantasy, but dozens of other shows and characters as well.

WORLDS COLLIDE

Critics and audiences were puzzled, at the very least. The *Chicago Sun-Times* called in a "bizarre twist ending," and it made the list of *TV Guide*'s "most unexpected TV moments." But more than a decade later, in 2002, TV writer and pop-culture blogger Dwayne McDuffie noticed another result of the final *St. Elsewhere* episode—if that show was in Tommy's mind, then every other show *St. Elsewhere* had a crossover with was a figment of the boy's imagination, too. Since McDuffie first wrote about it, hundreds of

Family Guy creator Seth MacFarlane missed his flight on one of the doomed 9/11 planes.

people have discussed and mapped out "the Tommy Westphall Universe" on the Internet.

Here are a few examples of how it works:

• *St. Elsewhere* character Dr. Roxanne Turner (Alfre Woodward) appeared on **Homicide: Life on the Street** in 1998. Because of that crossover, it's reasonable to conclude that *Homicide* was a creation of Tommy's imagination, too.

• *Homicide's* Detective John Munch (Richard Belzer) was moved to **Law & Order: SVU** in 1999, meaning that *that* show was also in Tommy's head, as are **all the various Law & Order programs,** because those all take place in a common TV universe.

• On a March 1985 episode of *St. Elsewhere*, Dr. Westphall and Dr. Auschlander visit the **Cheers** bar (both shows take place in Boston), bringing *Cheers* and its spin-offs and crossovers—**Frasier** and **Wings**—into the *St. Elsewhere* world of Tommy's brain.

• *Cheers* crossed over with **The John Larroquette Show** (1993–96). The main character of *Larroquette* worked at a bus station built by a company called Yoyodyne. Nearly a decade later, on the supernatural drama **Angel**, Yoyodyne was a client of the villainous law firm Wolfram and Hart. *Angel* was a spin-off of **Buffy the Vampire Slayer,** so both of them were Tommy Westphall's idea.

THE WESTPHALL-OUT

To date, 282 different television shows have been said to have been thought up by Tommy because of their connection to *St. Elsewhere*, including *I Love Lucy, Leave It to Beaver, Gilligan's Island, The Brady Bunch, M*A*S*H, Seinfeld, Home Improvement, Scrubs, Friends, Arrested Development, The Wire, Coach, The Drew Carey Show, Grace Under Fire, Ellen, Crossing Jordan, Six Feet Under, Las Vegas, The Office, Heroes, Passions, Nanny and the Professor, Betwitched, Three's Company,* and *Lost.*

"Someone did the math once," said *St. Elsewhere* creator Tom Fontana, "and something like 90 percent of all television took place in Tommy Westphall's mind. God love him."

*　　*　　*

Aw, shoot: Robert Stack, star of *The Untouchables* and *Unsolved Mysteries,* won the 1935 National Skeet Shooting championship.

LIFE WITH LUCY

*I Love Lucy and Here's Lucy are TV classics, but Lucille Ball's final
series, Life with Lucy, was a commercial and critical flop.
Nobody took it harder than Lucy herself.*

COMEDY TONIGHT
Lucille Ball was one of TV's first—and biggest—superstars.
Between *I Love Lucy, The Lucy and Desi Comedy Hour,
Here's Lucy,* and *The Lucy Show,* from 1951 to 1974 she was contin-
ually in a Top-10 show on CBS on Mondays at 9 p.m. Afterward,
she went into semiretirement, hosting specials, making talk-show
appearances, and occasionally starring in a movie.

Flash forward to 1986. The biggest TV story of the day was
the phenomenal success of NBC's *The Cosby Show.* Pundits had
declared the family sitcom dead (adult-oriented comedies like
Cheers and *Taxi* were in vogue), and NBC was in third place.
Then the network signed TV icon Bill Cosby and allowed him
to make whatever show he wanted. The gamble paid off, and his
family comedy became the #1 show on TV and took NBC to
first place (see page 423).

THE NEW COSBY
ABC yearned to imitate NBC's success, and executives brain-
stormed to come up with a list of TV icons who could headline a
new show. Someone suggested the biggest icon of all: Lucille Ball.

With experience as a star and as a producer (she once ran
DesiLu Studios, which made *Mission: Impossible* and other hit
shows), Ball knew that the road from idea to broadcast was long,
tiring, and complicated. And at age 74, she was in no mood to put
up with the usual preproduction process. So she told ABC that
she'd do a show only if several conditions were met:
• She wouldn't have to make a pilot episode.
• The show would be guaranteed a spot on the fall 1986 schedule.
• There would be no audience testing, notes for improvement
from network executives, focus groups, or prebroadcast retooling.
• She'd have the freedom to hire her own crew and staff—in

particular, writers Bob Carroll Jr. and Madelyn Davis, with whom she'd worked since *I Love Lucy*.

• It would be a pay-or-play deal, meaning that she would get paid for a whole season's worth of episodes, even if they didn't air.

• She would have complete creative control.

• For her efforts, she'd get a large salary (reportedly in the millions).

ABC was so eager to sign Ball, and so sure that any show she delivered would be a smash hit, that they agreed to all of her demands. What could they possibly lose?

MAKING IT

Carroll and Davis wrote some scripts for what they called *Life with Lucy*. Although conceived as a simple family comedy about a spry, meddlesome grandma, the plot was actually quite complicated: Lucy Barker (Ball) is a 70-year-old redheaded health nut who lives with her daughter, son-in-law, and their two kids in California. Lucy's husband recently died and left her with a 50 percent ownership of the hardware store he ran for decades. Bored and lonely, she decides to work at the store, much to the chagrin of Curtis, the guy who owns the other half. Curtis also moves in with Lucy's family because he's the father of Lucy's son-in-law.

Every episode would involve the standard Lucy situations: Lucy meddles in the affairs of her family, Lucy mishears something, Lucy gets tongue-tied around a celebrity, Lucy gets caught up in a slapstick situation.

Ball cast an ensemble of sitcom veterans. Co-starring as Curtis: her old *Here's Lucy* foil, Gale Gordon. He was 80 at the time, and he would agree to do the show only if he could get the same pay-or-play deal as Ball. He got it. Rounding out the cast: Ann Dusenberry as the daughter, Larry Anderson as the son-in-law, and Philip Amelio and Jenny Lewis as the kids.

ON THE AIR

ABC aired promos for Lucille Ball's triumphant return to television all summer long and debuted the show on Saturday, September 20, 1986, as the linchpin of its new fall season. (It led into *The Ellen Burstyn Show*, an attempt to siphon off some of the audience from NBC's *The Golden Girls*.) One of the highlights of the first episode was the standing ovation the studio audience gave Ball near the beginning of the show—edited down from five minutes of applause. It looked like *Life with Lucy* was going to be another hit and another big TV comeback story.

Then the rest of the show unfolded. As Ball attempted slapstick gag after slapstick gag, the studio audience reportedly cringed. Gasps can be heard on the soundtrack as they react to a brittle-looking 74-year-old woman performing physical comedy.

OLD SCHOOL

The first episode attracted more than 20 million viewers, enough to rank it in the Nielsen Top 20 for the week. Then the reviews started to come in. Critics were disappointed by the stale premise and the same old sight gags. One critic said that Ball, in an orange shock wig and heavy makeup, looked "like a kabuki performer."

Why was the show so bad? For one, ABC couldn't step in and change anything—it had to let Ball do whatever she wanted. The results showed onscreen: Instead of memorizing lines, Ball read them off of used cue cards, which hadn't been widely used on sitcoms since the 1950s; the episode directors were old associates who hadn't worked in more than 20 years and hadn't kept up with new directing trends and techniques.

Even the sound and picture were off. Ball insisted on hiring an *I Love Lucy* soundman who, by 1986, was going deaf. Ball herself was so concerned with not appearing old on camera that she instructed makeup artists to pull back her skin with adhesive tape, then hide the tape under her wig. She then had the camera crew outfit their equipment with soft-focus filters that gave the show a bizarre, hazy appearance.

YOU CAN'T BE IN THE SHOW, LUCY

The ratings fell further every week. A guest spot by John Ritter and the addition of *Honeymooners* star Audrey Meadows to the cast didn't attract new viewers. After eight episodes had aired, ABC bought out Ball's contract and canceled *Life with Lucy*. Ball never made another television show, privately confessing that she was convinced that America "didn't love her anymore." She died in 1989 at age 77.

EVERYBODY PANIC!

*Since the dawn of civilization, people have created wild
threats to be afraid of—witches, demons, and cradle-
robbing strangers, to name a few. In the last 50 years, it
seems like we've had more and more panics. Why?
Some say it's because of the power of TV.*

MODS AND ROCKERS
Background: In 1964 two rival youth countercultures
vied for turf in England. The Mods dressed in stylish
outfits, rode motor scooters, and listened to ska music. Rockers
preferred leather jackets, motorcycles, and rock 'n' roll. A few
scuffles and riots broke out between Mods and Rockers, and they
even favored different weapons: Mods reportedly used knives and
razor blades; rockers liked clubs and bats.

Panic! British TV news wildly overreported a handful of unrelated
dance-hall and pool-hall fights as a full-scale, nationally organized
gang war between unified fronts of Mods and Rockers. For a few
months, British citizens lived in fear of roving bands of Mods riding around on Vespa scooters, dressed in collared shirts, and armed
to the teeth with knives. Police stepped up patrols of seaside
towns, coming down especially hard on clubs and bars that were
popular hangouts for these groups. When the media ran out of real
fights to cover, they began linking unrelated fights, riots, and
deaths to the imaginary gang war.

BACKMASKING

Background: Rock music was deemed "the devil's music" pretty
much from its inception. During the 1980s, the scare went one
step further when artists such as Led Zeppelin, Queen, and even
the Beatles were accused of hiding subversive messages in their
songs...backward. A technology called "backmasking" supposedly
obscured them, making them sound like gibberish when played on
an LP. But, the theory went, when played backward, innocent
lines like "Another one bites the dust" became lines like "It's fun
to smoke marijuana"—subliminal ideas that could infiltrate the
minds of impressionable kids. Some Christian groups accused the

---

Animated, female, and African-American remakes of *The Odd Couple* were all produced.

Church of Satan of masterminding the whole operation in order to attract more converts.

Panic! In 1982 Dan Rather devoted a large portion of one of his first nights as host of *The CBS Evening News* to the controversy. He even played some of the alleged backmasked messages for the television audience. (Played backward, by hand, an LP produced an incoherent mess of sound.) By 1984 backmasking had been so widely reported that legislation was proposed in several states to ban it...even though there was no proof that it actually existed.

RAINBOW PARTIES

Background: In 2003 *The Oprah Winfrey Show* devoted an episode to the supposed spread of "rainbow parties," suburban teenage get-togethers in which boys competed to receive a certain sexual favor from girls, earning lipstick marks as proof of their conquest. One guest claimed the parties were being hosted by kids as young as 13.

Panic! It was the first time any mention of a "rainbow party" had appeared in the mass media, but a year later, they were still a hot topic among school guidance counselors and sexual education classes, and even spawned a cautionary young-adult novel. Still, there's no proof that these parties existed before the *Oprah* show. Some parents claim it was the show that put the idea in kids' heads.

SATANISTS

Background: The idea of satanic cults spawned a major panic in the 1980s. It began with the 1980 publication of *Michelle Remembers*, a "memoir" of repressed memories written by Michelle Smith, a woman who claims to have grown up in a cult in which she was subjected to ritualistic sexual abuse. Smith inspired others to undergo repressed-memory therapy, and many claimed to have discovered that they, too, had been victimized by satanic cults.

Panic! Never one to avoid sensationalism, tabloid TV journalist Geraldo Rivera produced a TV documentary in 1987 called *Satanic Cults and Children*. Without citing any sources, Rivera claimed that the United States was home to one million satanic cultists, all involved in a single organization that had chapters in every major city. To give perspective, Rivera claimed there were more satanists in the U.S. than police officers. In the end, Smith's recollections were proven to be a hoax...as was the satanic underworld.

Mister Ed's filming-day diet: 20 pounds of hay and a gallon of sweet tea.

SECRETS OF SUCCESS

TV stars and show creators tell how they do it.

"We don't want to be a goody-goody show and pretending we are nice people because we are not. Our number-one aim is to be entertaining."
—Simon Cowell,
judge on *American Idol*

"We ushered in a cycle of cynical shows. But we were probably the most mean-spirited. Everyone on our show was humiliated on a weekly basis."
—Amanda Bearse, Marcie on
Married...with Children

"We're making a show that sci-fi geeks like, but also has a human story that others can relate to. We don't underestimate people. You don't need a college degree to think."
—John Noble,
Walter on *Fringe*

"What made us different from other Westerns was the fact that *Gunsmoke* wasn't just action and a lot of shooting; they were character-study shows. They're interesting to watch all these years later."
—James Arness, Sheriff
Dillon on *Gunsmoke*

"We do fact-check, not because of any journalistic criteria; we do that because jokes don't work when they're lies."
—Jon Stewart, *The Daily Show*

"If you're afraid that people are going to flip the channel, tell a better story, write a better joke, add a subplot where someone is dressed like a wizard."
—Dan Harmon, creator
of *Community*

"I write the show straight through. And then we find, when we're editing, where the breaks go. You can do a lot with a commercial break—you can change days, you can suggest the passage of time."
—Matthew Weiner,
creator of *Mad Men*

"We try to stay away from sitcom-formula jokes, like a Lenny-Squiggy entrance. Someone says, 'Who would be stupid enough to wear that hat?' and they enter wearing that hat."
—Ray Romano,
Everybody Loves Raymond

Bonanza's David Canary (Candy the ranch hand) is a descendant of Calamity Jane.

NO WHAMMIES, BIG MONEY

When a humble-looking contestant named Michael Larson
appeared on a game show called Press Your Luck *in 1984,*
he won big—suspiciously big. Then his life came undone.

IT'S ALL PART OF THE GAME

In May 1984, Michael Larson, a 35-year-old ice-cream truck driver from Lebanon, Ohio, flew to California to audition for the CBS game show *Press Your Luck*. But what the show's producers didn't know was that Larson had an edge.

Most game-show contestants study the show they're about to appear on, but Larson had taken it one step further. According to his former partner, he'd filled the couple's home with TVs that played endlessly. He watched hours upon hours of television, trying to find a way to get rich, focusing on infomercial schemes and game shows. Then he found one.

PAUSE AND PLAY

Press Your Luck worked like this: A rectangular game board was filled with lighted squares indicating different cash amounts ($100, $200, $3,000, etc.). Contestants took turns "spinning" the board, the squares would light up in a seemingly random order, and the contestant would press a button to stop the "spin." Lights illuminated where they'd landed, and they won whatever amount was in the square. In addition, there were "Whammy" squares with a cartoon drawing of a little red devil that would wipe out their entire winnings. There were also "Prize" squares (a Brazilian vacation, a pool table) and "Extra Spin" squares. Object: Amass as much money as you could, keep your turn with as many free spins as possible, and avoid Whammies. (While they waited for a good spot to stop, contestants customarily chanted "No Whammies! Big money!")

But after watching the show for hours on end, Larson had figured out that the game's randomly blinking board wasn't as unpredictable as it appeared. He found, with lots of pausing and rewinding of taped episodes, that the board followed five distinct patterns, which he memorized. He thought that if he could get on the show, he'd be able to stop the board where he wanted, earning endless cash and free spins. He'd make a fortune.

PUTTING ON A SHOW

Larson knew that if he looked cocky or knowledgeable, he wouldn't make it on the show, so he put on an act for the producers. During the contestant-screening process in Los Angeles, he acted perky, excited, and self-deprecating—the way he had seen contestants on the show behave. It worked. He made it onto the show that same day.

Larson carried the act over to the show, smiling brightly, bouncing in his seat, and bantering with host Peter Tomarken about being out of work. When asked what he'd do with the money if he won, Larson said he "hoped to make enough money so I won't have to drive the ice-cream truck next summer." The two other contestants were a Baptist preacher named Ed Long and dental assistant Janie Litras.

Larson was up first to the board. He stopped his button and landed on...a Whammy. (Most likely, this was part of his plan. He didn't have any money to lose yet, and hitting a Whammy wouldn't arouse any suspicion.) On his next spins, he earned a modest $2,500. Long earned $4,080; Litras got $4,608 in cash and prizes. That was the end of the first round. After a commercial break, Larson controlled the board. On his first spin, he hit one of the best spots on the board: $4,000 plus a free spin. Then he hit $5,000 and a free spin. Then $1,000 and a free spin. And so on— he kept nailing the "sweet spots."

NO WHAMMIES, EVER

At first, Larson's "luck" did not look out of the ordinary. It was common for *Press Your Luck* contestants to get a lucky run—most players ran out of spins or hit a Whammy somewhere between their fifth and tenth attempts.

On set, the mood was fun and electric. But in the control room, things were more tense. Producers began to suspect that Larson wasn't just lucky—maybe he'd figured out how to beat the game. And yet they couldn't stop him because he wasn't breaking any rules.

Actor Mark Chapman lost the lead role in a 1985 TV movie about John Lennon...

Meanwhile, the other contestants' moods changed. At first they cheered Larson on, but as they sat helplessly, unable to compete, they lost their patience and, as Larson later said, "shot him daggers." When Larson reached $100,000, his winnings display had to drop the dollar sign in order to squeeze in the massive number. A few moments later, he bowed out and passed on his extra spins, effectively ending the game. Total winnings: $110,237 in cash and prizes.

OVERTIME

Press Your Luck contestants normally returned on the next episode to defend their title, but Larson wasn't allowed to do so—CBS rules stipulated that any contestant who'd won more than $25,000 couldn't come back. But he did technically appear on two episodes of the show—his winning streak had gone on for so long (39 spins in all) that the show exceeded its 30-minute running time. Producers decided that Larson's performance was newsworthy and potentially ratings-grabbing, so they decided to air his stint as two episodes.

To fill out two shows, Tomarken recorded an interview with Larson, who revealed that he'd had to borrow money to get his plane ticket to California, and that he'd bought the shirt he was wearing at a thrift store for 65 cents. Larson also mentioned that he'd probably invest his winnings in real estate.

Larson's *Press Your Luck* episodes aired on June 8 and June 11, 1984. And then they were put in a vault. CBS was so embarrassed by the incident that they banned the footage for years. When USA and the Game Show Network each bought the rights to air *Press Your Luck* reruns in the 1990s, CBS would not let them air the Larson episodes.

NOT SO LUCKY

Technically, Larson hadn't done anything illegal, so he went home with his $110,237. But his good fortune didn't hold. After shelling out $30,000 in taxes, he put about $30,000 into a real estate venture that turned out to be a Ponzi scheme. He lost about half of his *Press Your Luck* winnings.

Ever the opportunist, in November 1984, Larson saw a chance for another big windfall—a radio contest. Every day, a Dayton,

Ohio, station would read a serial number from a dollar bill on the air. If a listener could find a bill matching that number, they would win $30,000. Over a two-week period, Larson deposited the remainder of his *Press Your Luck* winnings in five different banks, then withdrew all of it in dollar bills. Eventually, he had tens of thousands of $1 bills—some in bundles, some in burlap sacks, some stuffed in plastic garbage bags.

Larson and his partner went to work, sitting down with the serial numbers the radio stations were still willing to pay on (listeners had a few days to find and turn in each serial number, so on any given day there were several chances to win). For hours every day, they checked the bills against the numbers. When Larson realized it would take about a week for them to go through just half of all those bills, he put some back in the bank, keeping about $40,000 in cash. After a few days of staring at serial numbers, the couple needed a break and went to a Christmas party. While they were gone, their house was robbed—and all the cash was stolen.

FROM WHAMMIES TO SCAMMIES

Larson's relationship with his partner went downhill after the robbery, which he suspected she'd orchestrated. "He kept watching me real close at night," she said. "I just had a feeling he was going to try to kill me." Eventually, she kicked him out.

Knowledge of Larson's whereabouts after the split are sketchy: At one point, he took a job with Wal-Mart as an assistant manager. In 1995 he suddenly left Ohio. His family later discovered he was under investigation for allegedly taking part in a lottery scheme that robbed 20,000 people of $3 million. He was never prosecuted. Larson died of throat cancer in 1999.

In 2003 the Larson episodes of *Press Your Luck* showed up on TV for the first time in nearly 20 years. That year, the Game Show Network produced a documentary about Larson called *Big Bucks: The Press Your Luck Scandal*, which included footage from the shows. The same night, GSN broadcast a special episode of its *Press Your Luck* revival, *Whammy!* The contestants: Larson's brother James, and his original competitors, Ed Long and Janie Litras. The winner: James Larson.

TV PORTMANTEAU QUIZ

A portmanteau is a word or phrase that results from two other words or phrases being combined—for example, "international" plus "network" forms "Internet." In this wordplay game, two TV show titles make a portmanteau. Can you guess the shows and their combined titles based on these wacky combined plots? (Answers are on page 498.)

1) Orange County, California, teenagers (Ben McKenzie, Adam Brody, Rachel Bilson) fall in and out of love with each other as they attend concerts by indie rock bands...and use advanced forensics equipment to solve heinous sex crimes and murders in Miami (theme song provided by the Who).

2) Groucho Marx tells jokes, improvises, and asks two contestants trivia questions for cash prizes...which they need to raise their two teenagers, Becca (Kellie Martin), a sensitive nerd; and Corky (Chris Burke), a boy with Down syndrome.

3) A man (Josh Radnor) in the year 2030 has flashbacks to his salad days in New York City in his 20s, all leading up to how he eventually met his kids' mother...which is a car that's possessed by a human spirit and speaks in the voice of Ann Sothern.

4) Two New York City police detectives (Gary Sinise and Melina Kanakaredes) fight crime and solve mysteries...with the assistance of two New York City police detectives (Dennis Franz and Jimmy Smits).

5) At a hip cocktail party in his mansion, *Playboy* publisher Hugh Hefner interviews cool, happening celebrities and flirts with attractive young women...who all end up being attacked by the Playboy Mansion's resident vampire, Barnabus Collins (Jonathan Frid).

6) A tame, 600-pound black bear is brought in from the wilds of the Pacific Northwest to live among humans, where he befriends a little boy (Clint Howard) and...an idealistic, handsome young surgeon (Vince Edwards) at County General Hospital.

7) Writer Dick Loudon (Bob Newhart) buys a Vermont inn for some peace and quiet, which he doesn't get because of the inn's neurotic staff...and his constant absences to jet off to Europe to solve international murders and jewel-heist mysteries with his wife (Stefanie Powers).

8) After they both get divorced, two best friends move in together to raise their children and face life. One (Susan Saint James) is the mother of a headstrong teenage daughter...the other (Calista Flockhart) is a flaky lawyer who wears extremely short miniskirts and hallucinates about dancing babies.

9) In this soap opera parody set in the midwestern town of Fernwood, a large family deals with infidelity, divorce, paternity disputes, sexual perversions, and the braided title character (Louise Lasser)...who has the ability to transform into any land animal she wishes, a power she uses to fight crime.

10) In a gritty drama about the issues facing the racially diverse students of a 1970s inner-city high school, each episode depicts... one hour of actual time, with each season occurring over the course of a single day, as the class tries to thwart a terrorist attack or presidential assassination.

11) A young, single executive (Christina Applegate) gets in an accident and has amnesia—she can't remember anything about her life...such as whether she or her live-in male housekeeper (Tony Danza), with whom she has lots of sexual chemistry, is the one *really* running the house.

12) On New Year's Eve 1999, a lazy pizza delivery boy (voice of Billy West) falls into a cryogenic freezing chamber and wakes up in the year 3000. The earth has transformed into a sci-fi utopia... but his family of redneck relatives, including the acerbic matriarch (Vicki Lawrence), is still around, butting their noses into each other's business.

*   *   *

3 actors whose voices introduce network evening news shows: Michael Douglas (*NBC Nightly News*), Morgan Freeman (*CBS Evening News*), and Mike Rowe (*ABC World News Tonight*).

DRIFTING AWAY

Many cable networks began as "niche" channels, featuring music, history, or classic movies. Then, over time, most of them evolved into something quite different. The TV industry term for this: "channel drift."

M TV
Original niche: 'Round-the-clock music videos.
Today: Reality shows about young people (*Jersey Shore, The Real World, Teen Mom*); music videos in the early morning hours.

Bravo
Original niche: High culture—opera, ballet, and films of Broadway plays and musicals.
Today: Reality shows targeted at or about wealthy consumers, such as *Project Runway, Top Chef,* and *The Real Housewives of Atlanta.*

TLC (The Learning Channel)
Original niche: A hybrid of PBS and the Discovery Channel, "the place for learning minds" offered historical documentaries, nature shows, science series, and instructional programs.
Today: Reality shows, including *Toddlers & Tiaras; What Not to Wear; Little People, Big World;* and *Kate Plus 8.*

A&E (Arts & Entertainment)
Original niche: Biographical and historical documentaries. Its most popular show, *Biography,* was spun off into a separate channel.
Today: Reality shows like *Gene Simmons: Family Jewels* and *Fix This Kitchen.*

VH-1 (Video Hits 1)
Original niche: Rock videos for audiences too old for MTV, and programs about classic rock and pop.
Today: In the late 1990s, it began featuring pop-culture nostalgia

(*Pop-Up Video, I Love the '80s*). After a successful run of "Celebre-ality" shows (see page 173), it switched to mostly reality TV—*Basketball Wives, Dance Cam Slam,* and *My Big Friggin' Wedding,* for example.

The History Channel

Original niche: Documentaries and interviews with historians.

Today: Renamed simply History, it still airs historical shows but has expanded to include reality shows like *Ax Men* and *Ice Road Truckers.*

Cartoon Network

Original niche: All cartoons, all the time

Today: It moved classic cartoons like *The Flintstones* and *Yogi Bear* to a sister channel called Boomerang. It still airs cartoons, but oddly enough, it now offers live-action shows, such as *BrainRush,* a game show for preteens in which contestants have to answer questions while riding a roller coaster.

American Movie Classics

Original niche: Classic Hollywood movies, primarily from the 1940s, '50s, and '60s.

Today: Movies primarily from the 1990s, as well as original, hour-long series, such as *Mad Men* and *Breaking Bad.*

CMT (Country Music Television)

Original niche: 24 hours of country music videos.

Today: Reality shows such as *Trick My Truck* and *World's Strictest Parents* share air time with reruns of *Green Acres, The Dukes of Hazzard,* and *Married...with Children.*

Game Show Network

Original niche: From 1994 to 2003, it aired only game shows.

Today: It has added reruns of competitive reality shows such as *The Amazing Race* and has an interactive call-in quiz show, both of which fall under the "games" heading. What doesn't: the reality show *Carnie Wilson: Unstapled,* which documents the Wilson Phillips singer's struggle to lose weight.

The judges' buzzers on *America's Got Talent* were recycled from *Press Your Luck* & *Family Feud*

REVENGE OF THE WRITERS!

Are TV writers thin-skinned? Well, whether you're an actor, a network executive, or even a member of the general public, don't ever upset one. You, your name, or your TV character may be ridiculed on the small screen in front of millions of viewers.

BACKGROUND
According to Amy Chozick, entertainment columnist for the *Wall Street Journal*, "In the movie business, writers hand over a screenplay and creative power to a director. In television, the writer rules. Writers often make the creative and day-to-day managerial decisions. They also possess a little-talked-about power: the written word as a way to settle scores." Here are some examples.

OFFENSE: As a writer on *Cybill*, Chuck Lorre had numerous run-ins with co-star Cybill Shepherd, who often complained about her lines. Later, while serving as executive producer on *Roseanne*, Lorre often clashed with Roseanne Barr over her character, her authority, the direction of the show, and just about everything else.

WRITER'S REVENGE: For a promotional stunt in 2008, two CBS shows, the crime-drama *CSI* and the sitcom *Two and a Half Men*, traded writers. Lorre, who oversaw *Men*, wrote the *CSI* episode, making the murder victim a thinly veiled amalgam of Shepherd and Barr. Before the fictional TV star (played by Katey Sagal) was killed, she yelled at her writer, "Don't argue with me. Just make me funny. And lovable!" Later, her dead body was discovered with a rubber chicken shoved down her throat. Detective Grissom (William Petersen) deadpans, "Dying is easy; comedy is hard."

OFFENSE: As the elegant Lady Marjorie, Rachel Gurney was a fan favorite on *Upstairs, Downstairs*, a British melodrama that ran from 1971 to 1975. Set in the early 20th century, the show followed the lives of the servants (downstairs) and the aristocrats

---

Hot Springs, NM, changed its name to Truth or Consequences to get the show aired there.

(upstairs) in a London mansion. But Gurney never liked her character and often said so: "I would much rather play one of the servants; they are much nicer people." In 1973 she quit.
WRITERS' REVENGE: "Lady Marjorie" was sent to America...on the *Titanic*.

OFFENSE: For four years, *Entertainment Weekly* critic Ken Tucker blasted the USA Network mystery series *Psych*. He wrote that it was "predictable," "unappealing," and "*Monk* for morons."
WRITERS' REVENGE: In 2009 *Psych* aired an episode about a deranged serial killer named...Ken Tucker. (The real Ken Tucker was reportedly thrilled to receive such an "honor.")

OFFENSE: Before creating *Mad Men*, Matthew Weiner was a writer on *The Sopranos*. Before that, he wrote for the CBS sitcom *Becker* alongside head writer and producer David Hackel. Judging by a scene at the beginning of *The Sopranos* episode "Chasing It," Weiner didn't particularly enjoy working for Hackel.
WRITER'S REVENGE: In the scene, some teenagers are kicking over headstones in a graveyard. One of the headstones belongs to "David M. Hackel."

OFFENSE: According to David Simon, who in the early 1990s was a police reporter for the *Baltimore Sun*, his bosses at the newspaper created a "hellish, futile bureaucracy" that focused more on sensationalism and awards than actual journalism. In 1995 Simon quit his job at the *Sun* after a bitter dispute with managing editor Bill Marimow. Simon found success elsewhere: his books about inner-city life became the basis for NBC's *Homicide: Life on the Street* and HBO's *The Wire*.
WRITER'S REVENGE: In season four of *The Wire*, a new and obnoxious character was introduced: police lieutenant Charles Marimow. He was pompous, bumbling, and cruel, with little regard for the rule of law. How did Bill Marimow respond to the unflattering portrayal? "This is a grudge which now extends more than a decade and is demeaning not to us but to [Simon]. To hold a grudge that long poisons the grudge-holder," he said.

OFFENSE: Early in his career, TV writer David Kohan (*The*

Wonder Years, Will & Grace) wrote jokes for stand-up comedian Elayne Boosler. They didn't get along.

WRITER'S REVENGE: On a 1996 *Boston Common* episode written by Kohan, Leonard (Steve Paymer) is detained at an airport security checkpoint and asks the guard: "You're going to arrest me for telling a stupid joke? Then why don't you arrest Elayne Boosler?"

OFFENSE: In 2005 *CSI* writer Sarah Goldfinger was all set to buy a new house in Los Angeles, but the deal between her and the sellers, a couple named Melinda and Scott Tamkin, soured, and she couldn't buy the house.

WRITER'S REVENGE: In 2008 Goldfinger wrote a *CSI* episode about a realtor couple named...Melinda and Scott Tamkin. Melinda gets murdered; Scott's a perverted drunk. Just before the episode was filmed, *CSI* producers decided to change the last name of the couple to avoid a lawsuit. Too late: A synopsis of the episode had already been posted online. The real-life Tamkins discovered that anyone who Googled their names could find that synopsis, which depicts them "engaged in a reckless lifestyle of sexual bondage, pornography, drunkenness, marital discord, depression, financial straits, and possibly even murder." The couple sued, asking $6 million for defamation. (The suit is pending.)

* * *

DAMMIT, JIM!

On *Star Trek*, Dr. Leonard "Bones" McCoy (DeForest Kelley) would get so exasperated when asked to do something out of his comfort zone that he'd grumble, "I'm a doctor, not a _____." It became an enduring TV catchphrase. Here are a few examples:

"I'm a doctor, not a bricklayer."

"I'm a doctor, not an engineer."

"I'm a doctor, not a coal miner."

"I'm a surgeon, not a psychiatrist."

"I'm a doctor, not an escalator."

SIGNING OFF

Traditionally, TV news anchors conclude broadcasts with a signature line they repeat each day, called a "sign-off." Here are parting words from some of TV's most enduring icons.

"**See you on the radio.**" CBS *Sunday Morning* anchor Charles Osgood got his start in radio, and for a while he juggled careers in both radio and TV news. His parting words on his TV appearances became "See you on the radio," and he kept the sign-off even after he had completely left radio.

"**Good night, Chet.**" "**Good night, David.**" When Chet Huntley and David Brinkley hosted *The Huntley-Brinkley Report* on NBC from 1956 to 1970, they weren't even in the same room, let alone the same city. Brinkley broadcast from Washington, D.C., and Huntley from New York. Rarely did they actually speak to each other during the news broadcast, but they always ended the show with this tagline.

"**And so it goes.**" Lloyd Dobyns coined the phrase (based on the line "So it goes!" from Kurt Vonnegut's *Slaughterhouse-Five*), but Linda Ellerbee popularized it when she succeeded Dobyns as the host of several NBC late-night news shows in the late 1970s and early '80s. The line was later used by fictional reporter Murphy Brown (Candice Bergen) on *Murphy Brown* (1988–98). Ellerbee guest-starred on an episode and argued with Brown over who originated the phrase.

"**Good night, and good luck.**" Possibly the most famous sign-off in TV history, this phrase was coined by 1950s CBS News personality Edward R. Murrow (*Person to Person, See It Now*). He had gotten his start on CBS Radio during World War II, broadcasting from the rooftops of London buildings during the German blitz. With the line, Murrow was earnestly reaching out to the audience in an attempt to provide comfort. He kept the line after the war.

"**Good night, and good news.**" Okay, it's not a *real* news anchor's sign-off. It was used by Ted Baxter, the fictional Minneapolis

---

Iceland enforces a TV-free day every Tuesday to encourage family interaction.

anchorman played by Ted Knight on *The Mary Tyler Moore Show* (1970–77). It's a parody of and homage to Murrow.

"And that's the way it is." *CBS Evening News* anchor Walter Cronkite never intended for this sign-off to become his signature line repeated nightly for decades. When he began anchoring the news in 1962, he'd planned to end each broadcast with a human interest story, followed by a brief off-the-cuff commentary or final thought. But producers told him there wouldn't be enough time to do all that, so he quickly came up with "And that's the way it is." Years later, he still thought it sounded "too authoritative."

"And that's a part of our world." Dan Rather took over for Cronkite in 1981, and by 1986 he was itching to create a tagline as memorable as Cronkite's. Without telling producers, he started using one he'd come up with. At the end of a broadcast in September 1986, he said just one word: "Courage." Two days later, following a story about Mexico, Rather said "*Corajé*" (Spanish for "courage"). It didn't work out; shortly thereafter, Rather switched to the modest "And that's a part of our world."

"We're in touch, so you be in touch." Hugh Downs, and later Barbara Walters, uttered this line at the end of ABC's newsmagazine *20/20*. Although Downs doesn't recall exactly why he started using the phrase, he has said it was probably a subtle request for viewer mail.

"If it's Sunday, it's *Meet the Press*." The late Tim Russert's closing phrase as host of the Sunday morning political discussion show *Meet the Press* sounded more like an introduction...for a show that had just ended. When interim host Tom Brokaw stepped in to host after Russert died in 2009, he kept Russert's line as a tribute.

*   *   *

Everybody loves Ray-man: Jamie Foxx imitated Ray Charles for years in his stand-up act and on *In Living Color*. In 2004 he was selected to play Charles in the dramatic biopic *Ray*... and won an Academy Award for Best Actor.

Flipper was played mainly by two dolphins named Suzy and Cathy.

THE GOLDEN GIRLS STORY

> **Dorothy:** Merry Christmas, Rose. Merry Christmas, Blanche.
> **Rose:** Merry Christmas, Dorothy, Merry Christmas, Blanche.
> **Blanche:** Merry Christmas, Rose, Mer...
> **Sophia:** What the hell is this—The Waltons?

WHATCHU TALKIN' 'BOUT, ROSE? TV was attracting predominantly younger viewers in the mid-1980s, thanks to breakout stars like Gary Coleman of *Diff'rent Strokes* and Michael J. Fox of *Family Ties*. Then came the senior-citizens brigade: *Matlock*; *Murder, She Wrote*; and *The Golden Girls*—shows about older Americans, made specifically for older Americans. All three were hits, and 25 years later, *The Golden Girls* still has staying power. Why? It attracted a much wider demographic than just the elderly, despite the fact that there were no kids or young adults on the show, no male leads, and no cast members under 50.

The series revolved around the lives of four "women of a certain age" living in Miami: Blanche (Rue McClanahan), a sexually active Southern belle; Rose (Betty White), a kindhearted dingbat; Dorothy (Bea Arthur), the wise, often bitter voice of reason; and Dorothy's mother, Sophia (Estelle Getty), a cranky octogenarian with a sardonic wit.

MIAMI NICE

The seed of the show was inadvertently planted at a 1984 party for NBC affiliates called the All-Star Lineup Dinner. Sixty-four-year-old Selma Diamond, then portraying a wisecracking bailiff on NBC's *Night Court*, performed a comedy routine in which she acted confused about *Miami Vice*, calling it "Miami Nice," and saying that it must be "about a bunch of old ladies in Florida playing pinochle." That joke got NBC programming chief Brandon Tartikoff thinking about how his elderly aunt had a contentious relationship with her elderly neighbor, but they were still best friends. Could NBC do a show about old ladies?

A few weeks later, Tartikoff and the network brass decided to go with the idea, with Diamond as the lead character. Warren

---

Q: In 1987, what product was advertised on TV by live models for the first time? A: The bra.

Littlefield, the senior vice president of comedy development, was keen on it, saying, "Society writes off people who are over the hill. Our people should be young in attitude, full of hormones, and take no bull!" Tartikoff knew exactly who to tap to create such a show: Susan Harris, creator of the sitcoms *Soap* and *Benson*.

THREE WOMEN AND A GAY GUY
Harris's first draft of the show featured three elderly women living in a house with a young gay servant named Coco. Michael Eisner, the head of Disney (which produced *The Golden Girls*), agreed that there should be a fourth character, but not a gay man in his 20s. So Harris went back to work and created Sophia, Dorothy's mother. Her backstory: She has suffered a stroke, which causes her to blurt things out. Harris felt that Coco's sarcastic lines would be funnier coming from an extremely old lady. Eisner agreed.

Next came casting. Sadly, Diamond had to drop out because of health problems and passed away shortly after. Harris, having written for *Maude* in the 1970s, suggested that show's star, Bea Arthur, for Dorothy. Rue McClanahan was originally cast as the naive Rose, similar to her ditzy character, Vivian, on *Maude*; Betty White was cast as Blanche, similar to the sex-starved Sue Ann she'd played on *The Mary Tyler Moore Show*. But, not wanting to be typecast, the women switched roles.

Finding Sophia was difficult, as there weren't many women in their 80s up for the rigors of a sitcom. So stage actress Estelle Getty was cast. At 62, she was actually a year younger than Arthur, who played her daughter. The five-foot-tall Getty underwent 45 minutes of makeup each day to look 20 years older.

A SITCOM FOR EVERYONE
The Golden Girls premiered in September 1985 to 44 million viewers, making it the #1 show of the week. Even airing on little-watched Saturday night, the show finished in the Top 10 for six of its seven seasons. All four leads won Emmy Awards, and some of today's most successful TV writers earned their chops on the show, including Mitch Hurwitz (*Arrested Development*) and Marc Cherry (*Desperate Housewives*). *Golden Girls* reruns are among the most-watched programming on the Lifetime and Hallmark Channels, and it's a safe bet it will live on in TV land to a ripe old age.

It was Rue McClanahan's idea to make Blanche a Southern belle.

TICKER SHOCK

aking news: The crawls and graphics you see on news channels sometimes get goofed u

Breaking News: Fire destroyed by home **(Fox 5)**

Bernanke on the Housing Market: BLAH blah BLAH blah BLAH
blah BLAH blah BLAH blah **(CNN)**

3,0000 pupils sat maths exams for 1976 **(BBC)**

Space Shuttle traveling nearly 18 times speed of light **(CNN)**

Will high gas prices cost your kids their eductaion? **(Fox News)**

Experts Agree: Al Qaeda Leader is Dead or Alive **(CNN)**

dsfgdfgfsfgdf sdfgsdfgsdfgsdfg **(Fox News)**

Authorities are reminding everyone to now allow impaired drivers
to get behind the wheel **(CNN)**

Breaking News: Many words should fit on this sentence bar. Do
not try to type in a paragraph to tell story **(KDKA 2)**

Fight over N.Y. Mosque Shits to D.C. **(CNN)**

Tiger Woods Takes Leave From the Game of Golg **(CNN)**

Los Angeles Lakers vs. Boston Knicks **(ESPN)**

Norah O'Donnell - The White Ho **(MSNBC)**

Sara Palin (R) Former Presidential Candidate **(CNN)**

Memorial Day Weekend: Buckle up,
Slow down & Drink & Drive **(KARE 11 News)**

Granny Clampett's (*The Beverly Hillbillies*) real first name was Daisy.

THE *SURREAL* CHAIN

The Surreal Life (2003–06) was a VH1 reality show that mixed Big Brother and The Real World. Instead of everyday strangers living in a house together, the housemates were all minor celebrities. And it had one other distinction: it was a spin-off machine.

SPIN-OFF CITY

During the 2005 season of *The Surreal Life*, two housemates, *America's Next Top Model* winner Adrianne Curry and former *Brady Bunch* cast member Christopher Knight, fell in love. In one episode, the cast is asked to pitch their own reality show concepts. Curry's idea: *Beauty and the Brady*, about her and Knight. Later that year, VH1 began airing a Curry/Knight reality show: **My Fair Brady**.

• The 2004 cast included rapper Flavor Flav (of Public Enemy) and Danish actress Brigitte Nielsen (*Red Sonja*). The two began a romance, and VH1 built a reality show around the odd couple, 2005's **Strange Love**. At the end of the show, the couple split, and Flav was heartbroken.

• Don't cry for Flav—he got another chance to find love (and to be on TV). In 2006 he was the focus of VH1's **Flavor of Love**, a *Bachelor*-style dating show. It went on to become the network's most-watched show ever, and prompted VH1 to move its programming away from music and pop culture and toward trashy reality shows.

• The female contestants on *Flavor of Love* were prone to drunken blackouts, drunken fistfights, drunken public displays of nudity, public defecation (seriously), and other unruly behavior, prompting VH1 to reunite them for 2007's **Flavor of Love: Charm School**, in which experts taught them proper, ladylike behavior. It was hosted by actress Mo'Nique (who would later win an Oscar for her role in *Precious*).

• Winner of *Flavor of Love*: an ex-stripper named Hoopz. (Flav gave all of his dates nicknames, because he couldn't remember their real ones—Hoopz wore big hoop earrings.) Runner-up: "New York" (Tiffany Pollard), who moved on to do the mate-picking on

I Love New York in 2007. When she didn't find a partner, VH1 produced a show for Pollard in which she tried to become an actress—*New York Goes to Hollywood* (2008), and then another on which she worked a different job each week, called **New York Goes to Work** (2009).

• Two guys not picked by New York on *I Love New York*, "Real" and his brother "Chance," got to star in a 2008 VH1 dating show called **Real Chance at Love**.

• Also in 2008, VH1 invited the most colorful, obnoxious, and memorable contestants from all of its reality shows back to TV for the unsubtly titled game show **I Love Money**.

• *Flavor of Love* was a dating show built around an '80s rap star. But what about an '80s rock star? Bret Michaels, lead singer of the hair-metal band Poison, was recruited to star on **Rock of Love**.

• Also following the *Flavor of Love* model, rejected *Rock of Love* contestant Daisy de la Hoya went on to headline **Daisy of Love** in 2009.

• Other contestants from *Rock of Love*—heavily tattooed rock 'n' roll groupies who were just as unruly as the contestants on *Flavor of Love*—returned to VH1 for **Rock of Love: Charm School**, hosted by Sharon Osbourne.

• Megan Hauserman, a losing competitor on both *Rock of Love* and *I Love Money*, got her own show in August 2009 called **Megan Wants a Millionaire**. The premise: Hauserman, an admitted gold digger, would choose from a group of men claiming to be wealthy. One of those contestants was a man named Ryan Jenkins. After taping the show, and before all but the first three episodes had aired, Jenkins killed his estranged wife and then committed suicide while on the run from police. VH1 pulled *Megan Wants a Millionaire* off the air. The fact that one of its contestants was involved in a murder/suicide effectively ended the VH1 spin-off chain…

• Until Michaels returned in October 2010 for **Bret Michaels: Life As I Know It**, a series documenting his life after a brain hemorrhage and heart surgery (and winning a reality game show on another network, NBC's *The Celebrity Apprentice*).

EVERYBODY'S TALKING

*Talk shows usually just comment on the headlines...but
sometimes they make headlines of their own.*

REESE IN PIECES

When Reese Witherspoon made her first appearance on
The Late Show with David Letterman, to promote the movie
Election, Letterman announced that the 22-year-old actress was
pregnant. She shyly told Letterman that "it was a big secret" and
asked him how he found out. He said, "I think maybe I screwed
something up." Witherspoon had no alternative but to confirm it,
adding, "Well, I guess now my grandmother knows. Thanks, Dave!"
She was not yet married to the baby's father, actor Ryan Phillippe.

THE RUNNING MAN

In the summer of 2003, Arnold Schwarzenegger was adamantly
denying rumors that he would run for governor of California.
Then, on the August 6 episode of *The Tonight Show*, Schwarzenegger announced he was entering the race. In the open election,
there were 135 candidates on the ballot (including *Diff'rent
Strokes* star Gary Coleman), but Schwarzenegger ultimately won.

REAL REALITY TV

Just before married actors Harry Hamlin and Lisa Rinna appeared
on *Today* to promote their reality show *Harry Loves Lisa* in 2010,
they received a call telling them that their Beverly Hills clothing
store was being robbed. Hamlin told host Kathie Lee Gifford, "I
have to keep my cell phone on, because our clothing store is being
robbed as we speak." Rinna interjected, "That's real life, baby!"
During a call he received on-air, Hamlin learned that the bandits
had made off with $10,000 in merchandise. (The crooks were
never found. And the store was robbed again a few days later.)

REAL FAKE NEWS

Many politicians have announced their candidacy for president on
news shows. In 2003 North Carolina senator John Edwards made
history when he announced his run on a *fake* news show, *The Daily*

Show. Edwards said he was keeping a promise he'd made to host Jon Stewart the previous year—when Stewart asked if he would run, Edwards replied, "I'm certain you'll be the first person I tell."

JOE COOL
In a joint interview with her husband in early 2009, Jill Biden, wife of Vice President Joe Biden, said on *The Oprah Winfrey Show* that Barack Obama had let her husband choose between serving as vice president or secretary of state, making it sound as if Secretary of State Hilary Clinton had been Obama's second choice. Joe Biden quickly tried to change the subject, but it was too late. A White House spokesperson denied it, telling reporters that Biden was offered only the VP spot, and Clinton only the State Department job. (Only Joe knows for sure.)

WALK THE LIE
Sporting a long beard and mumbling incoherently, actor Joaquin Phoenix (*Walk the Line, Gladiator*) appeared on *The Late Show with David Letterman* in October 2008 to announce that he was retiring from acting. His new career? Rap music. The bizarre interview instantly led to rumors that it was all staged. It was: Phoenix and a friend, actor Casey Affleck, were filming a mockumentary about Phoenix's "retirement" called *I'm Still Here.* Phoenix appeared on *The Late Show* again in 2010 to "apologize" to Letterman for the previous interview. It was later reported, however, that Letterman had been in on the joke all along.

DR. NO
On Dr. Laura Schlessinger's radio advice show in 2010, an African-American woman called in for advice in dealing with racial slurs from her white husband's friends. Schlessinger went on a tirade about the "double standard" of the usage of the "n-word," stating that "black guys use it all the time." Schlessinger herself used the *actual* n-word 11 times during the segment, then remarked, "If you're that hypersensitive about color, don't marry out of your race." She later apologized and went on CNN's *Larry King Live,* telling King that she didn't want "some special-interest group deciding this is a time to silence a voice of dissent." She then announced that she was taking her show off the air.

FELICITY AND URKEL TRAVEL THROUGH TIME

*"Jumping the shark" has become a TV industry cliché—it means
that an aging show has started adding crazy characters, implausible
storylines, or silly stunts as a last grasp for viewers' attention.
Here are some shows that went off the rails.*

Series: *Family Matters* (1989–98)
At first: *Family Matters* was a spin-off from the sitcom *Perfect Strangers*, centered around the Winslows, a middle-class African-American family in Chicago. But midway through the first season, the Winslows' nerdy teenage neighbor, Steve Urkel, appeared in an episode and became a pop-culture phenomenon. Before long, Urkel was everywhere—his catchphrase "Did I do that?" adorned T-shirts, and stores were deluged with talking Urkel dolls and Urkel-Os breakfast cereal.
What? By season six, the family sitcom had become a science-fiction show. Most episodes revolved around Urkel inventing crazy contraptions, including a time machine (to transport himself to a pirate ship) and a cloning device (to make a cool clone of himself named Stefan Urquel).

Series: *Roseanne* (1988–97)
At first: Starring smart-aleck comedian Roseanne Barr, the series was lauded as a realistic portrayal of an average, working-class family.
What? In the show's ninth season, the Conner family wins a $100 million lottery jackpot. Plot lines about the pitfalls of lower-middle-class life were replaced by the travails of living the good life. And things became increasingly surreal: In one episode, Roseanne fights terrorists on a train; in another, she encounters satanists. The series finale culminated in a bizarre monologue in which Roseanne's character reveals that the entire final season didn't really happen—it was the basis of a book she was writing to cope with her husband Dan's (John Goodman) death. In the timeline of the show, there had been no lottery and no terrorists, and Dan had died at the end of the second-to-last season.

On the original *Perry Mason*, Mason won 268 cases...and lost only 3.

Series: *The Flintstones* (1960–66)

At first: Essentially *The Honeymooners* set in the Stone Age, this show features regular guys Fred Flintstone and Barney Rubble, who work at a rock quarry, eat Brontosaurus burgers, and are subjected to a lot of rock-based wordplay.

What? Midway through *The Flintstones'* final season in 1966, Fred and Barney find themselves endlessly pestered by a new arrival named the Great Gazoo—a condescending, aristocratic-voiced alien who crash-landed in Bedrock after being exiled from his home planet. Ratings dropped as fans of the show found the futuristic visitor out of place in a cartoon about prehistoric times, and to make matters worse, annoying.

Series: *Felicity* (1998–2002)

At first: For its first three seasons, *Felicity* was a straightforward light drama about a New York City college student caught in a love triangle. But when the show's main character, Felicity Porter (Keri Russell), decided to cut her long curly locks, ratings dropped by 35 percent (the haircut was #19 on *TV Guide*'s "25 Biggest TV Blunders" list). But that wasn't the worst idea the producers of *Felicity* came up with.

What? In season four, Felicity convinces a Wiccan friend to cast a spell on her to send her back in time to right a romantic wrong. The rest of the characters continued on in the present. Viewers were perplexed by the tangled mess of conflicting parallel timelines and their central character's already complicated love life. In the show's final episode, a fever-ridden Felicity wakes up in bed surrounded by her concerned friends—the writers had resorted to the old "it was all just a dream" ploy.

*   *   *

MAKING *TIME*

Actress Whitney Blake (best known for the 1950s sitcom *Hazel*) became a TV writer in the 1970s. Her biggest success: co-creating the CBS sitcom *One Day at a Time*. She based it on her own experiences as a divorced single mother raising a teenage daughter. (Blake's daughter: future *Family Ties* star Meredith Baxter.)

DAVID CARUSO, MOVIE STAR?

*Some people in Hollywood feel that there are two kinds of
actors: movie stars and TV stars. Every so often, a TV star
leaves the small screen to try for big-screen stardom.
Some succeed...but most don't.*

Actress: Shelley Long
Small Screen: Long was virtually unknown when she
was cast as the intellectual barmaid Diane Chambers on
Cheers in 1982. The show went on to become one of the most
popular sitcoms of the 1980s, and Long won an Emmy and two
Golden Globes for her role. She balanced her *Cheers* shooting
schedule with starring roles in a string of hit film comedies,
including *Night Shift*, *Outrageous Fortune*, and *The Money Pit*. In
1987 Long left *Cheers* to focus solely on her movie career.
Big Screen: Long's departure from the sitcom made tabloid headlines, with reports that she was difficult to work with. Those
rumors may have hurt Long's chances of finding the movie work
she wanted. Between 1987 and 1992, she made only four films, all
of them forgettable flops. (Remember *The Boyfriend School? Frozen
Assets?*) Long later returned to TV with a string of made-for-TV
movies and short-lived sitcoms in the 1990s, but her most successful project was a movie after all: She played Carol Brady in *The
Brady Bunch Movie* (1995)—ironically, a movie remake of a TV
show.

Actor: David Caruso
Small Screen: Most of the critical acclaim heaped on Stephen
Bochco's gritty 1990s police drama *NYPD Blue* was focused on
Dennis Franz, the aging character actor who had starred previ-
ously on Bochco's *Hill Street Blues*. So did Franz leave *NYPD
Blue* after one season to become a movie star? Nope. But David
Caruso, the previously unknown actor who played Franz's young
partner, did.
Big Screen: In 1995 Caruso starred in two erotic thrillers: *Jade*

and *Kiss of Death*. Both were huge box-office bombs. That left Caruso in a bind—he couldn't get film work because people didn't go to his movies, and he couldn't get TV work because he'd signed a "will not work in TV for three years" agreement to get out of his *NYPD Blue* contract. So he waited it out and didn't work until 1997, when he could return to TV. He starred in the short-lived CBS legal drama *Michael Hayes* but didn't have a real success again until 2002, when he landed a starring role in *CSI: Miami*.

Actor: Jeff Conaway
Small Screen: Conaway started out as a movie star—his breakthrough role as Kenickie in 1978's *Grease*. He then moved to TV, to portray Bobby, the struggling actor who works as a cabbie on *Taxi*. After three seasons, Conaway left the show to restart his film career.
Big Screen: Life imitated art, and Conaway became an unsuccessful actor, just like Bobby; he didn't get cast in a single movie for two years. In 1983 he returned to TV in the fantasy series *Wizards and Warriors*, which was canceled after two episodes. Conaway acted sporadically since, but returned to TV in 2006...as a participant on VH1's *Celebrity Fit Club*, which he dropped out of due to a drug addiction, which he then sought help for on VH1's *Celebrity Rehab*.

Actor: George Clooney
Small Screen: Clooney appeared in several TV series in the 1980s, including *The Facts of Life* and *Roseanne*. But he became a major star in 1994 when he was cast as Dr. Doug Ross on *ER*. Before long, Clooney was in such demand that during breaks from the show, he starred in several movies, including *Out of Sight* and *Batman and Robin*. In 1999 he left *ER* to devote all his time to making films.
Big Screen: It worked out pretty well. By 2001, Clooney had become one of the biggest movie stars in the world. His trilogy of *Ocean's Eleven* movies earned $1.1 billion at the box office, and he won an Academy Award for Best Supporting Actor in 2006 for *Syriana*.

What did KAOS and CONTROL stand for on *Get Smart*? Nothing.

TV INSPIRATIONS

It's always interesting to find out where the architects of pop culture get their ideas. The sources of these TV characters may surprise you.

PHOEBE BUFFAY. Lisa Kudrow found it difficult to portray her flighty, hippie-ish character on *Friends*—she's nothing like that in real life. But co-star Jennifer Aniston is. Said Kudrow, "Jennifer introduced me to books that gave me an insight into that spiritual world." So Kudrow read the books…and studied Aniston.

MORK. In 1978 *Happy Days* creator Garry Marshall asked his young son Scott what would make him watch the show. Scott didn't like *Happy Days* but loved *Star Wars*, so he answered, "If it had a space alien in it." Marshall ordered his staff to write an episode about an alien. After auditioning more than 20 people, he gave Robin Williams the part when he sat on a chair upside down.

CORPORAL KLINGER. Jamie Farr's cross-dressing character on M*A*S*H was inspired by comedian Lenny Bruce's attempt to dodge the draft by dressing as a member of the WAVES (Women Accepted for Volunteer Emergency Service). The show's creator, Larry Gelbart, told Farr to play Klinger effeminately; it was Farr's idea to play him "straight and manly."

COLUMBO. The sly detective, who appeared in 69 made-for-TV movies on NBC and ABC from 1968 to 2003, wasn't based on a real cop but on the ancient Greek philosopher Socrates, who often won arguments by playing the fool. In the same way, Lt. Columbo (Peter Falk) tricked murderers into confessing. Richard Levinson and William Link, who created the character, borrowed the name from heavyweight boxer Rocky Marciano's corner man, Allie Colombo.

DAVID BRENT. Several years before creating the buffoon boss in BBC's *The Office*, Ricky Gervais was at a job interview when the interviewer interrupted him to take a phone call. The man pretended to be nice to the caller, while mouthing to Gervais that the guy was a "wanker." That moment laid the foundation for David Brent's pompous insincerity.

Bette Davis starred on the '80s soap *Hotel*, but said it was so smutty they should rename it *Brothel*.

JUST JOSSIN'

Some thoughts about making television from Joss Whedon, a onetime Roseanne *writer who has created some of the most popular cult shows of all time:* Buffy the Vampire Slayer, Angel, Firefly, *and* Dollhouse.

"The two things that matter the most to me: emotional resonance and rocket launchers. *Party of Five,* a brilliant show that often made me cry uncontrollably, suffered ultimately from a lack of rocket launchers."

"You can either watch TV or you can make TV."

"I *love* to write. There's nothing in the world I like better, and that includes sex, probably because I'm so very bad at it."

"Television got into an opening-weekend mentality that works in the movies but it doesn't make sense in television. If something doesn't hit right away, they pull the plug on it."

"I'd rather have a show that 100 people need to see than 1,000 people like to see."

"The English language is my bitch. Or I don't speak it very well. Whatever."

"I love fantasy. I love horror. I love musicals. Whatever doesn't really happen in life is what I'm interested in."

"The greatest expression of rebellion is joy."

"You get so many people out here with incredible technical expertise who have nothing to say, or no idea of the importance of having something to say, or the importance of understanding what they're saying."

On *Firefly:* "Two roads diverged in a wood, and I took the road less traveled by and they *canceled my frikkin' show!* I totally should have taken the road that had all those people on it."

"I don't enjoy dumb TV. I believe Aaron Spelling has single-handedly lowered SAT scores."

"Always be yourself. Unless you suck."

HOW TO GET YOUR SHOW ON TV

So you've got an idea for a new comedy series about an eccentric uncle who spends all his time reading in the bathroom, his beautiful if beleaguered wife, their two cage-fighting sons, and their talking dog. So now what?

BACKGROUND
It's no secret that television producers and networks receive scripts and pitches for new series all the time, so how can you stand out from the rest and get your show produced?

1. Develop a great original idea. Don't try to sell a TV show about a cynical ex-pro baseball player/bartender and the hilarious friends who hang out in his tavern—there's already been a *Cheers*. Develop something new, something that hasn't been seen yet, something that'll show producers that you're capable of original thinking (but just familiar enough that audiences will be willing to give it their time). And think the idea all the way through. Is it a drama? A comedy? A reality series? How many characters are there? Who are they? Where do they live? What are their jobs? How old are they? What kind of food do they like? Do they have any skeletons in their closets? How do their personalities mesh and clash in the show? Think of everything, and write it all down.

2. Write a short summary, or "logline." This is a one- to three-sentence overarching description of your show. It obviously needs to be concise, and it has to be very compelling because you want to grab the attention of someone who has read several thousand loglines today. A great place to see sample loglines is at the Internet Movie Database (IMDb.com). Here's an example: "An antisocial maverick doctor who specializes in diagnostic medicine does whatever it takes to solve puzzling cases that come his way using his crack team of doctors and his wits." What's that show? *House.*

3. Write a "treatment." This is a detailed description of the show: the general atmosphere, the plot arc of the series, the names and descriptions of the characters, etc. Treatments are usually four or five pages long, single-spaced with breaks between the

---

Youngest TV lead: Jay North of *Dennis the Menace*. (He was 7.)

relatively short paragraphs, and are usually in 12-point Times New Roman or Courier font. They're written in the present tense, and the characters' names are written in capital letters. Keep it quick-tempoed and "punchy," to quote more than a few professionals—and "sell" the characters and the story so the reader is compelled to see your pilot script. When you're done with the treatment, rewrite it. Polish it as many times as necessary, give it to a few trusted friends to read, and polish it again.

4. Write a pilot script. You need to write your script in the proper format or it'll make its way to the garbage can faster than you can say, "D'oh!" You can find many samples of TV scripts online to study the format details, and software such as Final Draft makes the process much easier. You've already developed the show's over-all idea and the treatment, so you just have to get to work actually writing the thing. And rewriting. And rewriting...until you've got a great show. The rule of thumb on page count: A page per minute of show. So an hour-long pilot script, subtracting for commercial time, should be about 45 pages long.

5. Register the project with the WGA. Make sure to register your treatment and pilot script with the Writers Guild of America. That's not because you'll be sending it to people who would steal scripts from the hands of their own bedridden mothers, but a registered script gives you legal recourse and ownership of your work, no matter what happens. You can find details online at wga.org. They make it very easy to register your work online; it'll cost you about $20.

6. Find and use some TV industry contacts. Before you send out your proposal, you'll have to figure out *where* to send it. A popular resource is the Hollywood Creative Directory (you can find it online). They have contact information for thousands of production companies. If you're really dedicated, move to Hollywood. It's where nearly all North American shows are made (a few are made in Vancouver and Toronto), and it helps to be close to the action if you ever get to pitch your show in person (see step 10).

7. Try to get an agent. This is very hard for unestablished writers. Begin by networking—talk to as many people in the business as you can until you finally convince an agent to represent you (or at least look at your script). If you're lucky enough to get one, it's going to make your job a whole lot easier. With his or her industry contacts, an agent greatly increases your chances of getting in front of a representative of a production company. (There's a list of agents at the WGA's website.)

8. Make your proposal. There is no one way to prepare a TV show proposal—different companies and different producers like different formats. The most important part is to make your proposal easy to read—and very compelling. A basic template includes the script's title, genre (comedy, drama, science fiction, etc.), WGA registration number, the series logline, the treatment, loglines for five to seven possible episodes, and your contact information. Some experts also recommend including a list of main and regular characters in the show, with short descriptions; others suggest a one-page synopsis before the treatment. Note: Don't send your pilot script along with the proposal. If and when they want it, they'll ask for it.

9. Send, send, and send again. Try to send out two or more proposals every day. Don't send them unsolicited: Call the companies first, ask for the development department, and get them to let you send a proposal in, or, if you're lucky, schedule a meeting to pitch the show. Again: This may be quite difficult for an unestablished writer, so your energy may be better used getting an agent.

10. Hone your pitch. If you're lucky, you'll get a production company interested and will be asked to come in and pitch your show. That means you'll have to stand in front of one or more people and tell them about your idea. You have to practice this. Tell an imaginary friend in your living room about this great new TV show you've got—use your own language and let your excitement about the project come through. If you can, record or even videotape yourself doing it, and listen to or watch what you've done, make your own critiques, and improve it. And then do it for friends, and let them critique you. Have two pitches ready: a short one, about 3 minutes, and a 10–15-minute one, too, just in case you get them really interested.

Congratulations! You've sold your show! Then what? It depends. You might be paid a sum for the rights to the show, and if it gets made, be credited as a creator. The studio may send you on your way...or hire you on as a staff writer on your very own show.

I WANT MY MTV!

*Usually it's a network's programs that become
a sensation. But here's one channel that
changed pop culture all by itself.*

• A New Zealand music video show, *Radio with Pictures*, inspired ex-Monkee Michael Nesmith to develop a show for Nickelodeon in 1979 called *PopClips*. Warner Cable, which owned Nickelodeon, spun off the idea into an all-music video channel later that year: Music Television (or MTV).

• When MTV launched at 12:01 a.m. on August 1, 1981, it was available to only about 10,000 cable subscribers in northern New Jersey.

• Today, MTV is the world's largest TV network, watched in 300 million households globally.

• First nonmusic program on MTV: the television-trivia game show *Remote Control* (1987).

• MTV was the first national media outlet to report the death of Nirvana lead singer Kurt Cobain in April 1994. (*The Week in Rock* host Kurt Loder cut into regular programming.)

• **Identifying text on videos (in this typeface, called "Kabel Black") first included artist, song title, album, and record label. Video directors were added in 1992.**

• On February 27, 2000, MTV aired its millionth video. It was the same one it played on its first day: the Buggles' "Video Killed the Radio Star."

• MTV initially followed a rock-only format, with no videos by black artists. In 1983 CBS Records threatened to pull its videos if MTV didn't air Michael Jackson's "Billie Jean." The network relented, and integrated the music.

• The original MTV theme—a hard-rock guitar riff—was written and performed by musician Jonathan Elias. (He later wrote the "Yahoo!" yodel.)

• Among the video shows that tried to compete with MTV (and failed): HBO's *Video Jukebox*, TBS's *Night Tracks* and ABC Rocks. KVMY was a local Las Vegas station that aired only music videos.

On January 19, 1953, 72% of all Americans tuned in for the birth of little Ricky in *I Love Lucy.*

ANYONE'S A STAR

Back before YouTube, the best way for an average Joe (or a not-so-average Joe) to get an audience was to book some time on a local cable-access channel. Here are some classic cable-access kooks from around the country (all of whom you can still see...on YouTube).

Program: *Jonathan Bell*
Location: Dallas (1992–93)
Details: Public-access cable has had more than a few televangelists—from the mild to the extreme—but none were quite like Jonathan Bell, a makeup artist who dropped everything to start a ministry on public access, reaching out directly to viewers at home, all of whom he thought needed to be "saved." What was unusual about Bell was his approach: He screamed at Satan, and about everything else, constantly. Here's a typical Bell rant (delivered, like everything he said, in a consistent shriek): "I read my Bible five to six to seven, eight hours a day. Every time I got a chance, my Bible tape is on in the car. Actually, I don't have a car right now, my car got stolen four weeks ago, and the Dallas police hardly do nothing to help me. I can't get my insurance money either, so right now I'm bussing it."

Program: *The Junior Christian Science Bible Lesson Program*
Location: Los Angeles (1985–2005)
Details: Once called "the most bizarre children's program ever conceived," this Los Angeles-based public-access show was just like the title says—a Christian Science children's program. Without any irony or satire, the show addressed topics such as the dangers of drugs and UFOs through the use of puppets that were variously described as "deformed," "frightening," and "creepy." Most of them were operated and voiced by David Liebe Hart, a self-described ventriloquist...whose lips were always moving. Amazingly, the show ran for more than 20 years (a favorite of viewers, not just children or religious types, who loved it because it was so bad). Hart went on to become a cast member on the bizarre Cartoon Network sketch show *Tim and Eric Awesome Show, Great Job!*

Program: *Let's Paint*
Location: Los Angeles (2002–08)
Details: Artist John Kilduff created and hosted this "variety" show. Dressed in a paint-spattered suit, he simultaneously jogged on a treadmill, painted pictures, blended smoothies, and chatted breathlessly with callers.

Program: *Mustafio*
Location: Queens, New York (1999–present)
Details: *Mustafio* consists of an image of a disembodied man's face, which stares, unspeaking, at the viewer. While the head moves (or remains eerily still), it's accompanied by stream-of-consciousness voice-over monologues, read in a vague European accent, along with miscellaneous sounds, such as clanging and moaning. Completely unlike anything else on TV (and fairly unsettling), *Mustafio* has become a cult hit in New York and has even spawned a couple of CD recordings of select monologues.

Program: *The Three Geniuses*
Location: Los Angeles (1996–2005)
Details: This was a true anything-goes show that happened in real time, live: The performers would arrive at the studio with no idea what they were going to do, and just wing it. The result was what most viewers considered just plain bizarre, with eerie sound effects and music, randomly interspersed images, and psychedelic camera work. The show attracted members of Los Angeles's underground/fringe art community, and one of the most popular performers was Stangelyne, a transvestite bodybuilder with Tourette's syndrome. *LA Weekly* compared watching it to taking LSD.

Program: *The Lone Shark*
Location: Bridgeport, Connecticut (1991–2001)
Details: Created and hosted by Jim Sharky and Sean Haffner, *The Lone Shark* was known for pushing the envelope of what was considered acceptable content for TV broadcasts. One particularly memorable episode was entitled "The Jeffrey Dahmer Children's Show" and featured the disembodied heads of the two hosts sitting inside a refrigerator; at one point, Sharky's head lip-synched to a

---

In many beer commercials, liquid detergent is added to the beer to make it foamier.

recording of "Mack the Knife." That episode wasn't the one that pushed *The Lone Shark* off the air, however. After a ten-year run, the show was finally canceled after an episode in which the hosts were using a file-sharing web application, as they periodically did, and downloaded and broadcast a brief segment of an extremely graphic porn video. Oops.

Program: *Chic-a-Go-Go*
Location: Chicago (1996–present)
Details: Calling itself "Chicago's dance show for kids of all ages!" and hosted by Ratso, a puppet rat, this show is G-rated fun. *Chic-a-Go-Go* follows the same format as *Soul Train* and *American Bandstand*, but the dancers range from young children to senior citizens, and all wear their own colorful costumes. It's such an institution that it attracts big-name musical guests such as Question Mark and the Mysterians, Neko Case, and Plain White Ts (lip-synching to their hits, just like they would have on *Bandstand*).

*   *   *

GAMES PEOPLE PLAY

Today, it's commonplace for video-game fans to download games over the Internet through services like XBox live or Wii Virtual Console. But the idea started in the early days of home video games, back in 1981. Cable companies across the U.S. began offering a service called PlayCable, which allowed subscribers with an Intellivision game console to download and play video games. Users paid $10 a month to rent a PlayCable Adapter, which plugged into the cartridge slot on their Intellivision. Then they tuned their cable boxes to the Intellivision Channel and selected a game—there were about four choices, which changed monthly. The system was slow—all of the game codes were sent out individually, so if a user wanted to play *Space Armada*, for example, the adapter would wait until the code for *Space Armada* cycled around, then download it. PlayCable was discontinued in 1983, when Intellivision games became too graphically advanced to send out over cable TV lines.

ANTIQUES ROADSHOW: THE TOP FINDS, PART II

On page 68, we told you about the most valuable items ever uncovered on PBS's Antiques Roadshow. Now here's a look at some objects that turned out to be spectacular finds.

A SKETCHBOOK
The owner, a habitual yard sale shopper, picked up a sketchbook of watercolors for 25 cents. A *Roadshow* expert determined that it was a lost workbook belonging to 19th-century landscape and nature painter Rufus Grider. Estimated worth: $20,000 to $30,000.

A PAINTING
While shopping at a Salvation Army store with her mother in New Mexico, a woman found an old cardboard box stuffed with oil paintings. They were having a half-price sale, and she took home one of the pieces for $1.50. She had no idea it was an original painting by 20th-century Western artist Fremont Ellis worth an estimated $10,000 to $15,000. "My brother told me it's ugly," the buyer said. "But I think my mom will want to go shopping with me again."

A BASEBALL JERSEY
At a sports memorabilia convention in 1984, a man purchased a 1951 Minneapolis Millers jersey (#28) for $50. He thought it was a fun relic of the long-defunct local minor-league baseball team. Then he found out who had worn it: Willie Mays. He could even verify it belonged to Mays because he found a picture of Mays wearing it. *Roadshow* estimated the jersey's worth at $80,000.

A BEATLES ALBUM
The 1966 Beatles album *Yesterday and Today* was initially produced with a cover image of the Beatles dressed in butcher smocks and covered with pieces of meat and doll parts. Shortly after it was

---

Cagney & Lacey was the first prime-time show to use the word "condom."

printed, Capitol Records decided it was too gruesome and ordered the sleeves to be destroyed or covered over with a sticker of the band in a more sedate pose. Only a few hundred originals made it to the public, such as the one brought to *Roadshow* by a man who bought it in 1966 at Sears for $2.99. The album was appraised at $10,000 to $12,000.

AN URN

In 1972 a man purchased what he thought was a porcelain urn for storing cremated remains at a Seattle garage sale for $10. When *Roadshow* came to town, he decided to get it appraised. It turned out not to be a funeral urn—it was a rare 17th-century Japanese tea urn. Almost no porcelain was exported from Japan at that time, which drove the item's value up to an estimated $15,000.

AN OLD BOOK

The owner bought an old, yellowed atlas at an auction, thinking that the old map plates could be torn out and sold individually at flea markets. But, as a *Roadshow* appraiser explained, it's actually an atlas compiled by mapmaker Frederick DeWitt in 1680. *Roadshow* appraised it at $50,000. "I think you've convinced me maybe we ought to keep it together," said the owner.

* * *

TV TOWN POPULATIONS

- *The Andy Griffith Show*'s **Mayberry**: pop. 1,800.
- *The Flintstones*' **Bedrock**: pop. 2,500.
- *The Simpsons*' **Springfield**: pop. 30,720.
- *Dawson's Creek*'s **Capeside** (Mass.): pop. 35,000.
- *Buffy the Vampire Slayer*'s **Sunnydale** (Cal.): pop. 38,500 at the beginning of the show; 32,000 at the end. (It's a dangerous town.)
- *SpongeBob SquarePants*' **Bikini Bottom**: pop. 50,000.
- **Twin Peaks**: pop. 51,201. Creator David Lynch wanted it to be 5,120, but ABC feared that urban viewers would be turned off by such a small town, so they made him add in the extra digit.

TV (TELEVISION)

You probably know that NBC stands for National Broadcasting Company and CNN for Cable News Network, but do you know the meanings of the rest of these TV acronyms?

QVC: This home-shopping channel's name boasts of "quality, value, and convenience."

TBS: In the 1970s, Ted Turner owned an Atlanta TV station called WTCG (for "Turner Communications Group"), which he put on early cable TV systems. Result: It's become one of the most-watched channels under its later name, TBS, short for Turner Broadcasting System.

G4: The network airs shows about technology, video games, and computers. The "G4" refers to "games, gear, gadgets, and gigabytes."

MSNBC: A joint venture between Microsoft and NBC, the name combines the "MS" of Microsoft with NBC.

WGN: A general entertainment cable channel, it began as a local Chicago station, where it was owned by the *Chicago Tribune*, whose slogan is "World's Greatest Newspaper."

CNBC: This cable news channel is operated by NBC...but its acronym does not mean "Cable NBC." According to NBC, it actually stands for Consumer News and Business Channel.

C-SPAN: Cable-Satellite Public Affairs Network.

The CW: This network is a joint venture of CBS (the C) and Warner Brothers (the W).

CMT: It began in 1983 as CMTV, for Country Music Television, but dropped the V after a complaint by MTV.

ESPN: Entertainment and Sports Programming Network.

FX: A Fox-owned cable channel, the name means "Fox EXtended."

MTV: It used to signify the Music Television network, but in 2010 the network officially changed its name to MTV, meaning the letters now technically signify...nothing.

An excerpt from *Gunsmoke* can be heard in the background of Pink Floyd's *The Wall* album.

REALITY SHOW REJECTS

You would think that people eating cockroaches on Fear Factor *would be as low as reality TV can go...but it isn't. Lots of reality show ideas get pitched to networks, but some are so offensive, disgusting, or just plain weird that they never even get made. Here are a few of those.*

BEYOND THE BIGGEST LOSER
On *The Biggest Loser*, extremely overweight contestants exercise, diet, and get healthier. But on *this* unproduced reality show (unnamed in media reports), contestants share a house and then walk out the front door when they've lost weight. But it's not that easy—at the beginning of the show, all the contestants are wider than the door; literally, the only way out is to lose weight.

ALL MICHAEL JACKSON, ALL THE TIME
Proposed around 2004, five years before Michael Jackson died, this takeoff on *The Real World* would have featured a bunch of strangers living in a house together. The twist: All the housemates would be Michael Jackson impersonators, and they'd be required to stay in costume, wear makeup, and behave like Jackson for the duration of the show, tentatively titled *House of Michael Jacksons.*

MONKEYING AROUND
CBS's popular reality game *The Amazing Race* sends pairs of people around the world on an elaborate scavenger hunt. On a proposed show called *Monkey on Your Back*, contestants would race around the U.S. on an elaborate scavenger hunt...and would have to travel with a capuchin monkey the entire time.

YOU GET AN ORPHAN! YOU GET AN ORPHAN!
On shows like *The Bachelor*, women compete for a (theoretical) romance with an eligible male. On a show reportedly called *Adoption Island*, childless couples were to compete against each other in stunts, games, and parental-skill-building exercises for the ultimate prize: the legal guardianship of an orphan.

Only actors to win an Emmy & Oscar the same year: Helen Hunt ('98) & George C. Scott ('71).

A FIRST TIME FOR EVERYTHING

The show: *Virgin Territory*. The contestants: self-described nerds and geeks who have trouble talking to girls, have very little dating experience, and are all virgins. The grand prize at the end of the series, for one entrant: losing his virginity…to a porn actress. This idea was pitched to a few networks by Kevin Platt, a producer best known for acquiring and distributing Paris Hilton's sex tape.

PRISON BREAK ISLAND

Stephen King's novel *The Running Man*, later made into a movie, is set around a futuristic TV game show in which criminals are hunted down for sport. In 2001 a TV producer tried to make the idea into a real show. His plan was to place a dozen convicted felons (but "no murderers") on a tropical island and force them to survive by themselves, as on *Survivor*. Then, it was planned, celebrities would track them down and recapture them. The last free convict would win $1 million, which would then be donated to one of his or her victims. Reportedly, the show had already booked one celebrity hunter: Lou Ferrigno (*The Incredible Hulk*).

THE DEVIL AT YOUR BACK

The Little Red Man was a show conceived to help people confront childhood bullies, cruel bosses, and other tormentors. How was that done? A "little person," painted red from head to toe, would find the people who had done bad things, follow them around for a day to creep them out (recorded by hidden cameras), and then confront them about their evil deeds. The subjects would then be shown the result of their cruelty, after which they were confronted by their victim. Producers hoped that "seeing the little red man" would become an exciting cultural phenomenon, so that people with sins on their conscience would fear getting caught by this reality show.

*   *   *

"One night I walked home very late and fell asleep in somebody's satellite dish. My dreams were showing up on TVs all over the world."
—Steven Wright

The San Francisco Zoo named a baby bald eagle "Stephen Jr." after Stephen Colbert.

VANITY PLATES

At the very end of a show's credits, the production company identifies itself with a picture or short clip. This is called a "production slate" or "vanity card," and producers often take the opportunity to get creative. Here are some of our favorites.

Company: MTM Enterprises
Details: Mary Tyler Moore and her husband Grant Tinker produced several classic '70s shows through their company, MTM, including *The Mary Tyler Moore Show*, *The Bob Newhart Show*, and *Rhoda*. The MTM logo that appears at the end of each program is a brief clip of a meowing orange kitten—a spoof of the MGM movie studio's roaring lion.

Company: Ubu Productions
Details: Gary David Goldberg produced *Family Ties* through Ubu, named after his black Labrador Retriever. The slate consists of a sepia-toned picture of the dog with audio provided by Goldberg and Ubu: "Sit, Ubu, sit. Good dog." "Ruff!"

Company: Mutant Enemy
Details: Joss Whedon's production company has made cult horror and science-fiction shows such as *Buffy the Vampire Slayer* and *Dollhouse*. Mutant Enemy's slate: a crudely drawn green monster moving jerkily across the screen while an announcer says, "Grr. Argh."

Company: Where's Lunch Productions
Details: Veteran TV writer and producer Phil Rosenthal named his company after what he says is "the most important thing" to a stressed-out sitcom writer: lunch. At the end of Rosenthal's *Everybody Loves Raymond*, a placemat printed with "Where's lunch?" appears onscreen. Each time, a different plate of food is set down on it, such as tacos, a sandwich, or spaghetti.

Company: Lottery Hill
Details: *Family Ties* star Michael J. Fox returned to TV in 1996

with the ABC sitcom *Spin City*. Fox's company Lottery Hill (named after his Vermont farm, once owned by a lottery winner) produced the show, and he provided the voice-over for the slate. As a drawing of a barn appears, Fox says, "Moo," an homage to Ubu's bark. "If I'd had more time, I would've said, 'Good cow,'" Fox later recalled.

Company: Ten Thirteen Productions
Details: Chris Carter's company (which produced *The X-Files*) is named for his birthday, October 13. The slate features "Ten Thirteen Productions" glowing eerily against a black background. A child's voice breaks the creepy vibe, proudly proclaiming, "I made this!" (It's 10-year-old Nathan Couturier, son of *X-Files* sound editor Thierry Couturier.)

Company: John Charles Walters Productions
Details: After the credits ran on *Taxi* (1978–83), viewers would see the back of an old man as he shuffled down an office hallway. A female voice said, "Goodnight, Mr. Walters," to which "Mr. Walters" would only grumble. *Taxi* was "A John Charles Walters Production," as the card said, but Walters isn't a real person—the show's producer was Ed Weinberger, who simply made up the name for his company. (He's also the actor portraying Mr. Walters.)

Company: Chuck Lorre Productions
Details: Lorre likes to reward hard-core fans who record his shows or watch them on DVD, such as *Dharma and Greg*, *Two and a Half Men*, and *The Big Bang Theory*. His vanity card (a different one is created for every episode of all Lorre's series) is usually a screen full of tiny text that shows up for a second or two. Viewers with recorders can pause the cards to see Lorre's messages, jokes, or explanations of math and physics references (for *The Big Bang Theory*). Sometimes the card is philosophical, such as on this one from *Dharma and Greg*: "If one were God, one would act toward all beings and all things as if they were one's own creations. And that, my friends, is the secret of life in a two-second vanity card. Of course, the secret could also be 'Sit, Ubu, sit.' We have to keep an open mind."

THE MONKEES, PART I

In 1966 the best-selling rock band in the United States wasn't the Beatles—it was the Monkees. And they weren't even a "real" band (at least at first); they were a Hollywood creation.

THE PRE-FAB FOUR

In 1953 a TV producer named Bob Rafelson was traveling through Mexico with a group of "four unruly and chaotic folk musicians" and thought their exploits would make for a fun TV show. He unsuccessfully pitched the idea to Universal in 1960. Five years later, Rafelson was working at Screen Gems, the TV division of Columbia Pictures, with another young producer, Bert Schneider. Both were fans of the Beatles' film *A Hard Day's Night* and marveled at how it had fused comedy and rock music. They wondered: Could that be translated to TV?

The two men formed Raybert Productions and began developing their series. At first, they wanted to hire an established band, such as Herman's Hermits, but decided they didn't want to deal with record company contracts. But through the magic of TV, the band didn't even need to be musicians—they wouldn't really be playing the instruments; they only had to look convincing. Acting experience wouldn't be necessary, either.

In 1965 they ran this ad in Hollywood Reporter and Variety: "MADNESS!! AUDITIONS. Folk & Roll Musicians, Singers for acting roles in new TV series. Running parts for 4 insane boys, age 17–21."

MICKY, DAVY, PETER, AND MIKE

Word spread around the L.A. music scene, and 437 "folk & roll musicians" and "insane boys" showed up to audition. After a three-month process in which the leading candidates were called back several times to perform in various groupings to see who had chemistry together, Raybert ended up with two professional actors and two professional musicians—all of whom could sing and all of whom were funny.

• **Micky Dolenz, 21,** a former child star (he'd starred as an orphaned acrobat on the 1956 show *Circus Boy*), was hired to be the drummer, even though he couldn't play the drums or even look like he could. His singing, however, was top-notch, so he ended up singing on most of the Monkees' hits.

• **Davy Jones, 21,** was an experienced stage performer who had toured with the musical *Oliver!* in 1962. (With that production, he had appeared on the same 1964 *Ed Sullivan Show* as the Beatles, had seen the girls going hysterical, and said to himself, "I want a bit of this.") Jones was under contract with Screen Gems and was urged to audition—he could sing, was good-looking, and had a British accent—in other words, he was Beatles-esque. He was hired as the "official" lead singer.

• Stephen Stills of the band Buffalo Fish (later Buffalo Springfield) was cast, but he backed out when he learned that Screen Gems would own the rights to any songs he wrote. He suggested an ex-bandmate named **Peter Tork, 24.** By the time Rafelson tracked him down, Tork was working as a dishwasher. He was primarily a guitarist; in this band, he'd be the bassist.

• **Mike Nesmith, 21,** was playing in a band called the Survivors. Already a successful songwriter—he'd written Frankie Laine's "Pretty Little Princess"—he was on his way to a successful music career when he auditioned for the show. Wearing his trademark wool cap and carrying a sack of laundry, Nesmith announced in his slight Texas drawl, "I hope this ain't gonna take too long, fellas, 'cause I'm in a hurry." He was named lead guitarist.

HEY, HEY, WE'RE THE CREEPS!

Raybert had their four musicians, but they were lacking one important detail—a name for the band. Some possibilities tossed around: the Creeps, the Turtles, and the Inevitables. Then Schneider suggested taking a cue from how the Beatles had misspelled "beetles," and he turned "monkeys" into Monkees.

Rafelson and Schneider now needed money to film a pilot. Former child star Jackie Cooper, then a Screen Gems executive, offered $250,000 before he even saw the script. It helped that Schneider's father was the president of Columbia Pictures, parent company of Screen Gems.

In early 1966, Rafelson and Schneider hired character actor James Frawley to conduct acting classes and direct the pilot. It would be his first directing job. They told him to relax and to

---

"dare to be wrong." So Frawley had the band members, who were quite stiff at first, watch Marx Brothers movies and perform improv exercises: "Swim around in slow motion! Now roll around on the floor! Now you're a crab! Now you're giraffes! Run around and talk like a giraffe would talk!" By the time they filmed the pilot in the spring, the Monkees' personas were in place and, perhaps more importantly, they'd become friends.

TEST PILOT

The plot of the pilot: The band's upcoming gig at a fancy country club is in jeopardy when the sweet-16 birthday girl falls for Davy, and her stuffed shirt of a father doesn't approve. The four stars—even Dolenz and Jones, who'd done some TV—were overwhelmed by the complexities of the shoot. Raybert wanted a fast show, so they brought in TV commercial production teams, who filmed the stars riding on motorized skateboards, running amok through hotels, and doing other silly things. The Monkees themselves were quite lost; the show, they were told, would be crafted later in the editing booth. "The narrative of the shows was never that important," recalls Nesmith. "What was important was a kind of kinetic energy."

Rafelson and Schneider loved the pilot, but test audiences hated it. Tork explained why: "When the audience didn't know who these kids were, the obnoxiousness was overpowering. They were like, 'What are these brats doing?'" But instead of making the Monkees more polite, Raybert simply showed the pilot again—this time with early screen tests from Jones and Nesmith tacked on at the end. That did the trick: "It gave the next audience enough identification with the kids that they forgave them for being obnoxious."

Raybert showed the pilot to NBC's programming chief Mort Werner. "I don't know what the hell we've just seen," he exclaimed, "but I think we should put it on the air."

MONDAY NIGHT MADNESS

The Monkees premiered on Monday, September 12, 1966, at 7:30 p.m. The show was an instant hit and ruled that time slot for two seasons. At the time, it seemed revolutionary. Some of the cutting-edge aspects:

- **Quick takes.** Most shows at the time had about 15 scenes per episode. *The Monkees* averaged about 60.
- **Surrealism.** *The Monkees* regularly featured dream sequences, visual gags (such as "stars" in Davy's eyes), wacky sound effects, rapid-fire scene transitions, and action that was sped up and slowed down.
- **Breaking the "fourth wall."** For example, when the boys find themselves in a tough situation, Micky looks at the camera and says, "Who wrote this?" The camera follows him as he leaves the set and walks into a smoke-filled room with old Asian men crouched around typewriters.
- **Music videos.** Elvis and the Beatles had done it on film, but until *The Monkees*, no TV sitcom routinely stopped telling its story—twice per episode—to feature a music video of the band's latest song. *The Monkees'* musical interludes proved that television could sell records.
- **Counterculture presented in a good light.** The Monkees had long hair and lived in a groovy beach house, but compared to real hippies (or the Beatles), they were square: on-screen, they didn't do drugs, didn't talk politics, and didn't disrespect young ladies. Ironically, that lack of an edge may have boosted the counterculture movement. "Kids could show their parents that there were long-haired people who *weren't* deviant," said Tork later.

The Monkees became overnight sensations...but they'd soon suffer the scorn of the music industry.

For Part II, turn to page 436.

*　*　*

TV BEER COMMERCIAL SLOGANS FROM THE '50s

- Schlitz: "The beer that made Milwaukee famous"
- Pabst Blue Ribbon: "33 fine brews blended into one great beer"
- Blatz: "Always the same good old Blatz"
- Shaefer: "The one beer to have when you're having more than one"

...IS LIKE A...

This page of TV wit is like a glass of orange juice—refreshing and full of pulp.

"Sex is like tennis. When you play an inferior opponent, your game suffers."
—Edie, *Desperate Housewives*

"Charlie may be prickly and crusty on the outside, but inside he's all soft and gooey, like a pudding-filled cactus."
—Alan, *Two and a Half Men*

"Marriage is like a coffin, and each kid is like another nail."
—Homer, *The Simpsons*

"Bob's just like a stray dog. He follows me around, scratches himself, and he keeps leaving nose prints on my windows."
—Linda, *Becker*

"The future is like a Japanese game show—you have no idea what's going on."
—Tracy, *30 Rock*

"Life is like a grapefruit. It's sort of orangey-yellow and dimpled on the outside, wet and squidgy in the middle. Oh, and some people have half a one for breakfast."
—Ford, *The Hitchhiker's Guide to the Galaxy*

"Saying there appears to be some clotting is like saying there's a traffic jam ahead. Is it a ten-car pileup, or just a really slow bus in the center lane? And if it is a bus, is that bus thrombotic or embolic? I think I pushed the metaphor too far."
—Dr. House, *House*

"A conscience is like a boat or a car. If you feel you need one, rent it."
—J.R., *Dallas*

"Looking at cleavage is like looking at the sun. You don't stare at it. It's too risky. You get a sense of it and then you look away."
—Jerry, *Seinfeld*

"What you and I did last night was perfectly natural, like the wind, or not trusting Canadians."
—Laurie, *Cougar Town*

"Now get in there and run that meeting like a shark driving an assault vehicle through a herd of seals wearing chum pants!"
—Veronica, *Better Off Ted*

STARS BEHIND BARS

It's not unheard of for a TV star to run afoul of the law and spend some time behind bars. What's more unusual is when a convicted criminal goes to prison...and later becomes a TV star.

STAR: Charles S. Dutton, who starred in *Roc* (Fox, 1991–94) and now has a recurring role on *House* as the father of Dr. Foreman (Omar Epps).

BEHIND BARS: In 1967 the 16-year-old Dutton killed a man in a knife fight and served time for manslaughter. Caught with a deadly weapon while on parole, he was sent back to prison. He attacked a guard, and more time was added to his sentence. While in solitary confinement for refusing a work assignment, Dutton read a book of plays from the prison library to pass the time. He credits *Day of Absence*, by Douglas Turner Ward, with inspiring him to turn his life around. "It was the first play I had ever read, and it struck a chord in me," he told an interviewer in 1992. "I formed a prison drama group and starred in the play in front of 1,200 inmates." After getting paroled in 1976, Dutton acted in local theater, earned a college degree, and won admission to the Yale Drama School. That led to a career on Broadway, in film, and on TV. "I consider myself a living testament to the power of the arts," he says.

STAR: Tim Allen, stand-up comedian, film actor, and star of *Home Improvement* (1991–99).

BEHIND BARS: In 1978 Allen was arrested for drug trafficking after he tried to sell 1.4 pounds of cocaine to an undercover cop. That was enough to get him sent away for life, but Allen copped a plea and testified against other drug dealers, so he served a little over two years in federal prison. It was while awaiting sentencing that Allen made his first appearance as a stand-up comedian, at the Comedy Castle in Detroit. "The judge suggested I get my act together, and I took him seriously," he says.

STAR: Duane Lee Chapman, a.k.a. Dog, star of the reality series *Dog the Bounty Hunter* (A&E, 2004–present).

First commercial aired in color: a Pall Mall cigarette ad in 1954.

BEHIND BARS: In the 1970s, Dog ("God spelled backwards") was a member of a Texas biker gang called the Devil's Disciples. They were the ones who gave Dog his nickname—he was a devout Christian even when he rolled with them. In 1976 Dog and another Disciple were involved in a drug deal that went bad; the other gang member killed the drug dealer while Dog, unknowing, sat in a car half a block away. Dog served 18 months in Texas's notorious Huntsville State Prison for his role in the murder. He caught his first fugitive while still incarcerated, when he ran down a fleeing inmate nicknamed Bigfoot to prevent guards from shooting him. Saving Bigfoot's life earned Dog a new nickname, "Bounty Hunter," and helped him win early release from prison, after which he made his living selling vacuum cleaners door-to-door. Dog was soon back in court, this time for nonpayment of child support—he's been married five times and has 14 children. While looking over Dog's criminal file, the judge found a letter from the warden of Huntsville Prison praising Dog for saving Bigfoot's life. That gave the judge an idea: He showed Dog a mug shot of a fugitive wanted by the court for skipping bail, and told him that if he caught the guy, the judge would personally pay $200 toward his child support. Dog caught the fugitive within days and was off and running on a new career as a bounty hunter and bail bondsman. An appearance on the 2003 A&E reality show *Take This Job* landed Dog his own series, which debuted in 2004 and was soon the top-rated program on that network.

STAR: Felicia "Snoop" Pearson, who played Snoop Pearson on HBO's *The Wire* (2002–08).

BEHIND BARS: In 1994 Pearson, then 14, was convicted of second-degree murder after she shot and killed another girl in a street fight. Pearson served six years and was released in 2000. By 2004 she had slid back into a life of crime, dealing drugs while working at a car wash. Her life changed when Michael K. Williams, who played a gangster named Omar on *The Wire*, spotted her in a Baltimore club. Williams was so captivated by Pearson's thug appearance that he talked *The Wire*'s producers into giving her an audition. They created the character of Snoop Pearson, a killer in a drug gang, for her (and used her name, too). Pearson credits the show with helping her turn her life around, but casting a real-life killer as a killer on TV, and using her real name to boot, has been painful for the family of Okia Toomer, the girl Pearson murdered. They only learned of Pearson's new life when a family member recognized her while watching *The Wire.* "I was devastated. It's like they're glorifying it," Toomer's mother, Carlene Smith, told the *Washington Post.*

STAR: Tony Sirico, who played Paulie "Walnuts" Gualtieri on *The Sopranos* (1999–2007)

BEHIND BARS: Sirico is probably the only *Sopranos* star whose real-life rap sheet is as long as that of the mobster character he played. Arrested 28 times for robbery and other crimes as a young man, Sirico was serving time in New York's Sing Sing prison in the early 1970s when an ex-con acting troupe called the Theater of the Forgotten staged a play there. "I was truly captured by the magic of the performance," Sirico told an interviewer in 2003. "It was the major step in me getting my life straight." After his release, Sirico called a friend, actor Richard Castellano (who played mobster Peter Clemenza in the 1972 film *The Godfather*), and asked for help breaking into acting. Castellano helped him land a part in the 1974 mob film *Crazy Joe.* "That film got me a Screen Actors Guild card, which gave me a life," Sirico said. "Instead of a life sentence."

EXTRA: Sirico says he got the best advice of his career at his very first acting class. "I was this 30-year-old ex-con villain sitting in a class filled with fresh-faced, serious drama students. [The instructor] leaned over to me after I did a scene and whispered, 'Tony, leave the gun home.' After so many years of packing a gun, I didn't even realize I had it with me in acting class. When he told me to leave the gun home, he meant for me to also leave my former life behind, to be an actor."

*　　*　　*

The Couric Effect: In 1998 Katie Couric's husband died of colorectal cancer, and she became an advocate for cancer awareness. She even had a colonoscopy on *Today* in 2000. After that, according to studies, 10 percent more American women underwent the procedure.

THE ROBOT REVOLUTION WILL BE TELEVISED!

*We try to write about robots in every Bathroom Reader so we'll be
in their good graces when they inevitably take over the world.
With that in mind, here are some notable TV robots.*

Robot: The Robot
Series: *Lost in Space* (1965–68)
Specs: His primary objective: to keep the Robinson family,
especially the youngest member, Will (Bill Mumy), safe as they
bumble their way through space. Despite giving the robot that
important task, the Robinsons never bother to give it a name,
though it's technically a Class M-3 Model B9, General Utility
Nontheorizing Environment Control Robot.
Memorable quote: "Danger! Danger!"

Robot: Rosie
Series: *The Jetsons* (1962–63, 1985–87)
Specs: Rosie, a Model XB-500 from U-RENT-A-MAID, diligently
serves as everything from a housekeeper to a nanny for "Mr. J's"
futuristic family, and, for reasons unknown, speaks with a Brooklyn accent. Sentient and caring, she even has a boyfriend, Mac,
the robot assistant of building superintendent Henry Orbit.
Memorable quote: "I swear on my mother's rechargeable batteries!"

Robots: Vicki and Vanessa
Series: *Small Wonder* (1985–89)
Specs: In this sitcom, inventor Ted Lawson has created a Voice
Input Child Identicant (code name "Vic(k)i") robot, which he
and his family pass off as a real human child. Even though Vicki
(Tiffany Brissette) always wears the same red-and-white dress,
speaks in a robotic monotone, and "eats" and "drinks" through the
use of a coolant system, nobody ever catches on. The Lawsons
send her to school, but also use her as a domestic servant and keep
her in a cabinet at night. And Ted repeatedly attempts to replace

Vicki with a newer model named Vanessa (also played by Brissette). Vanessa acts more human than Vicki, but has more independent thoughts—she gets mad at the Lawsons and tries to burn down their house, and, in the series finale, sabotages their trip to Hollywood.

Memorable quote (Vanessa): "I'm smart, I'm talented, and I'll step on anyone who gets in my way."

Robot: Twiki
Series: *Buck Rogers in the 25th Century* (1979–81)
Specs: Twiki, a cute Model 22-23-T Ambuquad, serves as a side-kick for the human Buck Rogers. Despite being an advanced, fully functioning humanoid robot during a time in which interstellar space travel is possible, Twiki suffers from (or is programmed with) a debilitating stutter, making him a source of comic relief.
Memorable quote: "Bidi-bidi-bidi!"

Robot: Data
Series: *Star Trek: The Next Generation* (1987–94)
Specs: Perhaps because the series is set in the more enlightened 24th century, Data, a sentient android, is treated as a near-equal by the *Enterprise*'s crew. He serves as a lieutenant commander and chief of operations. His superiority over his carbon-based colleagues enables him to pull the ship out of numerous jams over seven seasons. Despite this, Data inexplicably strives to become "more and more human" as the series progresses.
Memorable quote: "If you prick me, do I not...leak?"

Robot: Bender
Series: *Futurama* (1999–2003, 2010–present)
Specs: Built by Mom's Friendly Robot Company in a Mexican factory, Bender (his full name is "Bender Bending Rodriguez") is the face of the huge robot population in "New New York," circa the year 3000. Built to bend girders and powered by alcohol (he acts drunk if he ever *stops* drinking), Bender and millions of other robots live alongside humans, mocking them to their faces and entertaining them with robot-based soap operas like *All My Circuits*, while openly talking of overthrowing the planet.
Memorable quote: "Bite my shiny metal a**!"

BRITISH HUMOUR

Time to tune ye tellys to the other side of the pond for Bob's Your Uncle John's guide to the cheekiest of the Britcoms! (Translation: Here are some classic British sitcoms to check out on DVD.)

COUPLING (2000–04). A group of friends in their 30s hang out in a pub and attempt to navigate their dysfunctional sex lives. Steve (Jack Davenport) and Susan (Sarah Alexander) are a couple, but Steve is having trouble letting go of his youthful indiscretions. Sally (Kate Islett) and Jane (Gina Bellman) are Susan's best friends. Sally is so neurotic about aging that she can't even be around old people, and Jane is loopy and says things like, "For me, vegetarianism is about saying yes to things. Even meat." (Fun fact: *Coupling* was based on the NBC sitcom *Friends*. In 2003, NBC then made an American version of *Coupling*, which was canceled after four episodes.)

SPACED (1999–2001). Tim (Simon Pegg) and Daisy (Jessica Hynes) are flatmates who pretend to be dating to appease the "couples-only" clause in their lease. Not that their landlord, drunken divorcée Marsha, cares (she's too busy lusting after Brian, the tormented painter who lives downstairs). Tim aspires to be a comic-book artist, and Daisy a magazine columnist, but they usually just sit while Tim plays video games and Daisy dresses up her dog, Colin. *Spaced* was written by Pegg and Hynes, and directed by Edgar Wright, who would go on to make the films *Shawn of the Dead* (with Pegg) and *Scott Pilgrim Vs. the World*.

BLACK BOOKS (2000–04). Dingy London bookstore proprietor Bernard Black (Dylan Moran) hates customers because "they all come in here and want to buy things!" Bernard's friend Fran (Tasmin Greig) forces him to hire an assistant named Manny (Bill Bailey) to cheer him up. When not insulting customers, the trio usually get very drunk and embarrass themselves in public.

THE IT CROWD (2006–present). Roy and Moss are content running the IT department in the basement of a big company, instructing their superiors to "try turning it off/on again." Problem solved. Then they go back to their socially inept nerdfest. That is, until Jen becomes their boss. She knows nothing about computers, but that's not her biggest fault: Jen actually makes Roy and Moss "do things" like try to meet girls or assist her in a wacky scheme.

DAD'S ARMY (1968–77) Set during World War II in the village of Walmington-on-Sea, this show follows the soldiers of the Local Voluntary Defense brigade—men too old or otherwise unfit to go fight with the army. Some of those characters are Mainwaring (Arthur Lowe), the arrogant bank manager; Lance-Corporal Jones (Clive Dunn), a butcher prone to World War I flashbacks; and Godfrey (Arnold Ridley), who can't control his bladder. The show is equal parts kooky characters and slapstick, and nothing much happens as the men sit around their church hall headquarters, patrol the sleepy town, and bicker. One of the longest-running Britcoms ever, *Dad's Army* also spawned a successful radio show, a feature film in 1972, and even a stage version in 1975.

GREEN WING (2004–07). In this surreal show (think *Scrubs*, but loopier), the demented staff of a hospital lust after each other, mercilessly tease each other, dress up in squirrel costumes, do cartwheels in the hallways, bring camels to work…and rarely treat patients.

KEEPING UP APPEARANCES (1990–95) Hyacinth Bucket (Patricia Routledge) comes from lower-middle-class stock, but desperately wants to be thought of as a sophisticated lady, so she spends her time hosting fancy dinners, trying to meet aristocrats, improving her diction, and hiding away her relatives from the influential people in the social circles she's trying to break into. Oh, and she insists her name is pronounced "Bouquet."

AS TIME GOES BY (1992–2005) Lionel (Geoffrey Palmer) and Jean (Judi Dench) dated in the early 1950s, but split apart and lost touch when Lionel was drafted and sent to the Korean War. Four decades later, after both have married, raised children, built careers, and found themselves single, Lionel runs into Jean in London. The second-chance romance develops (and the couple marry) over nine seasons, much to the puzzlement of their respective families.

LET'S PORTEND

*Life imitated art when these TV shows predicted
things that actually came true.*

THE YEAR OF THE SEX OLYMPICS (1968)
Prediction: This BBC made-for-TV movie warned of a
future in which a select few will control all entertainment.
Strange TV shows emerge, one of which takes people to a tropical
island and films them as they try to survive.
What happened: That unnamed program sounds a lot like CBS's
Survivor (2000–present). One difference: on *The Year of the Sex
Olympics*, when viewers get bored of the show, producers dropped
a murderer onto the island. So stay tuned to *Survivor*.

MAX HEADROOM (1985)
Prediction: Set in the dystopian future world of 2004, this British
TV movie about totalitarian networks, insidious subliminal advertising, and computer-generated talking heads became an American series on ABC in 1987. The movie predicted that TV would
consist of hundreds of niche-based "micro-channels" (including
one that showed only court trials) and ratings could be measured
on a second-by-second basis.
What happened: Viewers today have hundreds of available channels, including Court TV (now TruTV). And while Nielsen can't
yet measure ratings down to the second, it can and does track
them minute by minute.

OIL STORM (2005)
Prediction: When this TV disaster movie aired on FX in June
2005, U.S. gas prices were hovering around a modest $2 per gallon
and New Orleans hadn't been hit by a major hurricane since
1965. In *Oil Storm*, a hurricane hits New Orleans in September
2005, causing extensive damage to both the city and Gulf Coast
oil platforms. Survivors take refuge in the Superdome, and the
resulting oil shortage causes gas prices to rise dramatically.
What happened: Less than three months after *Oil Storm* aired,

---

The *Gilligan's Island* theme song was recorded in a garage.

Hurricane Katrina made landfall near New Orleans in September 2005, caused extensive damage, sent refugees to the Superdome, and triggered an oil shortage that temporarily pushed gas prices over $5 per gallon.

THE LONE GUNMEN (2001)

Prediction: The pilot episode of this short-lived *X-Files* spin-off is one of the most eerily prescient sci-fi stories to hit the small screen. The show's three conspiracy-theorist heroes believe that an impending terrorist attack will be blamed on an anti-American extremist dictator. The Lone Gunmen thwart the attack—a passenger plane hijacked and flown into the World Trade Center.

What happened: The episode aired in March 2001, just six months before the events of 9/11.

SPOOKS (2005)

Prediction: Known as *MI-5* when it aired on A&E in the U.S., this topical British spy series often took its plots from the headlines. But one episode hit a little too close to the mark: On July 6, 2005, the cast filmed scenes of terrorist bombs exploding in London.

What happened: The day after the filming, an actual terrorist attack occurred in London. "We had to change quite a lot of it because it was all a bit tasteless," said star Rupert Penry-Jones, who played MI-5 section chief Adam Carter. "It seemed like we were cashing in on what happened, when we'd already shot it the day before." The episode was aired, but prefaced with a warning to viewers.

*   *   *

TWO GROSS TV FOODS

• **Cheesy blasters (30 Rock).** Liz Lemon's (Tina Fey) idea for a mass-produced snack product: "You take a hot dog, stuff it with some Jack cheese, wrap it in some pizza: it's Cheesy Blasters!"

• **Slurm (*Futurama*).** This green goo is the most popular soda of the 30th century. It's so addictive that sales aren't hurt when it's revealed that Slurm is made entirely out of slime trails left by giant space slugs.

Nolan Gould, who plays the dumb kid Luke on *Modern Family*, is a Mensa member.

SAVE OUR SHOW!

*No matter how much critical love and fawning Internet attention a
series gets, if it's just a cult hit with a low number of viewers, it will
probably be swiftly canceled. But sometimes, rabid fans band
together and lobby TV networks to give their favorite show
another chance. Sometimes it even works.*

Show: *Veronica Mars.* The CW canceled the critically
acclaimed mystery series in 2007.

Response: Fans sent more than 10,000 Mars Bars to CW
headquarters.

Result: The show stayed canceled. Currently, star Kristen Bell is
trying to acquire the rights from Warner Bros. to produce a
straight-to-DVD movie that would wrap up the series's loose ends.

Show: *Reaper.* The CW's 2007 dark comedy starred Bret Harrison
as the devil's 21-year-old son, whose job it was to collect souls that
had escaped from hell. His sidekick was a guy nicknamed Sock.
The show wasn't a hit (it aired at the same time as *American Idol*),
so the CW decided to cancel it at the end of its first season.

Response: Harrison posted a message on his website and on
social-media networks asking fans to send socks (get it?) to the
CW.

Result: Surprisingly, *Reaper* got a second season.

Show: *Chuck.* In April 2009, the comic spy show was "on the
bubble" with NBC, meaning that its ratings were neither good
enough to warrant renewal nor bad enough to warrant cancellation. Its fate was unclear.

Response: The Subway chain was the show's biggest sponsor, so
on April 27, 2009, fans of the show went to their local Subways,
bought a sandwich, and put a note in the store's comment box
asking to "Save Chuck!" Home videos of fan gatherings at Subways around the U.S. flooded YouTube.

Result: *Chuck* was renewed for the fall season, but NBC denied
that the "sandwich surge" had anything to do with the decision.

How about you? 49% of Americans polled say they watch "too much TV."

Show: *Roswell.* This teen drama about humanlike aliens living among us was canceled by UPN at the end of its first season in 2000.

Response: More than 6,000 fans sent bottles of Tabasco Sauce to UPN's offices. (It was the favorite drink of the alien characters.)

Result: It worked. *Roswell* remained on the air until 2002.

Show: *Moonlight.* The new vampire series premiered in 2007, but attracted a relatively small audience of two million people on Friday nights, so CBS canceled it.

Response: Vampires like blood, so *Moonlight* fans raised awareness of the show's cancellation by organizing blood drives. Thousands of gallons of blood were donated.

Result: *Moonlight* stayed dead. However, its cult popularity led CBS to sign star Alex O'Loughlin to a long-term contract—he currently plays Steve McGarrett on the network's hit revival of *Hawaii Five-O.*

Show: *Everwood.* Canceled in 2006.

Response: In the show's final episode, on-again, off-again teen lovers Ephram and Amy finally end up together and kiss on a Ferris wheel. Die-hard fans of the show protested the cancellation by pooling money to rent a Ferris wheel and running it in Burbank, California, near the WB's headquarters.

Result: *Everwood* didn't return.

*   *   *

AMERICA'S NEXT TOP EX-PITCHER

In 2008 pitcher Dinesh Patel signed with the Pittsburgh Pirates, becoming the first person born in India to play professional baseball in the United States. The only thing: Patel had never played the game before. How did he get signed to a pro contract? He was on an Indian reality TV show called *Million Dollar Arm*, where American scouts came to India to look for pitching phenoms. Patel came in second, was signed to the Pirates, and pitched seven innings in minor-league play before he was released from the team in 2010.

Geordi's eye visor on *Star Trek: The Next Generation* was a spruced-up engine air filter.

FIRED FROM TELEVISION

*TV actors have an easy job: say their lines, look pretty,
and enjoy the fame and fortune. So why do they have to
go and do something stupid and get themselves fired?*

Star: Mackenzie Phillips
Series: *One Day at a Time*
Fired: Phillips was the daughter of the troubled singer John
Phillips of the Mamas and the Papas, and she began using drugs
early in life. She kept her addictions secret for the first two years of
One Day at a Time but was arrested in 1977 for cocaine possession.
Phillips avoided jail time and kept her job, but she kept doing
drugs. Her behavior on the set grew increasingly erratic; she would
suddenly fall asleep and was habitually late for show tapings. One
day when she came to the set raving incoherently, she was suspended for six weeks. When she returned, nothing had changed, so
she was fired from the show and sent to rehab in 1980. She came
back to the show a year later, but was again using cocaine by 1982.
Producers demanded a drug test, and when Phillips refused, she was
fired. Her character was written out: It was explained that she had
walked out on her husband and child and moved away.

Star: Jessica Biel
Series: *7th Heaven*
Fired: After four years playing the squeaky-clean Mary on the
wholesome WB drama about a minister and his family, Biel wanted to be more like other teen stars. She was hoping to take on sex-
ier parts or appear in horror movies, and she was certain the show's
image had lost her a role in Oscar-winner *American Beauty*. Biel
tried to get out of her contract, but executive producer Aaron
Spelling wouldn't allow it. So she posed semi-nude in *Gear* magazine. Spelling was furious, and he removed Biel from the show—
exactly what she wanted. Biel's movie career then took off. She's
appeared in hit movies such as *I Now Pronounce You Chuck and
Larry* and *The A-Team*. As for *7th Heaven*, writers transformed
Mary from a clean-cut teen athlete into an alcoholic runaway and
wrote her out of the show.

Star: Andy Gibb
Series: *Solid Gold*
Fired: The younger brother of Barry, Maurice, and Robin Gibb of the Bee Gees, Gibb was a huge pop star in the late 1970s, with his first three singles going to #1, a feat never repeated. By 1981 his disco-oriented music career had fizzled, so he took a job as the host of the hit music series *Solid Gold*. It put him back in the public eye, but Gibb was dealing with a serious cocaine addiction; he began to behave erratically and missed rehearsals and tapings. After just one year, *Solid Gold* producers fired Gibb for his disruptive behavior, and his career was essentially over. Gibb would go on to make a handful of TV appearances before his death in 1988 from myocarditis, a heart condition that may have been aggravated by cocaine use. He was 30 years old.

Star: Casey Wilson
Series: *Saturday Night Live*
Fired: Wilson had been a popular member of the ensemble cast of *SNL* for two years, when she was surprisingly let go just before the beginning of the 2009–10 season. Why? According to insiders at *SNL*, Wilson was ordered to lose 30 pounds...or else. She didn't, and was fired. She was replaced with a more svelte comedian named Jenny Slate, who, during her first on-camera appearance, said the f-word on live TV. Slate was fired at the end of the year.

Star: Neal McDonough
Series: *Scoundrels*
Fired: McDonough is best known for a recurring role on *Desperate Housewives* as Dave, the crazy ex-husband of Edie (Nicolette Sheridan). His character was killed off in 2009, but he quickly signed on with another ABC show, *Scoundrels*, portraying the patriarch of a family of criminals. Even though he'd seen the script, and even though production had been underway for weeks, when it came time to film a sex scene with his co-star Virginia Madsen, McDonough refused. Reason: He's a devout Catholic and refuses to even kiss on-screen. Producers at *Desperate Housewives* had accommodated his no-love-scene policy, but the ones at *Scoundrels* didn't—they fired him, replacing him with David James Elliott.

HAPPY DAAAYYYS, PART I

*The landmark sitcom Happy Days (1974–84) was more than
just a show about a clean-cut teenager and his cool biker pal—
it bridged the gap between early TV sitcoms like Father
Knows Best and edgy modern comedies like The
Simpsons. Here's how Happy Days began.*

THE ALL-AMERICAN SITCOM

Tuesday night at 8:00 p.m. For nearly a decade, that time slot was owned by *Happy Days*. Debuting as a midseason replacement in January 1974 (in place of a hospital sitcom called *Temperatures Rising*), *Happy Days* ran for 255 episodes before signing off in 1984.

Millions tuned in each week to watch the Cunninghams, a 1950s family living in Milwaukee: naive teenager Richie (Ron Howard), his wise father Howard (Tom Bosley), doting mother Marion (Marion Ross), and precocious little sister Joanie (Erin Moran). Richie's friends were aspiring singer Potsie Weber (Anson Williams), cheesy jokester Ralph Malph (Donny Most), and the epitome of cool—Arthur "Fonzie" Fonzarelli (Henry Winkler).

Although *Happy Days* changed quite a bit over its 10-year run, its ratings were strong for most of that time. The nostalgia and innocence of the half-hour morality tales became a refuge for some Americans during a turbulent decade, even if it took viewers (and network executives) a while to realize that.

NEW FAMILY IN TOWN

The birth of *Happy Days* can be traced back to a conversation on a winter night in 1971. Two young TV executives, Michael Eisner (ABC) and Tom Miller (Paramount), were snowbound at Newark City Airport in New Jersey and began chatting. The duo lamented that there were no longer any family-oriented sitcoms like *Father Knows Best*. So they decided to create one.

After returning to Los Angeles, Eisner brought the idea to writer/producer Garry Marshall, who was enjoying great success with *The Odd Couple*. Marshall loved the idea but didn't think viewers would find such a show credible if it were set in modern

Peter Graves once fell asleep during a *Mission: Impossible* scene. No one noticed.

times—opinions about politics and the Vietnam War made the
generation gap an uncomfortable presence in many American
homes. Marshall's solution: set the show, which he called *Cool*, in
an idyllic, romanticized 1950s. The pilot, entitled "New Family in
Town," was about a family who became the first on their block to
own a TV, a 1950s rite of passage.

LOVE AND THE HAPPY DAYS
Eisner and Marshall convinced the bigwigs at ABC to finance the
pilot, but there was a creative snag: *Cool* took place in an Italian
neighborhood in the Bronx, where Marshall had grown up. The
studio nixed that—too "ethnic"—and asked them to pick a Midwest city to cater to average Americans. They chose Milwaukee,
where Miller's parents lived and owned a laundromat. So if the
producers needed to shoot on location, they'd get free lodging *and*
dry cleaning. Test audiences liked the pilot but not the title, so
Miller played on its warm nostalgia with a new name: *Happy Days*.

Marshall was sure they had a hit, but network brass viewed the
pilot...and passed. Official reason: "No one cares about the 1950s
anymore." In order to make their money back, ABC did what they
had done with a lot of rejected comedy pilots: turned it over to
producer Aaron Spelling to use as an episode of his anthology
series *Love, American Style*. Called "Love and the Happy Days,"
the segment aired on February 25, 1972.

THE FORCE WAS WITH THEM
Later that year, George Lucas began casting for a movie about
teen life and car culture in the early 1960s, *American Graffiti*, and
asked ABC for a copy of "Love and the Happy Days." In the pilot,
he spotted Ron Howard, a young actor already famous for his boy-
hood role of Opie Taylor on *The Andy Griffith Show*. He thought
Ron Howard might be right for the lead role of a naive teenager—
essentially the same part he'd played in the pilot. According to
Garry Marshall in his book *Wake Me When It's Funny*:

> George took one look at Ron's performance as Richie Cunning-
> ham, with his honest fifties face and freckled I-still-look-like-Opie
> innocence, and cast him in *Graffiti*. When the film was released in
> 1973, it became a big hit and ushered in a nostalgic era in film and
> television. Then one day an executive at ABC said, "Don't we
> have something gathering dust on our shelf that takes place in the

1950s?" Michael Eisner said, "Yes we do." Nostalgia was suddenly hot and my pilot was given a second life.

Marshall went back to work. Together with his producing partner Ed Milkis, they filmed a new pilot with most of the roles recast. ABC wanted teen heartthrob Robbie Benson to play Richie, but Benson didn't want to do TV, so he conspired with Marshall to flub his audition.

That left the door open for Marshall's first choice: the originator of the role, Ron Howard. But this time he turned it down because he wanted to become a director. And after *American Graffiti*'s success, he didn't want to play any more teenager roles (he was 20).

HAPPY DAYS ARE HERE AGAIN

In the first season of *Happy Days*, the writers and performers were still finding their collective voice. Mr. and Mrs. Cunningham were more jaded than they would later be portrayed; Joanie was brattier; Potsie was a deviant; and Richie's older brother, Chuck (Gavan O'Herlihy), did little more than hold a basketball and insult Richie. Most of those characters changed and developed; Chuck was written out of the show completely (see page 127).

Critics slammed the show for being a blatant rip-off of *American Graffiti*, not realizing that *Happy Days* actually came first. Viewers weren't impressed, either. As the show limped along, the ratings were so low that it was in danger of being canceled. Something was missing.

But it turned out that *Happy Days* already had the edge it needed—standing right there in a gray windbreaker.

For Part II, turn to page 365.

*   *   *

SUPPLIES ARE NOT AT ALL LIMITED!

Remember those TV ads offering albums "not available in stores, available only through this special TV offer"? The person who sold the most albums: country singer Boxcar Willie (10 million).

P*R*NT*L ADV*S*RY

Here's just a few of the breast—uh, best—
TV news bloopers of all time.

THE POWER OF SUGGESTION

In December 2006, Fox News anchor David Asman was delivering a story about how Miss USA contestant Katie Rees had been disqualified after naughty photos of her turned up on the Internet. Asman's script read, "She lost her title," but as a photo of Rees in a bikini came on-screen, Asman said, "She lost her tittle." He quickly corrected himself, saying "Her *title!* Her *title.*" He added, "Oh, the Internet. What they're gonna do with this one." Asman's assessment was correct—the clip has been viewed on YouTube more than eight million times.

BAD JOB

In November 2002, Shephard Smith of Fox News was doing a story on Jennifer Lopez and the fact that some people in the singer's home neighborhood in the Bronx were not happy with her. "Folks there," Smith said, "are more likely to give the singer a curb job than a b***job." He meant to say, "more likely to give her a curb job than a *block party.*" The unflappable anchor corrected his remarks and apologized to viewers as crew members giggled in the background.

VERY HAPPY MAN CLIMBS MOUNTAIN!

In June 2001, co-anchor Cynthia Izaguirre of KOAT in Albuquerque, New Mexico, was introducing an upcoming segment. "Right after the break," she said, "we're going to interview Erik Weihenmayer, who climbed the highest mountain in the world, Mount Everest. But...he's gay!" She followed that with, "I mean, excuse me, he's blind. So we'll hear about that." Izaguirre explained afterward that she had just finished an interview with a gay man and mixed them up. "Since that video went up on YouTube," she said, "I've gotten hundreds of e-mails from all over the world from people thanking me for making them laugh."

The vista behind Mr. Roarke as he greeted guests on *Fantasy Island* was the L.A. Arboretum.

BLACK AND GUS

News anchor Al Peterson of KEZI in Eugene, Oregon, was reading from his script about two cows that had escaped from a truck in Washington, D.C. "A tractor-trailer," he said, "transporting Black and Gus"—the screen went to a shot of one of the cows, and Peterson ad-libbed, "there's Black or Gus now"—then he continued, saying, "...was stopped on the side of the Beltway while the driver changed a flat tire." When he finished, co-anchor Jim Fisher commented, "Gee, I wonder if those cows named 'Black and Gus' were actually Black Angus cows." Peterson looked confused for a moment, then realized his mistake and looked at his notes. "It does read...Black Angus," he muttered (and then almost fell out of his chair laughing).

QUICK (MIS)TAKES

• Adrienne Alvarez of KTSM in El Paso, Texas, told viewers that police had arrested an ice-cream vendor who was on the city's most-wanted list. Except she called him an "an a** cream vendor." She apologized and carried on with the story.

• In May 2008, Sue Simmons, lead anchor at WNBC in New York, told viewers, "At 11:00, paying more at the grocer but getting less. We'll tell you how to get the most. What the f*** are you doing?" She thought she was off the air. Simmons later gave an on-air apology. (The person she was talking to was not identified.)

• In 2009 CNN's Zain Verjee reported that "Northwest Airlines has started serving penis again." She meant, of course, to say "peanuts." Later in the same episode, Verjee noted that Georgia was "the top penis-producing state in the U.S."

• In December 2007, Fox 13 News in Utah reported that an earthquake had struck Alaska's Aleutian Islands. The anchor said it was "a 7.2 magniturd earthquake"...after which his co-anchor and the rest of the news crew quickly broke into fits of laughter.

*　　*　　*

Fly away: What do superstar Jennifer Lopez and *Dancing With the Stars* judge Carrie Ann Inaba have in common? Both started as "Fly Girl" dancers on *In Living Color* (1989–94).

SPUN-OUT SPIN-OFFS

Many successful TV series were "spin-offs" of other shows—Cheers begat Frasier, Dallas gave us Knot's Landing, and Grey's Anatomy spawned Private Practice, for just three examples. Some spin-offs, however, never even make it to the air, even when an entire episode of the parent series is used to introduce the new show.

ORIGINAL SERIES: *The Cosby Show*
SPIN-OFF: Mr. *Quiet* (1985)
STORY: *The Cosby Show* was a surprise hit for NBC in 1984 and is even credited with lifting the network from third to first place. Show star/creator Bill Cosby had free rein at the network, and in 1985 he produced an episode of his show to serve as a pilot to star his friend, singer Tony Orlando, for whom he'd opened concerts in the 1970s. On that episode, the Huxtable family volunteered at an inner-city community center run by Orlando's character. Despite Cosby's pull, the pilot was never made into a series because, according to Orlando, his own performance "stunk."

ORIGINAL SERIES: *The Office*
SPIN-OFF: "Untitled *Office* Spin-Off" (2009)
STORY: In 2008 NBC executives asked producers of the hit comedy *The Office* to create a spin-off. They didn't want to split up the original show's ensemble, so the producers planned to introduce a new character to *The Office*, to be played by *Saturday Night Live*'s Amy Poehler, and then base a new, office-based show around her. NBC announced that the untitled show would debut in the plum, post-Super Bowl time slot in February 2009, but the show's writers were having a hard time creating a show that was different enough from *The Office*. So they scrapped the idea of the spin-off and made a show called *Parks and Recreation* "inspired by" *The Office* instead— shot in the same dry documentary style but this time set in the world of local politics. The show was a modest hit when it finally debuted in April 2009, and in January 2011 begun its third season.

ORIGINAL SERIES: *Emergency!*
SPIN-OFF: *905-Wild* (1975)

STORY: Writer/actor Jack Webb created the cop show *Dragnet* in the 1950s and revived it in the late 1960s. The new show then spun off another police drama called *Adam-12*, which in turn begat *Emergency!* (1972–79), about a pair of paramedics/firefighters. And a 1975 episode of *Emergency!* served as a pilot for yet another rung on the ladder of *Dragnet*-derived shows. *905-Wild*, as the show was to be titled (based on police code for "wild animal, loose and threatening"), followed a Los Angeles animal control worker (portrayed by Mark Harmon in one of his first roles). The *Emergency!* cast showed up briefly, but the rest of the episode showed Harmon fighting off a tiger in a grocery store and saving dogs caught in a brush fire. Apparently the *Dragnet* magic didn't transfer to the animal kingdom—NBC passed on *905-Wild*.

ORIGINAL SERIES: *Buffy the Vampire Slayer*
SPIN-OFF: *Buffy the Animated Series* (2002)
STORY: *Buffy* has a rich mythology, and successfully spun-off the 1999–2004 series *Angel*. Left on the drawing board: spin-offs about the vampire Spike (James Marsden), the vampire hunter Giles (Anthony Stewart-Head), and an animated spin-off for kids. The Fox Network commissioned it for a Saturday morning slot, and *Buffy* producers made a four-minute teaser video, with most of the original cast providing their voices. Fox ordered 13 full episodes, but just a few weeks later, in early 2002, the network shut down its Saturday morning cartoon division.

ORIGINAL SERIES: *Welcome Back, Kotter*
SPIN-OFF: *The Horshacks* (1977)
STORY: Next to John Travolta's Vinnie Barbarino, the most popular of the teenage delinquent Sweathogs on *Welcome Back, Kotter* was the scrawny, nerdy Arnold Horshack (Ron Pallilo). A two-part episode made during *Kotter*'s second season, "There Goes Number 5," was intended as a spin-off, focusing on Horshack and his equally weird family. When the family's fourth stepfather dies, Horshack has to take a job with his uncle to feed his brothers and sisters. The episode was among the lowest-rated *Kotter*s of the year, proving that a little Horshack goes a long way.

THIS IS YOUR BRAIN ON TV

*Just how much power does television have over our lives? Can TV
make us buy stuff we don't need? Can it make us more violent?
More intelligent? Or is TV turning our brains into tapioca
pudding? Here's what the experts have to say.*

SCATTERED PICTURES

The first brain-scanning studies on the psychological effects
of television were conducted in the mid-1960s by Herbert
Krugman, manager of public opinion research at General Electric.
His mission: To seek new ways to make advertisements more effective. The most surprising thing Krugman learned is that watching
commercials is a highly passive process, meaning it requires less
critical thinking than reading a print advertisement. That's due to
the visual element of TV—our minds are more receptive to any
message that has bright pictures. Did Krugman discover some subtle, insidious form of mind control? Not exactly. An ad only works
if it doesn't profoundly affect the way you already think. Can it
make you to buy a certain brand of soda? Sure. Can it sway a vegetarian to an all-bacon diet? No.

The point is: Your brain is an incredibly complex organ made
up of more than just electricity and chemicals; it's a living thing
that changes over time. Anything that you do for two to three
hours a day—such as vegging out in front of the tube—is bound to
affect your neural development...for better *and* for worse.

YOU TAKE THE GOOD...

• **TV keeps you company:** A 2009 joint study conducted by the
Universities of Buffalo and Miami found that watching favorite
TV programs can give you a feeling of "technologically induced
belongingness." As far as certain sections of your brain are con-
cerned, there's no difference between your real friends and your
TV "friends." Both can alleviate feelings of loneliness or despair.

• **"Smart" shows make you smarter:** Since the 1960s, IQ scores
have risen by several points throughout the developed world.

Known as the Flynn Effect (named for New Zealand researcher James R. Flynn), this rise in intelligence is attributed to smaller families, improved nutrition, increased literacy rates...and TV. According to Steven Johnson, author of *Everything Bad Is Good for You: How Today's Popular Culture Is Actually Making Us Smarter*, because modern TV shows, especially one-hour dramas, are more complex than shows of old, our brains are becoming more complex just trying to keep up with them. Johnson uses the Fox thriller show *24* to illustrate his point:

> During its 44 minutes, the episode connects the lives of 21 distinct characters, each with a clearly defined "story arc." Nine primary narrative threads wind their way through those 44 minutes, each drawing extensively upon events and information revealed in earlier episodes. Draw a map of all those intersecting plots and personalities, and you get structure that—where formal complexity is concerned—more closely resembles a complex 19th-century novel than a hit TV drama of years past like *Bonanza*.

• **"Dumb" shows make you smarter:** You can learn what *not to* do by watching *COPS*, *Supernanny*, or even *America's Funniest Home Videos* (such as not copping attitude with cops, not giving up on "time-out," and not leaping from your roof onto your torn trampoline). Consider this: A U.S. government study found that teen pregnancies fell "dramatically" in 2009 to a record low. Why? In part because of MTV's hit reality show *16 and Pregnant*. "Some critics say these shows glamorize teen pregnancy," said the study's spokesman, Bill Albert, "but our data shows that's not the case. While MTV is not in the teen pregnancy prevention business, we firmly believe they have developed two shows (including *Teen Mom*) that are probably the best teen pregnancy public service announcements ever made."

YOU TAKE THE BAD...
• **TV make Teen Hulk smash!** Researchers at the University of Maryland showed various violent acts from TV shows to male teenagers and measured their brain responses. According to lead researcher Jordan Grafman, those who watched the most aggressive shows became "less sensitive to violence, then more accepting of violence, and more likely to commit aggressive acts since the emotional component associated with aggression is reduced and normally acts as a brake on aggressive behavior." Grafman added

---

Canadian actor with most hours logged on American TV: Raymond Burr.

that this is especially risky to adolescents because their brains are constantly "changing and developing, particularly in the parts that control emotions."

• **TV is *not* for babies:** A 2008 joint study by Children's Hospital in Boston and Harvard Medical School found that "contrary to parents' perceptions that TV viewing is beneficial to their children's brain development, we found no evidence of cognitive benefit from watching TV during the first two years of life." They concluded that educational videos such as *Baby Einstein* can actually hamper cognitive growth. "Infants who watched the videos understood fewer words than those who did not watch them."

• **Too much TV makes life harder:** Psychologists at three universities in New York followed 700 families for 20 years. Subjects were interviewed at the ages of 14, 16, 22, and 33. The results:

> Youths who watched one or more hours of television per day were at elevated risk for poor homework completion, negative attitudes toward school, poor grades, and long-term academic failure. Youths who watched three or more hours of television per day were the most likely to experience these outcomes.

• **TV is like crack:** Have you ever said, "I shouldn't sit in front of the TV all night," but you do anyway? Have you ever tried to have a conversation in a room with the TV blaring…and not be drawn in by its alluring glow? That's because research has shown that habitual TV viewers exhibit the same conditions of euphoria and withdrawal experienced by habitual drug users.

THE FACTS OF LIFE

So it seems that Homer Simpson was right when he said that TV is our "teacher, mother, secret lover." According to *The Age of Television* author Martin Esslin, it's more than that: The boob tube is the most popular shared form of communication on Earth. "In the spiral of historic development, we have returned to a situation similar to that of tribal societies whose members all congregated in the village to listen to their leaders, priests, or shamans. The age of civilization based on reading, on a written literature, is over."

Now, as scientists continue to determine what more than 60 years of television has done to our brains, they remind us that we have a lot of control over this "TV effect," depending not just on what and how much we watch, but *how* we watch.

BRI SPORTS REPORT

For this tale, we take you back to the 1970s—to a time when the TV landscape was much more sparse, and political correctness was more than a decade away. It was the inaugural Battle of the Network Stars, a celebrity sports event chock full of drama, scandal, triumph, cigarettes, and a few ethnic slurs.

MALIBU, CALIFORNIA, 1976

Battle of the Network Stars was the brainchild of Barry Frank, president of CBS Sports. His goal: to make sports more entertaining by placing non-athletes in athletic events, which wouldn't be nearly as fun if they also weren't also beloved TV stars of the day. The success of the first broadcast spawned 18 more *Battles of the Network Stars*, aired every six months for the next nine years, rotating between CBS, NBC, and ABC. Filmed as if it were the Olympics, the event was hosted by the 1970s' most cherished sports personalities, led by the legendary Howard Cosell. Who. Said. Every. Word. As. If. It. Were. Its. Own. Sentence.

The sideline reporter was Olympic decathlon champion Bruce Jenner, who interviewed the stars after they competed in such events as swimming, kayaking, tennis, cycling, an obstacle course, golf, a slam-dunk contest, and the big final event, the tug-of-war. Although the announcers (somewhat) took the games seriously, the same couldn't be said for the stars, most of whom showed up merely to have fun and promote their shows. But one star took the proceedings *very* seriously. Let's go to the videotape.

WHO LOVES YA, BABY?

The three team captains: CBS's Telly Savalas of *Kojak*; ABC's Gabe Kaplan from *Welcome Back, Kotter*; and NBC's Robert Conrad of *Baa Baa Black Sheep*. After NBC won the 400-meter relay race, Savalas, with a cigarette hanging out of his mouth, complained to Cosell that NBC's Ben Murphy (*Gemini Man*) took the baton "a hundred feet early." For Savalas, this injustice was more than an insult to his network, it was an insult to his ethnicity. "I'm a Greek-American, a representative of my ancestry who started the Olympic Games," he said, only half-jokingly.

Meanwhile, echoes of "NBC cheated" reverberated throughout Pepperdine University, where the games were held. Cosell asked Savalas point-blank: "So you think NBC should be disqualified?" Savalas replied, "You mentioned that word, Howard, I didn't. But yes, I think so."

KNOCK IT OFF, I DARE YOU

When Conrad got wind of the news that his NBC teammate was accused of cheating, the diminutive tough guy—whose famous commercials dared America to "knock a battery off" his shoulder—complained to Jenner that ABC was merely looking for a scapegoat to blame for their poor performance. "If they're protesting the fact that we outran them," Conrad quipped, "then that's their problem."

Savalas and Kaplan, who'd remained on the sidelines up until that point, entered the fray. Savalas, wearing a red polyester sweatsuit and sparkling gold chains, said to Jenner, who was sporting casual wear, "It's like if I put my uniform onto you, Bruce, that's how vulgarly and flagrantly they broke the rules!" Conrad responded with a few racist comments about Kaplan and Savalas, ending with, "I'm German, so I want to kill them both!" Everybody laughed.

UP YOUR NOSE WITH A RUBBER HOSE!

Then came the ruling: In one of the earliest instances of instant replay being used to overturn a call on the field of a sporting event (seriously), NBC was given a two-second penalty, making ABC the winner.

Conrad was even more incensed. He challenged Kaplan to a one-on-one 100-yard race to determine the *true* winner. Kaplan, with his wry smile, took the challenge. (He didn't mention that he was a track star in high school.) After a tense wait, the runners left their marks and Kaplan left Conrad in the dust. Teammate Ron Howard (*Happy Days*) was the first to congratulate him. Conrad, out of breath, said, "That's the way (pant) I like it. The best man won." Then he slapped Kaplan on the face (twice) and walked away. In his trademark style, Cosell concluded: "And so Gabe Kaplan comes through in the clutch. He understands now why we call it the thrill of victory vis-à-vis the agony of defeat."

Neil Simon, Mel Brooks & Woody Allen all wrote for Sid Caesar's *Your Show of Shows* (1950–54).

PRIME-TIME PROVERBS

*More reflections on life from some of
TV's most popular shows.*

ON TV

"Imitation is the sincerest
form of television."

—Mighty Mouse, *The New
Adventures of Mighty Mouse*

ON ARTISTS

"Artists are always ready to
sacrifice for art—if the price
is right."

—Gomez,
The Addams Family

ON INTELLIGENCE

"The intellect is a much more
powerful weapon than the
gun, particularly when the
gun doesn't work."

—Dorian, *Blake's 7*

"A truly wise man never plays
leapfrog with a unicorn."

—Banacek, *Banacek*

ON DEDICATION

"My dad has this joke: 'How
do you get to the Van Clyburn
Orchestra? Practice.' Well, it
used to be a joke. Now he just
screams it."

—Connie, *King of the Hill*

ON RAISING KIDS

Fred: Didn't you learn anything being my son? Who do
you think I'm doing this all
for?
Lamont: Yourself.
Fred: Yeah, you learned
something.

—*Sanford and Son*

ON FASHION

Barney: Lesson one. Lose the
goatee. It doesn't go with your
suit.
Ted: I'm not wearing a suit.
Barney: Lesson two. Get a
suit. Suits are cool.

—*How I Met Your Mother*

ON EXPLORATION

"There's a time and a place
for everything, and it's called
college."

—Chef, *South Park*

ON HIGHER POWERS

Sheldon: In difficult times
like this, I often turn to a
force stronger than myself.
Amy: Religion?
Sheldon: *Star Trek.*

—*The Big Bang Theory*

On *Scooby-Doo*, Velma's last name was Dinkley. Shaggy's was Rogers.

NETWORK NEWS COMES OF AGE

On page 93, we told you the story of Camel News Caravan, NBC's first nightly television news program. Here's a look at what was happening over at CBS at the same time.

DAVID AND GOLIATH

By the time NBC's *Camel News Caravan* premiered in February 1949, the rival *CBS TV-News* had been on the air for nine months. It was a very different kind of program. The stories covered by CBS were more newsworthy, and because of that, the film footage was not always as compelling (or as violent) as what viewers saw on *Camel News Caravan*. And when someone in the news died from cancer, CBS *said* they died from cancer. It wasn't unheard of for a camel, a cigar smoker, or a "No Smoking" sign to find their way into a shot, or for Lucky Luciano to be mentioned on the air by name. The broadcast never ended with a live shot of a cigarette smoldering in an ashtray, either. CBS took TV news seriously, and it showed.

News had been a top priority for CBS from the founding of the company two decades earlier. In 1928 William Paley bought a controlling interest in a failing chain of 16 radio stations owned by the Columbia Phonograph Company. In those days, CBS was minuscule compared to NBC, which was owned by corporate giants RCA (Radio Corporation of America), General Electric, and Westinghouse. Paley knew he couldn't compete with cash-rich NBC when it came to hiring top talent for the entertainment side of his network, so he decided to compete against it in the one area where he could afford to: news.

THE BEST AND THE BRIGHTEST

In 1930 Paley hired Ed Klauber, an editor of *The New York Times*, and Paul White, a United Press wire service reporter, and set them to work applying the highest standards of print journalism to radio. In the process, Klauber, White, and the reporters

---

There is a chain of *Friends*-inspired Central Perk coffeehouses. Most are in the Middle East.

they hired largely invented the new field of broadcast journalism from scratch.

Over the next decade, CBS became the standard-setter in the industry. When war came to Europe at the end of the 1930s, the network's foreign correspondents, led by Edward R. Murrow in London, were in the best position to cover it. For millions of Americans following events at home, their most vivid memories of World War II were of sitting by the radio, listening to reports filed by Murrow and his "boys": Eric Sevareid, Charles Collingwood, William L. Shirer, and other giants of CBS News.

THE TIFFANY NETWORK
Paley's emphasis on quality and other shrewd moves paid off, not just in reputation but also in profits. By the late 1940s, CBS—the "Tiffany Network," a nickname it earned because of its high quality, inviting comparisons to the famous jewelry retailer—wasn't just the most prestigious broadcaster in America; it had also beaten out NBC to become the largest and most profitable network as well. So when the time came to begin moving into television, CBS wasn't about to abandon the high standards that had put it on top.

At CBS, unlike at NBC, sponsors had no say in how the news was presented. If they didn't like it, they could go someplace else. Smart advertisers were happy with this arrangement, because they understood that their products benefited from the association with quality journalism.

THAT DAMN PICTURE BOX
But the journalists who worked at CBS in the late 1940s did have one thing in common with their counterparts at NBC: None of them wanted anything to do with television. The future of TV seemed too shaky, and most of the top radio talent at CBS dismissed television journalism on principle, because they thought pictures were a gimmick and a distraction from serious news reporting. They'd never needed them before, so why did they need them now? "That damn picture box may ruin us all," Eric Sevareid groused to CBS president Frank Stanton.

Sevareid wasn't interested in hosting the nightly TV news, and neither was Edward R. Murrow or any of his other "boys." When the job was finally offered to a 30-year-old CBS reporter named Douglas Edwards, he turned it down, too. Edwards had the prospect of a long and fruitful career in front of him, and he was terrified of destroying his professional reputation by working in television.

Stanton finally had to call Edwards into his office. He predicted that radio would soon be eclipsed by TV and that Edwards, if he took the job, would become one of the best-known and most respected newsmen in the country. Hearing that, Edwards agreed to host *CBS TV-News*. He anchored the broadcast for the next 14 years; from 1950 on, it was called *Douglas Edwards and the News*.

SEEING IS BELIEVING

Frank Stanton's predictions about the growth of television were right on the mark. If anything, the changes that were about to hit broadcasting were even swifter and more drastic than he had imagined. The number of U.S. households with televisions grew tenfold between 1949 and 1950. By 1951 five million homes had sets; in 1956, 40 million did. The numbers just kept growing.

American consumers weren't the only people who discovered the wonders of TV. So did advertisers, who soon realized that *showing* a product in a TV commercial generated exponentially more sales than *describing* the product over the radio ever had. Advertising dollars that just a year or two earlier had been spent in radio began to pour into television.

MAKE ROOM FOR BIG BROTHER

In the years that followed, CBS, NBC, and ABC (which launched its evening news program in 1953) lavished millions on their news divisions, adding staff, increasing production values, and establishing bureaus all over the world. But they didn't do it because television news made money. The news divisions actually *lost* money every year, and most years they lost a lot of it. The real money was in entertainment—comedies, dramas, and variety shows. Sure, William Paley and the owners of the other networks enjoyed the prestige that their news programs brought to their businesses, but they also saw them as a necessary cost of doing business.

On *Bones*, Temperance Brennan writes books about a character named Kathy Reichs...

It's not as if they had much choice. For though the networks were for-profit private enterprises, they broadcast their product over the *public* airwaves, which were regulated by the Federal Communications Commission. In return for reaping the enormous profits generated by hit shows such as *I Love Lucy*, *Gunsmoke*, and Milton Berle's *Texaco Star Theater*, the FCC required networks to provide public service programming as well—like news. So the networks were in the news business for good, whether they liked it or not.

ANCHORS AWAY

Those first evening news anchors who feared that TV would kill their careers quickly discovered how lucky they were to have been shoved into it one step ahead of everyone else. Life at the top wasn't bad: You got famous, you made a lot of money, and you got to stay in your job...as long as your ratings didn't drop.

John Cameron Swayze was the first of those early news anchors to suffer the effects of a shrinking audience: In 1955 *Camel News Caravan* slipped to second place behind *Douglas Edwards and the News*. When it was still in second a year later, Swayze was canned and the show was replaced with *The Huntley-Brinkley Report*, co-hosted by Chet Huntley and David Brinkley. (Swayze, a distant cousin of actor Patrick Swayze, left journalism and became the pitchman for Timex watches. You may remember him as the guy in TV commercials who said, "It takes a licking and keeps on ticking.")

In 1958 *The Huntley-Brinkley Report* pulled ahead of *Douglas Edwards and the News* and stayed there. In 1962, after four years of trying to reclaim the top spot, CBS fired Edwards and replaced him with Walter Cronkite. It would take another five years to do it, but in the summer of 1967, the *CBS Evening News with Walter Cronkite* passed *Huntley-Brinkley* to claim the top spot—and never fell behind again. The golden age of network news had begun.

Tune in to Part III of the story on page 451.
(Film at 11:00.)

...In real life, Kathy Reichs is the author who wrote the books on which *Bones* is based.

A COMMON QUIZ

Only the most devout TV fans will know what the things in these questions have in common. Got what it takes? (Answers are on page 499.)

1) What do these Oscar winners have in common? Charlton Heston, Sean Penn, Susan Sarandon, Helen Hunt, Julia Roberts, Reese Witherspoon, Robin Williams, and George Clooney.

2) What unique viewing statistic do *AfterMASH*, *Cheers*, *Rhoda*, and *Lou Grant* have in common?

3) What do the shows *MacGruder and Loud*, *The Wonder Years*, *Hard Copy*, and *Airwolf* have in common?

4) What do Don Ameche, Dianne Wiest, Ed Harris, Kathleen Quinlan, Russell Crowe, Jennifer Connelly, Paul Giamatti, and Frank Langella all have in common?

5) These TV characters all accomplished what astounding athletic feat? Homer Simpson, Peg Bundy of *Married...with Children*, Howard Sprague of *The Andy Griffith Show*, Mort Goldman of *Family Guy*, and Obie of *Living Single*.

6) Who are Richard Ruccolo, Ryan Reynolds, and Traylor Howard?

7) What do the shows *Hill Street Blues*, *Malcolm in the Middle*, *Scrubs*, and *The Tick* have in common?

8) What abrupt change didn't affect *Baywatch*, *Punky Brewster*, *Charles in Charge*, or *Hee Haw*?

9) What sort-of creepy thing is shared by members of the casts of *Nash Bridges*, *Nip/Tuck*, *The Brady Bunch*, and *Dexter*?

10) John Lennon died in 1980. What is the only show since then that featured guest appearances by all three surviving Beatles?

11) What do TV legends George Reeves, Andy Griffith, and Jackie Gleason have in common by not having?

WHAT DID
JIM ROCKFORD DRIVE?

*A look at some cars that were so special, they were
almost co-stars. How many do you remember?*

Series: *The Saint* (1962–69)
Vehicle: Volvo P1800
Details: The show's producers asked Jaguar to provide an E-Type sportscar for use on the show, but Jaguar turned them down. So Volvo, who were trying to break into the sportscar market with their new two-seater P1800, happily supplied the British spy show with five cars—all in bright white—over the course of its run.
Bonus: In Leslie Charteris's *The Saint* book series, hero Simon Templar drives a red-and-cream Hirondel. If the producers of the TV show wanted one of those for the show's star, Roger Moore, they were out of luck…it was a fictional car make.

Series: *The Rockford Files* (1974–80)
Vehicle: Pontiac Firebird Esprit
Details: Private investigator Jim Rockford (James Garner) parked his gold Pontiac Firebird next to his mobile home on the beach in Malibu. Fourteen of the cars, models 1974 through 1978, were used over the series' run, each modified and painted to look like the original 1974 model. In an interview, Garner said that his agent thought up the car's license plate number of 853OKG. The "853" represents August 1953, when Garner got his first acting role; "OK" is his home state of Oklahoma; and "G" is for Garner.

Series: *Supernatural* (2005–present)
Vehicle: 1967 Chevrolet Impala
Details: Show creator Eric Kripke made the decision to have his two main characters, supernatural phenomena–hunting brothers Sam and Dean Winchester (Jensen Ackles and Jared Padelecki), drive around in Dean's black Impala: "It's a Rottweiler of a car,

---

Beginning in 1965, NBC was the first network to have nightly news broadcast 7 days a week.

and I think it adds authenticity for fans of automobiles because it's not a pretty ride. It's an aggressive, muscular car, and I think that's why it fits so well into the tone of our show."

Series: *Perry Mason* (1957–66)
Vehicle: 1957 Ford Fairlane 500 Skyliner; Cadillac Series 62
Details: The wily defense attorney played by Raymond Burr drives pretty hot cars for the time. The one seen in the very first episode is a brand-new black Ford Fairlane 500 Skyliner. The "Skyliner" in the name refers to the fact that it has a retractable hardtop roof that disappears into the trunk—it was the first American car with that feature. Over the course of the series, Mason also drives a 1958 or 1959 Cadillac Series 62 convertible, black with white top.

Series: *Columbo* (on and off between 1971 and 2003)
Vehicle: 1959 Peugeot 403 convertible
Details: Peter Falk, who played the rumpled Lieutenant Columbo, picked the dilapidated and rusting car himself because he thought it was the kind of vehicle his character would drive. He found it in a parking lot at Universal Studios only a day before shooting began. "I just saw the nose of a car sticking out," he said—but he knew it was the one (it turned out not to even have an engine). After the show was canceled in 1978, the Peugeot was sold off. When the show returned in 1989, producers found a similar Peugeot in Ohio.

Series: *The Mentalist* (2008–present)
Vehicle: 1972 Citroën DS 20
Details: Simon Baker—who plays Patrick Jane, consultant with the fictional California Bureau of Investigation, and former fake psychic—chose the car himself. Executive producer Chris Long told *Parade* magazine in 2009, "Simon wanted a car that reflected his quirky character. He's a longtime fan of Peter Falk, so we went looking for a Columbo car." Long says the downside of using the car is that "it stalls all the time, plus the taillights went out and had to be painted on."

I LOVE A PARADE

While countless turkeys roast each Thanksgiving morning, 3.5 million spectators bundle up and line the streets of New York, and another 50 million tune in at home to watch the Macy's Thanksgiving Day Parade. Here's how this TV tradition began.

MARKETING ON 34TH STREET
In 1924 Macy's department store came up with a novel idea to promote the upcoming Christmas shopping season: They would have a parade. After running a string of small notices in New York City newspapers, the store placed a full-page ad in the *New York Herald Tribune* on November 27, 1924—Thanksgiving Day. It read: "Today is the day! Big Christmas parade welcoming Santa Claus to New York." It went on to promise "elephants, bears, camels, monkeys, clowns, brass bands, and everything that makes a real Circus Parade so dear to everybody."

The ads worked: More than 250,000 people came out to watch the parade, then followed it to the Macy's flagship store in Herald Square at 34th Street. Santa Claus then unveiled the holiday window displays and declared the Christmas season (and the shopping season) officially open.

BIG BALLOONS
The parade was such a success that Macy's decided to host one every year. In 1927 it was renamed the Macy's Thanksgiving Day Parade and the zoo animals were replaced with gigantic helium balloons (almost as big as the ones used today) to be released at the end of the parade. Planners thought they would float gracefully into the sky, and figured they could be rounded up later. But that's not what happened—as the balloons rose, the helium inside them expanded, and they exploded one by one over Manhattan.

The next year, Macy's redesigned the balloons with safety valves and fitted them with return-address labels; a reward of $100 was offered to anyone who returned a balloon. Over the years, one disappeared over the Atlantic and others were torn to shreds by people vying for the reward money. In the interest of public safety, Macy's stopped the practice of releasing the balloons in 1933.

First cartoon character depicted in the Macy's Thanksgiving Day Parade: Felix the Cat.

SMALL SCREENS

The Macy's parade was already popular before television took off, but the two developed side by side. In 1939 an experimental local television broadcast of the parade was shot with cameras positioned above Central Park's Museum of Natural History. World War II put an end to further broadcasts, as the war effort claimed not just the broadcasting equipment, but also the rubber needed to make the balloons.

Television resumed in the U.S. in 1946, and so did local broadcasts of the Macy's Thanksgiving Day Parade. While much of early television is lost to history (programs were commonly broadcast live; recording technology was too expensive), footage of that parade survives because it was used in the 1947 movie *Miracle on 34th Street*. In fact, that movie's perennial broadcasts on television was one factor in introducing the parade to a national audience and helped make it a holiday tradition.

PLAYING IN PEORIA

An hour-long segment of the parade was first nationally broadcast—on a delay—in 1948. The broadcast was expanded to two hours in 1961, and the parade has been aired in full since 1969. But it's not live—a tape delay is still used to ensure that it's seen all over America at the same start time: 9 a.m.

CBS aired the parade until 1955, when NBC picked up the rights. But that doesn't mean other networks don't—or can't—air it. Because the parade is conducted on public streets, it's considered news, and other broadcasters may legally show it. Today CBS telecasts it to its affiliates without a tape delay, so viewers can see the parade hours before NBC begins airing the "official" broadcast.

THE BLACK PARADE

Since World War II, Macy's has considered calling off the parade only once: In 1963, Thanksgiving fell a few days after the assassination of President John F. Kennedy. Macy's didn't feel it was appropriate to stage the parade, but letters and calls poured in from people all over the country, including newly sworn-in President Lyndon Johnson, encouraging them to carry on. That year, parade flags were flown at half-staff, and black streamers accompanied many of the floats.

TV MU$IC

Since the rise of TV in the late 1940s, what's been the biggest obstacle in getting music into shows? Money.

THAT'S WHAT I WANT
In the early days of television, the budgets of most programs were very low, especially when compared to feature films. After the costs of the writers, actors, sets, and crew, very little was left over to spend on things like a musical score. The climate is similar today. Using existing, copyrighted musical works is often too expensive; hiring composers to score unique music costs even more. These limitations led television music supervisors over the years to come up with some pretty inventive solutions.

Solution 1: ALTER AN EXISTING WORK
Hardly anyone can listen to the "William Tell Overture" and not think of *The Lone Ranger*. But pioneering television music supervisor David Chudnow had to make sure that the opposite was also true. Why? Because the Rossini composition was actually owned outright by the *radio* version of *The Lone Ranger*. Securing the rights for the TV version in 1949 was beyond the show's budget. Chudnow worked around this by hiring NBC staff arranger Ben Bonnell to change a few notes and cues (the term for each individual piece of music within a film or TV score) just enough so that, legally speaking, it was a different song. Other early programs used the same tactic—the theme for the *Adventures of Superman* TV show was slightly altered from the original radio score.

Solution 2: USE THEMES OVER AND OVER AND OVER
Even for shows that could afford to compose an original opening theme song, having to score every episode presented a whole new challenge. Chudnow found one solution for this: He created MUTEL (short for "Music for Television"), a library of music that TV producers could use after paying a one-time fee. Most of the MUTEL entries were slightly tweaked scores from radio shows and B-movies. (Some early TV shows that mined MUTEL: *Racket Squad, Captain Midnight, Annie Oakley,* and *Ramar of the Jungle.*)

Makes sense: "Kukla" from the puppet show *Kukla, Fran and Ollie* is Russian for "doll."

Solution 3: HIRE A COMPOSER...ONCE

As television grew in the 1950s and '60s, so did advertising revenue. Higher-profile shows, such as CBS's *I Love Lucy*, could now afford a composer to score the opening theme and various cues— one that could be played when Lucy entered the apartment, one when she messed something up, another when she started crying, and so on. Once the composer's initial work was done, he was paid his fee, and then the show had its own unique musical library to cull from. This would be the norm in television for the next three decades.

Solution 4: BALLAD BREAKS

Ever notice how many of today's prime-time dramas include at least one pop song, often appearing over a montage? One of the first shows to do this was *Miami Vice* (1984–89). And, as one of NBC's most successful shows, its budget allowed producers to use well-known songs, such as "In the Air Tonight" by Phil Collins. But most shows don't have the budget for big-name music, so they hire a music supervisor to seek out and secure the rights for songs. One of the biggest in the industry is Alexandra Patsavas, who has found songs for *The O.C.*, *Grey's Anatomy*, and *Chuck*. In turn, bands whose songs are featured in shows get paid a hefty fee ($100,000 or more) and get great exposure—Snow Patrol and the Fray both received Grammy nominations after their songs were featured on *Grey's Anatomy*.

Solution 5: FAIR USE

Of course, a music supervisor's favorite song is a free song. Fortunately, there are thousands of tunes that fall in the category of public domain. The most frequent user of public domain songs: *The Simpsons*.

*   *   *

TV Irony: *60 Minutes* aired a segment in 2002 about corruption in the Jefferson County, Mississippi, judicial system. The program accused trial lawyers of urging their clients to sue corporations for outlandish sums. Two Jefferson County citizens were outraged at the report and sued the producers of *60 Minutes*...for $6 billion.

TREK STORY, PART I

*TV's Star Trek franchise was a four-decade-long roller-coaster ride, beginning
with two different shows helmed by two very different men—Gene
Roddenberry and Rick Berman. Here's the first installment
of their behind-the-scenes story.*

MACHO MAN
In his youth, Gene Roddenberry was a lot like Captain
Kirk—always looking for adventure. As a teenager in the
1930s, he wanted to be a cop and even volunteered for the FBI. In
World War II, he became a decorated bomber pilot who completed 89 missions in the Pacific. After the war, Captain Roddenberry
was piloting a Pan Am passenger jet over the Syrian desert when
the plane lost an engine and crashed. He fought off looting
nomads to keep his passengers safe until help arrived.

One day in the mid-1950s, Roddenberry, now a motorcycle
cop, walked into a Hollywood restaurant and interrupted a group
of TV producers at a lunch meeting. He dropped one of his scripts
on the table and said, "You'll want to read this." It was an uncon-
ventional, swaggering way to get his foot in the door...and it
worked.

WAGON TREK
By 1964 Roddenberry was a successful TV writer, having written
dozens of scripts for successful TV Westerns (*Have Gun – Will
Travel*) and police dramas (*Highway Patrol*). But his goal was to get
a show he created on the air, and he already had the first piece of
the puzzle—a great idea. From his official pitch:

> *Star Trek* is a new kind of television science fiction series. The for-
> mat will be "*Wagon Train* to the Stars"—built around characters
> who travel to other worlds and meet the jeopardy and adventure
> which become our stories.

Studio after studio said no. "Too risky," one executive said, "too
smart. And way too expensive to produce every week." In the
1960s, TV sci-fi was more fantasy than science-fiction; there was
little attempt at realism—with either the science *or* the storylines.

Combining a space adventure with serious drama was unheard of. But Roddenberry *knew* there was an audience for it.

GENE LOVES LUCY

Having been rejected by the major TV studios, Roddenberry turned to a smaller one, Desilu. There he succeeded. Although Herbert Solow, Desilu's vice president, wasn't completely sold on the *Star Trek* idea, he thought Roddenberry had great promise as a writer/producer and convinced his boss, Oscar Katz, to sign him to a three-year deal.

The studio needed a hit—its only show in production at that time was *The Lucy Show*. Lucille Ball herself (Desilu's president) convinced Katz to allow Roddenberry to pitch *Star Trek* to the networks, saying, "There aren't smart shows on TV." So Roddenberry went to CBS, home of *The Lucy Show*. After an impassioned, two-hour presentation, network president James Aubrey Jr. thanked Roddenberry for his time but turned down *Star Trek* because the network was already developing a similar show: *Lost in Space*. A meeting with ABC also ended in rejection. The only stop left: NBC.

This time, Roddenberry got the go-ahead. Mort Werner, NBC's vice president of programming, shelled out $500,000 to produce a pilot. Called "The Cage," it starred Jeffrey Hunter as Captain Christopher Pike and Majel Barrett as his female second-in-command. (There was also an alien character with pointy ears played by Leonard Nimoy.) Werner was impressed by the storytelling, the drama, the acting, and the attention to detail, but still said no to a series, using the same "too smart" and "too expensive" logic that Roddenberry had heard so many times.

But there was a glimmer of hope. Werner allowed Roddenberry to film a second pilot—with a few changes: 1) find a younger, better-looking actor to play the captain, 2) demote the woman, and 3) get rid of the "pointy-eared guy."

A REFLECTION OF THE TIMES

Roddenberry was dismayed about the changes but elated about having a second chance, so he compromised. William Shatner came in as Captain Kirk (replacing Pike), and Barrett was recast as Nurse Chapel. But Roddenberry refused to relinquish the

"Vulcan" character. And he made one other change without informing NBC: He added a female African-American officer to the bridge.

Roddenberry wanted *Star Trek* to reflect American society and modern, progressive culture. Uhura, played by Nichelle Nichols, became TV's first black female character in a position of authority during the civil-rights movement. Racism, militarism, pacifism—few topics were taboo for the original *Star Trek*. And it was an intelligent show, thanks to some of the day's best sci-fi writers, including Harlan Ellison, Theodore Sturgeon, and David Gerrold (who would become best known for writing the episode "The Trouble with Tribbles"). Whereas other space shows (like *Lost in Space*) featured mindless monsters, *Star Trek* aired an episode about a "Horta"—a rocklike thing that turned out to be a mother protecting her young.

STARDATE 1513.1

Star Trek premiered on September 8, 1966, and a whopping 40 percent of American homes tuned in. The size of the audience may have been because NBC launched their fall season a week before the other networks; CBS and ABC were airing reruns. When competitors put new shows against *Star Trek*, ratings dropped. By the end of the season, it ranked a disappointing #52. Desilu's Katz wanted to cancel it, but again Lucille Ball exerted her power to keep it in production for another year. At the end of the second season, NBC was all set to cancel the show, no matter what Ball said—it was losing badly to CBS's *Gomer Pyle USMC*—but *Trek*'s small, rabid fan base mounted a massive letter-writing campaign to keep it on the air. The show was saved again.

Ratings, however, did not improve. NBC never knew how to market *Star Trek*, or to whom—it was too grown-up for the *Monkees* audience and too far-out for the *Gunsmoke* crowd. Plus, Roddenberry constantly battled NBC and soon Paramount, which bought out Desilu, over everything from budgets to hemlines. Even the actors were fighting with each other (Shatner frequently stole lines from his castmates) and with Roddenberry (over scheduling and appearance fees).

By the third season, the budget was severely cut and the show's quality suffered. NBC was ready to let it go. The network put *Star*

Trek in the time slot where shows go to die: Friday night at 10 p.m. The final episode aired on June 3, 1969, a month and a half before the moon landing.

TOONING IN

Then something strange happened. Reruns of *Star Trek* in the mid-'70s attracted new fans and the show suddenly became a phenomenon. Fans assembled at *Star Trek* conventions, and spin-off novels were huge sellers in the sci-fi market. That proved to the brass at NBC that there *was* an audience for the show. Still, it was too risky to dive into another expensive production, and it would be too difficult to reassemble the cast to revive the series. So in 1973 NBC decided to make *Star Trek* into a Saturday morning cartoon.

Although it was cheaper to produce, *Star Trek: The Animated Series* was by no means a cheap knockoff. Roddenberry was still in charge; most of the original cast (including Shatner and Nimoy) voiced their characters; and veteran writers D.C. Fontana and David Gerrold wrote scripts. As many adults as kids tuned in, but there weren't enough of either to keep it on the air. Though the show was well received, NBC canceled it after two seasons.

PHASE II, ENGAGE

With reruns of *Star Trek*'s original 79 episodes still performing strongly in 1977, Paramount asked Roddenberry to develop a second live-action series. Called *Star Trek: Phase II*, it was to be a revival of the original series, with Shatner, Nichols, and other cast members (but not Nimoy—he was committed to starring in *Equus* on Broadway). Sets were built, scripts were written, and contracts were signed. Paramount even envisioned *Phase II* as the linchpin of the Paramount Television Service, a new broadcast network it was developing.

And then *Star Wars* was released.

Not only did *Star Wars* become one of the highest-grossing movies of all time, it renewed interest in big-screen science fiction, which hadn't been popular in a decade. Paramount saw bigger dollar signs on the big screen, so they retooled *Phase II* into 1979's *Star Trek: The Motion Picture*. That decision launched a big-screen *Trek* franchise that spawned four movies and earned half a billion dollars at the box office over the next nine years. The movies were such a success that in 1986 Paramount once again called on Gene Roddenberry to create a live-action television series.

Roddenberry decided he needed someone who knew not only how to get a show on the air but how to *keep* it on the air. His preferred choice for a producer was Harve Bennett, the man who wrote *Star Trek II: The Wrath of Kahn*, but Bennett was too busy working on the *Trek* film series.

That's when Roddenberry was told that he should talk to a young man rising up through the ranks at Paramount: Rick Berman.

GENERATION NEXT

If Gene Roddenberry personifies Captain Kirk, then Rick Berman takes after Captain Picard. Whereas Roddenberry made action shows, Berman made PBS kids' shows such as *Big Blue Marble*, as well as the very intellectual documentary *Space*. And Berman was coming into his own as a producer, having worked on ratings giants *Cheers*, *MacGyver*, and *Webster*. One thing Berman wasn't: a *Star Trek* fan. Roddenberry didn't mind—the new show was going to take place 80 years after the original series, and he thought that it should look and feel different from the 1960s version.

But from the get-go, Berman's relationship with Roddenberry was tumultuous. Their first major clash concerned putting a "bald Englishman" on the bridge of the *Enterprise*. Roddenberry agreed that Captain Kirk's "cowboy diplomacy" should be toned down for the new show, but he didn't like Berman's choice for the role of Captain Picard: classically trained Patrick Stewart. Nearly everyone else did, however, and Berman finally talked Roddenberry into it.

In September 1987, the two-hour premiere of *Star Trek: The Next Generation* attracted a massive 27 million viewers. Paramount's gamble had paid off. For the first time in nearly two decades, a new live-action *Star Trek* series was on TV.

But it wasn't very good (at first).

Beam yourself to page 398 for Part II.

LUKE HAD LAURA'S ALIEN LOVE CHILD!

Don't watch soaps? You're missing out on some delightfully weird TV.

Soap: *Days of Our Lives* (NBC)
Story: "The Swamp Girl" (1998–2002)
Details: Bo Brady (Peter Reckell) is looking for his wife, Hope (Kristian Alfonso), who was believed dead but was then spotted alive. His search takes him deep into the Louisiana bayou, where he finds a disfigured "cavewoman" the locals call "Swamp Girl" (Julianne Morris). It turns out she's Greta Von Amberg, a former magician's assistant who was horribly scarred by acid during a trick gone awry, after which she went to live in the swamp. Bo takes her home and pays for laser surgery to get rid of her scars—and she turns into a beautiful young woman...and she's a princess! (Bo stopped looking for Hope.)

Soap: *One Life to Live* (ABC)
Story: "I Was Blind, but Now I See...*Gunsmoke*" (1988)
Details: Clint Buchanan (Clint Ritchie) is shot in the head and goes blind. Later, while riding a horse in the desert (blind), he's thrown, hits his head, and is knocked unconscious. When he wakes up—he can see! But he's been transported back in time to the year 1888, to an Old West town called "Buchanan City." Luckily, Viki Lord (Erika Slezak), who loves Clint, travels back in time, finds him, and brings him back to the present. And not a moment too soon—he was about to marry Ginny, one of Viki's ancestors (also played by Erika Slezak).

Soap: *Passions* (NBC)
Story: "The Boy Toy" (1999–2002)
Details: Evil witch Tabitha (Juliet Mills) magically brings a doll named Timmy to life, and he helps her do evil things to residents of Harmony. (He turns himself back into a doll when other people are around.) Timmy longs to be a real boy, and that wish is eventually

---

On the soap opera *Ryan's Hope*, character Delia Reid Coleridge...

granted—by the Little Angel Girl, the spirit of a statue in a Harmony church. This bizarre story line unfolded over three years, until the death of Josh Ryan Evans, the diminutive actor who played Timmy. Eerily, Evans died on the day that Timmy's death scene aired (it had been filmed earlier). In typical soap opera fashion, Timmy was supposed to return from the dead some months later. But when Evans *actually* died, all future Timmy plots were canceled.

Soap: *General Hospital* (ABC)
Story: "The Ice Prince" (1981)
Details: Evil Mikkos Cassadine (John Colicos) steals the world's largest diamond, the "Ice Princess," and uses it to fuel a machine that can create "carbonic snow." He hides the machine on a tropical island and threatens to freeze the planet if world leaders don't give him millions of dollars. Fortunately, Luke (Anthony Geary) and Laura (Genie Francis) find out and go to the island. Luke throws Mikkos into an ice chamber, where he instantly freezes to death. Luke then turns off the machine, saving the world.

Soap: *Guiding Light* (CBS)
Story: "Clone-No!" (1998)
Details: Josh (Robert Newman) marries Reva (Kim Zimmer), but Reva dies. So Josh gets a doctor to use eggs that Reva left at a fertility clinic and create a clone of her. The clone is fed a special formula that makes her age quickly, so she's the same age as Reva in no time. And she falls in love with Josh. Unfortunately, Josh doesn't fall in love with the clone, so Reva 2.0 runs away to a desert island…where she finds the *real* Reva, who isn't really dead. Real Reva returns to Josh. Reva 2.0, distraught, kills herself.

Soap: *Neighbours* (Seven Network)
Story: "Dream a Litter Dream" (1989)
Details: In a 1989 episode of this long-running Australian soap, the character Bouncer falls asleep and has a dream about Rosie, the cute girl next door. In the dream, Bouncer and Rosie are flowers, cheerful flute music plays, and the couple gets married. Then they have babies. The end. But it was just a dream—Bouncer and Rosie are a Golden Retriever and a Sheepdog. (Human) cast member Anne Charleston later noted, "It was very strange."

DO YOU SPEAK TV?

Here are some words introduced to the lexicon by TV shows.

COWABUNGA. Originally spelled "kawabonga," the word is an expression of approval invented by TV writer Edward Kean and first uttered in the late 1940s by Chief Thunderthud, a character on *The Howdy Doody Show*. It also appeared in a 1965 *Peanuts* special, but it was used most notably by Michelangelo of the *Teenage Mutant Ninja Turtles* (1987), Bart Simpson (1990), and Cookie Monster (2004).

BIPPY. Introduced and popularized by *Rowan & Martin's Laugh-In* in 1968 via the catchphrase "you bet your sweet bippy," the word refers to an indeterminate body part (although you can probably figure out which one). Also introduced by *Laugh-In:* the phrase "the fickle finger of fate."

FRAK. It's the swear word of the future! Originally spelled "frack" when it was used on the 30th-century-set *Battlestar Galactica* in 1978, it was altered to "frak" for the 2003 revival of the show. It's since made its way into common usage as a substitute swear word. (It's also been used on other TV shows, including *30 Rock* and *Veronica Mars.)*

CRUNK. On a 1995 episode of *Late Night with Conan O'Brien*, O'Brien invented the word "crunk" as an obscenity he could use without being censored. Rapper Ice-T was a guest that night and peppered his speech with the word. By 2000 "crunk" had caught on as a slang term with other rappers, where it took on the meaning "crazy" combined with "drunk."

TWILIGHT ZONE. Imagine if you will: this phrase was originally a scientific term referring to the deepest, most dimly lit part of the ocean. But since the 1959 premiere of Rod Serling's *The Twilight Zone*, it's come to describe a dreamlike, otherworldy state.

WARP SPEED. Derived from "time warp drive" in the pilot episode of *Star Trek*, warp speed is faster than light speed (which isn't actually possible). Today it's commonly used as a way to describe extremely fast movement.

Dick Clark's middle name is Wagstaff.

STEAGLE COLBEAGLE

Via elaborate publicity stunts, producers of The Colbert Report *and its fan base, the Colbert Nation, have created a huge public profile for the show and its host, Stephen Colbert (the blowhard, arrogant, faux right-wing pundit character, not so much the comedian of the same name who portrays him).*

COLBERT GETS HIS OWN ICE CREAM FLAVOR
In 2007 Ben and Jerry's debuted Stephen Colbert's Americone Dream, described as "the sweet taste of liberty in your mouth," which, as Colbert announced on his show "is what I taste like." (It's actually vanilla ice cream with caramel and pieces of waffle cone.) Ben and Jerry's has based other flavors around such liberal icons as Wavy Gravy and Jerry Garcia of the Grateful Dead, so the Colbert character claims that his flavor "brings some balance back to the freezer case." Both the company and Colbert donate profits to charity.

COLBERT ALMOST GETS A BRIDGE IN HUNGARY

In 2006 Hungary's Ministry of Economic Affairs and Transport hosted a contest to name a new cable bridge in Budapest. Voting took place online, so Colbert pleaded with his viewers to get Hungary to name the bridge after him. In the end, Colbert garnered 17 million votes—14 million more than the 3 million votes for second-place finisher Miklós Zrínyi, a 16th-century Hungarian folk hero (and around 7 million more than the entire population of Hungary). Hungarian officials decided to ignore the results of the contest altogether and call it the Megyeri Bridge (combining the names of the districts the bridge connects).

COLBERT RUNS FOR PRESIDENT

During the 2008 presidential primary season, Colbert attempted to toss his hat in the ring by filing as a candidate in South Carolina—his home state—in October 2007. After early polls found that he was actually attracting more support than legitimate candidates Dennis Kucinich and Bill Richardson, the state's Democratic Party Executive Council voted to boot him out of the race.

In an interview on *Meet the Press*, Colbert confessed that he wasn't expecting to win the presidency. "I don't want to be president," he explained. "I want to *run* for president. There's a difference."

COLBERT GETS BUGS NAMED AFTER HIM

In 2008 Colbert mentioned on his show that a new spider species had been named after rock star Neil Young, and said he wanted one too. Later that year, Jason Bond, a biology professor in charge of naming newly discovered spider species, granted the request. Bond appeared on *The Colbert Report* to officially announce the christening of *Aptostichus stephencolberti*. While the real Colbert was pleased, his blustery TV persona wasn't; he pleaded with the world's scientific community to give his name to "something cooler than a spider. Maybe a giant ant or a laser lion." A year later, he got his wish, sort of…when researchers named a Venezuelan diving beetle *Agaporomorphus colberti* in his honor.

COLBERT GETS A HOCKEY TEAM MASCOT

The Saginaw Spirit, a minor-league team in Michigan, has an eagle named Sammy as its mascot. But as a publicity stunt in 2006, the team held an online vote to suggest a second mascot. Colbert put the word out on his show, and the winning entry was, per his suggestion, "Steagle Colbeagle the Eagle." Immediately after introducing Steagle Colbeagle, the Spirit won seven games in a row.

*   *   *

12 TV VEGETARIANS

Spock (*Star Trek*)	Kwai Chang Caine (*Kung Fu*)
Principal Wood (*Buffy the Vampire Slayer*)	MacGyver (*MacGyver*)
Phoebe Halliwell (*Charmed*)	Ricardo Tubbs (*Miami Vice*)
Sara Sidle (*CSI*)	Artie Fonzarelli (Fonzie's brother on *Happy Days*)
Dr. Peter Benton (*ER*)	Angela Martin (*The Office*)
Phoebe Buffay (*Friends*)	Rachel Berry (*Glee*)

According to a poll in *Bird Talk* magazine, parrots' favorite TV show is *SpongeBob SquarePants*.

BANNED!

Producers sometimes push the envelope of what they can get away with on TV. Result: episodes so controversial that the powers that be elect to never show them again...or to never air them in the first place.

Series: *The Twilight Zone*
Episode: "The Encounter" (1964)
Banned! A white World War II veteran (Neville Brand) hires a young Japanese-American man (George Takei) to help him clean his attic. The Takei character becomes possessed by a Japanese sword that the owner admits he took from the body of a Japanese soldier he killed. Not only is the episode graphically violent (both men ultimately die), but it also has sensitive themes—the Japanese-American man confesses that his father was a spy who helped the Japanese bomb Pearl Harbor. As a result of numerous complaints, the episode was banned by CBS from entering syndicated reruns.

Series: *Married...with Children*
Episode: "I'll See You in Court" (1989)
Banned! Neighbors Steve and Marcy Rhoades go to a hotel and are secretly videotaped having sex, and the Bundys end up seeing the video. Most of the episode takes place in a courtroom when the Rhoadeses sue the hotel, but because of the raunchy plotline, the otherwise edgy Fox network deemed it "way too controversial" and refused to air it. The episode finally showed up 13 years later, when the cable network FX ran the series. (FX, by the way, is owned by Fox.)

Series: *Seinfeld*
Episodes: "Puerto Rican Day" (1998); "The Invitations" (1996)
Banned! In "Puerto Rican Day," characters get caught up in New York's annual Puerto Rican Day parade, and Kramer accidentally burns and stomps on the flag of Puerto Rico. Though it did air, the producers got thousands of complaints that the episode was racist and disrespectful. It never aired again.

When "The Invitations" first aired, it instantly became one of

---

Seinfeld's darkest and most memorable episodes: George's fiancée Susan dies of poisoning from licking cheap wedding-invitation envelopes. That episode was pulled from reruns for a while in late 2001 due to the widespread fear of the anthrax virus.

Series: *The Simpsons*
Episode: "The City of New York vs. Homer Simpson" (1997)
Banned! The Simpsons go to New York to retrieve Homer's car, which his friend Barney made off with and abandoned at the World Trade Center. Most of the episode takes place there, so after the towers were destroyed in the 9/11 attacks, the episode was pulled from reruns. In mid-2002, it began airing again and has been included on *Simpsons* DVDs.

Series: *Buffy the Vampire Slayer*
Episode: "Earshot" (1999)
Banned! This episode, originally scheduled to air in May 1999, concerns a mass shooting at Buffy's high school in which many students are killed. But after the Columbine tragedy in April 1999, the WB postponed the episode for more than four months.

Series: *Family Guy*
Episode: "Partial Terms of Endearment" (2009)
Banned! *Family Guy* has been no stranger to controversy—a main character is a baby who repeatedly attempts to kill his own mother, and recurring characters include a "greased-up deaf guy" and a neighborhood pedophile. But with this episode, Fox executives felt that the show went too far. In it, Lois agrees to be a surrogate mother for a friend who subsequently dies in a car accident. Lois then decides to abort the now-motherless child. Because of the subject matter, Fox refused to air it. They did, however, release it on DVD as a stand-alone episode...and charged $14.99 for it.

*　　　*　　　*

"I've got two *TV Guides*, one on the table and one in the bathroom. I'm rich!"
—Al Bundy, *Married...With Children*

James Dean once worked as a stunt tester for the game show *Beat the Clock*.

NEW KID IN TOWN

The trouble with cute kids on a family sitcom: they get older, and aren't so cute anymore. Or the show ages, and ratings drop. So here comes a new cute kid in the cast to the rescue! Does it work? Not really.

Character: Cousin Oliver

Series: *The Brady Bunch*

Story: By the fifth season of the series in 1973, the six kids in the cast were all teenagers (or about to be), and the ratings reflected a major drop in young viewers. The producers' solution to bring them back: a new kid. Midway through the season, Mrs. Brady's brother and wife go away on an overseas archaeological dig and leave their towheaded eight-year-old son Oliver (Robbie Rist) in the Bradys' care. Oliver became the center of storylines previously served by the now-too-old Bobby or Cindy—breaking a lamp or making a mess, and trying to cover it up, for example.

Effect: The ratings kept dropping across all age groups, so ABC canceled *The Brady Bunch* in spring 1974. Cousin Oliver had appeared in only six episodes.

Character: Ricky Stevens

Series: *The Partridge Family*

Story: The *other* TV show of the early '70s about a family with a lot of kids was also fading in popularity in 1973—from #16 in the ratings a year earlier, to out of the top 30 entirely. *Partridge* producers' solution: a new singer to replace fading teen idol David Cassidy. That new singer was the Partridges' four-year-old neighbor Ricky (Ricky Segall), who would pop in to rehearse with the family band.

Effect: Viewers kept tuning out. *The Partridge Family* was canceled at the end of the season.

Character: Chrissy Seaver

Series: *Growing Pains*

Story: The series was still a top-30 hit in 1988, but more than a million viewers had left the show in less than a year. Seeking to inject some new story ideas, writers had mom Maggie Seaver (Joanna Kerns) get pregnant and give birth to a daughter named Chrissy.

Effect: Ratings continued to sag, so in fall 1990, the show reinvented itself again. Chrissy, previously two years old, was suddenly seven (and played by actress Ashley Johnson). That didn't bring in new viewers, nor did the Seavers' adoption of a teenage runaway named Luke (an early role for future superstar Leonardo DiCaprio). *Growing Pains* went off the air in 1992.

Character: Olivia Kendall
Series: *The Cosby Show*
Story: There were already five Huxtable children on *The Cosby Show,* and even in the show's fifth season it was still the #1 show on TV, so why was four-year-old Raven-Symone added to the cast? Because she'd auditioned for a role in Bill Cosby's movie *Ghost Dad,* and while Cosby thought she was too young for that part, he created a role in *The Cosby Show* just for her. The setup: Denise Huxtable (Lisa Bonet) marries a Marine named Martin (Joseph C. Phillips), who has a young daughter named Olivia from his previous marriage. The precocious youngster became a comic foil for Cliff Huxtable (Cosby), a role previously filled by the now preteen Rudy (Keshia Knight Pulliam).
Effect: Not much. Ratings slipped from 23 million to 21 million, but it stayed the #1 show on TV. Cosby decided to end *The Cosby Show* two years later, when it was still ranked in the top 20.

Character: Andy Moffet
Series: *The Facts of Life*
Story: At first, this show was about a girls-only boarding school, but the main four teenage characters had all graduated by the end of the 1985-86 season. It was still a hit show, so NBC renewed it, and writers moved the setting to a gift shop. Another change: Charlotte Rae (the headmistress Mrs. Garrett) left the show, replaced by Cloris Leachman as Mrs. Garrett's sister, Beverly. And to bring some youth back to the show, producers brought in 13-year-old Andy (Mackenzie Astin), a troubled foster kid who worked at the malt shop. Beverly then adopted him, which allowed him to appear in more scenes.
Effect: Ratings remained stagnant; the show was canceled in 1988.

Kevin Sorbo (*Hercules*) was almost cast as Fox Mulder on *The X-Files.*

THAT'S SPOOKY

*Can TV predict the future? No, but sometimes
it produces some pretty eerie coincidences.*

STORY: In a 2005 episode of *Extras*, actress Kate Winslet
plays herself filming a movie about the Holocaust with
Extras' main character, a movie extra named Andy (Ricky
Gervais). Andy says to Winslet, "I think you doing this is so com-
mendable, using your profile to keep the message alive about the
Holocaust." Winslet replies, "My God, I'm not doing it for that.
And I don't think we really need another film about the Holo-
caust, do we? You know, we get it—it was grim. Move on. No, I'm
doing it because I've noticed that if you do a film about the Holo-
caust—guaranteed Oscar!"
SPOOKY: Four years later, Winslet won an Oscar for *The Reader*.
Her role: a guard at a Nazi concentration camp.

STORY: *Life Is Worth Living* was one of the most popular shows
on prime-time TV in the 1950s. It consisted of Catholic bishop
Fulton Sheen delivering half-hour lectures on religious and political issues. Sheen spoke often of the evils of the Soviet Union, particularly its "state religion" of atheism. In a February 1953 episode,
Sheen read from Shakespeare's *Julius Caesar*, with the names of
the corrupt ancient Roman rulers replaced with the names of
modern-day Soviet leaders. (Joseph Stalin stood in for Caesar.)
The segment ended with Sheen ominously booming, "Stalin
[Caesar] must one day meet his judgment"…implying he would
pay for his political actions with death.
SPOOKY: About a week after that episode of *Life Is Worth Living*
aired, Stalin suffered a stroke and died.

STORY: Airing in May 1998, the fourth-season finale of *NewsRadio* was an elaborate fantasy/dream sequence that took place
aboard the *Titanic*. All of the show's regular characters "died" by
the end. As an afterword, cast member Phil Hartman appeared as
himself, explaining to viewers that no one in the cast really
died…until being told (as a joke) that actor Dave Foley did, in

fact, drown during the shoot. Hartman then says, "Okay, one cast member died."

SPOOKY: "One cast member" did die, but it wasn't Foley. Two weeks after the episode aired, Hartman was murdered by his wife.

STORY: In 1976, five years into the run of the husband-and-wife mystery show *McMillan & Wife*, co-star Susan Saint James left the series because of a salary dispute. The show, retitled *McMillan* (and still starring Rock Hudson), explained the sudden absence of Sally McMillan by saying she died in a plane crash along with her toddler son.

SPOOKY: In November 2004, Saint James's husband, NBC executive Dick Ebersol, and their two sons, Charles and Teddy, were flying in a small plane when it crashed in Colorado. Ebersol and Charles survived; 14-year-old Teddy died in the crash.

*   *   *

REAL (AND REAL DUMB) *FAMILY FEUD* ANSWERS

Q: Name something a husband and wife should have separate ones of.
A: Parents.

Q: Name a famous bad guy from the Old West.
A: John Wayne

Q: Name a month of spring.
A: Summer.

Q: Name a word that starts with "Q."
A: Cute.

Q: Name a yellow fruit.
A: Orange.

Q: Name something you wouldn't use if it was dirty.
A: Toilet paper.

CELEBRITY ROASTED

Beginning as a segment of The Dean Martin Show *in 1973 and running as periodic TV specials until 1984,* The Dean Martin Celebrity Roasts *are a showbiz relic: old-time Hollywood big shots leveling insults at one another.*

"This man was married to a great many women in his life. They're all flat now."

—Don Rickles, on Orson Welles

"Lucy always relied on slapstick, pratfalls, and physical comedy to make people laugh. And that was just on her honeymoon."

—Milton Berle, on Lucille Ball

"You couldn't ask for a better boss. If you did, he would fire you."

—Audrey Meadows, on Jackie Gleason

"There's a statue of Jimmy in the Wax Museum, and the statue talks better than he does."

—Dean Martin, on Jimmy Stewart

"Never has one man given so little to so few."

—Jimmy Stewart, on Jack Benny

"Bette Davis was the Queen of Hollywood, back in the days when queens were still ladies and Joan Crawford was king."

—Joyce Haber

"It's a very patriotic night. Dean is celebrating the bicentennial. Just this morning, he took his 1,776th drink."

—Jack Carter, on Dean Martin

"So as we remember Abbott and Costello, as Laurel and Hardy will never die / surely we can't forget Rowan and Martin, but, baby, we sure gonna try."

—Nipsey Russell, on Dan Rowan and Dick Martin

"Johnny's first wife was named Joan, second wife was Joanne, present wife is Joanna. He just won't go for new towels."

—Bob Newhart, on Johnny Carson

"His movies were so bad, they were shown at drive-outs."

—Martin, on Ronald Reagan

DUELING SERIES

Do great minds think alike...or merely jump on the bandwagon when other networks seize upon a great idea? Here are a few "twins" that hit the airwaves at the same time—and then had to duke it out for viewers.

THE SHOWS: *Studio 60 on the Sunset Strip* vs. *30 Rock*
THE BATTLE: In 2006 *The West Wing* creator and executive producer Aaron Sorkin announced his hotly anticipated follow-up series: *Studio 60 on the Sunset Strip*, an hour-long drama about the eccentric writing staff of a *Saturday Night Live*-like late-night variety show. Meanwhile, *Saturday Night Live* actress and writer Tina Fey was producing *30 Rock*, her own sitcom about the eccentric writing staff of a *Saturday Night Live*-like late-night variety show. Few TV insiders thought NBC would pick up both shows, and if they had to choose, it would be the one from the guy who made *The West Wing*.
THE VICTOR: *30 Rock*. NBC did end up airing both shows, and *Studio 60* was the network's most publicized new show of the 2006–07 season. But *Studio 60* struggled to find an audience and was canceled after 22 episodes. NBC stuck behind *30 Rock*, a critical darling that earned a spot on the *New York Times* list of the "Best TV Shows of 2006." While it still fights to attract viewers, *30 Rock* has won three straight Emmy Awards for Best Comedy Series.

THE SHOWS: *Transformers* vs. *Challenge of the GoBots*
THE BATTLE: The cartoon world of the early 1980s was dominated by sentient robots and the toy companies that made them. In 1983 Hasbro Toys bought the rights to two lines of popular robot toys from Japan and was planning to create the kids' cartoon series *Transformers* around them. Competitor Tonka found out and decided to offer its own line of robots with an animated series to promote them. Both *The Transformers* and *Challenge of the GoBots* debuted in the fall of 1984.
THE VICTOR: *The Transformers*. GoBots lasted one year, with 65 episodes, before slowly rusting away in repeats for two years on the USA Network. Meanwhile, *Transformers* ran for four seasons

and spawned a full-length feature film in 1986. Several spin-offs, updates, and reboots aired throughout the 1990s, ultimately leading to Michael Bay's live-action films *Transformers* (2007) and *Transformers 2: Revenge of the Fallen* (2009), which zapped $1.5 billion out of moviegoers' pockets.

THE SHOWS: *ER* vs. *Chicago Hope*

THE BATTLE: Super-producer David E. Kelley took viewers into a realistically portrayed hospital operating room on CBS's *Chicago Hope*, which debuted on Sunday, September 18, 1994. The next night, NBC's *ER* debuted, bringing viewers an even more intense emergency room. There were many similarities between the two shows: Both took place in Chicago hospitals, both were staffed by hunky doctors and flustered nurses, and both had the same time slot. *Chicago Hope* performed so well that CBS moved it to Thursday night at 10 p.m., opposite *ER*, for an all-out battle to the ratings morgue.

THE VICTOR: *ER*, but both programs proved popular. *Chicago Hope* finished the 1994–95 season as the #28 show on TV; *ER* came in at #2. CBS transferred *Chicago Hope* to Monday night, where it brought in moderate ratings for six seasons. *ER*, on the other hand, became one of the most popular dramas of all time—lasting 15 years and ranking in the Nielsen top 10 for most of that time.

THE SHOWS: *Bewitched* vs. *I Dream of Jeannie*

THE BATTLE: In one corner, witch Samantha Stephens (Elizabeth Montgomery) of *Bewitched*, capable of casting spells with a twitch of her nose. In the other, Jeannie (Barbara Eden), a 2,000-year-old genie whose magical powers caused headaches for her "master"-turned-husband. Samantha first materialized on September 17, 1964, on ABC. Eager to earn some ratings magic for NBC, producer Sidney Sheldon released Jeannie from her bottle a year later.

THE VICTOR: It was a draw. *Jeannie* lasted five seasons and 139 episodes. While it never bested *Bewitched* in the ratings, it was incredibly popular in syndication and returned for two reunion movies in 1985 and 1991. Meanwhile, *Bewitched* conjured up 254 episodes over the course of eight seasons and led to a spin-off—*Tabitha*—in 1977, and a feature film in 2005.

DOG'S BEST FRIEND

Higgins the dog (also known as Benji) was legendary for performing stunts on TV and in movies that no animal had done before. Who taught him every trick he knew? Frank Inn, the greatest animal trainer in history.

CUE THE DOG

One day in 1964 on the set of *Petticoat Junction*, a towering, snowy-haired man knelt beside Higgins, a shaggy Terrier mix sitting alertly at his side. "Okay," the man said, "when the director calls, 'Action!' I want you to cross the room, take a piece of paper out of the safe, take the phone off the hook, pull the lamp cord out of the wall, and go hide in the car. Got it?"

The director called the scene, and the dog performed the sequence perfectly, with no retakes. The dog then headed for his "trailer," a doghouse built to look like a Southern mansion, and sprawled out on a pillow to wait for the next scene. It was just another day at the studio for the world's greatest canine actor, Higgins, and his legendary trainer, Frank Inn.

CALIFORNIA, HERE YOU COME

Born Elias Freeman in Indiana in 1916, Frank Inn was raised by a traveling Quaker minister, and his youth was marked by a hand-to-mouth existence and lots of church. The strict religious upbringing became too much for Elias, so he ran away in 1934, a few weeks shy of graduating from high school. He rode the rails looking for work, acting as a rodeo clown and picking up other odd jobs. Along the way, he changed his name to Frank Inn to keep his family from finding him.

When Inn got to southern California, he found a job cleaning horse stalls in Culver City, just outside of Los Angeles. That's where he got his big break: As the stableowner was riding one day, the horse bolted, and Inn grabbed the reins and calmed the horse down. The owner happened to work at MGM, and he got Inn a job in the maintenance department.

CAR AND JEEP

Just a few weeks into his new job, Inn was hit by a car while standing on a street corner. Pronounced dead at the hospital, he was sent to a mortician school for embalming practice—until some of the students noticed he was alive.

Inn recovered but was stuck in a wheelchair for months. For company, an MGM co-worker gave him a puppy that he named Jeep. One day, while trying to encourage the pup to come closer to his wheelchair, Inn almost fell over. As he jerked up his hand to steady himself, the dog barked. Inn raised his hand again. The dog barked again. He repeated the sequence; same result. He had just trained his first animal. With a lot of time on his hands, he began working with Jeep to see what else he could get the dog to do. Frank Inn had stumbled upon his true calling.

"MY DOG CAN DO THAT"
In 1935 Inn returned to his job on the MGM lot. On a break one day, he went to observe Henry East, a top animal trainer, work with a dog actor. The dog was supposed to climb a flight of steps, enter a bedroom, jump onto a bed and get under the covers, and then stick out its head and bark. But the dog just couldn't get the sequence right, and each time he messed up, the director, and East, grew more frustrated.

Inn walked over, pointed to the dog, and stated bluntly, "My dog can do that." East told Inn to prove it. So he hurried home and got Jeep, brought him to the set, and went about training him to do the scene. Then he just told him, in plain English, what to do—and Jeep aced it on his first take. East hired Inn as his new assistant.

Inn's first assignment: handling Skippy, the wirehaired Terrier best known for playing Asta in the *Thin Man* movies. From there, Inn honed his natural ability to communicate with animals and found work all over Hollywood. He even trained the first few Lassies on TV.

ANIMAL FARM
In the 1950s, Inn and his wife, Juanita, bought a ranch in the San Fernando Valley and began accumulating a small menagerie of animals to train and offer for hire: dogs, cats, pigs, and chimps, most of which he rescued from shelters, circuses, and zoos. At one point, the couple was caring for more than 1,000

If Jackie Gleason patted his stomach on *The Honeymooners*, it meant he had forgotten his lines.

animals. At any given time, around 100 were being trained for TV and film work. Some of the animal stars he trained over the next 20 years:

• Orangey the cat, who played Minerva on *Our Miss Brooks* (1952–56).

• Bernadette, the Basset Hound who co-starred as Cleo on *The People's Choice* (1955–58) with Jackie Cooper.

• Arnold Ziffel, the extraordinarily talented pig on *Green Acres* (1965–71) who could fetch newspapers, drink from a straw, write his name, play the piano, and change TV channels.

• Tramp, a shaggy mutt who played Spud on *My Three Sons* (1960–72).

ENTER HIGGINS
Frank Inn always claimed there was no secret to training animals. His technique was summed up in three words: patience, kindness, and rewards. Armed with those, Inn felt he could train anything that breathed. But he had no doubt as to which of his animals was the most talented. It was Higgins, a shaggy little Terrier mutt he rescued from the Burbank Animal Shelter in 1960.

Higgins became one of the most famous animal actors of all time: He portrayed Dog on *Petticoat Junction* (1963–70) and starred in *Benji*, the hit 1974 film that started a movie franchise. Inn claimed that he never had to train Higgins to do a trick—he just had to show the dog what to do, and he did it.

"THE SMARTEST DOG THAT EVER WAS"
Most animal performers learn a few tricks, and that's their repertoire. For six years on *Petticoat Junction*, Higgins was required to perform a new trick each week, "which made that dog about the smartest that ever was, in my book," Inn declared. Later, when Higgins was 16 years old and retired, director Joe Camp convinced Inn to bring Higgins out of retirement to star in *Benji*. It became the role for which the dog—and Frank Inn—are best remembered.

Higgins died at age 17 in 1975, but the Benji franchise lived on, with several other dogs taking over the role. When Inn died in 2002, one of his last requests was that Higgins's ashes be buried with him in his casket.

A SHOW IS BORN

More origins of popular programs.

MODERN FAMILY (ABC, 2009–present)
Writer-producers Christopher Lloyd (*Frasier*) and Steven Levitan (*Just Shoot Me!*), were brainstorming new ideas in 2008 after the failure of their latest show, the TV-news comedy *Back to You*. None of the ideas they had were very interesting, so they kept getting off topic, telling funny stories about their home lives—and realized that their own families were more entertaining than any of their show ideas. Lloyd and Levitan wrote "My American Family" on a white board and started building an idea around that title. Then, Lloyd realized, "There is no single modern family that represents the American family." So they created three families, all related: one nuclear; one with an older divorcé, his younger wife, and his stepson; and a gay couple who adopt a baby. The premise: a mockumentary filmed by an unseen Dutch filmmaker. They later scrapped the filmmaker but kept the mockumentary format, and renamed the series *Modern Family*. It was a breakout hit for ABC and took home the Emmy for Best Comedy Series in its first season.

HOUSE M.D. (Fox, 2004–present)
In 2003 Paul Attanasio, a former TV critic turned TV writer, was reading Dr. Lisa Sanders's diagnostic-medicine column in *The New York Times Magazine*. That sparked an idea for a *CSI*-style procedural about a team of doctors who solve impossible-to-diagnose medical cases. Fox executives liked the idea, which Attanasio called *Chasing the Zebra, Circling the Drain* (doctor lingo for an unknown disease killing a patient). To develop the series, the network brought in David Shore—it was his idea to center the show around an irreverent genius who walks with a cane. Inspired by one of Shore's favorite characters, Sherlock Holmes, Dr. Gregory House is addicted to drugs and has difficulty relating to other people. To cast the lead, Shore and his partner, Bryan Singer, looked at Denis Leary, Rob Morrow, and several British actors. None of them worked. "If we don't do this right," said

---

President Truman's first televised speech was about food rationing. It began with a Jell-O ad.

Singer. "House will just come off as hateful." Plus, all of the Brits who read for the part had terrible American accents. Then Singer received an audition tape from Hugh Laurie, who was in Africa filming a movie. He was dirty and unshaven, and had an acerbic wit. "Now that's a *real* American," beamed Singer, unaware that Laurie was a famous British comic actor. Laurie took the role of Dr. House—without realizing that he would be the lead character. *House M.D.* has been both a ratings and critical success, and earned the distinction in 2008 of being the most-watched TV show in the world.

THE SOPRANOS (HBO, 1999–2007)

When he came up with an idea for a mob movie in 1995, David Chase was already a 15-year veteran of TV, having won a writing Emmy in 1979 for *The Rockford Files*. In his screenplay, he wanted to tell the story of his own New Jersey family and acquaintances as if they were mobsters. (Tony Soprano's mother and psychiatrist, for example, are similar to Chase's.) Chase's agent told him that the story would work better as a TV show than a movie, so Chase retooled it. None of the Big Three networks was interested in producing a mob drama, but HBO was. They loved the script and in 1997 commissioned a pilot, which they also loved, but then they put *The Sopranos* on hold for more than a year. When it finally premiered in January 1999, it was an instant sensation. The show received 21 Emmys and five Golden Globes over seven seasons. To date, it's the most profitable series in the history of cable television.

UGLY BETTY (ABC, 2006–10)

This show debuted a few months after the premiere of the hit movie adaptation of Lauren Weisberger's 2003 novel *The Devil Wears Prada*, in which an awkward young woman climbs the ladder at a fashion magazine. *Betty* was partially based on *Prada*, but series developers Silvio Horta and Salma Hayek modeled the show more closely on a 1999–2001 Colombian soap opera called *Yo Soy Betty, La Fea* ("I Am Betty, the Ugly One"). ABC's *Ugly Betty* was one of 18 international versions of the Colombian show.

GO (ADAM) WEST

Adam West first hit it big when he starred in the campy 1966-68 Batman TV series. Today he's on TV again as an insane mayor on Family Guy. But the road between was littered with numerous failures.

Legends of the Superheroes (1979). West reprised his role as Batman for this series of low-budget superhero specials. The premise of the first episode: comic book superheroes (Batman, Robin, Green Lantern, etc.) unite to defeat a supervillain. The second episode was a roast of superheroes hosted by Ed McMahon. West, along with Bert Ward as Robin, performed a sketch about Robin wrecking the Batmobile. Then the show was canceled.

Ace Diamond, Private Eye (1983). An unsold pilot, set in the 1940s. West played an actor who starred on a radio show about a detective. When he wasn't doing that, he would solve minor mysteries that occurred at the radio station.

The Last Precinct (1986). In this made-for-TV rip-off of the popular *Police Academy* movies, West played an exasperated police sergeant in charge of a band of unruly and incompetent police academy graduates. The cast included *Ghostbusters* co-star Ernie Hudson and famed character actor Keenan Wynn in one of his final roles. It lasted just seven episodes.

Lookwell! (1991). Co-created by Conan O'Brien, this comedy pilot lampooned the then-current TV trend of seniors solving mysteries they'd stumbled upon (*Murder, She Wrote; Father Dowling Mysteries*). West lampooned himself, too, starring as Ty Lookwell, an out-of-work ex-action star. NBC passed on the show.

1775 (1992). This was CBS's pilot for an American adaptation of the popular British historical comedy *Blackadder*, now set during the Revolutionary War. Ryan O'Neal starred as an innkeeper; West played his brother-in-law, George Washington.

Muscle (1995). Airing on the first night of programming on the WB, this comedy set in a health club was a parody of soap operas. West played the owner of the gym...and is murdered in the first episode. (*Muscle* was murdered after 13 episodes.)

IT'S A RECORD!

For longest-running...

Prime-time drama: *Gunsmoke* (CBS, 1955–75) and *Law & Order* (NBC, 1990–2010) both ran for 20 seasons, although *Gunsmoke* produced more episodes: 635 to *Law & Order*'s 456.

Prime-time comedy: *The Simpsons.* It's also the longest-running scripted series in prime time. In fall 2011, it will begin its 23rd year.

Daytime soap: When *Guiding Light* was canceled in September 2009, it completed a 57-year run on CBS. (And it was a radio series from 1937 to 1956, giving it a 72-year life span.)

Game show: The current version of *The Price Is Right* has aired since 1972—a total of 38 seasons.

Cooking show: *Ciao Italia with Mary Ann Esposito* has been shown on PBS stations since 1989, or 21 seasons.

Kids show: *Romper Room* aired in some part of the country—there were both national and local versions—from 1953 to 1994, for 41 seasons. In fall 2011, *Sesame Street* will beat that record when it enters its 42nd season.

Show of any kind: NBC's political-affairs show *Meet the Press* has been running on Sunday mornings since 1947, just after regular TV broadcasting began. That's 63 seasons.

Portrayal of a single role (prime time): Starring as Sheriff Matt Dillon, James Arness is the only cast member who stayed with *Gunsmoke* for its entire 20-year run. Kelsey Grammer played Frasier Crane for 20 years, but did so on three different shows: *Cheers* (1984–93), *Frasier* (1993–2004), and *Wings* in 1992 as a guest star.

Portrayal of a single role (all time): Helen Wagner began playing Nancy Hughes McClosky on the CBS daytime soap *As the World Turns* in 1956, and continued playing her for 54 years, until shortly before her death in 2010.

UNSEEN TV

Ever wondered what the network geniuses do behind closed doors? These TV shows were approved and produced...but never broadcast.

SHOW: *Aquaman* (2006)
STORY: The fifth season of Superman-based *Smallville* introduced another superhero, Aquaman (played by Justin Hartley), that producers intended to spin off into a new series. A pilot was filmed (co-starring Ving Rhames and Lou Diamond Phillips) that TV insiders called one of the best of the year. But when the fall 2006 schedule was announced, there was no *Aquaman*. Why? The WB network was merging with another network, UPN, and in consolidating their programming, had left a lot of shows on the sidelines, including *Aquaman*. Later that year, the pilot was quietly made available on iTunes and became its most-downloaded TV show. It still never became a series.

SHOW: *Snip* (1976)
STORY: In 1976 NBC gave comedian David Brenner his own sitcom. The premise: Brenner is a divorced hairdresser whose ex-wife moves back in with him. It looked like a sure-fire hit—Brenner was one of the most popular comedians of the time, and the show was created by James Komack (who also made *Chico and the Man* and *Welcome Back, Kotter*). Seven episodes were filmed, but at the last minute, NBC executives got nervous and pulled the plug. Why? The network feared controversy over another character in the show—an openly gay hairdresser. Brenner later bitterly quipped to a reporter, "Apparently, in 1976 there were no gay people in America."

SHOW: *Mr. Dugan* (1979)
STORY: In 1978 the title character in *Maude* got elected to Congress and moved to Washington, but after two episodes, star Bea Arthur decided to quit the show. Producer Norman Lear quickly reworked the show to make it about James Dugan, a freshman African-American congressman, played by Cleavon Little (*Blazing Saddles*). A few weeks before the show's heavily advertised 1979

debut, Lear screened the show for black members of Congress. They hated it, and found it to be full of stereotypes. One member called it "demeaning" and threatened to organize a boycott of CBS. Lear promptly ended production on *Mr. Dugan.*

SHOW: *Commando Nanny* (2004)
STORY: From 1989 to 1993, Gerald McRaney starred in *Major Dad* as a tough Marine drill sergeant who adopts his new wife's three children. In 2004 he signed up for the similar *Commando Nanny*, portraying a former Marine who goes to work as a child care provider. (Creator Mark Burnett based the show on his own experiences.) The WB network announced the comedy as part of its fall 2004 lineup. It was not to be: Teenage co-star Philip Winchester broke his foot during filming and had to drop out of the show. Then McRaney required emergency surgery to remove a cancerous lung tumor, and producer Rachel Sweet quit because of the delays. Down two actors and a producer, the WB had no choice but to cancel *Commando Nanny* before it aired.

SHOW: *Coastocoast* (1978)
STORY: Between 1976 and 1978, ABC president Fred Silverman brought the network from third place (out of three networks) to first. His strategy? Titillating programming, nicknamed "jiggle TV" by the media: shows with scantily clad women and adult themes, such as *Charlie's Angels* and *Three's Company.* In mid-1978, NBC lured away Silverman, hoping he'd work the same "sex sells" magic for them. The network had announced its new fall shows before Silverman came over, canceling family-friendly fare like *Chico and the Man* and *The Bionic Woman* in favor of sexy shows, including *Legs*, a sitcom about two promiscuous showgirls, and *Coastocoast*, a comedy about promiscuous flight attendants. Somewhere between ABC and NBC, Silverman made an about-face on his approach to TV. "It's time to move in another direction," he told reporters. "Television should present things of value." Silverman ordered *Legs* to be reworked into the family show *Who's Watching the Kids*—the main characters now raised their younger siblings instead of entertaining men. As for *Coastocoast*, which Silverman called "an abomination" behind closed doors, it was canceled in the summer of 1978.

A REALLY BIG SHEW

Some quick facts about the variety show that everybody watched on Sunday nights between 1948 and 1971: The Ed Sullivan Show.

• **Job history:** Prior to hosting his legendary show, Ed Sullivan wrote a Broadway gossip column called "Little Old New York" for the *New York Daily News*, the most widely read newspaper in the U.S. at the time. (The column was also syndicated to 200 other papers.) He parlayed that into a gig as emcee for the *Daily News*'s annual Harvest Moon Ball, which CBS aired. The network picked him to host a variety show in 1948 when one exec remarked that Sullivan "seemed relaxed and likeable with none of the brashness of a hardened performer."

• **Original title:** The show was named *Toast of the Town* when it debuted. The name that most people actually called it, *The Ed Sullivan Show*, became its official title in 1955.

• **Guests on the first episode:** The comedy duo of Dean Martin and Jerry Lewis, plus Broadway producers Rodgers and Hammerstein with a preview of their score to *South Pacific*.

• **Pre-show ritual:** According to Sullivan's publicist, Bernie Illson, the host drank a glass of wine mixed with Sweet'N Low.

• **Variety:** While Sullivan's show is largely remembered for bringing rock 'n' roll to mainstream America—episodes with Elvis Presley and the Beatles are among the most-watched programs in TV history—it included many different types of performers, from old-fashioned (jugglers, circus acts) to highbrow (opera singer Maria Callas, ballet troupes, and classical pianist Van Cliburn).

• **The act that appeared most:** Wayne & Shuster, a Canadian comedy duo who performed Shakespeare-based sketches. They were on *Sullivan* 67 times.

• **Studio audience:** Demand for tickets was so high that *The Ed Sullivan Show* admitted spectators to its Sunday-afternoon dress rehearsals.

More than 600 million people watched the *Apollo 11* moon landing on July 20, 1969.

• **Sullivan's favorite acts:** Señor Wences, a Spanish ventriloquist whose characters included a face named "Johnny" drawn on his hand (Johnny: "S'alright?" Wences: "S'alright.") and Topo Gigio, a mouse puppet controlled by five Italian puppeteers.

• **Ratings:** The show peaked in popularity in the mid-1960s. More than 50 million Americans watched *Sullivan* on CBS every Sunday night—more than half of the TV-viewing audience at the time.

• **Integration:** *The Ed Sullivan Show* supported black entertainers in an era when many television programs did not. The Supremes were the first black act to appear on the show, in 1964.

• **Feud:** Sullivan had a well-publicized quarrel with comedian Jackie Mason in 1964. Near the end of Mason's routine, Sullivan gave him a "wrap it up" gesture from offstage. Mason joked about it and waved it off; Sullivan mistakenly thought Mason's wave was obscene...and that the viewers had seen it. Sullivan exploded backstage and terminated the show's contract with Mason, canceling six upcoming appearances. Mason filed a lawsuit, which was later dropped, and Sullivan invited Mason back to the show in 1966, and publicly apologized.

• **Banned for life:** The Doors made an appearance on the show in September 1967. Just before the performance, Sullivan told the band they "ought to smile a little more," and a producer told them they had to alter lyric "girl, we couldn't get much higher" from their song "Light My Fire" because some saw it as a drug reference. The band agreed, went on live TV...and Morrison sang the original lyric anyway. Sullivan was furious. He refused to shake hands with the band members at the end of the song and banned the Doors from ever returning to the show.

• **And introducing...:** Among the performers who got their first TV exposure on *The Ed Sullivan Show:* Joan Rivers, George Carlin, Richard Pryor, and Marvin Gaye.

• **The end:** CBS unceremoniously canceled the program at the end of the 1970–71 season, denying its viewers (and Sullivan) the satisfaction of a series finale after 23 years.

Peter Jennings hosted a CBC radio show at age nine.

LICENSE TO WATCH

*If you're a James Bond fan, you know that agent 007 has a
license to kill. But did you know that he also has a license
to watch TV? So does everyone else in the U.K.*

COMMERCIAL FREE, BUT NOT FREE FREE
If you've ever been to Great Britain and spent time watching the eight channels of the British Broadcasting Corporation, it probably didn't take you long to notice that the BBC's
shows are never interrupted by commercials. The BBC doesn't
fund its operations by selling advertising time like American
broadcast networks do. So how do they pay their bills? By charg-
ing every household and business with a television license fee.

As of 2010, the cost of a license to watch a color TV is
£145.50 a year ($235), or just under $20 a month, and a license to
watch a black-and-white TV is £49 a year ($80). Seniors older
than 74 are entitled to free licenses, and the visually impaired
qualify for a 50% discount (presumably because they can hear the
TV but not see it). But everyone else who owns a TV—or a laptop, or a smart phone, or any other mobile device—and uses it to
watch any TV transmissions, whether they watch the BBC or not,
has to pay. Watching TV without a license is criminally equivalent to tax evasion and is punishable by up to £1,000 ($1,614) in
fines.

DEATH AND (TV) TAXES
The BBC is a public corporation created and run by the British
government. As such, it has more in common with the U.S.
Postal Service than with the American TV networks. The BBC's
charter requires it to collect the licensing fee, and it takes this
duty very seriously: For more than 60 years, the BBC has
employed a fleet of "television detector vans" that roam neighbor-
hoods, scanning for emissions from illegally operated TVs. The
technology they use to detect TV emissions is a state secret as
closely held as nuclear weapons codes. Another secret: the number of detector vans in the BBC fleet, and exactly how and where
the vans are deployed to catch offenders.

BBC B.S.

That's the official story, anyway. The vans actually exist—for years, they'd had have TELEVISION DETECTOR painted on their sides in big letters and giant antennas popping out of their rooves. But it's not clear whether they really contain "TV-detecting equipment." It's debatable whether TVs even emit any signals that can be picked up by a passing van. Such a vehicle would presumably pick up emissions from all of the TVs in the neighborhood, so it would need to be able to distinguish an emission from a single unlicensed TV from all the licensed ones.

Many people in the U.K. believe that the entire TV-detector van program is just an elaborate, six-decade-old publicity stunt—the BBC's attempt to terrorize scofflaws into paying their license fee. But the BBC claims that, since 2003, the newest generation of vans has been able to "detect the use of TV receiving equipment at specifically targeted addresses within 20 seconds...and pinpoint the actual room that the television set is in." These stealth vans are said to have removable signage and no external antennae, which makes them almost impossible to spot. "Any van in the street could be a TV detector van these days. We tend to work more undercover than in the past," warns the BBC. Hand-held scanner wands, supposedly issued to enforcement officers beginning in 2007, "make it easy for us to locate TV receiving equipment in even the hardest-to-reach places," says the BBC website.

SIGNAL CORPS

Even if the van technology is questionable, the enforcement officers sent out to catch license evaders are very real. They work from a database of every household and business in the U.K.—nearly 30 million addresses—that is cross-referenced against a database of license holders to produce a list of addresses with no TV licenses. Each day thousands of enforcement officers make unannounced visits and look for signs of televisions in use. Sometimes they simply stand in front of the house, looking through windows and listening for TV noises.

The officers can also ask to enter the premises and inspect the TV equipment, to verify that a holder of the cheaper license really is watching on a black-and-white TV, for example. Or they might feel a "broken" TV for warmth, to see if it was in use right up until they rang the doorbell. But the occupants of a household are under no obligation to allow an officer to enter the premises, or even to answer questions. Any officer refused entry must go to court and obtain a search warrant.

BBC enforcement personnel visited more than 3.5 million addresses in 2007 and caught an average of 1,000 license evaders each day. In all, about one in four households that claim they don't need a license are later found by enforcement officers to need one. Offenders must pay the license fee in full or risk prosecution and the £1,000 fine.

* * *

EXCUSES, EXCUSES

Each year the BBC's TV Licensing division releases a list of excuses given by license evaders caught red-handed watching TV without a government license. Some recent examples:

"My 11-year-old son must have bought the TV during the night. It wasn't there when I went to bed."

"I've got a marriage license and that's no good, so why should I bother with one for the TV?"

"We don't watch the TV; it's just a piece of furniture that the cat likes to sleep on because it's always nice and warm."

"I've not bought a license as I dreamt I didn't have to, and the saying is you've got to follow your dreams."

"I can't think straight. My girlfriend hit me on the head with a hammer, but I thoroughly deserved it."

"I don't need a license because I only watch Australian soaps."

"My son stopped making the payments. He's run off with someone he met on the Internet."

"I can't get the TV out of the box."

"I'm not watching the TV. I'm just recording shows to watch later, when I've got a license."

"The TV hasn't been on. It's warm because we put a turkey on top of it to rest before being carved."

"I can't afford the license. I have to pay my cable TV subscription."

SOAPY MONIKERS

Why do soap opera characters always seem to have such fancy names? Because it's more dramatic to say, "Your real father is...Alexander Channing!" than, "Your real father is...Gus Lipshitz!" Here are some of our favorite soap names.

Bascombe Moody
(*One Life to Live*)

Lance Cumson (*Falcon Crest*)

Felicia Gallant
(*Another World*)

Brock Hayden (*The Doctors*)

Meredith Lord Wolek
(*One Life To Live*)

Alexis Carrington Colby
(*Dynasty*)

Abby Fairgate Cunningham Ewing Sumner
(*Knots Landing*)

Quinn McCleary
(*Search for Tomorrow*)

Phoebe Tyler Wallingford
(*All My Children*)

Palmer Cortlandt
(*All My Children*)

Maggie Fielding Van Alen Powers (*The Doctors*)

Claude Charbonneau
(*One Life to Live*)

Chase Kendall
(*Search for Tomorrow*)

Greenlee Smythe
(*All My Children*)

Roland Saunders
(*Falcon Crest*)

Mortimer Bern
(*One Life to Live*)

Gwendolyn Lord Abbott
(*One Life to Live*)

Margo Montgomery Hughes
(*As the World Turns*)

Clayton Boudreau
(*Guiding Light*)

Prunella Witherspoon
(*General Hospital*)

Edward Louis Quartermaine
(*General Hospital*)

Malcolm Scorpio
(*General Hospital*)

Therrese Lamonte
(*Another World*)

Brooke Logan Forrester
(*The Bold and the Beautiful*)

Penelope Hughes Cunningham
(*As the World Turns*)

Angelica Deveraux
(*Days of Our Lives*)

Most expensive commercial: $20 million for a 2004 Chanel ad starring Nicole Kidman.

CUT!

*When the director yelled "Cut," these
people took it a little too seriously.*

CUT! On October 30, 1976, comedian Buck Henry was performing a scene with John Belushi on *Saturday Night Live*. It was called "Samurai Stockbroker" and featured Belushi's recurring Samurai character. At the end of the sketch, Henry's character has lost all of his money and remarks, "If this office had a window, I'd jump out of it." Belushi, as the Samurai, pulls out his sword and uses it to hack through a wall of the set, to create a window for Henry to jump through. But as Henry stood behind Belushi, watching him swing his sword around, a stray sword stroke slashed his forehead. A dazed-looking Henry starts to walk off set, and then turns back and jumps out the "window" to finish the scene. Henry performed the rest of the *SNL* episode with a bandage on his head. (In solidarity, the rest of the cast wore bandages on their heads, too.)

AND...CUT! Jimmy Smits was filming a murder scene on *Dexter* in 2008 when he pretended to plunge a prop knife into the heart of stuntman Jeff Chase. Chase appeared as though he'd really been stabbed in the heart...because he almost had. Smits had somehow grabbed a real knife rather than one of the retractable ones. Luckily the knife hit right on a piece of protective plastic Chase described as "the size of a Post-It note" taped to his chest, and the knife didn't enter his body. The veteran stuntman must have been doubly terrified: He was wrapped in plastic wrap and had duct tape over his mouth (prepped for a ritualistic murder by a killer portrayed by Smits), and Smits, deep in character, hadn't noticed. Luckily another actor saw what had happened and yelled at Smits to stop. "I really thought I'd been stabbed in the heart," Chase said afterwards, "but I didn't have a scratch. Jimmy was devastated and couldn't stop apologizing. I told him I felt more sorry for him than me."

AND...CUT! Circus performer Jayde Hanson appeared on the

Actor Edward D. Murphy appeared on 10 *Law & Order* episodes as 12 different characters.

British show *This Morning* in 2003 demonstrating his record-set-
ting knife-throwing skills by throwing as many as he could at his
assistant, Yana Rodianova. With just a few seconds left in their
segment, Rodianova suddenly stopped smiling and the show's host,
Fern Britton, yelled, "Oh my God, there's blood!" Hanson had
struck his assistant in the head, hadn't noticed, and had kept
throwing knives at her. He finally stopped, and Rodianova was
rushed off the set. She said afterward that there was just a small
cut on her head. "It's happened twice before," she said, "but never
that bad. But I forgive him because it's our job." She added that
she had a "splitting headache." Bonus: Hanson and Rodianova
were later married. "I think he'll be aiming a bit wider now I am
his wife," Rodianova joked after the ceremony. "He'd better not do
it again."

AND...CUT! BUT DON'T CUT! Michael Pitt, while filming a
fight scene for HBO's 1920s drama *Boardwalk Empire*, hit another
actor on top of the head with a stunt bottle. It wasn't supposed to
break, but it did. The other actor was fine, but the broken bottle
slashed Pitt's hand open. Executive producer Martin Scorsese
checked up on him and asked how bad the wound was. Pitt
showed him, and Scorsese replied, "That's pretty bad. Can you do
it again?" Pitt had to reshoot the scene another 15 times before he
could get stitches.

*   *   *

STUPID LAWYER TRICKS
After David Letterman moved from NBC late night to CBS in
1993, NBC refused to allow him to take his most famous comedy
bits with him, claiming they were the network's intellectual property. Instead of dropping the bits, Letterman renamed them:

• **Viewer Mail** became the **CBS Mailbag.**

• **Paul Shaffer and the World's Most Dangerous Band** became
the **CBS Orchestra starring Paul Shaffer.**

• **The Top Ten List** became **The *Late Show* Top Ten List.**

• The recurring character **Larry "Bud" Melman** used his real
name, **Calvert DeForest.**

BIG-SCREEN SMASH, SMALL-SCREEN FLOP

M*A*S*H, Friday Night Lights, and Fame are successful TV shows that began life as movies. But not all adaptations of popular movies worked out on television.

Movie: *Fargo* (1996)
To TV: The dark comedy about a sunny, very pregnant small-town Minnesota sheriff trying to solve a series of grisly murders won Oscars for Best Actress (Frances McDormand) and screenwriting (Joel and Ethan Coen). In 1997 CBS commissioned a TV version. Cast as Sheriff Marge Gunderson was then-little-known actress Edie Falco. It didn't get picked up for a series, but that worked out well for Falco—had the show kept running, she might never have starred on *The Sopranos*.

Movie: *Casablanca* (1942)
To TV: Some movies are so adored and critically acclaimed that remaking them is unthinkable. *Casablanca* is one of them. Yet in 1983 NBC aired a series designed as a "prequel" to the film. Who did they get to fill the shoes of screen legend Humphrey Bogart, whose portrayal of Rick Blaine was his most famous performance? David Soul, the guy who played Hutch on *Starsky and Hutch*. The film's other central character, Ilsa Lund (played by Ingrid Bergman) wasn't even in the TV show...which lasted five weeks.

Movie: *Dirty Dancing* (1987)
To TV: A pop-culture juggernaut in 1987, *Dirty Dancing* earned $80 million at the box office, the soundtrack sold 10 million copies, and even a live touring version sold out arenas. CBS execs wanted to cash in, too, so in 1988 they produced a weekly TV series of the same name. The show followed the same plot as the movie, unfolding over many weeks instead of two hours, and with some necessary changes designed to keep the all characters in the same setting, a Catskills resort, indefinitely. Prime example: Baby (Jennifer Grey in the film, Melora Hardin in the show) was made

---

During the show's four-year run, the word "sex" was uttered on *The Brady Bunch* just twice.

the daughter of the resort's owner, instead of a guest. *Dirty Dancing* the TV show was the only part of the franchise to flop—it was canceled after 11 episodes.

Movie: *Parenthood* (1989)
To TV: The movie, a look at the triumphs and troubles of family life, included just as much drama as comedy—characters contemplate divorce, one has a gambling addiction and abandons a child, another gets in a car accident, and Steve Martin's character learns his son has learning disabilities. That was too heavy for TV, so when NBC turned *Parenthood* into a show for the fall 1990 season, the network made it into a wacky family sitcom (and replaced Martin with Ed Begley Jr.). It lasted 12 episodes. In 2009 the movie's original producers, Ron Howard and Brian Grazer, decided to give it a second try. This time they made the TV series less of a comedy and more of a drama. It was NBC's most successful new show of the year.

Movie: *My Big Fat Greek Wedding* (2002)
To TV: The romantic comedy was a surprise box-office hit in 2002, earning more than $240 million. It was written by the film's star, Nia Vardalos, based on the real-life experiences of her husband, who was overwhelmed by her colorful Greek relatives. Before writing it as a film, however, Vardalos pitched the idea as a TV series to CBS, which turned her down. When the film became a hit, CBS made Vardalos an offer. It looked like a can't-miss premise, and it had a great lead-in, *Everybody Loves Raymond*. With most of the movie's main cast reprising their roles, the first episode of *My Big Fat Greek Life* attracted a large audience. But after seven episodes, viewers grew tired of the broad ethnic comedy, the ratings plummeted, and CBS canceled the show.

More movies turned into TV flops: *Tremors, Weird Science, Rambo, F/X, Robocop, Uncle Buck, Harry and the Hendersons, House Calls, Down and Out in Beverly Hills, Little Shop of Horrors, Dangerous Minds, The Magnificent Seven, Stir Crazy, Fast Times at Ridgemont High, The Crow, Clueless, Baby Boom, Police Academy, Private Benjamin, Logan's Run, The Client, Working Girl, Breaking Away, Serpico, Planet of the Apes,* and *Ferris Bueller's Day Off.*

DR. DOCTOR

We're not doctors; we just quote fake ones from TV.

"Treating illnesses is why we became doctors. Treating patients is what makes most doctors miserable."
—**Dr. House,** *House, M.D.*

Patient: You're a kid.
Doogie: True, but I'm also a genius. If you have a problem with that, I can get you someone who's older but not as smart as me.
—*Doogie Howser, M.D.*

Dr. Fishman: It looks like he's dead.
Michael: Just to be clear: *looks* like he's dead, or he *is* dead?
Dr. Fishman: It just looks like he's dead. But he's going to be fine.
—*Arrested Development*

"Don't worry, you won't feel a thing....till I jam this down your throat."
—**Dr. Nick,** *The Simpsons*

"My dear girl, I'm a doctor. When I peek, it is in the line of duty."
—**Dr. McCoy,** *Star Trek*

Hurley: How is it called again, when doctors try to appease their patients?
Jack: You mean "doctor-patient relationship"?
Hurley: Yeah, that. You suck at that.
—**Lost**

Dr. Fiscus: I have a hunch.
Dr. Craig: So did Quasimodo.
—*St. Elsewhere*

Henry: I was never very good with my hands.
Radar: Guess that's why you became a surgeon, huh, sir?
—**M*A*S*H**

"Each and every one of you residents is going to kill a patient....Cross your fingers and hope that the guy that you murder is a jackass with no family. Great to see you, kids. All the best!"
—**Dr. Cox,** *Scrubs*

Nurse Piggy: May I remind you that this is a hospital?
Dr. Bob: I'm glad you did. The way these jokes are dying, I thought it was a morgue!
—*The Muppet Show*

The phrase "I'm not a doctor, but I play one on TV" was first said in a 1986 aspirin commercial.

CLOSED CAPTIONS: A TIMELINE

*When movies got sound in the late 1920s and text
captions disappeared, the deaf and hard-of-hearing
were left out of screen entertainment. That
wouldn't change until the 1970s.*

1970s. Malcolm "Mac" Norwood is made head of Media Services and Captioned Films (MSCF), a program run by the U.S. Department of Education that superimposes captions on film prints as a service to the deaf. Norwood, who is deaf himself, lobbies a flagship PBS station, Boston's WGBH, to work with the MSCF to make television accessible to the deaf and hard of hearing. WGBH officials jump at the idea, and the job is assigned to a production assistant, Phil Collyer. He throws himself into the project, consulting not only television experts but linguists as well, and even immerses himself in deaf culture to understand the needs of the community. Before long, Collyer is head of WGBH's "Caption Center," the first TV captioning operation. .

Around the same time, the National Bureau of Standards (NBS), another government agency, makes advances in digital electronics that allow television transmitters to send electronic data along with the television signal. NBS officials decide to use the technology to transmit the time, and they present "TvTime," as they call it, to the FCC. The FCC deems it useless.

October 1971. NBS then tries a different tack: They give ABC executives a TvTime demonstration, in which they send written messages, that, like the time, appear as text on TV screens. One of the executives suggests that the technology might work to provide captions, allowing people with hearing impairments to read dialogue, bringing them into the television experience. NBS decides to develop the idea.

December 1971. Mac Norwood and MSCF hold the first National Conference on Television for the Hearing Impaired in Nashville. Both the MSCF/WGBH team and the NBS/ABC

---

team get the chance to demonstrate their different captioning technologies.

Collyer and his Caption Center team have figured out how to digitally encode caption information onto prerecorded videotape, which can then be broadcast like any other prerecorded show. They show the conference crowd one of the shows they produced for PBS, Julia Child's *The French Chef*, with captions. This type of captioning, which cannot be turned off, becomes known as "open captioning."

NBS/ABC wows the crowd by showing a TV tuned to the local ABC affiliate, Nashville's WKRN, where *The Mod Squad* is on. It looks like any other *Mod Squad* episode until the TvTime decoder is turned on. Suddenly, captions of the show's dialogue appear at the bottom of the screen. This technology is "closed"— it can be turned off if the viewer doesn't want to see it, leading Norwood to coin the name "closed captioning."

1972. Although most hearing-impaired people involved prefer the closed-captioning option, TvTime technology isn't yet developed enough for public use. So the first to make it to the small screen is the Caption Center team at WGBH. In August they begin airing open-captioned episodes of *The French Chef* as a test. A total of eight episodes are aired on PBS stations all over the country for two months, and are well received.

1973–1975. Open captioning remains the only technology available for the rest of the 1970s, during which time WGBH captions more programs for PBS, including several children's shows. The first are *Zoom* and ABC's *World News Tonight*, which airs on PBS stations all over the country just hours after the original ABC broadcasts. But the days of open captioning are numbered.

1976. The NBS/ABC team, in collaboration with Collyer and the Caption Center, continue to develop closed-captioning technology. As a result, the FCC agrees to reserve a section of the television broadcast spectrum exclusively for closed-caption transmission.

1979. The FCC creates the National Captioning Institute (NCI), with a mission to develop and provide closed-captioned television on a national level.

1980. The National Captioning Institute begins selling "TeleCaption" decoder boxes to the public. (Cost: $250) and on March 16, PBS, ABC, and NBC, begin broadcasting the first nationally aired closed-captioned television shows in history. The first shows: *Masterpiece Theatre* (PBS), *Sunday Night Movie* (ABC), and *The Wonderful World of Disney* (NBC). (CBS doesn't join in, as they are developing their own technology, which doesn't pan out. They finally joined the other networks and air closed-captioned shows in 1984 after protests by deaf activists.)

"When television finally began to be closed captioned," hearing-impaired actress Marlee Matlin recalls, "I watched everything that came on, and I'm telling you, everything. Who wouldn't? Imagine having to watch TV all your life without any sound, and then someone suddenly turning on the sound for one hour. It was really a shock."

1982. The first real-time closed captions appear (before now, all captions were prepared in advance). To accomplish this, trained "captioners"—often court reporters who can type as many as 225 words a minute—are hired to type TV show dialogue into a captioning computer as it is spoken, giving viewers a gap of only a second or two between the spoken words and the captions.

Today: Most TV sets are already programmed with a captioning feature—simply press a button or two, and the captions appear on the screen, eliminating the need for a caption converter box. And captions aren't just for the hearing-impaired. Their availability and ease of use makes them a common device in noisy public places like gyms, bars, and airports.

* * *

BOTTOMS UP!

In 2001 Comedy Central aired a sitcom called *That's My Bush!*, a parody of cheesy 1970s and '80s comedy centered on a dumb but lovable President George W. Bush. Character actor Timothy Bottoms, a dead ringer for the president, starred. The show ran for 13 episodes. In 2003 Bottoms returned to television...as President George W. Bush in *DC 9/11*, the first made-for-TV movie about the events of 9/11.

PRETENDERS TO THE LATE-NIGHT THRONE

The third host of The Tonight Show, Johnny Carson, *didn't invent the late-night talk show. But he did dominate it. Over his 30-year-run as host, Carson turned the program into the single largest revenue-generator in TV history. No wonder networks and syndicators tried to come up with their own versions of NBC's juggernaut. Here's a look at the many who tried—and failed—to get a piece of late-night television glory.*

The Les Crane Show (1964–65). By late 1964, Carson was already NBC's late-night powerhouse, but ABC was ready to fight. In November 1964, it began airing *The Les Crane Show,* a confrontational political-issues and interview program hosted by Crane, a San Francisco radio personality. Crane interviewed celebrity guests and political figures, including Robert F. Kennedy and Malcolm X, and invited audience members to ask questions. It didn't make a dent in Carson's ratings, so Crane was fired from the show in March 1965, and it was renamed *Nightlife.* Guest hosts filled in, but the ratings sank even lower. Crane returned in June before the show was finally canceled that November.

The Joey Bishop Show (1967–69). In 1967 ABC tried again with *The Joey Bishop Show.* Hosted by Bishop, a comedian and member of Frank Sinatra's "Rat Pack," the show wasn't politically oriented like *The Les Crane Show,* it was an unabashed *Tonight* clone...and it lasted only two years. (Bishop's sidekick: a young Regis Philbin.)

The Dick Cavett Show (1969–75). An intellectual, stand-up comedian, comedy writer, and actor, Cavett replaced Bishop in 1969. *The Dick Cavett Show* was intended to appeal to younger, hipper viewers by featuring rock musicians and artists, the kinds of people you wouldn't see on *The Tonight Show.* Some memorable moments: bands that performed at Woodstock gathered for a discussion about the event a day after it ended; a single show in 1970 offered guests Salvador Dali, Lillian Gish, and Satchel Paige. Still,

---

Before deciding on Johnny Carson, NBC almost hired Groucho Marx to host *The Tonight Show.*

it wasn't a hit. ABC stuck with it for five years, although airings were gradually cut back from five nights a week, to five nights a month, to just two nights a month. It left the air for good in January 1975.

The Merv Griffin Show (1969–72). Griffin, the affable singer, composer, and TV entrepreneur who created *Jeopardy!* and *Wheel of Fortune*, among numerous other hits, hosted a daytime variety show from 1962 to 1969. It was so popular that CBS hired Griffin to air the show at 11:30 p.m. Fewer than half of CBS affiliates carried it—running old movies and sitcom reruns proved more profitable than trying to sell ad space for a direct competitor to Johnny Carson. *The Merv Griffin Show* returned to daytime in 1972, where it stayed for another 14 years.

Goodnight America (ABC) (1974–77)

ABC went in a more newsy direction with this show, which aired sporadically from 1974 to 1977 and was hosted by *Good Morning America* correspondent Geraldo Rivera. Notable moment: In 1975 *Goodnight America* aired the Zapruder footage of the assassination of President Kennedy for the first time on TV. The program didn't bring in high ratings but did well enough that ABC decided to try another late-night news show in 1980: *Nightline*.

Thicke of the Night (1983–84). In September 1983, a huge newspaper, billboard, and TV ad campaign heralded the first serious challenger to Carson in more than a decade: Alan Thicke, star of the new syndicated show *Thicke of the Night*. America's response: "Who?" Thicke was a Canadian actor and musician (he wrote the theme song to *Diff'rent Strokes*) who'd hosted the most popular daytime talk show in Canadian TV history and had served as head writer on the '70s talk-show parody *Fernwood 2-Night*. But all that talk-show experience—real and fake—didn't quite resonate with Americans; on its first night on the air, *Thicke* was clobbered by a Carson rerun. *Thicke of the Night* holds a dubious TV record: In the Philadelphia area, it scored a Nielsen rating of zero. That means that theoretically, on that night, not one of the three million people in the Philadelphia metropolitan area watched *Thicke of the Night*. (Uncle John was a guest on

Thicke of the Night in 1983—he hopes it wasn't that episode.) The show was canceled in June 1984. On the same day, Thicke's wife filed for divorce. (Bad day.)

The Jerry Lewis Show (1984). Jerry Lewis's loud, boisterous comedy was extremely popular in the 1950s. By the early '80s, he was enjoying an unlikely comeback after starring in Martin Scorsese's *The King of Comedy*, and in 1984 he landed a syndicated talk show. While other Carson competitors tried to shake up the talk-show format or appeal to younger viewers, Lewis's show was similar to *The Tonight Show*'s old-time showbiz feel, but with zany humor and overblown sentiment. Lewis began his first show by opening a spring-loaded can of coiled snakes and laughing wildly; he ended that episode by saying, "The best wish I could ever wish you—to have people in show business as friends—it's a gift—it's a wonderful frustration, not being able to thank them all." *The Jerry Lewis Show* was canceled after just five weeks.

Nightlife With David Brenner (1986–87). This contender had the benefit of a host associated with *The Tonight Show*—Brenner had performed on Carson's show more than 100 times. And Brenner was a younger stand-up comedian (41 at the time) with a hip, observational style. Even the bandleader was cool—former Beatles sideman Billy Preston. It didn't matter; the show was canceled after a little-noticed year on the air.

The Late Show (1986–87). Joan Rivers became Johnny Carson's permanent guest host in the early '80s, filling in for him on his many days off (contractually, he only had to make four shows a week). In 1986 Rivers left *The Tonight Show* for the brand-new Fox Network, which gave her a late-night show called *The Late Show*. Carson was so offended that she took the job without telling him about it first that he never spoke to her again. (To this day, Rivers hasn't appeared again on an NBC late-night program.) Rivers was too abrasive to appeal to most viewers, and the show was on a network that most people didn't even know existed. After seven months of declining ratings and contract disputes, Rivers was replaced by a string of guests hosts, and then by 28-year-old African-American comedian Arsenio Hall. Ratings improved, but Fox canceled *The Late Show* in favor of a more ambitious late-night option that it already had in production...

The Wilton-North Report (1987–88). Producer Barry Sand, who'd worked on the quirky post-*Tonight Show* program *Late Night with David Letterman*, wanted to make Fox's next late-night show "unlike anything else that's ever been on television." And he did, because *The Wilton-North Report* was downright bizarre. With only three months to develop the show and get production going, Sand had an "anything goes" approach—segments included remote reports, comedy sketches, interviews with celebrities and everyday people, and even interviews with inanimate objects (such as a Pee-wee Herman doll). The hosts of the show were *not* named Wilton and North (the show was produced in the Wilton-North Building in Los Angeles); they were actually Phil Cowan and Paul Robins, two DJs from Sacramento with no TV experience. Among the people they beat out for the starring roles: future talk-show hosts Rosie O'Donnell and Ellen DeGeneres. The show debuted in December 1987...and was gone by January 1988. Neither Cowan or Robins ever worked in TV again.

The Pat Sajak Show (1989–90). In early 1989 Carson was over 60, and TV insiders thought he'd probably be retiring soon. CBS's strategy: establish a new talk show that couldn't possibly challenge Carson, but that would naturally ascend to the top once Carson stepped down. CBS hired *Wheel of Fortune* host Pat Sajak for the job, who got good reviews as a host, but couldn't generate the second-place ratings the network had hoped for— that spot was occupied by *The Arsenio Hall Show. The Pat Sajak Show* didn't even air on a quarter of CBS stations—they showed *Arsenio* instead. *Sajak* aired until April 1990, with the last few months hosted mainly by guest stars—the last episode was hosted by comedian Paul Rodriguez.

The Arsenio Hall Show (1989–94). A little more than a year after Fox canceled *The Late Show*, its final host returned to the air with a talk show produced by Paramount Television. It was an instant hit, and the first legitimate challenger to Carson, drawing millions of under-40 viewers away from *The Tonight Show. Arsenio* had youth appeal—it attracted rap, hip-hop, and rock acts that would never have appeared on *Tonight,* and Hall cultivated a party atmosphere. The show is probably best remembered for the signature waving fist-pump Hall and his audience (which Hall called "The Dog Pound") used at the beginning of each episode. Insiders thought Hall would be the new king of late night once Carson retired, but his ratings actually suffered when Carson left the airwaves. The media frenzy generated by CBS's new host, David Letterman, who'd left NBC's *Late Night* after being passed over as the new host of *The Tonight Show* in favor of Jay Leno, made those two shows neck and neck for #1. Hall was left out of the competition, and his show was canceled in the summer of 1994. A decade later, Hall returned to late-night TV as a "man on the street" interviewer for *The Tonight Show with Jay Leno.*

Into the Night with Rick Dees (1990–91). In 1990 Carson was 65 years old, and the average age of his viewers was advancing, too. ABC tried to cater to a younger audience by shaking up the late-night format with *Into the Night,* which included youth-oriented comedy sketches, rock bands, and Rick Dees, a former host of *Solid Gold* and a radio DJ who had one of the most popular morning radio shows in the country. *Into the Night* appealed to younger viewers…but only those who weren't already watching the similar *Arsenio Hall Show. Into the Night* went into the night permanently in summer 1991.

THE END?
Johnny Carson retired in 1992…which made late-night fair game for the first time. For that story, turn to page 378.

*   *   *

TRY TO KEEP UP

In 2010 D.J. Goodson, an inmate at a Pennsylvania prison, sued reality-show stars Kourtney, Khloe, and Kim Kardashian for "extreme emotional distress." The prisoner said other inmates wanted to watch *Keeping Up with the Kardashians* on the prison lounge's only TV, forcing him to sit through it, and claimed the experience left him permanently scarred. He is seeking $75,000.

GAME SHOW GOOFS

*Being on a game show may look easy from the comfort
of your living room, but under those hot television lights,
contestants' mouths sometimes disconnect from their brains.*

Anne Robinson: What insect is commonly found hovering above lakes?
Contestant: Crocodiles.
—*The Weakest Link*

Alex Trebek: If a Japanese *isha* (doctor) asks you to stick out your *shita*, he means this.
Contestant: What is…your behind?
—*Jeopardy!*

Anne Robinson: Who is the only Marx brother that remained silent throughout all their films?
Contestant: Karl.
—*The Weakest Link*

Todd Newton: Bourbon whiskey is named after Bourbon County, located in what state?
Contestant: England.
—*Press Your Luck*

The Puzzle: TOM HANKS AS _ORREST GUMP
Contestant: Tom Hanks as Morris Gump.
—*Wheel of Fortune*

Richard Dawson: Name something a blind man might use.
Contestant: A sword.
—*Family Feud*

Eamonn Holmes: Name the playwright commonly known by the initials G.B.S.
Contestant: William Shakespeare?
—*National Lottery Jet Set*

Steve Wright: What is the capital of Australia? And it's not Sydney.
Contestant: Sydney.
—*Steve Wright Radio Show*

Bob Eubanks: What is your husband's favorite cuisine?
Contestant: *All in the Family*.
—*The Newlywed Game*

Kevin O'Connell: What moos?
Contestant: A car.
—*Go*

Richard Dawson: Name an occupation whose members must get tired of smiling.
Contestant: Game show host.
—*Family Feud*

Reporter Walter Winchell was told he couldn't wear a hat on TV because "it wasn't polite."

TASTES LIKE TV

When TV characters cook, the results are often disgusting.

Drink: Flaming Homer
Show: *The Simpsons* (1991)
Origin: Homer is bored at home one night—forced to watch his in-law's vacation slides—and he doesn't have any beer, so he makes a cocktail from whatever he can find. He pours the leftover bits from several liquor bottles into a blender, along with the accidental addition of "Krusty's Non-Narkotic Kough Syrup." Homer thinks it tastes okay…but it's even better after it's lit afire by a stray cigarette ash. "I don't know the scientific explanation, but fire made it good," Homer says when he recreates the "Flaming Homer" at Moe's Tavern. Moe then steals the idea and starts serving the drink (for $6.95) and renames it the "Flaming Moe."

Food: Chocolate Salty Balls
Show: *South Park* (1998)
Origin: When the Sundance Film Festival comes to town, the soul-singing school cafeteria cook Chef (voice of Isaac Hayes) opens a stand to sell cookies to tourists. His most popular item: his "Chocolate Salty Balls." It's a blatant double entendre, and Chef even sings a song about them: "Hey, everybody, have you seen my balls? They're big and salty and brown!" The song (which reached #1 in England) gives the recipe: cinnamon, egg whites, melted butter, flour, unsweetened chocolate, brandy, vanilla, and sugar. (Curiously, it doesn't call for salt.)

Drink: Thankstini
Show: *How I Met Your Mother* (2005)
Origin: This cocktail, a martini, invented by booze-swilling playboy Barney (Neil Patrick Harris), combines Thanksgiving food with booze. It's made from two ounces of potato vodka, four ounces of cranberry juice…and a bouillon cube for that poultry flavor. Barney remarks that it "tastes just like a turkey dinner."

In 11 years of operation (1995–2006), UPN never made a profit, and lost more than $1 billion.

Food: Skip's Scramble
Show: *Arrested Development* (2005)
Origin: On one episode, characters eat Sunday brunch at a bistro called Skip Church's (the joke being that people "skip church" to go there). A brief shot of the menu shows standard brunch fare, along with an omelet called Skip's Scramble. Its description: "Too many choices? Menu too big to swallow? Let Skip serve you up a scram that has something from every dish on the menu. It will knock you into next week!" Price: $47.95. The dish includes eggs, ten slices of bacon, ham, peppers, onion, sausage, and a chocolate glazed doughnut. (The menu also features the disclaimer that Skip Church's is "not responsible for medical bills or deformities resulting from the digestion of its menu items.")

Drink: Killer Shrew
Show: *Mystery Science Theater 3000* (1992)
Origin: On an episode of the movie send-up show revolving around the 1959 movie called *Killer Shrews*, Joel (Joel Hodgson) and his robot companions devise the "Killer Shrew," a cocktail that's nonalcoholic but not very healthy. The recipe: combine chocolate ice cream, Cap'n Crunch with Crunchberries, Peanut M&Ms, pancake syrup, Circus Peanuts, Mr. Pibb, Marshmallow Peeps, Sweet Tarts candies, vanilla cake frosting, and Good & Plenty in a blender. Then, "pour into a plastic tulip vase" and throw in a wind-up toy shrew. Joel took one sip... and fell into a diabetic coma from all the sugar. (Note: If you throw in wax lips, it's no longer a Killer Shrew; it's a "Vulcan Mind Probe.")

Food: Spaghetti Tacos
Show: *iCarly* (2009)
Origin: On one episode of this popular Nickelodeon comedy, Spencer (Jerry Trainor) had no idea what to make for dinner. So he invented spaghetti tacos, hard taco shells filled with noodles and marinara sauce. Since that episode aired in 2009, the food became a cultural phenomenon both on the show and in real life. In one episode, characters oversee a spaghetti-taco-making contest on a cable show, and in the real world, spaghetti tacos were the most-requested food item at American school cafeterias in

2010. "Spaghetti tacos make it possible to eat spaghetti in your car," said Syracuse University pop-culture professor Robert Thompson in *The New York Times*. "It's a very important technological development."

Drink: Bloody Awful
Show: *Top Gear* (2008)
Origin: This British show about cars and other manly stuff is co-hosted by Jeremy Clarkson, who came up with this recipe for what he calls "a man's V8 smoothie." And that's not V8, as in the vegetable drink—that's V8, as in the high-powered car engine, which he used to power a blender. Into that blender were placed a few pounds of raw beef with the bones, a dozen hot chilies, a half gallon of Bovril (a meat flavoring agent and tenderizer), two cups of Tabasco sauce...and a brick.

Food: Shepherd's Pie Trifle
Show: *Friends* (1999)
Origin: In a Thanksgiving episode, chef Monica (Courteney Cox) makes the holiday feast, while Rachel (Jennifer Aniston) volunteers to make a trifle for dessert. The British dish is traditionally made up of cake, custard, and fruit, but when the pages of Rachel's cookbook get stuck together, she inadvertently mixes in the ingredients of shepherd's pie with the trifle, making for a disgusting crossbreed of the two. Joey (Matt LeBlanc), who has a huge appetite, doesn't think there's anything wrong with the dish, and eats the whole thing himself. "What's not to like? Custard, good. Jam, good. Meat, *good*." Ross disagrees, saying that it "tastes like feet."

*　　*　　*

TWO TV RECORDS

• **Most cartoon characters voiced by one person:** Kara Tritton provided the voices for 198 different *Blues Clues* characters.

• **Youngest TV show host:** Luis Tanner, host of the Australian show *Cooking for Kids with Luis*, began hosting the show in 2004, when he was six years old.

THE TV BLACKLIST

In the 1950s, television was capturing the American consciousness. But then it collided with another craze that was sweeping the nation: the "Red Scare."

RED DAWN
On June 22, 1950, *Counterattack*, an anti-Communist newsletter put out by former FBI agents, published "Red Channels: The Report of Communist Influence in Radio and Television." At a time when Senator Joseph McCarthy was seeking to expose Communists working in the government, *Counterattack* aimed to expose Communists working in television. The report named 151 show-business people said to be "under the Communist influence," along with a brief summary of their "questionable ties," which included advocating for or working with organizations that promoted civil rights, anti-nuclear proliferation, the New Deal, and censorship.

In fact, none of the alleged activities mentioned were illegal, and few of the accusations were substantiated. But the damage was done. Within a year, most of the 151 named were fired and blacklisted in both film and TV. Some were even forced to testify before the House Un-American Activities Committee (HUAC) and "name names" of left-leaning or "suspicious" colleagues.

LIFE ON THE "C" LIST

It's difficult to gauge just how many people were denied work in TV because of real or imagined communist sympathies. Some of the people affected by the blacklist:

• Jazz singer **Lena Horne** was unable to perform in films or on TV for seven years after being named in "Red Channels" because of her involvement with the Civil Rights movement.

• *The Honeymooners* began as a sketch on Jackie Gleason's 1952 variety show *Cavalcade of Stars*. Actress **Pert Kelton** originated the role of Alice Kramden. In 1955 she was rumored to have Communist ties, so when *The Honeymooners* debuted as a stand-alone series in 1955, Kelton was replaced by Audrey Meadows.

The first Emmy Awards were not televised—they were broadcast on the radio.

- Sanka Coffee sponsored CBS's top-10 sitcom *The Goldbergs* but pulled support in 1951 because co-star **Philip Loeb** had been listed in "Red Channels." CBS recast his character against the wishes of the show's star and creator Gertrude Berg. Loeb never found work again, and took a fatal dose of sleeping pills in 1955.

- From 1948 to 1950, **Irene Wicker** hosted ABC's popular kids' show *The Singing Lady*. It was canceled because Wicker was listed in "Red Channels" for having once supported a Communist candidate for office. She'd never heard of him, and *Counterattack* issued a retraction. Still, Wicker's career never recovered.

- **Aaron Copland**, probably the most prominent American composer of the mid-century, wrote and conducted an original piece called "Lincoln Portrait" for the Eisenhower Presidential Inaugural Concert TV special in 1953. But Copland was shunned in Hollywood because of Communist ties (he'd openly supported the Communist Party USA in the 1930s), so his segment was cut out of the special. His career later rebounded and he was awarded the Presidential Medal of Freedom in 1964.

- Tap dancer and rumored Communist sympathizer **Paul Draper** performed to "Yankee Doodle Dandy" on Ed Sullivan's *Toast of the Town* show in 1950. After the telecast, conservative newspaper columnists and the American Legion led a telegram- and letter-writing campaign protesting Draper's appearance. Sponsor Ford Motors forced Sullivan to issue an apology. Sullivan was so embarrassed that all future guests were screened for Communist ties by Theodore Kirkpatrick, an editor of *Counterattack*. Draper never worked in the U.S. again, and later moved to Europe.

RETURN TO REASON
Blacklisting continued throughout the 1950s, even as public sentiment turned against McCarthy and *Counterattack*. In May 1954, Edward R. Murrow used an entire episode of his CBS news program *See It Now* to present a point-by-point critique of McCarthy and red-baiting. Afterward, the network received thousands of phone calls and letters—15 to 1 in support of Murrow.

Partly as a result, some blacklisted actors and writers began to find work again in TV. By 1960, the Red Scare was a thing of the past.

HONEST SHOW TITLES

Television show names can be misleading, so we're suggesting these new, 100% accurate ones.

42 Minutes, Plus Commercials

Dancing with the Recognizable Names

Deal or Yelling at Briefcases?

Why Aren't You Smarter Than a 5th Grader?

I Tolerate Lucy

Urkel Matters

How I Hung Out With My Friends for Years Before I Eventually Met Your Mother

Two and 3/4 Men

The Wildly Disparate States of Tara

Knight Driver

Who's the Boss? Angela, Because She Hired Tony

He Has a Camera Crew, So He's Not Exactly an Undercover Boss

My Only Martian

Not Very Good Times at All

Mindy Reacting to Mork

The Grey Girls

Saturday Night on a Seven-Second Delay, Taped for the West Coast

Sex in a City

Mission: Quite Possible

In-Need-of-a-Makeover-Is-All Betty

The Resident of Queens

Fairly Large House on the Prairie

With a Slight Trace

The Doesn't-Want-to-Be-a-Bachelor-Anymore

It's Always Misanthropic In Philadelphia

They Promised Cougars in This Town, But It's Just a Bunch of Humans

Major Stepdad

The Flirting and Bickering Boat

In Japan, **Jersey Shore** is called **The New Jersey Life of the Macaroni Rascals**.

SIMON SAYS, SUE ME

*Being Simon Cowell isn't a bed of roses. He's had to put up with
out-of-tune singers, Paula Abdul... and lots and lots of lawsuits.*

FALLEN IDOL
During the live finale of *American Idol*'s 2010 season, Simon
Cowell's last episode, comedian Dane Cook put some of
Cowell's best put-downs to music as a tribute. Toward the end
of the song, about a dozen former contestants ran onstage, as
planned. What was unplanned was season 7 reject Ian Bernardo
taking the microphone from Cook and yelling, "No one cares! It's
all about Ian Bernardo tonight and I'm gonna replace you,
Simon!" *Idol* quickly cut to commercial.

Later, Bernardo filed a lawsuit against *Idol*, claiming that
Cook's bodyguards verbally assaulted and forcibly removed him.
Bernardo said that he was just doing what the *Idol* producers
had told him to: "They said, 'Go out there and act gay and outrageous.'" Bernardo is seeking $300 million for emotional distress.
Idol's lawyers have countersued him for legal fees. Bernardo won't
budge: "I will see them in court. I'm not going to back down just
because they are a major TV show." The case continues.
Simon says: "Despite the interruption, I loved the song."

GENDER NEUTRAL
In August 2010, *Britain's Got Talent* contestant Philip Grimmer,
57, donned a purple leotard, knee-high boots, and a blond wig for
a tribute to Madonna. After Grimmer sang Madonna's "Hung
Up," Cowell called the performance "horrendous" and Grimmer
a "hard-of-hearing and shortsighted Madonna." Grimmer, who is
partially deaf in one ear, claimed that Cowell was discriminating
against his disability. He also claimed that the show referred to
him as a "transvestite," which he is not. "I'm a female impersonator! That's what I put on my application," he explained. "It's my
niche. I'm not gay or a transvestite. Now my family thinks I'm a
cross-dresser." Grimmer filed suit against Cowell for defamation.
"This is David against Goliath! Madonna against Simon Cowell!"
He is seeking the equivalent of $380,000.

Bruce Lee was passed over for the lead in *Kung Fu*. (He was considered "too Asian" for U.S. TV.)

Simon says: "Madonna at 95 would look better and dance better than you."

IF THE SHOE FITS...

In 2009 a woman (whose name wasn't released to the press) applied for a job as chef at Cowell's Los Angeles estate. When she arrived for her interview, she was told to remove her shoes and was given a "substitute pair" to wear. When she left, she forgot to get her shoes, so a few days later, she went back to pick them up. She then claimed that members of Cowell's staff tried to give her the wrong shoes. She sued for the cost of the shoes and their orthopedic insoles, plus $9 for gas. Total amount: $661.59. In court, Cowell's lawyer returned her shoes. The woman was awarded $75 in court costs plus the $9 for gas.

Simon says: "This is a ridiculous story."

BRITAIN'S GOT ATTITUDE

Emma Amelia Pearl Czikai barely lasted a minute singing the inspirational "You Raise Me Up" on Cowell's *Britain's Got Talent* in early 2010 before all three judges gave her the thumbs-down. "You should give people a chance," she said. "This song is a really lovely0 song!" Cowell replied, "Not when you sing it." He then added, "I think I speak for everyone: You have a horrible singing voice, Emma." Czikai blamed "this particular microphone" for her poor performance and said the backing music was so loud she couldn't hear herself. She filed a suit against Cowell and the other producers for the equivalent of nearly $4 million, stating: "This program makes a select number of people very, very rich on the backs of the ordinary man and woman in the street through exploitation, humiliation, degradation, and a re-emergence of modern-day barbarism with all its inherent cruelty." The case is pending.

Simon says: "Emma, Emma, reality check here. It's not the music; it's not the microphone; it's you."

*   *   *

Random fact: In 1997 there were 16 TV comedies about African-American characters on the broadcast networks. In 2010 there were none.

TV's Davy Crockett (Fess Parker) wore a coonskin cap; the real one never did.

THE NICKNAME QUIZ

Try to match these TV characters' "real" (and rarely heard)
names with their nicknames. (Answers on page 500.)

1. Cockroach, *The Cosby Show*

2. Skippy, *Family Ties*

3. Beaver, *Leave It to Beaver*

4. Spike, *Buffy the Vampire Slayer*

5. B.A., *The A-Team*

6. Screech, *Saved by the Bell*

7. Corky, *Life Goes On*

8. Coach, *Cheers*

9. Bones, *Star Trek*

10. Bones, *Bones*

11. Boner, *Growing Pains*

12. Venus Flytrap, *WKRP in Cincinnati*

13. Hawkeye, *M*A*S*H*

14. Punky, *Punky Brewster*

15. Red, *That '70s Show*

16. Krusty, *The Simpsons*

17. Thirteen, *House*

18. Toofer, *30 Rock*

19. Crabman, *My Name Is Earl*

20. Bull, *Night Court*

a) Gordon Sims

b) Charles Thatcher

c) William Pratt

d) Walter Bradley

e) Remy Hadley

f) Penelope

g) Nostradamus Shannon

h) Herschel Krustofski

i) Bosco Albert Baracus

j) Leonard McCoy

k) Ernie Pantusso

l) Richard Stabone

m) Irwin Handelman

n) Temperance Brennan

o) Samuel Powers

p) Theodore Cleaver

q) Benjamin Franklin Pierce

r) James Spurlock

s) Darnell Turner

t) Reginald Foreman

Jack Benny's will provided for a red rose to be sent to his wife every day for the rest of her life.

RENAMED RERUNS

Hey, who put their Ponderosa *in my* Bonanza?!

ASHOW BY ANY OTHER NAME
If you watched daytime TV back in the 1970s, you
might remember a show called *Ponderosa* that looked
just like *Bonanza*...because it was. Why change the name of a
show for reruns and risk confusing (and losing) viewers? Because
it was better than the alternative—angering the viewers.
Reruns are so commonplace today that it's hard to imagine TV
without them, but in the '60s and '70s, viewers would complain
loudly if they thought they were watching a new episode of
their favorite show only to realize that they'd seen it before (and
the networks' switchboard operators and mail clerks could attest
to that).

But then the networks and television distribution companies
realized that reruns were a potential cash cow—reruns could
earn more money than a show could in its original run. Here's
how it works: A distribution company purchases old episodes of
a show from its network, then sells it directly to individual local
stations or cable channels. The network—and everyone who
worked on the show—receives a residual every time a rerun airs
anywhere, which adds up fast. (For example, *Seinfeld* reruns have
generated $2.7 billion in revenue; $800 million of that went to
Jerry Seinfeld.)

But what if new episodes of a series are still running in
prime time while older episodes are airing during the day? In the
1960s, the Federal Communications Commission ruled that a
TV show *had* to change its name if new episodes were still in
production for nighttime airings. That rule was designed to alleviate viewers' confusion, but really it only created more. Here
are some classic TV shows...and the names they were presented
under in reruns.

WHAT'S OLD IS NEW AGAIN

• Reruns of 1950s **Dragnet** episodes were called **Badge 714**,
which refers to Sgt. Joe Friday's badge number.

Disc jockey Casey Kasem was asked to be the voice of *Scooby-Doo*'s Shaggy...

- *Highway Patrol* was a 1955–59 cop show starring Broderick Crawford. In the 1960s, repeats of the show aired as **10-4**.

- *Laverne & Shirley* became *Laverne & Shirley & Company* to capitalize on the popularity of sidekicks Lenny and Squiggy.

- The Western anthology *Death Valley Days* was reran as *The Pioneers, Trails of the West*, and *Western Star Theater*.

- Ever watched *Sgt. Bilko*? That's the rerun name for *The Phil Silvers Show*, but even *that* wasn't the show's original title. It first aired on CBS from 1955–59 as *You'll Never Get Rich*.

- *The Andy Griffith Show* began airing daytime reruns in 1964 as *Andy of Mayberry*.

- Raymond Burr's *Ironside*, in which he played a wheelchair-bound private detective, was renamed *The Raymond Burr Show*.

- The James Garner-starring show *The Rockford Files* was renamed *Jim Rockford, Private Investigator*.

- *Gunsmoke's* rerun name was taken from its main character: *Marshall Dillon*. (In the U.K., reruns were called *Gun Law*.)

- *Have Gun–Will Travel* was renamed *Paladin* after the show's "gentleman gunfighter" played by Richard Boone.

- *Three's Company* spin-offs *The Ropers* and *Three's a Crowd* were included in *Three's Company* rerun packages, renamed as *Three's Company's Friends: The Ropers* and *Three's Company, Too*, respectively.

- Here's a case of a new show getting a name change so as not to be confused with its reruns. Say what? In 1982 CBS revamped the 1970s game show *The $25,000 Pyramid*, while reruns of the original program were still highly popular. To avoid confusion, the '80s version was called *The New $25,000 Pyramid*.

- The most unimaginative name change in the history of daytime reruns: *The Dick Van Dyke Show* became *The Dick Van Dyke Daytime Show*.

...in 1970, but refused to do it until the character was made a vegetarian.

LET'S GO FOR A SPIN(-OFF)

What's a really effective way for TV producers to get a new show on the air? They spin off a show from one that's already a hit. Here are some stories about the most famous (and weirdest) spin-offs in TV history.

SWITCHING GENRES

By the mid-'70s, *The Mary Tyler Moore Show* (1970–1977) had already launched two hit sitcoms based on supporting characters: *Rhoda* (starring Valerie Harper) and *Phyllis* (with Cloris Leachman). When MTM ended its run, Ed Asner's character, Lou Grant, got his own spin-off, *Lou Grant*. What was different about this show? It was the first dramatic series spun off from a comedy series. (And Lou switched, too, from working in TV news to editing a newspaper.) Over the course of the two series, Asner won five Emmy Awards—he's the only actor to ever win in both the sitcom and drama categories for the same part.

SWITCHING GENRES THE OTHER WAY

Hill Street Blues was a serious and somber police drama, with Dennis Franz as Sgt. Norman Buntz. When *Hill Street Blues* went off the air in 1987, the Buntz character continued on and moved to Beverly Hills to became a private detective on *Beverly Hills Buntz*—a comedy. It was the first time a drama series had spawned a sitcom. (It lasted for 13 episodes.)

A REAL-LIFE CARTOON

In 1994 *The Simpsons* creator Matt Groening began work on a show all about Bart Simpson's hero: Krusty the Klown, a bitter, self-loathing, chain-smoking TV kiddie-show host. But Groening didn't want to make another cartoon—so *Krusty the Klown* was slated to be a live-action show starring Dan Castellaneta (the voice actor behind Krusty, among other *Simpsons* characters). In Groening's pilot script, Krusty moves away from Springfield to Los Angeles, where he hosts a talk show. Fox loved the script but

---

Longest TV character name ever: Dr. Vijayaraghavensatanarayanamurthy (*Crossing Jordan*).

turned it down on the grounds that it would be too expensive to produce. What was so expensive about a *Klown* show? Beavers. As with *The Simpsons*, Groening packed *Krusty the Klown* with silly sight gags, one of which was a running joke about how Krusty lived in a house on stilts that beavers were always gnawing away at. Fox refused to foot the bill for the beavers, either trained or mechanical ones.

THE ROCKFORD FILES FILES

In May 2008, the Fox medical show *House* introduced a new character, a private detective named Lucas (Michael Weston) whom Dr. House hires to spy on his co-workers. Lucas served as comic relief to the intense medical scenes, and show creator David Shore based him on the scruffy, off-kilter private eye Jim Rockford from *The Rockford Files*. Shore planned to spin the character off into a new, *Rockford*-like detective series, but Fox passed on a Lucas show, and the project died. (Lucas remained a recurring character on *House*.) Two years later, Shore signed a deal with NBC to make a pilot for the fall 2010 schedule. Shore's idea: a remake of *The Rockford Files*. It didn't get picked up.

THE HURRICANE

Spin-offs are common; spin-offs of spin-offs are rare. NBC's 1985–92 hit about Miami retirees, *The Golden Girls*, yielded the spin-off *Empty Nest*, about pediatrician Harry Weston (Richard Mulligan) who lives next door. And the Miami hospital where Dr. Weston worked was the setting of *Empty Nest*'s own spin-off, *Nurses*. NBC engineered a ratings-grabbing "crossover event" in 1991: All three sitcoms dealt with the onslaught of a hurricane, and characters from *The Golden Girls*, *Empty Nest*, and *Nurses* appeared on each others' shows.

THE HAPPY DAYS CHAIN

Few TV shows have produced more spin-offs than *Happy Days*, which ran from 1974 to 1984 (see page 215). But *Happy Days* wasn't the first show in the chain—even it was a spin-off.
• *Love, American Style* was a 1969–74 anthology series, with a new story about new characters every week. In 1972 an animated *Love* segment called "Love and the Old-Fashioned Father" was made

into a syndicated series called *Wait Till Your Father Gets Home*, starring the voice of Tom Bosley as a suburban dad. Bosley then went on to star on *Happy Days*, which also began as a *Love, American Style* episode.

• In a 1976 *Happy Days* episode, Richie and Potsie double-dated some rough-around-the-edges friends of Fonzie's named Laverne and Shirley—who were then immediately transplanted into *Laverne & Shirley*, which ran for eight years.

• In February 1977, *Happy Days* introduced Nancy Blansky (Nancy Walker), Howard's (Tom Bosley) cousin who was a landlady for a group of Las Vegas showgirls. That fall Walker starred in the spin-off *Blansky's Beauties*. While *Happy Days* was set in the 1950s, *Blansky's Beauties* was confusingly set in the present. It was canceled after 13 episodes.

• An alien named Mork (Robin Williams) appeared on a 1978 episode of *Happy Days* to launch the 1978–82 series *Mork & Mindy* (also set in the present day).

• From aliens to angels: Chachi (Scott Baio) met his guardian angel, Random (Jimmy Brogan), in a September 1979 *Happy Days* episode. That same month, *Out of the Blue*, about Random, debuted; it lasted only five episodes.

• Long-time teenage lovers Chachi Arcola and Joanie Cunningham (Erin Gray) got engaged…and got their own show, the 17-episode bomb *Joanie Loves Chachi*.

❋   ❋   ❋

THE FLINTSTONES ROCKED THE ROCK PUNS

- Cary Granite (Cary Grant)
- Stony Curtis (Tony Curtis)
- Ed Sulleystone (Ed Sullivan)
- Perry Masonite (*Perry Mason*)
- Ann-Margrock (Ann-Margret)
- The Rolling Boulders (The Rolling Stones)

TV STARS AND THEIR DISEASES

We figured that in a book about TV it was not only okay—it was entirely appropriate—to get a little tacky now and then. This is one of those times.

Patrick Duffy. Best known for playing Bobby Ewing on *Dallas*, Duffy has Morton's neuroma, a condition that causes nerve tissue between toes to thicken, resulting in numbness and pain in the toes and feet. Duffy developed swollen nerves while wearing an uncomfortable, web-footed costume on the set of *The Man From Atlantis* for the show's two-year run in the '70s. He had surgery in 1989 to remove the swollen nerves, but it failed to relieve the problem.

Kim Cattrall. The *Sex and the City* star has Hashimoto's disease, an autoimmune condition in which the body attacks and damages the thyroid gland. This can result in the production of too much or too little thyroid hormone production, which leads to a wide variety of symptoms, including fatigue, weight fluctuation, migraines, rapid heartbeat, and depression.

Shannen Doherty. The *Beverly Hills, 90210* and *Charmed* star suffers from Crohn's disease, a condition that causes inflammation of the lining of the intestines. It can cause bowel pain, diarrhea, intestinal ulcers, and malnutrition, among other symptoms. "It can kind of mess with you," Doherty says. "There's nothing sexy about women saying: 'I've got to go to the bathroom right now.'" There is no cure, but Crohn's can be successfully treated with drugs. (Joe Rogan of *Fear Factor* and *NewsRadio* also has the disease.)

Jimmy Kimmel. It's kind of ironic that the host of *Jimmy Kimmel Live!*, a late-night talk show that airs when a lot of people are going to sleep, suffers from narcolepsy, a genetic neurological disorder that causes excessive drowsiness and even sudden sleep. "Truth be told, I'd rather have narcolepsy than not have it,"

Ray Bradbury helped develop *The Addams Family* comic strip for television.

Kimmel told *Esquire* magazine. "When I get on a flight to Vegas, I'll fall asleep before the plane takes off and wake up after it's landed. I'm always very close to sleep."

Kiki Shepard. The host of the live music show *It's Showtime at the Apollo* from 1987 until 2002 has sickle-cell disease, a genetic blood disorder that causes red blood cells to become fragile and C-shaped rather than round, which can result in numerous health problems—some mild, and some very dangerous. Shepard has been working since the early 1990s to raise awareness of the disease, which is especially prevalent among people of African descent.

Annette Funicello. The one-time "Mouseketeer" of the children's show *The Mickey Mouse Club* has the central nervous system disorder multiple sclerosis. Symptoms can range from fatigue to tingling and numbness around the body to pain, loss of muscle control, loss of balance, and cognitive problems. Funicello kept the condition a secret for many years, but publicly acknowledged she had it in 1992, and has worked to raise money for a cure since 1993. Other personalities with the disease include talk-show host Montel Williams and David "Squiggy" Lander of *Laverne & Shirley*.

Jon Hamm. The star of *Mad Men* has vitiligo, a disease that causes the patient's skin to gradually lighten. (Michael Jackson famously suffered from it.) The cause is unknown, and there is no real treatment. Hamm said it only affects his hands, that it comes and goes, and that it was brought on by the stress of doing the award-winning show.

Kristin Chenoweth. The singer and actress best known on TV for her roles in *The West Wing* and *Pushing Daisies* has Meniere's disease, an abnormal fluid buildup in the inner ear that can cause several symptoms, including severe dizziness and vertigo, tinnitus, and hearing loss. There is no cure, and treatment usually consists of trying to prevent or alleviate the severity of the symptoms. Chenoweth says that she has often had to endure symptoms such as vertigo while performing on stage in front of an audience. She adds that the disease "sucks a big fat corn cob."

NETWORK ORIGINS: ABC

*When NBC was forced to break up its radio broadcasting monopoly
and spin off one of its two networks (see page 46), it decided to
get rid of the least profitable one. The result: ABC.*

FEELING BLUE

In 1940 the FCC issued a report stating that commercial
radio in the United States was unfairly dominated by CBS,
Mutual Broadcasting, and the two networks of NBC (NBC Blue
and NBC Red). The government agency ordered NBC to get rid
of one of its networks. So NBC kept NBC Red, its cash cow and
home of its most popular shows, and in 1942 it put NBC Blue,
which aired mostly news and public affairs programs, up for sale.

The network sold immediately for $8 million ($104 million in
today's money) to Edward J. Noble, head of Life Savers Candy. His
first order of business: change the name. NBC Blue was rechristened the American Broadcasting Company, or ABC.

THE NETWORK WITH A HOLE IN IT

Noble was out of his element running a radio network. He had no
experience in broadcasting, and wasn't willing to spend any
money to pull ABC out of the ratings gutter (it was in fourth
place out of four networks). Not only would he not invest in stars
and writers for top-shelf programming to compete with CBS,
NBC, and Mutual, but he actually cut wages. At the end of 1943,
his employees opened up their bonus packages and instead of a
check found…a ten-pack of LifeSavers.

Noble had good reason to be worried about money. As television became the hot new medium in 1946, radio ad revenues began
dropping, but there wasn't enough money in TV yet to make up for
the costs of buying the expensive technology, much less the programming. ABC, evicted from the NBC-owned RCA Building in
New York, bought a riding academy on 66th Street and set up
offices and radio studios in what had been horse stalls. The riding
ring in the middle became the fledgling TV network's studio. A
20-year-old pie delivery truck was the vehicle for remote shoots.

ABC programming was equally low-budget. In 1948 its weekly

schedule featured only five total hours of programming that aired over Sunday, Monday, and Wednesday. Most of that time was taken up with roller derby and wrestling, but ABC also had *Hollywood Screen Test*, in which promising young actors played out scenes in front of a camera, hoping to get "discovered." The popular show lasted until 1953, and gave exposure to such up-and-coming stars as Jack Lemmon, Grace Kelly, and Jack Klugman.

THE HAPPIEST PLACE ON EARTH

In 1953 ABC-TV was still struggling to compete with CBS and NBC and was nearing bankruptcy...until it found a cash windfall. Just as ABC had been the result of a broken-up monopoly, the United Paramount Theaters cinema chain had been jettisoned from Paramount Pictures in 1949. UPT merged with ABC, installing its chief executive, Leonard Goldenson, as head, displacing Edward Noble as owner, who remained on the network's board of directors. Goldenson's experience was in the movie industry, and that's what he relied on to build up ABC. He couldn't participate in the movie business because of the antitrust ruling, but he could convince studios to work for TV. The studios, viewing television as a threat to the movie business, had boycotted the medium, but Goldenson went about changing that, convincing some of them that there was significant money in producing programming for his network.

One studio head who called back: Walt Disney. Disney was trying to finance a new theme park he planned to call Disneyland. At the time, amusement parks were viewed as disreputable places filled with dangerous rides, surly carnies, and rigged midway games. Disney couldn't get banks or other investors interested in his idea, so he came to ABC with a deal: In exchange for a $15 million loan, ABC would get a 35% stake in the park. And in exchange for producing a weekly show hosted by Walt Disney, ABC would pay Disney $35 million in licensing fees over seven years. Disney got his theme park, and ABC got its first Top 10 show: the Disney anthology series *Disneyland* (1954–61).

In 1986 media conglomerate Capital Cities Communications bought ABC. But in 1996 the Disney deal of the 1950s came full circle when the Walt Disney Company paid $19 billion for Capital Cities/ABC...or, factoring in inflation, about 250 times what Edward Noble paid.

First African-American sitcom star: Ethel Waters on 1950's *Beulah*. (She played a maid.)

WACKY TV

Every year, TV executives hear hundreds of ideas for new shows.
We all know the great ones; here are a few of the clunkers.

SIT OR MISS (1950)

A fast-paced daytime game show in which five contestants competed for cash and prizes by playing musical chairs.

TONI TWIN TIME (1950)

Basically a 15-minute commercial trying to pass itself off as a talent show. Hosted by a young Jack Lemmon, it featured pairs of teenage twin girls. First came the talent portion: girls would sing a song, perform a dramatic recital, or play an instrument. Next, though completely unrelated to the talent portion, the audience would guess which girl had had her hair done professionally and which had used a Toni Home Permanent kit. The program aired in prime time.

THE UGLIEST GIRL IN TOWN (1968)

In order to stay in London with his British girlfriend, an American man dresses in drag and lands work as a fashion model. Despite looking nothing like a woman (his face wasn't even shaved), he becomes the toast of the swinging '60s fashion world because of his "unique" appearance. It ran for 20 episodes.

GREAT DAY (1977)

Al Molinaro ("Al" in *Happy Days*) and Billy Barty play two homeless alcoholics trying to survive on the streets of New York City. A compelling tragic drama? No—*Great Day* was a comedy. It aired only once.

THE CHARMINGS (1987)

Premise: Snow White, Prince Charming, a magic mirror, and some dwarves are accidentally transported through time to 1980s Burbank, California. The show featured live actors, not animation, and the comedy arose mostly from Snow White's difficulty in dealing with the 20th century—especially modern appliances. It ran for 20 episodes.

Highest possible cash prize playing "Plinko" on *The Price is Right*: $50,000. No one has won it.

LIFE IMITATES TV

Coincidence or fate? Who knows…but either way, it's fascinating.

TV: *Chappelle's Show* poked fun at the home renovation show *Trading Spaces* in a 2003 parody sketch called "Trading Spouses."
LIFE: A year later, ABC premiered *Wife Swap*. Fox rushed a knockoff onto the air called *Trading Spouses*.

TV: On *The Mary Tyler Moore Show*, Murray (Gavin MacLeod) is the only member of the news team not to win a "Teddy" award.
LIFE: MacLeod was the only cast member without an Emmy win.

TV: In 1982 *SCTV* ran a parody ad for an album called *Stairways to Heaven*, featuring 30 versions of the Led Zeppelin classic covered by big stars.
LIFE: In 1995 the Australian variety show *The Money or the Gun* released "Stairways to Heaven," featuring several versions of the song in different genres.

TV: *Mad TV* sketches included a *Friday the 13th* sequel called *Jason in Space*, a fake ad for a vacuum cleaner with an iPod dock, and a fake ad for an "iPad" (though it wasn't a computer).
LIFE: The 2001 slasher film *Jason X* featured Jason in space, in 2009 Electrolux released a vacuum with an iPod dock, and in 2010 Apple released the iPad (though it wasn't a feminine napkin).

TV: In 2009 *The Big Bang Theory*'s Howard (Simon Helberg) designs a toilet for the International Space Station, and it breaks.
LIFE: Not long after the episode aired, the ISS toilet broke.

TV: On a 1993 *Seinfeld* episode, Elaine's (Julia Louis-Dreyfus) boyfriend shares the name of a killer, so she suggests he change it to something more "innocent," like O.J.
LIFE: A year later, O.J. Simpson (allegedly) murdered two people.

Q: Who nicknamed Jackie Gleason "The Great One?" A: Orson Welles.

TV DRUNKS

Alcoholism in real life: sad and self-destructive.
On TV: a laugh riot!

Character: Otis Campbell
Series: *The Andy Griffith Show* (CBS, 1960–68)
Details: Otis worked in a glue factory, and every weekend he'd find himself some bootleg liquor—Mayberry was a dry town—and go on a brain-cell-demolishing bender. Afterward, he'd save Sheriff Andy Taylor the trouble of throwing him in the drunk tank by locking him in one of the jail cells to sleep it off, then let himself out in the morning. Otis disappeared from the show for its last two years (rumor had it that sponsors weren't happy with a drunk character prone to hallucinations and pratfalls), only to reappear in the 1986 reunion movie *Return to Mayberry*—all sobered up and now the town's ice cream man. Fun fact: Hal Smith, who portrayed Otis, never had a sip of booze in his life.

Character: Patsy Stone
Series: *Absolutely Fabulous* (BBC, 1992–2004)
Details: Of the two drunken, debauched main characters on *Absolutely Fabulous*, Patsy (Joanna Lumley) is the more drunken and debauched. She's rarely seen without a drink in her hand, and she is always depicted in some stage of inebriation. She is such a lush that she consumes virtually *nothing but* alcohol: in one episode she claims to have not eaten since 1973.

Character: Karen Walker
Series: *Will & Grace* (1998–2006)
Details: The billionaire's wife who still works as the personal assistant of interior designer Grace on *Will & Grace*, Karen (Megan Mullally), manages to keep that job even though she barely does any work—and is always either gleefully drunk, unabashedly high on prescription drugs, or both. At one point, she travels to Las Vegas, where she remarks, "I may lose $100,000, but the drinks are free so it evens out!"

Richard Simmons once appeared as a dancing meatball in an Italian TV commercial.

Characters: Don Draper and Freddy Rumsen
Series: *Mad Men* (AMC, 2007–present)
Details: Most of the ad industry professionals on *Mad Men* drink copious amounts of booze—to celebrate, to socialize, because they're macho. But Don (Jon Hamm) is almost always drinking, even, or especially, at work. In one episode, he downed 13 glasses of whiskey and forgot what day it was, then woke up with a waitress he didn't recognize. (At that point, he cut back to only beer…for a while.) Don's drinking wreaks havoc on his home life, but he holds onto his job at Sterling Cooper. Copywriter Freddy Rumsen (Joel Murray) isn't so lucky. In a 2008 episode, he gets so drunk that he pees his pants and passes out before a meeting with a big client. That got him fired. He returned a year later…and joined Alcoholics Anonymous.

Character: Father Jack Hackett
Series: *Father Ted* (Channel 4, U.K., 1995–98)
Details: The semi-retired priest (portrayed by Frank Kelly) usually found sleeping in an armchair in the back of the priests' communal living room is such a drunk that he appears to be brain-damaged, as he has lost the ability to clean himself, or even speak more than a word or two at a time (most commonly an obscenity, or just "Drink!") In one episode, Father Jack dies and is prepared for burial—only he's not really dead—he just drank a bunch of floor polish and only *appears* to be dead.

*   *   *

MMM-HMM

Even devoted *King of the Hill* fans have a hard time understanding Hank Hill's fast-talking, drawling friend Boomhauer. To voice the character, actor Mike Judge did an impression of an irate caller who left a message on his answering machine in the early 1990s. The message went something like this: "I tell you what, man, that dang ol' Beavis and Butt-head talkin' crazy, man, blowin' up stuff and killin' frogs with bats, man, and that's messed up and you should be shamed o' yerself, man."

WHAT TV STARS EARN

Full disclosure: Uncle John gets nine rubber ducks an hour plus all the free break-room cake he can eat. He should have gone into TV.

• In 2008 **Katie Couric** left *Today*, the top-ranked network morning show, for a $15 million annual deal to anchor *The CBS Evening News.*

• Big, breakout stars earn more, but the **starting wage for an actor on a daytime soap opera** is $700 an episode. A supporting character actor who's been on the show five years can make about $3,000 an episode.

• **Jeremy Piven** plays the supporting role of talent agent Ari Gold on *Entourage* and gets $350,000 per episode. That's almost double the $200,000 paid to the show's star, **Adrien Grenier.** Why the big discrepancy? Probably because Piven has won three Emmys for the role.

• Movie stars who come to TV are well-compensated for the move. **Steve Carell,** who before joining *The Office* starred in movies like *Bruce Almighty* and *Anchorman*, brought in $297,000 an episode.

• When NBC opted to restore the host duties of *The Tonight Show* to Jay Leno in January 2010, it paid current host **Conan O'Brien** $30 million to buy out his contract. He reportedly used $10 million of that to help out writers and staff also left without a job, then brought them along to TBS, where he was paid an initial $10 million annually to host his new talk show, *Conan.* **Jay Leno,** meanwhile, returned to a $25 million yearly salary.

• One star who doesn't make much (relatively speaking): *Hannah Montana* star **Miley Cyrus.** While she's made nearly $1 billion for Disney in ticket sales and merchandising, she earned only $15,000 per episode on the TV series.

• When he was governor of New York, **Eliot Spitzer** took in $179,000 a year, the highest-paid governor in the United States. Forced to resign after a prostitution scandal, Spitzer now works as a pundit and host on CNN...where he makes $500,000 annually.

Remington (throat of) Steele: Pierce Brosnan got his show-biz start working as a circus fire eater.

TV HITS

Sometimes a TV show gets so popular that its audience can't get enough of it, even pushing a song from the show onto the pop chart.

SHOW: *Cheers*
SONG: "Where Everybody Knows Your Name"
STORY: In 1982 songwriter Gary Portnoy was working with collaborator Judy Hart Angelo on tunes for a Broadway musical called *Preppies* when the producer of a new TV sitcom, *Cheers*, asked if he could use one of the songs ("People Like Us") as the show's theme. *Preppies'* producers said no, so Portnoy and Angelo wrote another song for the *Cheers* producers. They didn't like it. So Portnoy and Angelo wrote another one. They didn't like that one, either. Finally, the duo wrote a song called "Where Everybody Knows Your Name." The producers loved it, and used it (sung by Portnoy) to play during *Cheers'* opening credits. The song quickly became a radio hit, but the show, initially, didn't catch on. Eventually, thanks in part to the song's popularity, *Cheers* went on to become one of the biggest shows on TV.

SHOW: *Family Ties*
SONG: "At This Moment"
STORY: L.A.-based pop band Billy Vera and the Beaters had a minor hit in 1981 with this ballad. But they hit the jackpot when the song was featured in three episodes of the show *Family Ties* in 1985 and '86—Alex (Michael J. Fox) and his girlfriend Ellen (Tracy Pollan) called it "their song." Radio stations across the country began getting requests for the once-forgotten song, dug out their copies, and in January 1987, "At This Moment" was the #1 song in the country.

SHOW: *The Greatest American Hero*
SONG: "Believe It or Not"
STORY: In the late 1970s and early '80s, Joey Scarbury was a session singer and songwriter for hire. Then TV composer Mike Post gave him his big break, selecting him to the sing the theme song

for a new show called *The Greatest American Hero*. The song, whose official title is "Theme from *Greatest American Hero* (Believe It or Not)," went to #2 in 1981. The show ran for three seasons, and though Scarbury never had another hit, he continued to write songs for radio and TV.

SHOW: *Welcome Back, Kotter*
SONG: "Welcome Back"
STORY: In 1975 TV producer Alan Sachs was preparing a sitcom called *Kotter*, about a man who returns to his rough Brooklyn neighborhood to teach high school. Sachs told his agent, Dave Bendet, that he wanted a "Lovin' Spoonful or John Sebastian type of song" to use for the theme. The Lovin' Spoonful (with Sebastian as its lead singer) had had a string of pop hits in the 1960s, such as "Do You Believe in Magic?" and "Summer in the City." Coincidentally, Sebastian was also a client of Bendet's, so Sachs quickly hired him. Sebastian wrote a minute-long song called "Welcome Back," which he feared would get rejected because it didn't have the word "Kotter" in it. But Sachs liked the song so much that he changed the name of the show to fit the song—*Kotter* became *Welcome Back, Kotter*. The show was an instant hit in the fall of 1975, fueling demand for the song. Sebastian wrote and recorded a second verse, and the song was released as a single. It went to #1 on the pop chart.

❉   ❉   ❉

HEAD SHOT

In October 1984, filming was underway on the seventh episode of the CBS spy series *Cover Up*. A scene called for actor Jon-Erik Hexum, as CIA agent Mac Harper, to load a gun. Filming was delayed, and Hexum got bored, so he started playing Russian roulette with what he thought was a harmless prop gun. But at close range, blanks can be deadly. Hexum placed the gun to his temple, pulled the trigger, and a blank discharged into his brain. He died six days later. Production on *Cover Up* continued—a new character, portrayed by actor Antony Hamilton, was substituted for the rest of the season. (Hexum's absence was left unexplained.)

QVC's top-selling item in its first year (1977): a helmet that held two cans of beer, with a straw.

LET'S GET *LOST*, PART II

In Part I (page 79), we put all the people in place and summarized season 1. Hold on—the story gets even more complicated (and bizarre).

THE STATION

The hatch is found to be the entrance to the Swan Station, which was originally manned by a group of scientists called the Dharma Initiative, short for "Department of Heuristics and Research on Material Applications." (*Heuristics* is a method of solving problems through testing out various solutions.)

After discovering the island in the late 1960s, a wealthy Danish scientist named Alvar Hanso helped create and fund Dharma. Gathering the world's best minds, Dharma built a neighborhood on the island along with several science stations, one of which—the Hydra—housed polar bears. (Mystery solved!) Shrouded in secrecy, as explained in an unearthed orientation film, Dharma studied the island's "unique electromagnetic properties."

Living inside the hatch is Desmond Hume (Henry Ian Cusick), the one who turned on the light when Locke asked for a sign from the island. (Another mystery solved!) Several years earlier, Desmond quit a Scottish monastery and fell in love with Penelope Widmore (Sonya Walger), but Penny's rich father, Charles Widmore (Alan Dale), didn't approve—he thought Desmond was a coward. So Desmond entered an around-the-world yacht race...and crashed on the island. (While training for the race, Desmond met Jack in L.A. and somehow knew they'd meet again.) Desmond's yacht was given to him by Libby (Cynthia Watros), who would later crash on the island in the tail section of Flight 815 and fall for Hurley before being shot and killed by Michael at the end of season 2. (Got it?)

DHARMA BUMS

When Desmond awoke on the beach in a haze, he was taken to the Swan by a Dharma member named Kelvin (Clancy Brown), the same man who'd taught Sayid how to torture prisoners in Iraq a decade earlier. Kelvin informs Desmond that he can't go outside because the air is radioactive. Desmond later discovers that that's a lie, but is uncertain as to whether the rest of Kelvin's story is true: Kelvin tells him that the Numbers (remember them?) must be entered into an old computer every 108 minutes in order to "save the world." Kelvin shows Desmond the Dharma orientation film, which explains that an "Incident" occurred at that site many years earlier that nearly destroyed the island... and the world. But then Desmond accidentally kills Kelvin and must enter the Numbers alone every 108 minutes for three mind-numbing years to prevent another Incident.

THE LEADER

During season 2, Michael negotiates with the Others for Walt's return. In exchange, the Lostaways have to turn over a man named Henry Gale (Michael Emerson), who says his hot air balloon crashed on the island. As season 3 develops, it becomes very clear that freeing Henry Gale would turn out to be a very, very bad idea. He is big liar. First of all, his name isn't Henry Gale; it's Benjamin Linus. And he didn't crash in a balloon—he's the leader of the Others, who have had a civilization on another part of the island for years. Ben is also a master manipulator (a potent quality in a leader), and once freed, he kidnaps Jack and threatens to kill Jack's girlfriend Kate if Jack doesn't remove the cancerous tumor Ben just found out he has on his spine.

LOVE RECTANGLE

Ben's right-hand man is the mysterious Richard Alpert (Nestor Carbonell), who, through what is apparently another mystical effect of the island, does not age. Flashbacks show Richard's back-story—before island life, he was in Miami, trying to recruit Dr. Juliet Burke (Elizabeth Mitchell) to work with the Others' scientific community on trying to unlock the secrets of the island.

Juliet had once cured her sister's cancer and made the infertile woman fertile again. The Others wanted to know how she did it, and whether it has anything to do with why women who get pregnant on the island happen to die during their second trimester. Juliet comes to the island and the Others hold her captive, but she doesn't find a cure for any of the Others' problems.

At this point in season 3, Juliet and Jack convince their captor, Ben, to free them and let them go home on a submarine the Others happen to have lying around. Oops! They can't go, because Locke blows up the sub. Why? Ben *made* him do it, in a complicated, manipulative attempt to get Juliet to stay on the island—Ben loves her. But Juliet doesn't love Ben—she loves Jack, but falls out of love with Jack when she realizes that Jack loves Kate. Juliet tries to love Sawyer, but he also loves Kate. Result: Everyone is miserable.

THE VALENZETTI EQUATION

After the Cuban Missile Crisis nearly led to nuclear war in 1962, the Hanso Foundation (at the behest of the U.N.) hired a Princeton University professor named Enzo Valenzetti to formulate a mathematical equation that could predict the end of the world. He came up with six numbers, each one a "core value" that represents human and environmental factors: $4 + 8 + 15 + 16 + 23 + 42 = 108$. It became known as the Valenzetti Equation. Dharma mathematicians ran this over and over with different variables in the hopes of changing one of the six numbers, thus staving off our extinction. They could not.

Making matters worse, Dharma inadvertently broadcast the Numbers off the island, and they were picked up half a world away by two soldiers. One went crazy and killed himself. The other went crazy and ended up in a mental hospital…where he passed on the Numbers to Hurley. Lesson: Do not mess with the Numbers. Hurley did, and they brought him misery. The first time Desmond failed to enter them into the computer—in September 2004—flight 815 was flying over the island. The electromagnetic pulse that followed caused the plane to crash.

When the numbers don't get entered a second time, the sky turns purple, the Swan implodes, and Desmond sees the future. He tells Charlie, "No matter what I do, brutha, you're gonna die." So Charlie sacrifices his life to warn his friends that an approaching freighter, which they've just spotted, may not be there to help them. (And that's where season 3 ends.)

HOSTILE TAKEOVER

So what happened to Dharma? Most of the workers were destroyed in the "Purge of 1992" by a group that Dharma called the Hostiles (a.k.a. the Others). The Hostiles believe that *they* are the island's protectors.

In fact, years before he became an Other, Ben was in Dharma.

He actually grew up in their island colony, but when he saw the ghost of his dead mother in the jungle one day, he yearned to know what was on the other side the sonic fence that Dharma had built to keep out the Hostiles. He eventually did find the Hostiles and was looked after by Richard, who was much kinder than his own abusive, alcoholic father. When Ben grew up, he rejoined Dharma and orchestrated the Purge, gassing all but two of the Dharma folk (the last surviving member was Kelvin).

TIME BANDITS

A big revelation with major ramifications in season 4 of *Lost*: The island can be moved through both space and time. How? All you have to do is turn an ancient frozen wheel deep underground in another Dharma station ("Orchid")—it's right next to a chamber of glowing light.

Ben knows about this, and turns the wheel to save the island from a fleet of Charles Widmore's invading mercenaries that arrive on a freighter. Ben is transported to the Sahara Desert three years in the future. But Ben doesn't turn the wheel far enough; it gets stuck and causes the island to start skipping through time, taking the Lostaways with it. They go back about 1,000 years, to when a 250-foot-tall statue still stood on the island. It depicted Taweret, the Egyptian goddess of birth and rebirth.

The island continues time-jumping, and the Lostaways are taken to the 1940s, shortly after a U.S. Army regiment brought a nuclear bomb to the island. Coincidentally, those soldiers were killed by the Others/Hostiles, under the direction of a young Charles Widmore, who would later be banished by Ben and spend his considerable wealth trying to locate and return to the island. What happened to the nuclear bomb? It got buried. (Don't worry—it'll come up later.)

THAT '70s SHOW

Among the time-traveling Lostaways is Daniel Faraday (Jeremy Davies), an eccentric physicist who came to the island in late 2004 aboard Widmore's freighter. Faraday informs Locke that the only way to stop the island from skipping is to turn the wheel again. Locke does so and disappears. The remaining Lostaways—Sawyer, Juliet, Jin, and Faraday, among others—end up in 1974.

Posing as shipwreck victims, they convince Dharma that they are *not* Hostiles, don their beige uniform jumpsuits, and join the Initiative. Sawyer becomes chief of security, and he and Juliet fall in love, get engaged, and live together in the same house that Ben will live in 30 years later.

THE REUNION

When Ben turned the wheel, the island disappeared to a new location, leaving Jack, Kate, Sun, Hurley, Sayid, and Aaron (still a baby in this scenario) stranded in a helicopter...with no fuel. The freighter they were supposed to land on had just blown up (because Ben recruited Michael from the mainland to infiltrate Widmore's freighter crew and destroy the ship). The 'copter crashes in what has suddenly become the middle of the ocean, but the survivors are soon saved by Penny, who, like her father, had been looking for the island. (She'd actually been looking for her lost love, Desmond.)

The six Lostaways are rescued. (The "ghost" of Christian separated Claire from Aaron in the jungle—Claire goes nuts and "raises" a dead squirrel instead, while Kate adopts Aaron.) To protect the island from being found by Widmore, Jack, on Locke's advice, orders the "Oceanic Six" to lie and say they're the only survivors of the crash. It leads to a rough three years back home: Hurley returns to the mental institution; Jack marries Kate, but he gets addicted to pain medication and she leaves him. Then Locke shows up after turning the wheel and convinces the Oceanic Six that they must go back to the island and save their friends.

Somehow, Ben is also in L.A. After he convinces Sayid to assassinate Widmore's group, Ben learns from Locke that the Oceanic Six are preparing to return. Ben murders Locke and puts his body on Ajira Airlines flight 316, trying to set up the same scenario that got Oceanic Flight 815 to the island. With Locke's body on board, as well as the Oceanic Six (sans Aaron) and a few other interested parties, the plane crash-lands on the island. However, only some of the passengers—including Ben, Sun, and dead Locke—remain in the present. Jack, Kate, Sayid, and Hurley find themselves stuck in 1977, setting up a reunion with their fellow Lostaways in the Dharma Initiative.

If your brain hasn't completely seized up, turn to page 494 for the final installment.

THE TEST PATTERN

A blast from the late-night-television past.

SAY GOOD NIGHT, GRACIE

People of a certain age remember when television broadcasts ended late at night. Until they resumed early the next morning, all that could be seen on the TV was a "test pattern" or "test card." These were configurations of lines and black-and-white shades used to calibrate both transmission equipment and old-style TV sets. They're rarely seen today; most TV stations now broadcast 24 hours a day, and televisions no longer require calibrating. (Modern "color bar" patterns are still used by broadcasters, and once in a while you can see them pop up late at night.)

The most widely used of the old test patterns was the "Indian Head Test Card," so named because it included an image of a Native American man, complete with feathered war headdress. Created in 1938 by RCA, it became a standard part of television broadcasts in many parts of the United States from the late 1940s until the 1970s, the end of the test-card era.

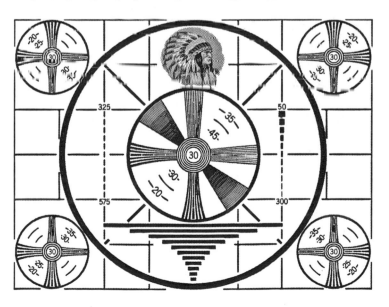

The Indian Head Test Card was also used in Canada, Sweden, Rhodesia, and Venezuela.

HELLO, LARRY

Larry David, the co-creator of Seinfeld, *went on to write and star in* Curb Your Enthusiasm, *which has an even quirkier take on the minutiae of daily life. Here are some observations from his* Curb *character (also named Larry David).*

"I'd rather have thieves than neighbors. The thieves don't impose. Thieves just want your things; neighbors want your time."

"Switzerland is a place where they don't like to fight, so they get people to do their fighting for them while they ski and eat chocolate."

"Do you think we really needed Alaska and Hawaii? They ruined the continental United States. Ruined it!"

To the president of ABC: "Here's a question for *Who Wants to Be a Millionaire:* What kind of an idiot is running ABC?"

"Grape works as a soda. Sort of as a gum. I wonder why it doesn't work as a pie."

"What is this compulsion to have people over to your house and serve them food and talk to them?"

"It's silly to put a napkin on an old pair of pants."

"An employee is told that the customer's always right and, in fact, the customer is usually a moron."

"I just can't stand the sound of the human voice."

"I'm not really too worried about the global warming. People like it a little warmer, don't they?"

"Nobody likes to fly. I don't even like to drive. And I don't like walking."

"Anyone can be confident with a full head of hair. But a confident bald man—there's your diamond in the rough."

"I pee sitting down. It's more comfortable. When you get up during the night you don't have to turn on the light and wake up. And you get to read. While you're peeing all over your shoe, I'm learning something."

Courteney Cox was the only cast member of *Friends* never to earn an Emmy nomination.

CASTING COINCIDENCES

Hollywood is a small town.

BILL MURRAY AND LORENZO MUSIC

When the 1984 film *Ghostbusters* was adapted into a TV cartoon called *The Real Ghostbusters* in 1986, star Bill Murray declined to provide the voice for his character, Dr. Peter Venkman. So producers used actor Lorenzo Music, best known for voicing comic strip cat Garfield in several TV specials. (He actually sounded a lot like Murray.) Murray still had veto power over who would get the job, though, and upon seeing the finished cartoon, he quipped that Dr. Venkman sounded too much "like Garfield." Music was fired and replaced. Music died in 2001, so producers needed someone new for the voice of Garfield for 2004's big-screen *Garfield: The Movie*. Who got the role? Bill Murray.

LAUREN GRAHAM AND MAURA TIERNEY

The 1995–99 sitcom *NewsRadio* co-starred Maura Tierney as reporter Lisa Miller. In 1997 Lauren Graham joined the cast for four episodes as an "office-efficiency consultant." Flash forward seven years to Bravo's *Celebrity Poker Showdown* tournament. Who won? Tierney. Who'd she beat? Lauren Graham. And the program was hosted by Dave Foley…who was also in the *NewsRadio* cast. Five years later, Tierney was signed to star in the NBC series *Parenthood*, but had to drop out when she was diagnosed with breast cancer. Her role was recast…with Lauren Graham.

ADRIAN PASDAR AND MILO VENTIMIGLIA

In 2003 *Gilmore Girls* producers devoted two episodes of the series to introduce a proposed spin-off featuring teen character Jess (Milo Ventimiglia), who movies to California to live with his father, whom he has just met. A casting agent almost cast character actor Adrian Pasdar (*Judging Amy*, *Profit*) as Jess' father because of his striking resemblance to Ventimiglia. Remarking that they looked more like brothers than father and son, the agent hired Rob Estes for the role instead. (The spin-off didn't get picked up.) In 2006 Ventimiglia and Pasdar both got roles on NBC's superhero drama *Heroes*, in which they played…brothers.

Annette O'Toole played Superman's girlfriend in *Superman III*, and his mother on *Smallville*.

LOST TV PILOTS

More ill-fated TV shows that were interesting enough for a single episode…but too strange (or awful) to be picked up as a series.

Alias Sherlock Holmes (1976)
A Los Angeles motorcycle cop (played by Larry Hagman) whose hobby is reading Sherlock Holmes novels gets injured in a crash, wakes up with amnesia, and thinks that he actually *is* Sherlock Holmes. Despite the mental condition, he returns to his police beat and solves crimes with his newly acquired "master detective skills." His sidekick is a psychologist (Jenny O'Hara) who happens to be named Dr. Watson.

Time of the Devil (1977)
Writer Andy Stuart (Dack Rambo) has an ill-advised love affair with a woman who's already spoken for—she's Satan's girlfriend. When a cabal of satanists kidnap her, Andy hires an exorcist (Dan O'Herlily) to find his lost love and help him vanquish demons along the way.

Divided We Stand (1988)
By the 1980s, families split apart by divorce were increasingly common, and TV producers tried to respond to the cultural trend with shows like this one. On this hour-long show, the first half focuses on the adventures of 10-year-old Cody (Seth Green) at his dad's house. In the second half, he heads over to mom's place.

Chain Letter (1988)
Acting on behalf of Satan, "The Messenger of Death" (Ian McShane, who later played Al Swearengen on *Deadwood*) sends out letters to humans offering various temptations. If the recipient takes the bait, they die and go to hell.

Crash Island (1981)
A charter flight carrying a high school swim team to Hawaii crashes on a deserted island. The teens (along with the plane's

mechanic, played by Harlem Globetrotter Meadowlark Lemon) are forced to fend for themselves and create a new society. Helping the them survive is a lost Japanese soldier (Pat Morita) who has learned to live off the land, having been stranded there for decades. *Variety* called *Crash Island* "a cross between *Gilligan's Island* and *The Bad News Bears*."

The Stranger (1973)
Astronaut Neil Stryker (Glenn Corbett) returns to Earth after a long voyage in outer space. Only he doesn't land on Earth—he lands on Terra, an alternate Earth that's "hidden behind the sun." It's exactly like Earth, except it's under global fascist rule. Once Stryker starts speaking out about the values of freedom and liberty, he's forced to go on the run from the totalitarian leaders and attempt to return home.

Ben Blue's Brothers (1965)
In this wacky family comedy, four brothers clash because they're all so different: one is a hobo, another an aristocrat, one's a vaudeville performer, and another is a regular guy. The kicker: all four brothers were portrayed by comedian and character actor Ben Blue (*The Big Broadcast of 1938*). The only character not portrayed by Blue is the brothers' mother.

The Many Wives of Patrick (1980)
Think *Lost* had a lot of characters and plots to keep track of? This show is about a man who has been married six times and has to juggle relationships and visitation schedules with his six ex-wives and more than a dozen children.

Superpup (1958)
Adventures of Superman ended production in 1958, but producer Whitney Ellsworth had an idea for a spin-off that would allow him to continue producing shows in the Superman universe, and more importantly, to reuse the old show's sets to save money. His idea: *Superpup*. This show, set in a dog-populated Metropolis, featured human actors in dog suits playing dog versions of Superman characters such as reporter "Bark Bent" and newspaper editor "Terry Bite."

SHOWS WITHIN SHOWS

TV characters tune into TV, too. Here's what they watch.

- **Futurama** takes place in the year 3000, when the world has become a very different place. The most popular show on TV is *Everybody Loves Hypnotoad*, starring an alien toad who emits a hypnotic electronic noise while his eyes swirl around, entrancing all who watch…which is precisely why it's the most popular show.

- **South Park** hit the airwaves in 1997, and family and TV decency advocates decried its pervasive scatological humor and foul-mouthed grade-schoolers. To satirize the controversy, the *South Park* creators made up a TV show for the kids of *South Park* to watch:
Terrance and Philip, which consists entirely of two Canadian men farting, then laughing uproariously.

- **Oz**, set in a maximum-security prison, is one of the darkest, most violent shows ever to air. The characters watch an educational show for preschoolers called **Miss Sally's Schoolyard**, starring a young blond woman who is very well endowed.

- **The O.C.** was a teen soap set in wealthy Newport Beach, in Southern California; characters on *The O.C.* watched **The Valley**, a teen soap also set in a wealthy area of Southern California. *The Valley*, then, is a parody of *The O.C.* The lead actor on *The Valley* is in his late 20s and plays a 16-year-old (just like his O.C. counterpart, Ben McKenzie), and two actors from the *Valley*, the ingenue and the nerd, date in real life—just like O.C. stars Rachel Bilson and Adam Brody.

- **Dinosaurs** was a 1991–94 Jim Henson-produced satire of family sitcoms—all the characters were dinosaurs. **Ask Mr. Lizard** was its parody of *Watch Mr. Wizard*, a kiddie science show from the 1950s hosted by Don "Mr. Wizard" Herbert. Herbert would always have a child assist him, and so did Mr. Lizard, although every week, "Timmy" would be killed or maimed by an experiment gone awry. "We're gonna need another Timmy," Mr. Lizard would yell to a stagehand at the end of every segment.

THE TOP 10

A look at the top 10 shows on TV over the past 60 years.

1949–1950
1) *Texaco Star Theater*
2) *The Ed Sullivan Show*
3) *Arthur Godfrey's Talent Scouts*
4) *Fireball Fun for All*
5) *Philco Television Playhouse*
6) *Fireside Theatre*
7) *The Goldbergs*
8) *Suspense*
9) *Ford Theater*
10) *Cavalcade of Stars*

1954–1955
1) *I Love Lucy*
2) *The Jackie Gleason Show*
3) *Dragnet*
4) *You Bet Your Life*
5) *The Ed Sullivan Show*
6) *Disneyland*
7) *The Bob Hope Show*
8) *The Jack Benny Program*
9) *The Martha Raye Show*
10) *The George Gobel Show*

1959–1960
1) *Gunsmoke*
2) *Wagon Train*
3) *Have Gun–Will Travel*
4) *The Danny Thomas Show*
5) *The Red Skelton Show*
6) *Father Knows Best*
7) *77 Sunset Strip*
8) *The Price is Right*
9) *Wanted: Dead or Alive*
10) *Perry Mason*

1964–1965
1) *Bonanza*
2) *Bewitched*
3) *Gomer Pyle, USMC*
4) *The Andy Griffith Show*
5) *The Fugitive*
6) *The Red Skelton Hour*
7) *The Dick Van Dyke Show*
8) *The Lucy Show*
9) *Peyton Place*
10) *Combat*

1969–1970
1) *Laugh-In*
2) *Gunsmoke*
3) *Bonanza*
4) *Mayberry R.F.D.*
5) *Family Affair*
6) *Here's Lucy*
7) *The Red Skelton Hour*
8) *Marcus Welby, M.D.*
9) *The Wonderful World of Disney*
10) *The Doris Day Show*

1974–1975
1) *All in the Family*
2) *Sanford and Son*
3) *Chico and the Man*
4) *The Jeffersons*
5) *M*A*S*H*
6) *Rhoda*
7) *The Waltons*
8) *Good Times*
9) *Maude*
10) *Hawaii Five-O*

TV *Guide*'s pick for best commercial ever: Apple's "1984," which aired only once. (In 1984.)

1979–1980
1) 60 Minutes
2) Three's Company
3) M*A*S*H
4) Alice
5) Dallas
6) Flo
7) The Jeffersons
8) The Dukes of Hazzard
9) That's Incredible!
10) One Day at a Time

1984–1985
1) Dynasty
2) Dallas
3) The Cosby Show
4) 60 Minutes
5) Family Ties
6) The A Team
7) Simon & Simon
8) Murder, She Wrote
9) Knots Landing
10) Falcon Crest

1989–1990
1) Roseanne
2) The Cosby Show
3) Cheers
4) A Different World
5) America's Funniest Home Videos
6) The Golden Girls
7) 60 Minutes
8) The Wonder Years
9) Empty Nest
10) Monday Night Football

1994–1995
1) Seinfeld
2) ER
3) Home Improvement
4) Grace Under Fire
5) Monday Night Football
6) 60 Minutes
7) NYPD Blue
8) Murder, She Wrote
9) Friends
10) Roseanne

1999–2000
1) Who Wants to be a Millionaire?
2) Who Wants to be a Millionaire?
3) Who Wants to be a Millionaire?
4) ER
5) Friends
6) Monday Night Football
7) Frasier
8) 60 Minutes
9) The Practice
10) Touched By an Angel

2004–2005
1) American Idol (Tues.)
2) CSI
3) American Idol (Wed.)
4) Desperate Housewives
5) Survivor: Palau
6) Survivor: Vanuatu
7) CSI: Miami
8) Without a Trace
9) Everybody Loves Raymond
10) Grey's Anatomy

2009–2010
1) American Idol (Tues.)
2) American Idol (Wed.)
3) Dancing With the Stars (Mon.)
4) Sunday Night Football
5) NCIS
6) Undercover Boss
7) The Mentalist
7) CSI
9) NCIS: Los Angeles
10) Dancing With the Stars (Tues.)

First coronation on TV: King George VI (1937). First broadcast live: Queen Elizabeth II ('53).

BACK FROM THE DEAD

Not even cancellation can keep a good show down.

The New Adventures of Perry Mason (1973–74)
Viewers were riveted by the original *Perry Mason* during its 1957–66 run, and CBS revived the courtroom drama in the early '70s, not that long after it left the air. Not returning: the iconic theme song "Park Avenue Beat," star Raymond Burr (TV veteran Monte Markham took over the role), and viewers. Succumbing to stiff competition (NBC's *The Wonderful World of Disney* and ABC's *The F.B.I.*), *New Adventures* was canceled after 15 episodes. However, the crafty attorney eventually did return to TV in 1985 with a string of 30 made-for-TV movies on NBC, with Raymond Burr back in the title role.

The New Leave It to Beaver (1983–89)
Riding a wave of '50s nostalgia, in 1983 CBS aired a *Leave It to Beaver* reunion movie called *Still the Beaver*, which updated the stories of all the comedy's characters. Now an adult, Beaver (Jerry Mathers) was divorced and living at home with his widowed mother (Barbara Billingsley). Wally (Tony Dow) lived next door with his family. Eddie Haskell still lived down the street, and his son, Freddie, was as smarmy and manipulative as his father had been as a kid. Ratings were so good that the Disney Channel decided to make a series based on the show. It fit in with the network's family programming and lasted for one season there before Ted Turner purchased the rights. It ran for another four seasons on TBS, now called *The New Leave It to Beaver*. Though the new show was little-watched, it's technically the most successful sitcom revival in TV history, with 104 episodes produced.

The Twilight Zone (1985–89, 2002–03)
In 1983 Steven Spielberg produced a feature-film version of the classic paranormal anthology *The Twilight Zone*, remaking well-known segments of the 1959–64 series. Box-office sales were tepid, but in 1985 CBS went ahead with a new TV incarnation. Because creator and main writer Rod Serling died in 1975, the new series

featured stories based on the works of major horror and science-fiction authors Stephen King, Arthur C. Clarke, and Harlan Elli-son. (The first episode starred Bruce Willis in a story about a mean-spirited businessman battling his good-natured doppel-gänger.) An old *Twilight Zone* bit player named Charles Aidman filled Serling's role as host. The Grateful Dead rerecorded the show's famous theme song. Despite its pedigree, this new *Twilight Zone* was clobbered in the ratings by ABC's Friday-night family shows *Webster* and *Mr. Belvedere*. CBS canceled it in early 1987, midway through its second season, although new episodes were produced for syndication until 1989. In 2002 the struggling UPN network revived *The Twilight Zone* yet again, remaking episodes from the original series. Forrest Whitaker took over as host, and rock band Korn updated the theme song. It lasted a single season.

The Fugitive (2000–01)

The 1993 film version of the 1963–67 TV series brought in a whopping $180 million at the box office. So making an updated series of it seemed like a no-brainer for CBS. Actor Tim Daly (*Wings*) was cast as the new Dr. Kimble, but his efforts to find the mysterious "one-armed man" who killed his wife were cut short after a single season. Why did it fail? Probably for the same reason that locally aired reruns of the original *The Fugitive* flopped in the 1970s—everybody knew how it was going to end. (Bonus: CBS was so sure that *The Fugitive* would be a hit that it placed an unas-suming new crime show directly after it, hoping to boost its rat-ings. That show: *CSI.*)

Knight Rider (2008–09)

Despite previous failures to revive the 1980s action series with made-for-TV movies in 1991 and 1994, and the short-lived 1997 action series *Team Knight Rider,* NBC dusted off KITT, the talking car, and tried once again in 2008. The supercharged car was fitted with impressive upgrades, including fancier weapons, the ability to change colors, and the voice of Val Kilmer. Justin Bruening starred as Mike Traceur, son of the original *Knight Rider*'s Michael Knight (played by David Hasselhoff, who makes a cameo appear-ance). A highly rated TV movie kicked off the series…which nonetheless flopped, and was tossed on the scrap heap after just 16 episodes.

STRANGE TIE-INS

Tie-in products are supposed to promote a TV show. But sometimes the merchandisers pick some really odd things to sell.

The Show: In a 2008 plot arc on *The Office*, paper company manager Jan Levinson (Melora Hardin) gets fired and moves in with her boyfriend, Michael Scott (Steve Carell), the show's lead character. Bored at home with nothing to do all day, Jan starts a candlemaking business: Serenity by Jan. They're foul-smelling candles—one character remarks that, when lit, they smell "like fire."
Weird Official Merchandise: NBC, which airs *The Office*, has a real website—serenitybyjancandles.com—where fans can buy actual candles, supposedly made by "Jan." Price—$15.

The Show: The premise of the popular HBO series *True Blood* is that vampires now live openly alongside humans due to the invention of a bottled synthetic blood substitute called Tru Blood. A running joke is that it tastes terrible—and not like blood at all—so most vampires end up finding ways to drink human blood instead.
Weird Official Merchandise: A soft drink called Tru Blood, produced by Omni Consumer Products, is now available in stores. (One reporter noted that it must have been a challenge to "mimic the taste of badly-mimicked blood.") The drink is actually just blood-orange-flavored soda and doesn't look or taste like blood at all.

The Show: Comedy Central's *The Jeff Dunham Show* was a variety program starring ventriloquist Jeff Dunham and his various puppets. His humor is like the "redneck" or politically incorrect humor of comedians like Larry the Cable Guy. He's even been accused of racism—his puppets include a Muslim one named Achmed the Dead Terrorist and a Mexican one named José the Jalapeño.
Weird Official Merchandise Surprisingly, one of the products released to promote the show was a line of expensive wines named after the crude puppets. Varietals include an "Achmed Syrah" for $45 and a "Peanut Riesling" for $26, named after another of Dunham's dummies. (It's not made from peanuts.)

During the 2007 Super Bowl, Hallmark Channel aired a marathon of Hallmark card commercials.

COPS STORY

COPS has been a Saturday night TV staple for so long—23 seasons as of September 2010—that it's easy to forget what a groundbreaking show it was when it debuted in 1989.

FIRST-PERSON PERSPECTIVE

In the early 1980s, an aspiring filmmaker named John Langley began work on *Cocaine Blues*, a documentary about the crack cocaine epidemic sweeping the country. As part of the project, he filmed law-enforcement operations, including drug busts and police raids.

At first Langley obtained the footage as an objective bystander, but that ended when an officer invited him to suit up in tactical gear and follow the police as they moved in. For the first time, Langley understood the stress and danger (and the adrenaline rush) that police experience daily. And the footage he shot during the raid was some of the most compelling he'd ever seen. He thought it might be possible to build an entire show around it.

KEEPING IT REAL

As Langley developed the idea for a show he called *Street Beat*, he decided it should be presented in a minimalist, *cinema verité* style—the edited footage would be presented as-is, without a narrator, script, music, staged reenactments, much editing, or any other standard TV storytelling conventions to distract the viewing audience. He didn't want a host or anyone else telling people what to think about what they were seeing.

Langley believed that such a show would be successful, but ABC, CBS, and NBC weren't convinced and passed on the idea. Even Langley's business partner, Malcolm Barbour, was skeptical. The concept was *so* unusual, and even if it was a good idea, it wasn't clear that a beginner like Langley would be able to pull it off.

With no takers for *Street Beat*, Langley and Barbour's production company spent the next few years producing a series of crime-themed syndicated TV specials (which included footage of police

---

First choice to play Marshall Matt Dillon on *Gunsmoke*: John Wayne.

ride-alongs) hosted by Geraldo Rivera. The specials were very successful and helped to raise Langley's profile in the TV business. But if he thought that would make it easier for him to find a buyer for the show he now called *COPS*, he was wrong: ABC, CBS, and NBC still said no.

THE ROOKIE

By 1987, however, there was a new player in network television: Fox. The upstart network had been on the air since October 1986, but few of its shows were successful. Fox was struggling not just to stay afloat but also to forge an identity distinct from the Big 3 networks—its survival strategy was to put unusual new shows on the air. And thanks to a looming TV writers' strike that looked like it might drag on for months, Fox was particularly interested in shows that didn't require writers or scripts.

Langley and Barbour put together a reel of the best police-raid footage from the Geraldo crime specials and made a sales pitch to three Fox executives: CEO Barry Diller; programming head Steve Chao; and a third, unidentified man who sat in the corner taking notes—Langley assumed he was an accountant. After they made their presentation, the man taking notes, who turned out to be Fox chairman Rupert Murdoch, told Diller, "order four of 'em." Langley and Barbour had a deal.

COP-SPAN

To film the pilot, Langley went to the same person he'd gone to when he needed police footage for his Geraldo specials: Sheriff Nick Navarro of Broward County, Florida. Navarro was bothered by the fact that the public's understanding of law enforcement was informed by fictional and wildly inaccurate movies and TV shows such as *Dirty Harry* and *Miami Vice*. He saw *COPS* as an almost C-SPAN-like chance to depict law enforcement as accurately and honestly as possible, and he believed that such transparency was essential in a free society. He happily allowed Langley to film his officers at work.

If you watch the hour-long *COPS* pilot, you may be surprised at how different it is from the modern version of the show. The most glaring difference is the inclusion of scenes of the officers in their own homes—cooking dinner with their families, watching

TV, and playing with their children. One officer and his wife even argue about their relationship in front of the COPS camera crew. Langley says Fox forced him to insert the cops-at-home footage into the pilot against his better judgement, theorizing that if the *cinema verité* footage didn't hook the audience, the real-life soap opera storylines would. The COPS pilot aired on Saturday, March 11, 1989. Ever since then, the show has aired on Saturday night.

ONE, TWO, THREE

Fox didn't promote COPS very heavily, but the show still managed to find an audience, which grew quickly thanks to positive word of mouth. As it did, Langley set to work stripping out all the features the network had forced on him—background music, the "soap opera" subplots, and the scenes shot at police headquarters, which he believed were unnecessary and much less interesting than scenes of police in the field. In the process, he also developed the three-stories-per-episode format that continues to this day:

• The first segment is a dramatic "action" sequence of some kind, often involving a police chase of a vehicle, or of a suspect on foot.

• The second segment is slower and often contains emotional or humorous content (such as the scene where a suspect repeatedly denies that he uses drugs, not realizing that he has a marijuana cigarette tucked behind his ear until the officer plucks it out).

• The third segment aims to give the audience something to think about, such as the methods used to take an uncooperative suspect into custody, or the social costs associated with treating drug addiction as a criminal problem instead of a public health issue.

BAD BOYS, BAD BOYS

Twenty-three years and more than 800 episodes later, COPS remains the most successful reality series on network television. Its role in shaping the public's perception of law enforcement has been profound, and it has produced an entire generation of officers who first developed an interest in police work while watching COPS when they were kids.

Perhaps the show's most unusual claim to fame is how it turned its "Bad Boys" theme song into the most quotable, if not the most famous, reggae song in history. From the beginning, Langley wanted *COPS* to be the first-ever network show with a reggae theme song, and while filming the pilot in Florida he had his field producers scour local record stores in search of just the right song. Someone found "Bad Boys," sung by the Jamaican band Inner Circle. "I said, 'That's it, that's the song,' Langley remembers. 'I mean, it was just too good. You know, "…bad boys, bad boys, what you gonna do, what you gonna do when they come for you?" It was just too perfect.'" The song was released as a single in 1993 and hit the Top 10.

MAKING THE SHOW

• In a typical week of production, as many as a dozen two-person COPS film crews are riding along with police officers all over the U.S. Most production takes place during warmer months, when crooks are more likely to be out and about. That explains why you hardly ever see a police chase in the snow…but you see plenty of suspects who are sweaty and shirtless.

• On average, it takes about 18 hours of unedited police footage to produce the 22 minutes of material that make up an episode.

• COPS has been filmed in Hong Kong, Great Britain, Russia… but never in Canada. Why not? "Canada has far less crime than we do in the States," Langley told the *Ottawa Citizen* in 2008.

"I'M ON TV!"

• If you (like Uncle John) live in terror of *COPS* filming in your town on that one worst day of your life, when you're drunk, half naked, and screaming in the middle of the street, fear not: COPS can't show your face on TV without your consent. Every face shown on the program is the face of a person who has signed a release form.

• In the early years, getting suspects to sign the release forms wasn't easy; many faces had to be digitally blurred as a result. But now that the show is famous, more than 90% of suspects sign them. "When they hear that we're not a news camera, that we're COPS, they generally exclaim, 'Oh, that's great! When will I be on?'" Langley says.

WORST SHOW TITLES

Many shows don't make it past season one. And some seem doomed right from the start—because of their awful titles. Like these.

Heil Honey I'm Home (1990). This British show, a parody of 1950s sitcoms, was about Adolf Hitler and Eva Braun, who get upset when a Jewish couple moves in next door. After thousands of callers complained that it trivialized the Holocaust, the show was canceled after one episode.

Testees (2008). On this FX comedy, two slackers work as research subjects for a company that tests drugs, chemicals, and other products.

Tattooed Teenage Alien Fighters From Beverly Hills (1994). Shortly after Fox's *Mighty Morphin' Power Rangers* became the hottest thing in kids' TV (and tie-in merchandise) in 1993, more kung-fu-and-robots shows weren't far behind. Fox's *VR Troopers* and *Big Bad Beetleborgs* and USA's *Tattooed Teenage Alien Fighters From Beverly Hills* all centered around teenagers using martial arts to fight giant robot aliens. *Power Rangers* lasted more than 17 years—the others, two or less.

Poochinski (1990). An NBC comedy about a cop reincarnated as a talking bulldog.

Whoops! (1992). The six survivors of an accidental worldwide nuclear apocalypse try to rebuild society in this ill-conceived sitcom. It was killed off after 10 episodes.

Having Babies (1978). A title change to *Julie Farr, M.D.* couldn't save this short-lived ABC medical drama about an obstetrician.

Too Something (1995). Creators of this short-lived Fox buddy comedy couldn't come up with a name for it by the time it hit the air, so they used its vague working title. A month into its run, Fox held a Rename the Show contest as a promotion. When it returned to the air six months later, the show had been renamed *New York Daze*. Then it was canceled.

Network TV's first female/female romantic kiss was on…

The Rerun Show (2002). This NBC summer-replacement series had an interesting concept: Veteran comedy actors remade old episodes of popular sitcoms (including *Saved By the Bell*, *The Facts of Life*, and *Bewitched*) using the actual scripts and faithfully recreated sets and costumes. But since summer is traditionally when networks air actual reruns, a series called *The Rerun Show* confused audiences. It was canceled after three episodes.

$#! My Dad Says* (2010). This was America's first sitcom based on a Twitter feed, and also the first to feature profanity in the title (although CBS promoted it as "Bleep My Dad Says").

Manimal (1983). An NBC crime-drama about a guy who helps cops solve crimes by transforming himself into various animals, such as dolphins and cougars. One of the most legendary bombs in TV history, it lasted eight episodes.

The Nutt House (1989). Mel Brooks developed this NBC sitcom about a run-down New York hotel. Cloris Leachman starred as proprietor Edwina Nutt, as well as the maid Mrs. Frick. The show lasted six weeks.

The Hat Squad (1992). A drama about three twenty-something orphans who team up to fight crime. Why the title? They all wear fedoras, all the time.

Shasta McNasty (1999). Three lazy rock musicians (one played by Jake Busey, Gary Busey's son) share a loft in Venice Beach. None of them was named Shasta McNasty. It was canceled after one season.

Johnny Bago (1993). A low-level mob criminal flees his enemies by traveling across the country in a Winnebago. (His name was Johnny, at least.)

It's Like, You Know (1999). This fish-out-of-water comedy was about a cynical New York writer (Chris Eigeman) who moves to Los Angeles, where he encounters nothing but flaky New Age types. Faded movie star Jennifer Grey co-starred as...faded movie star Jennifer Grey. Every episode featured somebody saying, "It's like, you know."

PAUL LYNDE'S GREATEST HITS

On the original Hollywood Squares *game show (1966–81), host Peter Marshall would ask one of the star panelists a question, and the star would give a joke response before the real answer. Comedian Paul Lynde, in the center square, usually delivered the best lines. Like these.*

Marshall: According to the *World Book Encyclopedia*, what is the main reason dogs pant?
Lynde: Because they can't talk dirty.

Marshall: What are "dual purpose" cattle good for that other cattle aren't?
Lynde: They give milk and cookies. I don't recommend the cookies.

Marshall: True or false: Research indicates that Columbus liked to wear bloomers and long stockings.
Lynde: It's not easy to sign a crew up for six months.

Marshall: Burt Reynolds is quoted as saying, "Dinah Shore's in top form. I've never known anyone to be so completely able to throw herself into a..." what?
Lynde: Headboard.

Marshall: Do female frogs croak?
Lynde: If you hold their little heads under water long enough.

Marshall: If the right part comes along, will George C. Scott do a nude scene?
Lynde: You mean he doesn't have the right part?

Marshall: What is the name of the instrument with the light on the end, that the doctor sticks in your ear?
Lynde: Oh, a cigarette.

Marshall: Is it normal for Norwegians to talk to trees?
Lynde: As long as that's as far as it goes.

Marshall: Who are more likely to be romantically responsive: women under 30, or women over 30?
Lynde: I don't have a third choice?

In 1998 employees of the FCC formed an ultimate frisbee team called "Seven Dirty Words."

Marshall: Pride, anger, covetousness, lust, gluttony, envy, and sloth are collectively known as what?
Lynde: The Bill of Rights.

Marshall: The Great White is one of the most feared animals. What is the Great White?
Lynde: A sheriff in Alabama.

Marshall: What do you call a man who gives you diamonds and pearls?
Lynde: I'd call him "darling"!

Marshall: It is the most abused and neglected part of your body. What is it?
Lynde: Mine may be abused, but it certainly isn't neglected!

Marshall: Who stays pregnant for a longer period of time, your wife or your elephant?
Lynde: Who told you about my elephant?

Marshall: Paul, can you get an elephant drunk?
Lynde: Yes, but he still won't go up to your apartment.

Marshall: Nathan Hale, one of the heroes of the American Revolution, was hung. Why?
Lynde: Heredity!

Marshall: Can chewing gum help prevent a child from catching a cold?
Lynde: No, but I know it'll plug a runny nose.

Marshall: Eddie Fisher recently stated, "I'm sorry. I'm sorry for them both." Who or what was he referring to?
Lynde: His fans.

Marshall: If you were pregnant for two years, what would you give birth to?
Lynde: Whatever it is, it would never be afraid of the dark.

*   *   *

NOT PLAYING BALL

On a 2010 episode of *Desperate Housewives*, Renee (Vanessa Williams) and Gabrielle (Eva Longoria) talk about past loves. Renee quips, "Never marry a basketball player." It's an in-joke: Williams's husband was NBA star Rick Fox; Longoria was married to NBA star Tony Parker…until she filed for divorce a few days after the episode aired.

DOCTOR WHO?

In recent years, the British sci-fi legend Doctor Who has enjoyed a resurgence in popularity in the U.S and the U.K. Still, most Americans know little about the Doctor. Here are a few facts to get you going.

WHOVILLE

Doctor Who premiered on England's BBC One on November 23, 1963, and has aired almost continuously ever since (although new episodes weren't produced between 1989 and 2005), making it by far the longest-running science-fiction program on television. With 770 episodes and counting, it's among the longest-lasting prime-time dramas as well.

In the 1970s, it was one of the first British series to air on American TV and became a cult hit. And in England, it's a pop-culture phenomenon—it's spawned radio series, novels, and several tie-in movies. Eavesdrop for long enough in any British pub, and you'll hear patrons arguing over who the best Doctor was. In both countries, *Doctor Who* has had a substantial influence on television. Here's a primer:

The premise. The Doctor (who is known *only* as "the Doctor") is the last of a race called the Time Lords, who are near-omnipotent, hyperintelligent, and keep a strict non-intervention policy—a law the Doctor breaks when he sets out to explore the universe. Along with a human companion (usually a teenager or young woman), the Doctor travels through time and space.

The TARDIS. This time-travel machine (an acronym for "Time and Relative Dimension in Space") resembles a telephone booth on the outside. On the inside, it's the size of several rooms. (Producers originally planned for the TARDIS to change shape and blend with its surroundings wherever it landed, but their paltry budget precluded building a new TARDIS each week, so the phone-booth format was made permanent.)

The Doctor. The role was originated by William Hartnell, who portrayed the Doctor as a cantankerous old man. Three years into the role, however, Hartnell grew ill and had to quit the show.

Quentin Tarantino's showbiz debut was as an Elvis impersonator on *The Golden Girls*.

Rather than end the series, script editor Gerry Davis came up with the idea that the Doctor could "regenerate" when he grows old or gets injured. That conceit has allowed for lead actors to come and go every few years, contributing to the show's longevity. To date, 11 actors have portrayed The Doctor.

The Daleks. The Doctor is pursued by this evil race of mutant aliens, who wear conical metallic suits that make them look like big pepper shakers. They yell "Exterminate!" before blasting their foes with ray guns. (The Doctor doesn't carry a gun—only a "sonic screwdriver.") One of the charms of *Doctor Who* is its cheesy special effects and low-budget soundstage sets, but that's something the show's creator—BBC head of drama Sydney Newman—didn't intend: He wanted *Doctor Who* to be an educational show to teach kids science. But the Daleks, introduced in 1963, proved so popular that the show settled into a serialized drama format. It was soon a Saturday-night ritual for kids and adults alike.

POPULARITY AND DEMISE

The series' peak of popularity was from 1974 to 1981 in both the U.K. and U.S. (It was reportedly PBS's most-watched series.) Its success was due in part to Tom Baker, the curly-haired Doctor with a trademark scarf and witty, exasperated attitude. Ratings hit a high of 16 million viewers in 1979, then slid steadily after Baker "regenerated" into Peter Davison. There was an 18-month production hiatus from 1985 to 1986, and with regular viewers at just three million in 1989, the BBC canceled *Doctor Who* after 26 years and 697 episodes.

REGENERATION

But *Doctor Who* didn't go away. The cottage industry of *Who* radio specials, albums, video games, and merchandise still attracted millions of fans. So, in 1996, the BBC decided to revive it, and to do so in a big way: in the U.S. and the U.K. at the same time. The BBC co-produced a flashy, well-funded made-for-TV movie with the Fox network to serve as a pilot for a new series, although it was technically a continuation of the old series. The May 1996 broadcast was heavily hyped by Fox, but ratings were poor in the United States (it aired against ABC's *Roseanne*).

In 1958 a law was passed prohibiting the use of actors posing as doctors in commercials.

It fared better in the United Kingdom—nine million viewers tuned in—but since Fox paid for the majority of the production, they got the say-so on whether to continue the series, and decided not to. The immortal Doctor looked to stay dead.

But the BBC became interested in *Doctor Who* again in 2003, as the show approached its 40th anniversary. Retrospectives in print and on television inspired them to relaunch *Doctor Who*. Debuting in 2005, with Christopher Eccleston as the roguish Doctor, the series was updated for the new millennium—filmed in high definition on location instead of in a studio, with a bigger budget and better special effects. David Tennant took over as the Doctor from 2005 to 2010, then Matt Smith took the reins. It's a Top 10 show in the U.K.; in the U.S., it's BBC America's top-rated series.

*   *   *

OOPS DOWN UNDER

It was the dramatic finale of the 2010 season of *Australia's Next Top Model*. The competition had came down to two contestants: Kelsey Martinovich and Amanda Ware, and host Sarah Murdoch prepared to announce the winner. "Australia's next top model for 2010 is," she said, pausing to get the news from her earpiece, which had been malfunctioning throughout the episode, "It's you, Kelsey." A stunned Martinovich then gave a brief speech on the live broadcast, gushing and thanking her family and friends.

Runner-up Ware also said a few words. But as she spoke, Murdoch's grin suddenly froze. Then she pulled her earpiece closer to her head, her eyes began darting back and forth, and her jaw dropped open. "Oh, my god. I don't know what to say right now. I'm feeling a bit sick about this. No, I'm so sorry about this. It's Amanda, I'm so sorry." Because of a technical glitch with her earpiece, Murdock had announced the wrong name on national TV.

"It's alright!" Martinovich said cheerfully. "It's an honest mistake." And although she didn't take home the big prize—a spread in *Harper's Bazaar*, a $25,000 Levi's campaign, and a new car—apologetic execs from Granada Television gave her $25,000 and a free trip to New York.

AN AWKWARD CONVERSATION

*Most TV talk shows are filled with mundane chit-chat by
stars plugging their latest movies or books. But every once
in a while, things get a little more intense.*

JOAN RIVERS VS. VICTORIA PRINCIPAL

While guest-hosting *The Tonight Show* in 1983, comedian
Rivers interviewed the *Dallas* star. Principal remarked that
she had just celebrated her 33rd birthday, then later claimed
that she was the first American baby born in Japan immediately
after WWII...which ended in 1945, meaning she was really 38.
Rivers called her out on it, and Principal left in a huff. From
then on, Principal's white lie became regular joke fodder for
Rivers, who went on to host *The Late Show* on Fox in 1986.
While interviewing *Dallas* co-star Ken Kercheval, Rivers got the
idea to call Principal at home to mockingly wish her a happy
birthday. Rivers dialed the number and got a busy signal, so she
asked an operator to break into the line, saying the phone number on TV. Principal still didn't pick up, but was later inundated
with prank phone calls; she successfully sued Rivers and Fox for
$3 million.

BURT REYNOLDS VS. MARC SUMMERS

When Reynolds and *Double Dare* host Summers were both guests
on a 1994 episode of *The Tonight Show*, Summers made a joke
about Reynolds's recent divorce from Loni Anderson. Reynolds
reacted by picking up his mug of water and dumping it in Summers's lap. Summers then tried to dump his mug on Reynolds, but
the actor blocked it, sending it back into Summers's face and
nearly knocking out a tooth. Host Jay Leno quickly cut to a commercial, and when the show returned, he gave each man a cream
pie to duke it out. The pie fight worked, and the two eventually
called a truce. (Summers later claimed that as their faces were
covered in pie, Reynolds whispered to him, "I only did that
because I really like you.")

On NBC's 1985 schedule, *Highway to Heaven* was followed by *Hell Town*.

HOWARD STERN VS. MAGIC JOHNSON

Basketball superstar Magic Johnson went into entertainment in June 1998 with a late-night talk show called *The Magic Hour*. Ratings were low and critics were cruel, criticizing Johnson's mumbling, wooden demeanor, and tendency to fawn over celebrity guests. Nobody was more critical than Howard Stern, who spent a few minutes almost every morning on his radio show detailing and mocking the previous night's *Magic Hour*. Looking for a ratings-boosting confrontation, Johnson invited Stern onto his show in July 1998. Stern accepted, and gave Johnson more than he bargained for by asking explicit questions about his sexual activities, how he contracted HIV, and whether he practiced safe sex with his wife. Johnson, for his part, didn't confront Stern. Instead, he smiled, chuckled, and mumbled.

GORE VIDAL VS. NORMAN MAILER

The Dick Cavett Show often showcased intellectual and literary guests, and in 1971 it hosted authors Gore Vidal and Norman Mailer, but unbeknownst to Cavett, the two men hated each other. Mailer refused to greet Vidal with a handshake, and Mailer, angry about an article Vidal had written about him in *The New York Times Review of Books*, remarked that he was "intellectually shameless" and likened his work to "the contents of the stomach of a cow." Vidal remained calm during Mailer's extended attack, but Cavett was not so cool; after Mailer curtly asked the host to look at his question sheet for a new topic to discuss, Cavett replied, "Why don't you fold it five ways and put it where the moon don't shine?"

*　　*　　*

YOUR TV IS TRYING TO KILL YOU

What would happen if you consumed only foods advertised on prime-time TV? According to a recent study by the American Dietetic Association, you'd get close to your monthly recommended intake of calories and sugar in *one day*. You'd also get 20 times the recommended servings of fat and fewer than half of the recommended servings of vegetables, dairy, and fruits.

TV INDUSTRY TERMS

*From the "bible" to time shifting, here's some more insider
lingo from the TV biz. (For more, see page 58.)*

Hot switch: When the ending of one show leads immediately into the beginning of another with no commercial break. It's hoped that viewers won't change the channel and will watch the next show.

Bug: Channel-identifying logo, usually placed in the lower-right corner of the screen.

Time shifting: Watching a show at a time other than when it is broadcast. It was coined to describe taping shows with a VCR, but now applies to online viewing and DVR (e.g., TiVo) use.

Burning off: When a show has been canceled but unaired episodes remain, a network may "burn them off"—show them with minimal fanfare during little-watched time slots or over the summer.

Syndication: TV networks provide programming to local stations that have agreed to be their affiliates. But syndication companies produce and package shows that are sold directly to individual stations to fill the hours of the day that aren't given over to the big network's schedules. Stations may pay millions to air syndicated reruns of *Everybody Loves Raymond* or original programming like *Jeopardy!*, but with a syndication deal, they get to keep all of the advertising revenue generated.

Fringe hours: For most of the country, prime time is 8 p.m. to 11 p.m. Fringe hours refer to the hour just before and just after prime time, when local channels usually air the most popular syndicated shows.

Happy talk: Improvised news-anchor banter.

Bottle: An episode of a show in which all action takes place in one room or on existing sets, with no guest stars or extras.

Bible: A book given to TV scriptwriters containing the official canon of a show—important background, plot

---

Bob Hope appeared on *The Tonight Show* 132 times—more than any other guest.

continuity, and extra character information. It is especially important for intricate fantasy and sci-fi shows, such as *Fringe* or *Doctor Who*.

Product displacement: In product *placement*, a company pays for its product to be featured (e.g., the prominently displayed Coca-Cola cups on the *American Idol* judges' table). Product *displacement* is the opposite: obscuring logos on prop items because the manufacturer didn't pay for their use.

Bumper: A still image, brief message, or bit of music leading into and out of commercial breaks. Examples: a photo of that week's host on *Saturday Night Live*, or "*Kate & Allie* will return after these messages."

* * *

MASONIC TRADITION

In an age where a show's time slot can change five times a year and daytime TV choices change every fall, Portland, Oregon, station KPTV has aired the same show every weekday at noon since 1970: reruns of the 1957–66 courtroom drama *Perry Mason*. (And for the four years before that, it aired at 7:00 p.m.) KPTV was an independent station, then became a UPN affiliate, and is now a Fox station. *Perry Mason* has stayed on the air, at noon, throughout.

If the show doesn't air precisely at noon, viewers get very upset. When the station moved the show to 12:30 p.m. in 1974, ratings dropped and angry calls flooded in. (It was moved back to noon 10 months later.) In 2008 the show was preempted for 30 minutes so KPTV could show President Barack Obama signing the economic stimulus bill. Irate *Mason* fans began phoning the station at 12:05. "It's untouchable," station manager Patrick McCreery told the Portland *Oregonian* in 2009. "We can add shows and take others off the air, but we can't fool with *Perry*." When McCreery was hired, KPTV management specifically told him that he could do anything he wanted...except cancel or reschedule *Perry Mason*, which still brings in about 10 percent of all Portland viewers watching TV at that time of day.

The odds of a three-way tie occurring on *Jeopardy!*: 1 in 25 million. (It's happened only once.)

DÉJÀ VIEW

*More TV actors and writers who tossed in self-referential nods
to their former works. (For part 1, see page 61.)*

Scott Bakula: He guest-starred on *Chuck* as Chuck's
estranged father. Accused of abandoning his kids, Bakula
responds, "Oh, boy," his catchphrase from *Quantum Leap*.

Don Most: In 1989 Most (Ralph Malph on *Happy Days*) had a
cameo on fellow *Happy Days* alum Scott Baio's show *Charles in
Charge*. Most's character wins the lottery and exclaims, "Happy
days are here again!" Charles retorts, "*Happy Days* got canceled."

Nathan Fillion: On a 2009 *Castle* episode, Castle (Fillion) tries
on a Halloween costume: tall boots, gun holster, and long brown
coat. He looks exactly like the character Fillion played on the
2002 cult classic *Firefly*. His daughter tells him, "Didn't you wear
that, like, five years ago? Don't you think you should move on?"

Richard Roundtree: He appeared on *Desperate Housewives* as Mr.
Shaw of Hafts Detective Agency. "Hafts" is an anagram of "Shaft,"
Roundtree's star-making role from the 1970s.

Barry Williams and Christopher Knight: They show up on *That
'70s Show* as the Formans' gay neighbors. They mention that they
once hid their homosexuality by posing as brothers. Williams
laughs and says, "Who would believe we're actually brothers?"
Williams and Knight starred as brothers Greg and Peter Brady on
The Brady Bunch.

Carrie Fisher: The actress who played Princess Leia in *Star Wars*
appeared on *30 Rock* as Rosemary Howard, a TV writer who
inspired Liz Lemon (Tina Fey). But when Liz realizes that Rosemary is kind of crazy, she flees. Rosemary yells after her, "Help me,
Liz Lemon! You're my only hope!" paraphrasing one of Leia's most
famous *Star Wars* lines.

Alan Alda: Guest-starring on *30 Rock* as Dr. Milton Greene, he

---

Dorf on college: Tim Conway donated his personal papers to Bowling Green University.

overhears Tracy (Tracy Morgan) crying, "It's true! There was no baby! It was a chicken!" Greene comments, "A guy crying about a chicken and a baby? I thought this was a comedy show!" It's a reference to a horrific moment on the last episode of Alda's M*A*S*H (see page 381).

David Ogden Stiers: Best known as Winchester on M*A*S*H, Stiers guest-starred on *Star Trek: The Next Generation*. In one scene, he activates computer terminal #4077, the number of Winchester's M*A*S*H unit.

Neil Patrick Harris: At the end of a *How I Met Your Mother* episode, Barney (Harris) writes on his blog about what he learned that day...while the *Doogie Howser, M.D.* theme plays quietly in the background. *Howser* ended each week with Doogie (Harris) typing a newly learned lesson into his computer journal.

Hugh Laurie: Observant viewers of *House* can find many subtle references to Laurie's early career in British comedy shows. In one episode, House attends a 1980s party, but comes dressed up like it's the 1880s, wearing a nearly identical costume to the one he wore on *Blackadder*. It's a joke on two levels, because Laurie wore the costume on television in the *actual* 1980s.

Michael J. Fox: *Spin City* had three great in-jokes:
• Fox's *Back to the Future* co-star Christopher Lloyd guest-starred on *Spin* as Owen, a politician who mentored Fox's character, Mike. After the two old friends embrace, Mike says, "This is like stepping back in time!" Lloyd, as Owen, replies in his trademark gravelly voice, "The past is prologue, Michael. Men like us have to keep looking...to the future!" Mike asks, "What the hell are you talking about?" Lloyd replies, "I don't know."
• On Fox's final episode of *Spin City*, he references the role that made him famous: Alex, the conservative son of liberal parents on *Family Ties*. Mike complains about a Republican Congressman named Alex P. Keaton, remarking, "What a stiff!"
• Meredith Baxter played Fox's mother on *Family Ties*. She played his mother on *Spin City*, too.

THE PROPHETIC *CRITIC*

A strange little animated show…that predicted the future of movies.

IT STINKS!

On the short-lived animated series *The Critic* (ABC/Fox 1994–95), TV movie critic Jay Sherman (voice of Jon Lovitz) hated almost every film he reviewed. (His catchphrase: "It stinks!") *The Critic* included short clips of these movies, which were parodies of real Hollywood movies and familiar movie genres. But strangely, several of *The Critic's* parodies later came to the *real* big screen.

The Merchant of Venice Beach. In a parody of a famous line from Shakespeare's *The Merchant of Venice*, *The Critic's* version has a slack-jawed Keanu Reeves saying, "Hath not a dude eyes? If you prick us, do we not get bummed?" A year later, *William Shakespeare's Romeo + Juliet* was released, set near modern-day Miami Beach.

Hunch! Sherman and his makeup lady Doris attend *Hunch!*, a stage musical based on Victor Hugo's dark 19th-century novel *The Hunchback of Notre Dame*. Sherman pans it as "inappropriate." In 1996 Disney released a musical cartoon adaptation of *The Hunchback of Notre Dame*.

Jurassic Park II: Revenge of the Raptors. In a clip of the "film," a velociraptor looks ready to attack…but then says, in a British accent, that he "and the other raptors have constructed a crude suspension bridge to Venezuela." The real *Jurassic Park* sequel, 1997's *The Lost World*, depicted the vicious velociraptors getting off the park's remote island and invading the civilized mainland (but they don't speak English).

Rabbi P.I. Arnold Schwarzenegger stars in this action "film" about "a Chicago cop who goes undercover" as a stereotypical Hasidic Jew. He goes on a spree, killing one man with a bris knife (saying, "Hava Nagila, baby") and shooting a mugger (quipping, "That's not kosher"). The 2003 movie *The Hebrew Hammer* is very similar. The plot: An orthodox Jewish renegade (Adam Goldberg) saves Hanukkah by killing off bad guys, including Santa Claus's evil son. His catchphrase: "Shabbat shalom, m*****f*****!"

Pro sports teams on *The Flintstones*: Bedrock Giants, Bedrock Dodgers, Green Bay Pachyderms.

VIVA VARIETY!

In the 1960s and '70s, TV variety shows were all the rage. They offered something for everyone: songs, dancing, jokes, sketches, and affable hosts. But for every Donny and Marie or Carol Burnett Show, there was a mime couple, or a Japanese pop duo who didn't speak English.

PINK LADY AND JEFF (NBC, 1980)
In late 1970s Japan, the most popular musical act was Pink Lady, a pop duo consisting of two 20-year-old women named Mie and Kei. They had only one American Top 40 hit, "Kiss in the Dark," but NBC chief Fred Silverman thought they were the perfect act to headline a variety show—he'd devised *Sonny and Cher* for CBS in the 1970s, and that had been a huge hit. Producers Sid and Marty Kroft had been told Mie and Kei spoke fluent English. They didn't. So added into the mix was comedian Jeff Altman, who was told to be purposely bad, even fairly racist, in serving as "translator" for Pink Lady's barely intelligible performances of songs sung in Japanese and English with thick Japanese accents. Translating involved sputtering Asian-sounding gibberish, along with jokes like, "You girls just love my big, round American eyes." At the end of every episode, Pink Lady sat in a hot tub and pulled Altman, still dressed in his tuxedo, underwater. It was an unmitigated disaster for NBC, who canceled after five episodes. "In the history of bad TV," writes Craig Nelson in *Bad TV*, "many are called, but only a very few reach the staggering heights of *Pink Lady and Jeff*."

SHIELDS AND YARNELL (CBS, 1977)
In the late 1970s, mime enjoyed a brief period of popularity, triggered in part by the many network TV variety shows that filled time with mime skits. The husband-and-wife mime duo Shields and Yarnell appeared on many popular programs, including *The Tonight Show*, *The Muppet Show*, and *The Sonny & Cher Comedy Hour*. (Their signature bit was a routine about married robots.) CBS eventually gave the couple their own show in the summer of 1977. Consisting of live mime performances, pre-taped mime per-

formances, mime-based comedy sketches, and mime performances set to music, *Shields and Yarnell* lasted nine months.

MARY (CBS, 1978)

In 1978 Mary Tyler Moore was out of work for the first time in over 20 years, having ended *The Mary Tyler Moore Show* the previous season. She was so bored that she was willing to try anything to get back on TV, even the singing and dancing required for a variety show (for which she had no experience). Moore and her husband, producer Grant Tinker, pitched *Mary* to CBS, and network executives thought it was such a no-brainer that they scheduled it in the prime-time slot of Sunday at 8:00 p.m. A cast of repertory players hired to sing, dance, and goof around included young unknowns Michael Keaton and David Letterman. Despite the quality of acting, the jokes were corny and Moore was visibly uncomfortable singing and dancing. It lost so much of the audience from its lead-in, *60 Minutes*, that CBS pulled the show after only three episodes.

The whole cast—except for Moore and Keaton—was fired, and the show returned in March 1979 as *The Mary Tyler Moore Hour*, a completely different concept. The first 30 minutes were about the backstage world of *The Mary McKinnon Show*, an unpopular, subpar variety show (like *Mary*). The second 30 minutes was the actual *Mary McKinnon Show*, a spoof of subpar variety shows (like *Mary*). The revamped incarnation lasted six episodes.

SATURDAY NIGHT LIVE (ABC, 1975)

NBC's long-running sketch show was first called *NBC's Saturday Night*, because ABC already had a Saturday-night variety show called *Saturday Night Live*. Hosted by sportscaster Howard Cosell, famous and popular for his sports coverage laced with biting wit and cynicism, ABC's *SNL* was an entertainment spectacle that truly defined "variety show." Acts included exotic animal training by Siegfried and Roy, comedy from Bill Murray, political commentary from John Wayne, songs by tennis player Jimmy Connors, and a remote shoot of Cosell interviewing Shamu, the killer whale at Sea World. The show lasted four months. In 1976, NBC bought the rights to the name and renamed its late night series *Saturday Night Live* (which also co-starred Bill Murray).

DON'T KILL THE TV!

It's only the messenger.

• In 2010 a 67-year-old Wisconsin man made headlines after he became so upset that he shot his TV. Why? Because Bristol Palin had advanced to the finals on *Dancing with the Stars*, and he didn't think she deserved to.

• A Georgia man walked into a Wal-mart in early 2010, grabbed an aluminum bat from sporting goods, and proceeded to smash 29 flat-screen TVs before workers could subdue him. Police gave no motive for the attack.

• In December 2009, a man from Albany, Louisiana, bet his friends that if the New Orleans Saints beat the Washington Redskins that Sunday, he would let them shoot his TV. Barely a few minutes after the Saints won in overtime, 12 of his friends, all Saints fans, arrived with a case of beer and various firearms. They took his 60-inch flat-screen TV to the backyard and shot it up.

• When Indianapolis Colts center Jeff Saturday was pulled from a game (which the Colts later lost) in the final week of the 2009 season, he came unglued. After the season ended, Saturday sheepishly admitted that following the game, "I went home and broke my TV."

• In 2009 after the big switch from analog to digital, a 70-year-old Missouri man couldn't get his new digital converter to work. He got so frustrated that, according to police, he "peppered his television with bullets." His wife said he'd been drinking.

• First rock musician to throw a TV set out of a hotel window: Keith Richards. It happened in 1972 when the Rolling Stones were staying on the 10th floor of the Hyatt West Hollywood. After that, tossing TVs became a rite of passage for touring rock stars. Thousands of innocent televisions have since been killed in the name of rock 'n' roll. (Thanks, Keith.)

Game-show host Wink Martindale had a top-10 song in 1959 with "Deck of Cards."

A SHOW IS BORN

More origins of popular programs.

EVERYBODY LOVES RAYMOND (CBS, 1996–2005)
After Ray Romano performed his stand-up routine on *The Late Show with David Letterman* in 1995, Letterman was so impressed that he offered Romano a development deal for a sitcom. The comic was teamed up with TV writer Phil Rosenthal to put something together that they could pitch to CBS. Rosenthal asked Romano to tell him about his life. Romano said he lived in Queens with his kids, and that his parents lived close by. "They live with my older brother, who's a police sergeant, and he's kind of jealous of me. One day he saw my Cable Ace Award for stand-up and he goes, 'It never ends for Raymond. *Everrrybody* loves Raymond!'" With that, Ray Barone was born. Romano didn't like the title, fearing no one would get the joke. He was wrong—at its peak, *Everybody Loves Raymond* averaged 19 million viewers per episode, placing it among the highest-rated sitcoms of all time.

BEVERLY HILLS, 90210 (Fox, 1990–2000)
Darren Star, originally from Maryland, wanted to create a TV show set on the West Coast about the "shared experience" of the "struggles" of affluent kids at a posh high school. The fledgling Fox network picked up the show in 1990, but ratings were low (even for the early days of Fox) and the series was nearly canceled...until the network brass learned that 75 percent of teenage girls who watched TV tuned in to the show. That, they knew, was a demographic that advertisers wanted. Result: *Beverly Hills, 90210* stayed on the air and enjoyed a successful 10-year run, covering such taboo subjects as alcoholism and drug use, domestic violence, gay rights, AIDS, date rape, teen suicide, pregnancy, abortion, and bulimia. In 1992 Star developed the *90210* spin-off *Melrose Place* for Fox, a "shared experience" about post-college life.

THE BEVERLY HILLBILLIES (CBS, 1962–71)
In 1959 veteran TV writer Paul Henning (*The Real McCoys*, *The Burns & Allen Show*) took a trip to visit Civil War historical sites

Bowled move: In 1997, *Ally McBeal* was the first series to feature a public unisex bathroom.

in the South. This gave him an idea for a series: What if someone from the rural South was placed in a sophisticated, wealthy neighborhood? In 1962 he sold the concept to CBS. Premise: A Missouri mountain family strikes it rich (by discovering oil, that is) and moves to New York City. CBS made Henning move the family to Beverly Hills because California scenes would be easier to film in their L.A. facilities. That move also inspired a title: *The Beverly Hillbillies.* Henning wrote main character Jed Clampett as a dumb yokel, but the star he sought for the part, Buddy Ebsen (who'd played a similar role in the 1961 film *Breakfast at Tiffany's*) wouldn't do it unless Jed was smarter. Within three weeks of its debut in 1961, *The Beverly Hillbillies* was the #1 show on TV. The eight episodes that aired in late 1963, immediately after the assassination of President Kennedy, proved such welcome escapism that they still rank among the 30 most-watched scripted shows ever.

MONDAY NIGHT FOOTBALL (ABC, 1970–2006)
Although they're the most-watched programming on TV today, in 1964 NFL games brought in only moderate ratings, almost entirely in the Northeast and upper Midwest. But league commissioner Pete Rozelle had an idea to increase football's popularity: a weekly game, broadcast on Friday night. It was a hard sell—the defunct DuMont Network had unsuccessfully aired games in 1953, and the rights holder, CBS, didn't think it could compete with viewers going out to attend high-school football games. Rozelle decided Monday was a better option and went about slowly promoting the idea. He scheduled a Green Bay Packers vs. Detroit Lions game for a Monday in September 1964, and it attracted a sold-out crowd. He continued to lay the groundwork by scheduling the occasional Monday game over the next five years. In 1969, when negotiating a new TV contract for the NFL, Rozelle proposed *Monday Night Football* to CBS and NBC, both of which passed because they had hit shows on Monday already (*Gunsmoke* and *Laugh-In*, respectively). But third-place ABC had nothing to lose and bought the rights. *Monday Night Football* debuted in September 1970. (First game: Cleveland Browns over the New York Jets, 31–21.) Ratings were low at first, but the exposure helped popularize pro football, which in turn made *MNF* a huge hit—within three years, it was a top-20 show. In 2006 the NFL negotiated a new TV contract, which sent their weekly network prime-time games to NBC and Sunday night.

TROUBLE ON THE SET

More behind-the-scenes disputes, shenanigans, and meltdowns.

THREE'S A CROWD

Four seasons into the run of ABC's *Three's Company* in 1980, co-star Suzanne Somers was due to renegotiate her contract. She made a staggering demand: a raise in salary from $30,000 an episode to $150,000, and 10 percent of the show's profits. Somers argued that she deserved it—*Three's Company* was an important part of the network's "jiggle TV" fad, and Somers played a ditzy, scantily clad sexpot. In other words, she thought she was a bigger draw and a more-valuable asset to the show than co-stars John Ritter and Joyce DeWitt. Producers called her demands "laughable" and refused. In protest, Somers called in sick for the taping of two episodes. The producers immediately fired back: Her character, Chrissy, was relegated to a 60-second appearance in the form of a phone call at the end of each of that season's remaining episodes, with the explanation that her character had moved away to care for her sick mother. Somers wasn't even allowed to interact with Ritter or DeWitt—an armed guard escorted her to an isolated part of the set, where she filmed her weekly scene. At the end of the season in 1981, Somers was fired. She later sued ABC for $2 million, claiming that her credibility in the TV industry had been damaged. (She was awarded $30,000.) *Three's Company* kept going for three more years.

DUKES DUDES DUMPED

It's rare for a series to survive the loss of one of its main characters, much less two, but that's exactly what happened when Bo and Luke Duke missed almost the entire fourth season of *The Dukes of Hazzard* in 1982–83. The actors who played the fast-driving cousins, John Schneider and Tom Wopat, walked out during a contentious contract dispute with producers. Schneider and Wopat were replaced by Byron Cherry and Christopher Mayer, who played Bo and Luke's cousins, Coy and Vance—dead ringers for the original duo. (Bo and Luke were said to have joined the NASCAR circuit.) Viewers didn't care for the two new Dukes—

the show dropped from #6 in the ratings to #50. Wopat, Schneider, and *Dukes* producers patched things up, and the original Dukes came back in 1983, but the show failed to rebound and was canceled in 1985. Bonus: Barbara Bach, who played Daisy Duke, had been at that fateful contract meeting, too. Producers later admitted that had Bach also walked out, they likely would have met the actors' demands because the series wouldn't have survived the additional loss. Bach stayed with the show, however, because Wopat and Schneider had advised her that contract negotiations were "man's work."

DELTA BLUES

Trouble on the set of the 1980s CBS comedy *Designing Women* began when star Delta Burke gained a noticeable amount of weight in 1989. With headlines like "Delta Bulk" screaming from tabloids, Burke asked series co-creator Linda Bloodworth-Thomason to write an episode addressing her weight. In it, Burke's character goes to her high-school reunion, where she overhears classmates mocking her for having gained weight. It earned Burke an Emmy nomination for Best Actress in a Comedy. Despite that, Burke claimed that the producers and cast members of *Designing Women* spread rumors about her and fed information to tabloids. In an interview with Barbara Walters, she let loose on producer Harry Thomason, saying he was so demeaning after she got heavier that he "screamed and yelled and threw things" at her as a matter of course. For her part, Burke played the diva, often missing rehearsals, forcing the writers and cast to juggle two scripts each week, one to use if she showed up and one for if she didn't. The producers became so exasperated that they held a private poll of cast and crew to decide whether she should be fired, and she was given the boot after the show's fifth season in 1991. In a note to the producers regarding her termination, Burke wrote, "Thanks for hiring me. Thanks for letting me go. It's the in-between part that we had problems with." Eventually the former co-workers made amends, and Burke appeared on a 2003 reunion special. She blames immaturity and personal problems for her behavior, saying, "I'm older now and on a lot of medication."

tick-tick-tick-tick-tick-tick-tick-tick

The most successful of all TV news magazines is 60 Minutes.
*On the air for more than four decades, the show has
won a record 87 Emmy awards. Here's where
it came from and the impact it's had.*

NEWS MAN

Before Don Hewitt created *60 Minutes* in 1968, he was already a 20-year veteran at CBS News. He was the first news producer to use two cameras to film a broadcast, to send reporters into the field to give live reports, and to display the reporter's name at the bottom of the screen. Hewitt even coined the term "anchorman." He also produced and directed the first televised U.S. Presidential debate in 1960 between Nixon and Kennedy. However, Hewitt's greatest talent was his ability to tell a complex story in a straightforward yet dramatic way.

LIFE OR SOMETHING LIKE IT

Hewitt didn't so much invent the TV news magazine as perfect it. (A British satire show from the early 1960s called *That Was The Week That Was* was first to use the format.) When CBS tasked him with creating a weekly news show, he looked to *Life* magazine for inspiration. It featured long character studies, photo essays, and had more of a narrative feel than the other leading news magazine, *Time.* So Hewitt utilized the "60 minutes" the network allotted him to create a show that would "package reality as attractively as Hollywood packages fiction." Just like a magazine, Hewitt formatted his show into "chapters," each with a one- to three-minute introduction "page" with magazine-style graphics.

Focusing on human interest, *60 Minutes* would tell the stories of a sympathetic figures, perhaps a rising star or a whistle-blower who was fired for exposing corruption, while also outing corrupt CEOs and politicians. Crucial to Hewitt's formula was maintaining a balance between the lighter fare and the more serious stories. "We could look into Marilyn Monroe's closet," he said in his pitch, "so long as we look into Robert Oppenheimer's laboratory, too."

FROM WORST TO FIRST

60 Minutes was slotted for every other Tuesday night at 10:00 p.m., alternating weeks with *CBS News Reports*. Premiering in September 1968, viewers of the first episode (not a lot) watched an interview with U.S. Attorney General Ramsey Clark about police brutality, got a tour of Nixon's convention headquarters, watched a short film by famed graphic designer Saul Bass, and saw the first informal "Point/Counterpoint" debate between correspondants Mike Wallace and Harry Reasoner about perception verses reality (this was the late '60s, after all). Ending the broadcast was humorist Art Buchwald with a pithy commentary (Andy Rooney was still a decade away).

Up until the mid-1970s, *60 Minutes* drew very low ratings and was shuffled around CBS' schedule. After the show and its iconic ticking stopwatch finally landed on Sunday nights at 7:00 p.m., a steady stream of viewers tuned in. Airing directly after NFL games on the East Coast was a big help, too.

60 Minutes entered the Top 20 in 1976. On several occasions, it's achieved something that no other scheduled news program has ever done—led the week in viewers for all shows. At its peak in 1979, an estimated 28 million viewers regularly tuned in. Entering its 44th season in 2011, *60 Minutes* is the longest-running and most watched prime-time show in history.

EYE WITNESSES

Hewitt's handpicked correspondents have become celebrities themselves, including Reasoner, Wallace, Ed Bradley, Dan Rather, Diane Sawyer, Charles Kuralt, Anderson Cooper, Leslie Stahl, and Meredith Vierra. Some highlights:

• *60 Minutes* pioneered "gotcha journalism"—now commonplace on shows such as *Dateline* and *To Catch a Predator*. An early example: *60 Minutes* producers set up a fake health clinic in Chicago. When a crooked drug company representative entered the clinic looking for a kickback, Wallace emerged from behind a one-way mirror and confronted the man. The correspondents became so adept at using trickery and subterfuge that in the 1980s, Herb Schmertz, VP of the Mobil Oil Corporation, wrote a guide for corporate executives on what to do if they see a *60 Minutes* journalist running toward them with a microphone.

- Wallace perfected his tough interviewing style in the 1950s on a New York show called *Night Beat*. His goal: to gain a tactical advantage over his subject, either by a revealing previously unknown hidden camera footage, or just straight bullying...no matter who sat opposite him. Here's an exchange from 2000 with Jiang Zemin, the General Secretary of China. Wallace: "You are the last major Communist dictatorship in the world. Am I wrong?" Zemin: "This is a big mistake. I don't agree with your point I'm a dictator." Wallace: "There's an old American phrase that if it walks like a duck and quacks like a duck and so forth, it's a duck."

- In 2010 *60 Minutes* used incurable cancer and ALS patients to infiltrate a "21st-century snake oil salesman" named Lawrence Stowe. He was captured on a hidden camera trying to convince a terminal patient to pay $125,000 for a cure of "stem cell injections." After the segment exposed Stowe as a fraud who didn't even have a medical license, the Attorney General's office, the California Medical Board, and the U.S. Food & Drug Administration all launched investigations. Stowe's clinic shut its doors.

- Hewitt nearly left the show after the 1996 debacle that inspired the film *The Insider*, about a scientist at the Brown & Williamson Tobacco Co. who blew the whistle on his company's disregard of scientific evidence that proved smoking was unhealthy. CBS pulled the story at the last minute, fearing billions of dollars in liability suits for convincing the scientist to break his confidentiality agreement. After Hewitt begrudgingly agreed to cut the interview, Wallace was so infuriated he threatened to quit. Hewitt convinced him to stay. "We could have left, of course," he later wrote, "But I had spent too much of my life making *60 Minutes* what it was."

LOVE, HEWITT

As the news magazine entered the 20th century, it found itself a victim of its own influence—*Inside Edition*, *20/20*, *Dateline*, and even CBS' own *60 Minutes II* and *60 Minutes Wednesday*. Hewitt wasn't happy about it: "We started a trend, and we ruined television by making this format profitable." Though he was in his 70s, Hewitt had hardly slowed down. Even still, the network replaced him. He died in 2009 at the age of 81. Though his show's numbers are lower than in their heyday, *60 Minutes* is still a Top 20 show. It's certainly taken its fair share of lickings, but it's still ticking.

60 Minutes was in the Nielsen top 10 for 23 straight seasons, a TV record.

A BEER AND A SMOKE

*What kept TV alive through its birth and early decades
of life? Beer and cigarette commercials.*

BELLY UP TO THE BAR
In 1946 a 10-inch, black-and-white RCA television set
cost $400. In 2010 dollars, that's $4,300, enough to buy
two big-screen plasma TVs and a Blu-Ray player. Most post-World
War II Americans wanted to own a TV, but few could afford it.
Besides, there weren't many TV shows to watch in 1946.

In those early days, networks found that sports were a cheap
way to fill up air time. All they had to do was train a camera on a
baseball game, boxing match, or roller derby bout, and people
would watch. And bar owners realized that a TV over the bar
would pay for itself (and then some) when patrons showed up to
watch sports and buy beer. Neighborhood taverns all over the
country posted signs promising, "We have TV!" In 1946 and 1947,
half of all televisions sold in the United States were to bars.

The first major sporting event to air on TV took place on
June 19, 1946: a heavyweight title bout between Joe Louis and
Billy Conn (Louis knocked out Conn in the eighth round). The
boxing match set a TV viewing record: 140,000 people watched,
most of them in bars. A year later, that record was shattered
when a *million* people watched the Joe Louis/"Jersey Joe" Walcott
title fight. When the 1947 World Series aired on TV, bars around
the nation reported lines winding around the block. Television
had found its first mass audience.

ALL ADS ARE BEER ADS

With so many people buying drinks while they watched TV,
advertising beer on TV was a natural fit—viewers could order the
product while the ad was still on. Unlike today's system of selling
blocks of ad time, back then, individual companies would sponsor
an entire program and get all the advertising spots. Regionally
dominant beers quickly snapped up sponsorship rights for local televised sports. Narragansett Beer was the first sponsor of televised
Boston Red Sox games, Goebel Beer sponsored Detroit Tigers

baseball, Griesedieck Brothers Beer backed several sports shows in St. Louis, Iron City Brewing sponsored the Pittsburgh Pirates, and Ballantine Beer sponsored New York Yankees games.

Into the 1950s, beer commercials continued to appear during sporting events, but as television sales grew, the ads popped up all over the airwaves. In 1951 Blatz Beer paid a whopping $250,000 to sponsor the TV debut of the hit radio show *Amos 'N Andy*. Pabst Blue Ribbon backed the sitcom *The Life of Riley*. And then there was *The Ken Murray Budweiser Show*, a talk show in which Murray and his guests drank a few cold ones while they chatted.

SMOKE GETS ON THE AIR

Revenue from all those beer ads helped keep the fledgling television industry in business. But it was another popular product that really launched prime-time programming: tobacco.

As beer and sports seemingly went together (then and now), in the 1940s and '50s, cigarettes and sophistication went together. At that time, there were few scientific reports linking tobacco with health problems, and cigarettes enjoyed a fairly positive public image. A burning cigarette looked glamorous in black-and-white movies, and millions of men had gotten hooked on smoking thanks to the cigarettes in their soldier ration kits in World War II.

FLAVOR COUNTRY

Cigarette-company sponsors shows, from the 1940s well into the '60s, aggressively pushed their shows' stars and scripts to promote their brands and depict cigarettes as modern, affluent, high-class accessories. It was product placement before such a term existed.

• Camel sponsored the 1949–56 police drama *Man Against Crime* (in addition to a nightly news broadcast; see page 93). The show was forbidden from showing bad guys, and even nervous-looking characters, from smoking. The cool and collected series star, Ralph Bellamy, however, was often seen smoking Camels.

• Leo G. Carroll and Lee Patrick, stars of the sitcom *Topper*, were required to smoke Camels on the show, and Carroll concluded each show by exclaiming, "They have flavor the way I like flavor!"

• One of the most popular variety shows of the '50s was *Lucky Strike Presents Your Hit Parade*, which featured a troupe of singers

---

...were all designed by "car customizer" George Barris.

starting each show with a rendition of the commercial jingle, "Be Happy, Go Lucky Strike."

• *The Chesterfield Supper Club* (1948–50) featured host Perry Como hawking Chesterfields between songs, and during them, too—he opened each show with a song called "Smoke Dreams."

• The familiar "valentine" logo at the beginning and ending of *I Love Lucy* wasn't added until the show went into syndicated reruns. When the show first aired on CBS in the 1950s, it was sponsored by Philip Morris, and began with Lucy and Ricky dancing around a huge pack of cigarettes. The show's ending had Lucy lighting Ricky's cigarette, chirping, "You see how easy it is to keep a man happy? Why not give your husband a carton of Philip Morris cigarettes?" Reportedly, *I Love Lucy* writers were even forbidden from using the word "lucky" in dialogue because it might remind viewers of Lucky Strike...a brand of rival American Tobacco.

SMOKE UP, KIDS

In spite of the number of shows sponsored by tobacco companies, there were also plenty of stand-alone cigarette ads on TV, too, airing at all hours of the day. John Wayne appeared in Camel ads (he died of lung cancer in 1979), Rod Serling of *The Twilight Zone* pitched Chesterfields (he died of a heart attack in 1975), and even Santa Claus got into the cigarette business. Okay, it was *Talent Scouts* host Arthur Godfrey in a Santa suit, but he did tell viewers that "the best Christmas gift is a carton of Chesterfields."

And long before Camel's cartoon mascot Joe Camel was accused of marketing cigarettes to children, animated characters populated tobacco ads, including Willie, the cartoon penguin who smoked Kools; Marlboro's Harry and Juggernaut Jones; and even, in 1961, Fred Flintstone and Barney Rubble for Winston.

The ads worked. In 1949 half of American men smoked cigarettes. By 1955, 59 percent did, despite the landmark 1952 *Reader's Digest* article "Cancer by the Carton," which marked the unofficial end of guilt-free smoking.

YOU'VE COME A LONG WAY, BABY

In 1962, the tide began to turn against the advertising of cigarettes on TV. That year, Surgeon General Luther L. Terry announced a review of scientific findings on cigarette smoking. Representatives from medical organizations, plus others from the Food and Drug Administration, the American Medical Association, the Federal Trade Commission, and the Tobacco Institute, were called on to study the findings. In 1964, after the representatives had gone over 7,000 scientific studies, Terry issued the report: Cigarette smokers were up to 20 times more likely to develop cancer than nonsmokers, smoking was a contributor to heart disease, and smoking during pregnancy was known to reduce the weights of newborns.

In 1965 Congress required all cigarette packs to carry a health warning label. The government was so adamant about getting out the information about the health effects of cigarettes that in 1967 the FCC required any TV network that aired a cigarette ad to also air an antismoking public service announcement.

Finally, in 1970, despite pressure from lobbyists, broadcasters, and the tobacco industry, Congress passed the Public Health Cigarette Smoking Act. It completely banned cigarette advertising from television and radio as of midnight, January 2, 1971. The last cigarette commercial, for Virginia Slims, was aired on *The Tonight Show* at 11:59 p.m., January 1, 1971.

(The beer ads, however, continue.)

*   *   *

A BANNED AD

In a 1996 Levi's commercial, a woman rushes into a public bathroom to change her clothes. In one corner, a man sits on a bench, wearing dark glasses and holding a white cane. Since he's obviously blind, the woman decides to change anyway, standing a few inches from him while buttoning up her jeans. He never reacts. When she hears a toilet flush in a nearby stall, she hurries out of the bathroom. Another man with dark glasses opens the stall door and feels his way out toward the sink, while the first man hands him the cane. He isn't blind—he was just helping out his friend. The spot aired briefly on British television before being yanked for its racy content.

TV QUIZ: THE NAME GAME

*See if you can remember high schools, workplaces,
hangouts, and hospitals from popular TV shows.
(Answers on page 500.)*

HIGH SCHOOLS
Match the high schools to the shows in which they appeared.

1. *The Facts of Life*	**a)** Buchanan High School
2. *Welcome Back, Kotter*	**b)** Neptune High School
3. *Veronica Mars*	**c)** Bayside High School
4. *Freaks and Geeks*	**d)** Fillmore High School
5. *Boy Meets World*	**e)** Eastland School
6. *Saved by the Bell*	**f)** McKinley High School
7. *Head of the Class*	**g)** John Adams High
8. *Our Miss Brooks*	**h)** Sunnydale High School
9. *Buffy the Vampire Slayer*	**i)** Madison High

WORKPLACES
Who works where?

10. Who works at McMann/Tate?
a) Don Draper (*Mad Men*)
b) Michael Steadman (*thirtysomething*)
c) Darrin Stevens (*Bewitched*)

11. Carrie Bradshaw (*Sex and the City*) writes for what newspaper?
a) *The New York Star*
b) *The New York Herald*
c) *The New York Ledger*

12. Who co-owns and manages the Dragonfly Inn?
a) Dick Loudon (*Newhart*)
b) Lorelai Gilmore (*Gilmore Girls*)
c) Julia Sugarbaker (*Designing Women*)

Maxwell Smart's shoe phone number was 306. Dialing 117 would turn the shoe into a gun.

13. On *Ugly Betty*, Betty Suarez works as a personal assistant, then junior editor, at which fashion magazine?
a) *Mode*
b) *Blush*
c) *Waif*

14. Where do Laverne and Shirley work?
a) Mel's Diner
b) Shotz Brewery
c) Wellman Plastics

HANGOUTS
Name the places identified with these shows.
15. The bar where Jack, Janet, and Chrissy hang out on *Three's Company*.
16. The bar where Ted, Marshall, Robin, Barney, and Lily drink on *How I Met Your Mother*.
17. The coffee shop where the *Friends* become friends.
18. The espresso bar favored by Frasier and Niles Crane on *Frasier*.
19. The diner on *Seinfeld*.
20. The *Cheers* bar's crosstown rival bar.

DOCTORS AND HOSPITALS
Match the TV doctors to their hospitals.

21. Gregory House	a) Sacred Heart
22. Meredith Grey (*Grey's Anatomy*)	b) San Francisco Memorial
23. John Carter (*ER*)	c) Seattle Grace-Mercy
24. John Dorian (*Scrubs*)	d) Lang Memorial
25. Marcus Welby	e) Eastman Medical Center
26. Doogie Howser	f) Blair General
27. James Kildare	g) County General
28. Trapper John, M.D.	h) Princeton-Plainsboro Teaching Hospital

Alka-Seltzer sales nearly doubled when their commercials began showing two pills instead of one.

THE WRITERS' ROOM

What's it like to write for TV? Here are some thoughts from the experts.

"In the writers' room, we talk about the most embarrassing, most personal things in our lives, things we would never publicly reveal. I've seen people locked in a room for 16 hours, laughing, screaming, crying."
—Jeffrey Stepakoff
(*The Wonder Years, Dawson's Creek*)

"As a writer, you love immediacy, being able to weigh in on something that's on everyone's mind. And with rare exceptions, you only get to do that with TV. With a movie, even if everything goes perfectly, I can write a joke today and have to wait two years to hear the laughter."
—Aaron Sorkin
(*The West Wing, Sports Night*)

"The only way to succeed is to write something from your heart, something that you feel strongly about, and hire a great cast, and after that, it is really up to the gods."
—Christopher Lloyd
(*Frasier, Modern Family*)

"As writers, a lot of us are very active politically, and want to make social statements. You're reaching like, 15 million viewers, and that's really exciting, but you want to find a balance between not being didactic and not hitting people over the head."
—Monica Macer
(*Lost, Prison Break*)

"My feeling is that we're not going to have interactive TV to the level that was originally predicted. When you're watching, do you really want to rewrite the story? Or do you want to be entertained? I'm an expert writer—I'm going to be able to do it better than somebody in his living room."
—Stephen J. Cannell
(*Hunter, The A-Team*)

"We've done jokes on AIDS, 9/11, farts, the Iraq War. We don't live in a bubble here. Every one of us has been touched by one of those things, just like our audience has. In fact, I was just touched by a fart moments before this interview."
—Brian Scully
(*The Simpsons, Family Guy*)

Of the 363 episodes of *Alfred Hitchcock Presents*, Alfred Hitchcock directed only 18.

ONLY ON TV

At some point in your life, you've no doubt been watching a television show and muttered, "That would never happen in real life." And yet these things happen on the tube...a lot.

• Someone mutters something under their breath—and the person standing right next to them can't hear it.

• The bad guys will get away, because they'll get caught up in a parade.

• There are three kinds of children: rude, disobedient, and precocious.

• When being questioned by the police in the middle of performing some job, dockworkers, housekeepers, school principals, etc., will continue doing that job.

• If someone does something stupid, their dog will cover its head with its paws in shame.

• Insensitive, dumb, overweight guys are married to smart, thin, beautiful women.

• If camping, there will be bears.

• Gifts aren't wrapped. Box tops are wrapped; box bottoms are wrapped separately.

• Nobody ever wears the same clothes twice.

• Massive, well-furnished apartments are affordable to the young and underemployed.

• Nobody says "goodbye" when they hang up the phone.

• Best friends or duos are the complete opposite of each other.

• If a woman is pregnant and suddenly stuck in a confined space (elevator, taxi, etc.) she'll give birth immediately.

The theme song for *The Beverly Hillbillies* reached #44 on the pop chart in 1962.

• If a woman is pregnant and makes it to a hospital, it will take hours or even days to deliver the child, during which she will yell, scream, and hurl insults at the man "who did this to her."

• Kids who get caught lying or screwing something up are not punished; they are praised for telling the truth.

• Grandmas act "young"—they know the new slang, the famous people, and have dates lined up for every night of the week.

• If it's just about Christmas, that never-before-seen, kindly old man just might be the real Santa.

• Whenever someone goes grocery shopping, they will return with one sack, from which a baguette will protrude.

• A surprise party is underway, and everyone hides. Someone comes in, turns on the lights, and everyone screams "surprise!"...to the wrong person. While everyone is milling about, the guest of honor slips in unnoticed.

• A man will schedule two dates on the same night at the same restaurant. He will run back and forth between the two tables until both women catch on and storm out.

• If a man engages in suspicious, secretive behavior, his wife or girlfriend will fear he's cheating. But he's actually planning either a surprise birthday party or a marriage proposal.

• Two people who share a room or apartment get in a fight and draw a line down the middle of the area, separating it into two spaces.

• A person goes on vacation, leaving their beloved pet in the care of a friend. The pet will die, and the friend will replace the pet, thinking the owner won't notice. They notice.

*   *   *

TV Word Origin: Hulu.com, the popular TV website, gets its name from a Mandarin Chinese word with two meanings: "hollowed-out gourd" and "interactive recording."

Donald Bitzer and H. Gene Slottow invented the plasma TV screen in 1964.

HAPPY DAAAYYYS, PART II

*The 20th century had its share of "cool" pop-culture icons:
Marlon Brando, James Dean. And then there was
the Fonz. (Part I is on page 215.)*

GREASING IT UP

In 1973 *Happy Days* got a second chance, thanks to the successes of *American Graffiti* and the stage production of *Grease* fueling a '50s-nostalgia wave. Naturally, ABC wanted producer Garry Marshall to imitate those blockbusters and write in a gang of "greasers." He refused, believing the show was already too derivative, but compromised by adding a single tough guy named Arthur Masciarelli (Marshall's real last name), who went by "Mash." But because of CBS's M*A*S*H, ABC feared that viewers might be confused, so the name was changed to Fonzarelli, "Fonzie" for short.

Marshall's first choice for the role was Micky Dolenz of the Monkees, whom Marshall thought had made a good biker during a guest turn on *Adam-12*. Dolenz read well, but there was one problem: He was a head taller than Ron Howard and Anson Williams.

THIS IS MY FONZIE?

So an audition call went out for a tough guy—a *short* tough guy. That's when a 5'6 ½" actor named Henry Winkler—a self-described "New York Jew with a big nose"—read for the part. Winkler, 27, wasn't really interested in TV; he wanted to make serious films and be the next Dustin Hoffman. But he had played a 1950s leather-jacket-wearing tough in the movie *The Lords of Flatbush*, so when a similar role came up in ABC's new sitcom, his agent urged him to audition.

Winkler didn't think he was tough enough, so he borrowed some of the mannerisms of his *Flatbush* co-star, Sylvester Stallone. Producer Tom Miller loved Winkler. Marshall responded: "*This* is my Fonzie?" He reluctantly agreed to cast Winkler but didn't give him any lines in the first episode.

AAAYYY...

Much of the credit for Fonzie's development goes to Winkler himself. As a trained dramatic actor, he was interested in exploring the character's emotional side. And there were a few scripted character traits that he changed because they didn't ring true:

• In the script, Fonzie was supposed to wear a cloth jacket and penny loafers. Winkler showed up on set wearing black leather boots and a leather jacket. But ABC censors considered leather too "hoodlum," so the Fonz wore a gray windbreaker instead. He was only permitted to wear his leather jacket while riding his motorcycle, because then it would be "safety gear." Marshall's solution: Put Fonzie on his bike as often as possible. (Winkler, ironically, was afraid of riding the motorcycle. He almost crashed into the director of photography on his first solo ride, so for the rest of the series, Fonzie's motorcycle rides were staged—he was towed on a flatbed truck.)

• Winkler invented Fonzie's most famous catchphrases by "reducing language to sound," as he put it. In an early scene, Fonzie had several lines that were supposed to convey how cool he was. Instead, Winkler simply said, "Aaayyy."

• Every other '50s thug in movies and TV kept a pack of cigarettes in the sleeve of his white T-shirt and was constantly combing his hair. Winkler refused to do either. When series director Jerry Paris instructed Fonzie to comb his hair in the bathroom at Arnold's, Winkler asked if he could try something else: Fonzie walks up to the mirror, pulls out his comb, shrugs as if to say, "Hey, it's perfect," and puts the comb away without using it.

"The Fonz was my alter ego," recalled Winkler. "He was everybody I wasn't. I was a bowl of jelly; he was in charge."

FINDING A GROOVE

With Winkler's input, the Fonzie character became a big draw and got more and on-screen time. Fonzie moved into the Cunninghams' garage and became Richie's mentor and best friend, teaching him how to stick up for himself. In turn, Richie taught the Fonz the importance of family. The pairing of this unlikely duo—a dropout and a square—added dimension to both characters. (Off-screen, Winkler and Howard became close friends as well.)

Another big boost for the show came at the beginning of the third season, when *Happy Days* switched from a single-camera closed-set shoot—each scene was shot three times from a different angle, like a movie—to a three-camera setup in front of a studio audience. Performing live allowed the cast to get instant feedback, which improved their comic timing. Viewers noticed, and the ratings steadily grew. The show moved up to 10th place in its third season. By the following year, it was #1.

FONZIE FEVER

In the show, Fonzie snapped his fingers and girls flocked to him. With a knock on the jukebox, he got music to play. Guys wanted to be him; girls wanted to be with him. School kids, carrying their Fonzie lunch boxes, gave each other the thumbs-up and said, "Correctamundo!" *People* magazine wrote in 1976: "The Fonz has become TV's super-character, cooler than Kojak, hotter than Mr. Kotter's 'sweathogs,' more explosive than *Good Times* dyn-o-mite." Winkler received nearly 50,000 fan letters per week. After an episode in which Fonzie got a library card, U.S. libraries recorded a 500-percent increase in cards issued.

ABC even considered changing the name of the show to *Fonzie's Happy Days*, or simply, *Fonzie*. However, Ron Howard and Garry Marshall threatened to quit if that happened. Even Winkler protested it. So ABC left the title alone.

Happy Days was cruising along at the top of the ratings, the cast was having a blast, and it seemed like Marshall and company could do no wrong.

And then Fonzie jumped over a shark.

SIT ON IT

Fans and critics are still debating whether the beginning of the end for *Happy Days* came during the three-part season premiere in September 1977. In a now-infamous scene, Fonzie, awkwardly dressed in swim trunks and his leather jacket, donned a pair of water skis and jumped over a shark to "overcome his fear of sharks." A few years later, two college students coined the phrase "jump the shark" to describe "the moment when you know that your favorite show has reached its peak. From then on, it will simply never be the same." About a decade later, they created a website, Jump the Shark, where TV fans could weigh in on where other TV shows jumped the proverbial shark.

Whether or not the quality of *Happy Days* declined after the shark episode is a matter of debate, but there's no doubt that the show remained popular. As Henry Winkler often points out, "We were #1 [in its time slot] for four more years after I jumped over that shark." The episode's writer, Fred Fox Jr., has also defended it: "It was huge, ranking No. 3 for the week and an audience of more than 30 million viewers." Most critics point out that if *Happy Days* ever truly did "jump the shark," it occurred three years later when Richie and Ralph left the show and Potsie was demoted to the role of a bumbling store clerk in Howard Cunningham's hardware store. Fonzie "grew up," becoming a shop teacher at Jefferson High and even entering a monogamous relationship. His main focus shifted to helping Joanie and Chachi keep out of trouble.

THE END OF AN ERA

The show's final years brought even more changes. Ted McGinley joined the cast as Roger Phillips, a coach at Jefferson High. But Roger never really meshed with viewers, and the ratings dropped considerably. Erin Moran and Scott Baio left in 1982 to star in the short-lived spin-off *Joanie Loves Chachi.*

Furthermore, Fonzie was no longer a cool rebel—he got a job teaching high school shop class and adopted a troubled boy—and nothing had replaced the Richie-Fonzie dynamic that had made the show so popular. But the strangest choice was that *Happy Days* didn't take its characters into the turbulent 1960s. Nothing was mentioned of Kennedy's assassination. When Richie and Ralph joined the Army in 1962, they weren't shipped to Vietnam but to Greenland.

Happy Days ended after the 1984 season with a bittersweet series finale, in which Ron Howard returned as Richie, and Joanie and Chachi got married. In the final scene, Howard Cunningham gave a toast, during which he turned to the camera and said to the viewers, "Thank you all for being a part of our family." Then he raised his champagne glass and said, "To happy days."

ALTERNATE TV GUIDE

Some actors are so closely associated with a specific role or TV series that it's hard to imagine he or she wasn't the first choice. But it happens all the time.

THE BRADY BUNCH. Gene Hackman almost got the part of Mike Brady. Producers cast Robert Reed instead—they didn't think Hackman was well-enough known.

GILLIGAN'S ISLAND. Among the actors almost cast: Jayne Mansfield as Ginger, Dabney Coleman as the Professor, and Raquel Welch as Mary Ann.

THE DICK VAN DYKE SHOW. Writer Carl Reiner originally sold this show about a TV comedy writer and his young wife as *Head of the Family.* Reiner's choice for the lead role: Johnny Carson.

BEWITCHED. When baby Tabitha got old enough to be played by a toddler, two child actresses were initially considered: Helen Hunt and Jodie Foster. (The part went to twins Diane and Erin Murphy.)

THE DUKES OF HAZZARD. Dennis Quaid almost landed the part of Luke Duke, but it went to Tom Wopat instead.

MURDER, SHE WROTE. The role of Jessica Fletcher was written with Jean Stapleton (Edith in *All in the Family*) in mind. She turned it down (so did Doris Day), so it went to Angela Lansbury.

DESPERATE HOUSEWIVES. Calista Flockhart, Heather Locklear, Sela Ward, and Mary-Louise Parker were all almost cast in the role ultimately given to Teri Hatcher.

THREE'S COMPANY. Billy Crystal auditioned for the part of Jack Tripper, which eventually went to John Ritter.

DYNASTY. Elizabeth Taylor, Raquel Welch, and Sophia Loren were all passed over for the part of Alexis; Angie Dickinson was offered the role of Krystal. The roles went to Joan Collins and Linda Evans.

CHARLIE'S ANGELS. They were almost Angels: Kim Basinger, Michelle Pfeiffer, and Kathie Lee Gifford.

THE PARTRIDGE FAMILY. After four seasons, David Cassidy was exhausted and wanted to leave the show. Rick Springfield was scheduled to replace him—until the network decided not to renew the show for a fifth year.

THE ODD COUPLE. Tony Randall's first choice to play Felix's slovenly roommate was Mickey Rooney (they'd worked together on Broadway). Creator Garry Marshall cast Jack Klugman instead.

HOUSE, M.D. On an episode of *Arrested Development*, actor Tobias (David Cross), an actor looks at old license plates commemorating parts he auditioned for. One of them reads "HOUSE." In real life, Cross read for the part, which eventually went to Hugh Laurie.

ARRESTED DEVELOPMENT. Two actors made the final cut for the part of Gob Bluth. The winner: Will Arnett. The loser: Rainn Wilson, who would later play Dwight on *The Office*.

FAMILY TIES. The role of Alex P. Keaton was offered to Matthew Broderick, who turned it down for a movie career. Michael J. Fox was cast instead.

BUFFY THE VAMPIRE SLAYER. Sarah Michelle Gellar read for the part of Cordelia; Charisma Carpenter read for Buffy. Creator Joss Whedon liked both actresses, but not in the parts for which they auditioned, so he switched them.

STAR TREK: THE NEXT GENERATION. Considered for the part of Geordi LaForge, a role that ultimately went to LeVar Burton: former baseball star Reggie Jackson.

In 1959 the U.S. Treasury produced a *Father Knows Best* episode that promoted savings bonds.

TV TREASURES

*Some more TV props, costumes, and memorabilia bought
by regular folks at not-so-regular prices.*

Lost: After filming on the series wrapped in 2010, more than
1,100 props were auctioned off, bringing in close to $1 million. One of the big-ticket items: a piece of fuselage from
the series' crashed plane went for $3,000.

The Sopranos: At a *Sopranos* costume auction at Christie's in
2008, an outfit worn by Tony (James Gandolfini) sold for $43,750.
All three pieces (black shirt, black pants, white undershirt) were
stained with fake blood—the costume was from an episode where
Uncle Junior accidentally shot Tony.

The Dukes of Hazzard: *Dukes* star John Schneider put up on
eBay his orange 1969 Dodge Charger "General Lee." It wasn't
used in the original show, only in a TV movie. It didn't matter—
a man named William Fisher came in with a winning bid of $9.9
million. It would have been the most expensive item ever sold on
eBay...but Fisher failed to pay and closed his eBay account. A
year later, the car sold at an auction house for $450,000.

Late Night With Conan O'Brien: From 1993 until 2009, O'Brien
kept a mug shaped like the head of General Dwight Eisenhower
on his on-set desk. (It's very rare—2,000 were made in 1950, and
only a handful still exist.) He actually had two, and he sold off the
spare in a 2009 charity auction. Final price: $500.

Arrested Development: A Segway scooter costs around $3,000.
But the one Will Arnett's character Gob on *Arrested Development*
rode around? The final price was not disclosed, but at a prop sale
after the show was canceled in 2006, the Segway sold for more
than $11,000.

Batman: At a Hollywood costume auction in 1994, the costumes
worn by Adam West (Batman) and Burt Ward (Robin) in the
1966–68 series sold together for $23,000...despite the fact that the
Batman suit didn't include the eye mask, boots, utility belt, and
shorts, and Robin's lacked a mask, gloves, and utility belt.

THE SPACE BRIDGE

No, it's not how Uncle John got from Oakland to San Francisco in '68—it's the story of how TV helped end the Cold War.

I WANT MY PEACE TV

On September 5, 1982, a small group of performers and students gathered in a TV studio in Moscow, in what was then the Soviet Union, to watch some television. Why a studio, and not at somebody's home? Because they weren't just watching TV, they were creating it. The studio was linked via satellite to the US Festival, a massive outdoor concert in San Bernardino, California. Performers on both sides took turns playing for the other, each being able to watch and hear the other in real time. (On the Soviet side they used regular TV screens in the studio; at the festival it was huge screens like they use at concerts and sporting events today.)

Even more: Hosts on both sides (Phil Donahue for the Americans) took questions from their respective audiences and relayed them to the other, then relayed responses via translators. It was the very first "telelink" between groups of regular citizens in the U.S. and the Soviet Union, and one of the first signs that relations between the two nations were easing. One of the Russian organizers, Joseph Goldin, dubbed it a *telemost*—Russian for "Space Bridge."

BRIDGE OVER TROUBLED WATER

The telelink had been organized with the goal of increasing understanding between the Soviet and American people. "Misconceptions between the Soviet Union and the United States," Joseph Goldin said, "can only be dispelled by direct and spontaneous contact between large groups of Russians and Americans." Coming as it did during an especially tense period of the Cold War (three months earlier, President Ronald Reagan had dubbed the Soviet Union the "evil empire"), the event was considered an enormous success—but very few people in the Soviet Union heard anything about it: the government refused to air it on television, or even mention its existence.

William H. Macy auditioned for the role of Brian the dog on *Family Guy*.

But a second Soviet-linked US Festival was held in May 1983, and this highlights of it were aired on Soviet TV—where it was watched by millions. It had an enormous effect on the Soviet people, most of whom were seeing regular American people for the very first time (and Americans seeing Russians, too). It caused a huge demand for similar links, which almost immediately began occurring at an ever increasing rate—hundreds a year at various public events by the end of the decade.

Two significant later Space Bridge events:

• In October 1983, American astrophysicist and author Carl Sagan hosted a link between American and Soviet scientists—to talk about the dangers of nuclear war. It was aired in full in both countries. American physicist Robert Fuller, who was in Moscow for the event, later said, "Nobody watched it in the U.S. except my dad. But the whole Soviet Union paid attention to this broadcast, and they learned for the first time that their country had missiles pointed at America, which hadn't been publicly known there."

• In 1987 ABC News anchor Peter Jennings hosted as journalists from both nations peppered each other with questions for two hours. It was aired live via closed-circuit TV at 50 American universities, and to the general public in the U.S.S.R., where it was viewed by 130 million people.

GOOD NIGHT, SPACE BRIDGE

After the breakup of the Soviet Union in 1991, the era of the Soviet-American Space Bridges naturally came to a close. Just how much of an effect the events had on Cold War relations is impossible to measure, but nobody involved doubts that they brought people in both nations closer together, and that they played at least a co-starring role in the eventual demise of the U.S.S.R.

Satellite television continues to bring groups of people around the world together, and today there are several channels dedicated to promoting understanding between peoples of different countries. (Do you have satellite TV at home? Peruse the channels—you just might find a Space Bridge-inspired TV show yourself.)

On 4/1/97, *Wheel of Fortune* and *Jeopardy!* Hosts Pat Sajak and Alex Trebek switched shows.

THE URICH EFFECT

The team behind the website Jump the Shark named Ted McGinley
as their patron saint because the actor appeared in so many TV
shows during their waning years. But who's our hero?
Robert Urich: the actor with the most TV flops.

ACTOR: FOR HIRE
Robert Urich was a TV fixture from the early '70s until
the late '90s. He's best known for his roles in two popular
dramas that ran for three years each: as casino boss Dan Tanna in
Vega$ (1978–81), and as the detective Spenser in *Spenser: For Hire*
(1985–88). But for all his popularity, Urich also holds the distinction of being the lead actor on 10 series that flopped—a TV
record.

• ***Bob and Carol and Ted and Alice* (1973)** Based on the controversial 1969 movie about wife-swapping, the TV version had to be
toned down—it was less about swinging and more about sexy situations like skinny-dipping. In his first major acting role, Urich was
Bob Sanders, played by Robert Culp in the film. In a sign of
things to come, ABC dumped the show after 12 episodes.

• ***S.W.A.T.* (1975)** Urich's next show was about a highly trained
special police task force. The funky theme song made the Top 10,
and the series was later turned into a movie (Colin Farrell played
the Urich role). But the show itself was never a hit—its run ended
after two half-seasons.

• ***Tabitha* (1977)** When *Bewitched* went off the air in 1972, the
character Tabitha was seven years old. This spin-off, about a 22-
year-old Tabitha's adventures in Los Angeles, launched in 1977.
(How did she age 15 years in a third of the time? Maybe it was
magic.) Urich played Tabitha's befuddled boyfriend Paul, essentially reprising the role of Samantha's befuddled husband Darrin
from *Bewitched*. *Tabitha* disappeared after 13 episodes.

• ***Gavilan* (1982)** Here, Urich portrayed Robert Gavilan, a cynical, hard-bitten ex-CIA agent working as an oceanographer to
help recover treasures lost in shipwrecks. *Gavilan* was sunk after
six airings.

In the 1959–60 season, there were 26 westerns on prime-time TV.

• **American Dreamer** (1990) In this sitcom conceived by *Family Ties* creator Gary David Goldberg, Urich plays a guy who quits his glamorous jet-set job as a foreign news correspondent to write a folksy newspaper column in a tiny Wisconsin town. It aired in the little-watched time slot of 10:30 p.m. on Saturdays...for one season.

• **Crossroads** (1992) In a premise similar to *American Dreamer*, Urich plays a successful guy—this time, an assistant D.A. from New York—who trades his busy lifestyle for a simpler one, reconnecting with his troubled teenage son on a motorcycle trip around the U.S. The show was gone after nine episodes.

• **It Had to Be You** (1993) Faye Dunaway played a blue blood, and Urich played her handyman and unlikely love interest. Besieged with production difficulties, the series was pulled off the air after four episodes to recast Dunaway's role...and never returned.

• **The Lazarus Man** (1996) Urich plays a man who wakes up in a shallow grave in post–Civil War Texas and doesn't remember who he is or how he got there. Viewers didn't care who he was or how he got there either. CBS canceled it after 18 episodes.

• **The Love Boat: The Next Wave** (1998) In a revival of the popular series, Urich played Captain Kennedy, subbing for Gavin MacLeod's Captain Stubing. Twenty-five episodes aired on the little-watched UPN network. It finished the season ranked #152.

• **Emeril** (2001) One of the most notorious flops in TV history, this NBC sitcom was built around real-life TV chef (and non-actor) Emeril Lagasse. It took place on the set of a TV cooking show, with Urich playing a sleazy agent. The series was gone after seven episodes. Even if it had lasted the full season, Urich wouldn't have been around: Sadly, he died of cancer in April 2002.

RUNNER-UP

Actress Paula Marshall has had starring roles in nine network TV series, the first eight of which were canceled after one season or less: *Wild Oats* (1994), *Chicago Sons* (1997), *Cupid* (1998), *Snoops* (1999), *Cursed* (2000), *Hidden Hills* (2002), *Out of Practice* (2005), and *Shark* (2007). Finally, in 2008, Marshall co-starred on the CBS sitcom *Gary Unmarried*, which was renewed for a second season. (Then it was canceled.)

1st person eliminated on the 1st episode of *Dancing With the Stars: The Bachelorette's* Trista Rehn.

EYE ON EYE ON SPRINGFIELD

In its 20-plus years on the air, The Simpsons has skewered just about every aspect of American life, including TV itself. Here are some of the shows the family watches, all absurd but...actually not that far from what's really on TV.

Do Shut Up: The Simpsons see this British sitcom on public television during a pledge drive. The on-air host notes that *Do Shut Up* is England's longest-running comedy, and that they'll be airing "all seven episodes."

MTC: Short for Monkey Trauma Center, it's *ER* with monkeys.

Admiral Baby: Even Homer thinks this show about a baby put in command of a U.S. Navy fleet is "a bit stupid."

President Clown: Krusty the Clown stars in this short-lived sitcom in which he plays a clown who becomes president. (Krusty mentions that the actress who plays his daughter "held up a liquor store last year.")

Law and Order: Elevator Inspectors Unit: A fake entry in the ever-growing *Law and Order* franchise.

Knightboat: The Crime-Solving Boat: A parody of the '80s action show *Knight Rider*, but with a talking, crimefighting boat instead of a talking, crimefighting car. Bart and Lisa think the show is contrived because it shouldn't be that easy for something that's confined to water to track down criminals. But "every week there's a canal. Or an inlet. Or a fjord."

Promiscuous Idiots Island: A parody of Fox's 2001 reality show *Temptation Island*, it's a show airing on Fox (like *The Simpsons*) that the show's announcer calls "the home of promiscuous idiots."

Touch the Stove: A game show in which contestants win prizes based on how long they can keep their hands on a hot stove top.

Ben: The bear from the 1967–69 series *Gentle Ben* returns to TV

On the '50s sitcom *I Married Joan,* sisters Joan Davis & Beverly Willis played mother & daughter.

to host a talk show. With a microphone and camera attached to his head, he roams his studio to allow audience members to ask questions until he gets distracted by a snack table...and then mauls the trainer who tries to pull him away from the food.

Tied to a Bear: A reality show in which contestants must complete challenges while...tied to a bear.

Eye on Eye on Springfield: Eye on Springfield is a news-magazine show about life in the Simpsons' town. *Eye on Eye on Springfield,* based in Springfield's rival town, Shelbyville, reports inaccuracies made on *Eye on Springfield.*

Battling Seizure Robots: A Japanese cartoon show about robot battles. The strobe-like special effects cause everyone who watches it to have a seizure.

The Bohring World of Niels Bohr: Niels Bohr was a Danish particle physicist in the early 20th century who studied subatomic particles. In other words, not very good television.

Trans-Clown-O-Morphs: A children's cartoon that exists solely to sell Trans-Clown-O-Morphs Cereal.

Chop Shop'd: In this parody of the celebrity prank show *Punk'd,* celebrities' cars are stolen and dismantled, and the parts sold off.

The New Adventures of Gravey and Jobriath: A parody of the 1960s stop-motion Christian kids' show *Davey and Goliath,* about a little boy and his talking dog. *Gravey and Jobriath* is the only show that ultrareligious Ned Flanders lets his children watch (although one of them thinks the idea of a talking dog is "blasphemous").

More *Simpsons* TV shows:

Are You Fatter Than a Fat Guy?
America's Funniest Tornadoes
When Animals Attack Magicians
When Surgery Goes Wrong
When Buildings Collapse
Mystery Injection

Soul Mass Transit System
Secrets of National Security Revealed
That '30s Show
A Connie Chung Christmas
Sumo Babies
The Drowningest Catch
Police Cops

THE LATE-NIGHT WAR

On page 281, we told you about all the late-night show hosts who tried to knock off Johnny Carson during his 30-year run as host of The Tonight Show. Nobody could. The real battle for late-night began when Carson retired in 1992.

L ENO VS. LETTERMAN
NBC forced Johnny Carson to retire in 1992 and gave his job to *The Tonight Show's* permanent guest host, Jay Leno. David Letterman, who for 11 years had hosted *Late Night* in the time slot following *The Tonight Show*, had assumed that he would be Carson's successor. Letterman was furious, and threatened to leave the network. So NBC went back on its deal with Leno and offered *The Tonight Show* to Letterman. That upset Leno, so NBC tried to appease him with a chance to host a nightly show in prime time, which he turned down. (He later took them up on it when he briefly resigned from *The Tonight Show* in 2009 and Conan O'Brien became host.)

In the end, Letterman jumped to CBS, where he began hosting *The Late Show with David Letterman*, an 11:35 p.m. show that competed directly with NBC's *The Tonight Show with Jay Leno*. While Leno and Letterman both enjoyed huge, loyal audiences (Letterman won the ratings race until 1995; Leno has topped him ever since), neither dominated late-night the way Carson had. This left the wide open, with a lot of new shows jockeying for ratings:

The Jon Stewart Show. In 1993 Stewart was a young comedian with a half-hour talk show on MTV. When Paramount canceled its syndicated *Arsenio Hall Show* in 1994, they replaced it with an hour-long version of *The Jon Stewart Show*. The show couldn't compete with Leno or Letterman, and it was canceled in 1995. (Stewart re-emerged in 1999 as the second host of Comedy Central's *The Daily Show*, which in 2010 surpassed *The Tonight Show* and *The Late Show* as the #1 late-night show among viewers under the age of 50.)

Late Night with Conan O'Brien. Lorne Michaels, producer of *Saturday Night Live*, had a clause in his contract that granted him control of *Late Night* should Letterman ever leave the show. Letterman bolted to CBS in 1993, so Michaels gave the host spot to a 29-year-old writer for *The Simpsons* and *Saturday Night Live* named Conan O'Brien. Despite O'Brien's complete lack of performing experience, the show eventually became a cult favorite and ratings leader, but O'Brien, an unlikely host to begin with, hadn't been Michaels's or NBC's first choice. The show was first offered to *Saturday Night Live* star Dana Carvey, who was announced publicly as the new host of *Late Night*...until they were unable to close the deal and Carvey stated that he had no interest in "following Jay Leno." Comedian (and one-time *Tonight Show* permanent guest host) Garry Shandling was also offered the show, but he opted instead to make *The Larry Sanders Show*...an HBO comedy about life behind the scenes of a late-night talk show.

In 2004 NBC was afraid *Late Night* host Conan O'Brien would sign a deal to host a late-night show on Fox, so they gave him his dream job, host of *The Tonight Show*. The catch: He'd have to wait until 2009 to get it. He succeeded Jay Leno in June 2009, but after seven months of declining ratings (due in part to a little-watched prime-time daily talk show hosted by Leno), NBC asked O'Brien to push back *Tonight* a half-hour to 12:05 a.m. because it wanted to give Leno the 11:35 to 12:05 slot. O'Brien refused and NBC fired him, restoring Leno to *The Tonight Show*. After fielding offers from several networks and studios, O'Brien launched a new show at TBS.

The Late Late Show with Tom Snyder. When Letterman moved to the 11:35 p.m. slot at CBS, he was given the opportunity to produce the show that followed it at 12:30. In 1995 he offered it to Tom Snyder, a newsman and reporter who'd had a thoughtful, late-night interview show called *Tomorrow* on NBC in the 1970s. Snyder hosted *The Late Late Show* until 1999, after which Craig Kilborn took over, followed by Craig Ferguson in 2005.

The Chevy Chase Show. Fox returned to late night in 1993 with this show—one of the most notorious flops in TV history. Chase was a popular film actor and comedian, well liked for his work in the *Vacation* movies and *Saturday Night Live*. But Chase's comic persona was that of an aloof jerk—not the best guy to host a show where celebrities came on to promote their latest projects. The Chase show tanked and was off the air just six weeks after its debut.

TV ANAGRAMS

An anagram is when you rearrange the words in a word or phrase to get a new word or phrase. Sometimes the anagram is a pretty fitting commentary on the original phrase, or it's just funny. Here are some anagrams of the names of some popular TV shows and characters.

*THE PATTY DUKE SHOW becomes…*HOW PESKY, THAT DUET

*GREGORY HOUSE becomes…*SORRY, HUGE EGO

*BUFFY THE VAMPIRE SLAYER becomes…*PITHY FEMALE BRAVES FURY

*THE HONEYMOONERS becomes…*OH, THERE'S NO MONEY

*LITTLE HOUSE ON THE PRAIRIE becomes…*THEIRS THE LONELIER UTOPIA

*AMERICA'S FUNNIEST HOME VIDEOS becomes…*OH, NO! FAD MISUSES CINEMA VERITÉ

*AMERICAN BANDSTAND becomes…*DANCERS AIN'T BAD, MAN

*THE SOPRANOS becomes…*A PERSON SHOT

*THE DATING GAME becomes…*GET A DAME NIGHT

*MY THREE SONS becomes…*MESSY THRONE

*THE ROCKFORD FILES becomes…*OFT-FIRED SHERLOCK

*MYTHBUSTERS becomes…*TRUTH BY MESS

*THE OPRAH WINFREY SHOW becomes…*HERO WORSHIP, THEY FAWN

*LOU GRANT becomes…*A LONG RUT

*RYAN SEACREST becomes…*NECESSARY RAT

*SIX FEET UNDER becomes…*EXIT FEEDS URN

*THE APPRENTICE becomes…*PATHETIC PREEN

*LOST IN SPACE becomes…*SO LET'S PANIC

Experts say: cats enjoy TV more than dogs do. (Cats are more visual; dogs rely primarily on smel

GOODBYE, FAREWELL, AND A*M*E*N

The final episode of M*A*S*H aired on February 28, 1983. It wasn't just a "TV event"...it was the most-watched episode in scripted TV history.

WAR IS SWELL

M*A*S*H was a sitcom based on a cynical movie inspired by a cynical book about an unpopular war. It was also one of the most successful TV shows of all time. Chronicling the doctors and nurses of the 4077th Mobile Army Surgical Hospital during the Korean War (1950–53), the first season in 1972 drew such low ratings that CBS nearly canceled it. But they gave it a chance, and by season two, M*A*S*H was a top-10 show. For the remainder of its 11-year run, it never fell out of the top 20.

Until 1983 M*A*S*H was a fixture on Monday at 9:00 p.m. on CBS. But by the time it ended, it had evolved into a much different show than it had been at the start.

FROM SILLY TO SERIOUS

The biggest reason for M*A*S*H's change in tone was Alan Alda, who starred as Captain "Hawkeye" Pierce, the unit's chief surgeon. After series creator Larry Gelbart left the show in 1976, Alda took over as head writer. He, along with executive producer Burt Metcalfe, convinced CBS to phase out the laugh track and focus less on the doctors' womanizing and pranks and more on character development and honest depictions of the horrors of war.

Result: M*A*S*H was no longer a comedy with occasional drama, but a drama with occasional comedy. "We're recreating a time of suffering and joy and revelation that happened to real people at a real time," said Alda. "We know what they went through. We can't be casual in the face of that."

THE BEGINNING OF THE END

M*A*S*H remained popular through all of the changes, but after 10 seasons, Alda and company were running out of stories to tell

---

Gabe Kaplan (*Welcome Back, Kotter*) gave up acting in the '80s and became a pro poker player.

about a three-year war. CBS wasn't willing to call it a day, though, and convinced Metcalfe and Alda to return for a final season that would conclude in February 1983 with a movie-length finale.

That wasn't Alda's first choice. He wanted the last M*A*S*H to be a regular 30-minute episode. At the end of his version, the audience would hear the director yell, "Cut!" and the camera would move back to reveal the crew. Alda would take off his surgical mask and address the viewers directly with a short, heartfelt tribute to veterans.

CBS nixed that plan, so Alda and eight other writers began penning "Goodbye, Farewell, and Amen."

THE WAR AT HOME

When M*A*S*H's end date was announced in the fall of 1982, it became the biggest story in entertainment. Many fans mourned the show's end. "The general viewing audience will feel a tremendous disappointment when M*A*S*H finally goes off the air," reported Dr. Robert London, a psychiatrist at the NYU Medical Center, adding that viewers might even suffer withdrawal symptoms. (CBS mourned the end of its hit show by selling 30-second advertising spots in the finale for $450,000 each—about a million dollars in today's money.)

In fact, M*A*S*H fans were so eager to find out what would become of Hawkeye, B.J., Col. Potter, Charles, Margaret, Klinger, and Father Mulcahy that a Fall 1982 edition of the *National Enquirer* promising exclusive scoops on the final episode sold out: "One character goes crazy, one is wounded in action, one leaves early, and one remains in Korea!" (They were right.)

PLAYING CHICKEN

While the final episode was being filmed, a forest fire swept through the outdoor set in the hills outside Malibu, leaving only a burned-out Jeep and the "Best Care Anywhere" sign standing. And only half of the scenes had been shot. Undeterred, Alda wrote the fire into the story: North Koreans had set off incendiary devices, causing a blaze and the evacuation of the 4077th.

On February 28, 1983, "Goodbye, Farewell, and Amen" aired on CBS. Directed by Alda, it was unlike any other M*A*S*H episode. It opens with Hawkeye in a mental institution, recalling a horrific experience to Dr. Sidney Freedman (Allan Arbus), M*A*S*H's psychiatrist. Over the course of the first hour, Hawkeye reveals a horrific ordeal he experienced while hiding in a bus with some Korean refugees. (A chicken was making noise, putting them all in danger of being captured by the Chinese, so Hawkeye told a woman to "shut that chicken up!" Hawkeye soon remembers that it wasn't a chicken but a *baby*, and that the mother had smothered it.) Later, he's deemed fit to return to duty, but it's obvious that he's damaged—especially when he risks his life to drive an abandoned tank out of camp to draw enemy fire away from the hospital.

That took up the first hour; the second hour and a half was all about the cease-fire ending the Korean War, and saying goodbye. In the iconic final scene, Hawkeye boards a helicopter and looks down at the camp from above. He sees someone has written "GOODBYE" in rocks on the ground. The helicopter flies away.

THE AFTERM*A*T*H

Even now, 28 years later, "Goodbye, Farewell, and Amen" still holds the record for most-watched scripted TV episode. (The previous record holder was 1980's "Who Shot J.R.?" episode of *Dallas*.) It's estimated that between 105 million and 121 million people tuned in, more than half of the U.S. population at the time. No single American TV broadcast surpassed the finale until the 2010 Super Bowl. And it's likely that M*A*S*H will hold on to this record for a long time, perhaps forever. Why? In the early 1980s, network television was the biggest thing going in home entertainment. But today, audiences are divided among hundreds of cable channels, DVDs, video games, and the Internet.

The M*A*S*H finale was such an event that it even affected everyday life. Newspapers reported that more than a million New Yorkers all flushed their toilets at once immediately after the show ended (they'd all waited until the end). According to "The Straight Dope's" Cecil Adams, it nearly brought on a plumbing catastrophe: "The resultant pressure drop caused a pronounced surge in the two huge tunnels that bring water into New York each day." And according to *New York Magazine*, classical radio stations across the country were inundated with requests for a Mozart piece called "Quintet for Clarinet and Strings, K. 581" just

---

...was in a car accident. She auditioned while still pulling glass from her hair.

after the show. The music figured into a poignant subplot where the snooty Major Charles Emerson Winchester III (David Ogden Stiers) teaches a group of Chinese prisoners of war how to play it.

F*A*C*Ts

• Each main character exits the show in a different type of vehicle: Hawkeye in a helicopter; B.J. on a motorcycle; Col. Potter (Harry Morgan) on his horse; Charles in a garbage truck; Margaret in a Jeep; Father Mulcahy (William Christopher) in an ambulance; and Corporal Klinger (Jamie Farr) in the back of an ox cart.

• Klinger, Potter, and Mulcahy reunited in the CBS spin-off series, *AfterMASH*, which lasted two seasons (1983–85). In 1984 CBS aired a pilot called *W*A*L*T*E*R* about Radar (Gary Burghoff), the camp's original company clerk, but the show was not picked up.

• During the filming of the finale, the Smithsonian Institution requested that set pieces, props, and costumes be set aside for the Museum of American History in Washington, D.C. Later, the M*A*S*H exhibit broke so many attendance records that it was extended for six months, and a few items are still on display today. And if you go to Malibu Creek State Park, about 25 miles north of Los Angeles, you can touch a piece of TV history—a burned-out Jeep carcass from the old 4077th.

*   *   *

THE HARDEST JOB IN SHOW BUSINESS

…is being Murphy Brown's secretary. During the comedy's 1988–98 run, Murphy (Candice Bergen) went through 93 secretaries, including a crash-test dummy, an adult chat line operator, John F. Kennedy Jr., and even Kramer from *Seinfeld*. (Murphy's secretaries had such a hard time that they formed their own support group.) In one episode, she did get a great secretary, but it was Carol (Marcia Wallace) from *The Bob Newhart Show*—and Bob swooped in and stole Carol back. In a final bit of karma, when Murphy was imprisoned for refusing to name her source, she was given a job as the warden's secretary. She performed horribly.

WACKY FAN THEORIES

Lots of TV viewers discuss their favorite shows at length on Internet message boards, blogs, and websites, covering plot developments, new characters, and backstage gossip. But some fans take it a step further and come up with their own radical ideas about what a show is really about. Here are some of the kookier ones we found.

Series: *Friends* (NBC, 1994–2004)

Wacky Theory: In the show's final season, Monica (Courteney Cox) struggles (and ultimately fails) to conceive a child naturally. Some fans say that this was foreshadowed eight years earlier. On a 1995 episode, Monica gets a job creating recipes made with Mockolate, a bad-tasting imitation chocolate. None of the other Friends will eat any (they won't touch her "Mockolate-chip cookies"), but she eats a lot of it while devising recipes. At the end of the episode, Monica loses the job because the FDA bans Mockolate, according to her boss, due to "something to do with laboratory rats." Fans see a link between the detrimental health effects of Mockolate and Monica's inability to get pregnant.

Boring Truth: Soap operas may be that complicated, but sitcoms aren't.

Series: *The Andy Griffith Show* (CBS, 1960–1968)

Wacky Theory: The series takes place in the South in the 1960s, and the main character is a sheriff. And yet there's no hint of the racial tension of the era: no segregated water fountains, no mention of the civil-rights movement gripping America…but then, there are no African Americans in Mayberry *at all*. Some fans think this means that Mayberry, North Carolina, is set in an alternate dimension in which Africans were never taken from Africa and enslaved to work in the New World.

Boring Truth: *The Andy Griffith Show* was a light comedy about a sleepy small town. The show didn't address the civil-rights movement because it wasn't a socially challenging or political show.

Series: *Scrubs* (NBC/ABC, 2001–10)

Wacky Theory: The character known only as the Janitor (Neil Flynn) relentlessly antagonizes main character Dr. Dorian (Zach Braff) and tells people far-fetched, conflicting stories about his life, his past, and even his name. On a 2003 episode, Dorian catches the 1993 movie *The Fugitive* on television and notices that an actor playing a transit cop looks exactly like the Janitor. (It really is footage of Flynn, who was in the movie.) The Janitor confirms that it was, in fact, him. Because Neil Flynn is a real actor from the real movie, and the fictional character he plays also claims the identity, fans think that this means that Neil Flynn and the Janitor, are, in fact, the same person.

Boring Truth: It was just supposed to be a funny reference to a cast member's previous role.

Series: *Mad Men* (AMC, 2007–present)

Wacky Theory: In the show's animated opening credits, a man in a suit jumps out of a window and falls to the ground as advertisements from the 1960s float past him. Some fans believe that the sequence is a preview of the show's eventual finale: The main character, ad exec Don Draper (Jon Hamm), will succumb to his many personal demons and jump to his death. Don has dealt with a lot in the show, including stolen identity, divorce, alcoholism, the social upheaval of the '60s, and severe depression.

Boring Truth: This theory grew so popular that *Mad Men* creator Matthew Weiner has addressed it in multiple interviews, stating specifically that the character falling in the credits is *not* Don Draper.

Series: *The Simpsons* (Fox, 1989–present)

Wacky Theory: Is the show presented through the eyes of baby Maggie Simpson? It *would* explain many curious elements of the show. For example, over 20-plus years of episodes, nobody on the show has aged—because babies have no sense of time. And why is Springfield's state never given? Because babies have no knowledge of anything beyond their immediate surroundings. As for the monster-themed Halloween episodes, adherents of the theory say those are Maggie's nightmares.

Boring Truth: It's a cartoon—things don't have to make sense.

FIRST LINES QUIZ #2

*Some more first lines of classic TV shows. (Quiz #1
is on page 36; answers are on page 501.)*

1. "In every generation, there is a Chosen One."

2. "How 'bout a beer, chief?"

3. "Alright, Jim, your quarterlies look very good. How are things going at the library?"

4. "Kids, I'm gonna tell you an incredible story."

5. "Yep." "Yep." "Yep." "Mmmm-hmmmm."

6. "Tell me what you don't like about yourself."

7. "My name is Mary Alice Young. When you read this morning's paper, you may come across an article about the unusual day I had last week."

8. "Once upon a time, an English journalist came to New York."

9. "So, if a photon is directed through a plane with two slits in it and either slit is observed, it will not go through both slits."

10. "Binford Tools is proud to present Tim 'the Toolman' Taylor!"

11. "If I had a remembrance book, I would mark down what it was like when we left our little house in the big woods to go west to Indian territory."

12. "1968. I was 12 years old; a lot happened that year."

13. "There's nothing to tell. It's just some guy I work with."

14. "Somebody answer the door!" "Hey Chip, Dad wants you to answer the door."

15. "The following takes place between midnight and 1 a.m., on the day of the California presidential primary."

16. "Well, Mary, what do you think?"

First female nudity on TV: Valerie Perrine in a 1973 PBS broadcast of *Steambath*.

LET'S CHANGE SOME THINGS

Network executive: "We love your new show!" Producer: "Fantastic!"
Executive: "But we're going to completely change everything about it."
Producer: "Huh?" Executive: "Relax, it's just a little retooling."

A VERY BRADY SPIN-OFF

First attempt: In 1974 producer Sherwood Schwartz wrote an episode of his show *The Brady Bunch* around friends of the Bradys named the Kellys, a childless couple who adopt three kids, each a different race. Schwartz was actually testing the waters for a spin-off called *Kelly's Kids*. ABC wasn't interested, but Schwartz didn't give up on what he thought was a great idea for a show—12 years later, he rewrote the script, and CBS agreed to make it into a series. Debuting in September 1986, Schwartz's *Together We Stand* starred Dee Wallace Stone and Elliot Gould. Ratings were low, and after six episodes (in five different time slots), CBS yanked the show off the air for "retooling."

Do-over: When *Together We Stand* returned in January 1987, it was no longer about a racially diverse blended family...it was about a widowed single mother raising four kids by herself—because Gould's character had been killed off. Appropriately, the series was retitled *Nothing Is Easy*.

Result: Viewers still weren't interested. After another seven episodes, Schwartz's old idea was gone for good.

SAVED BY RETOOLING

First attempt: The Disney Channel debuted a sitcom titled *Good Morning, Miss Bliss* in 1988. The show revolved around an Indiana middle school teacher (Hayley Mills), her friendships with other teachers, and (barely) her classroom and students. It was a vehicle for Mills, a former Disney child star, but the breakout characters turned out to be the kids: scheming Zack (Mark-Paul Gosselaar), fashion-obsessed Lisa (Lark Voorhies), and a nerd nicknamed "Screech" (Dustin Diamond).

Do-over: NBC bought the rights to *Good Morning, Miss Bliss* with

---

Only 3 *SNL* featured players have become full cast members...

an eye toward airing it on Saturday mornings after cartoons, to attract a teenage audience. The show was completely revamped: The location switched to a high school in Southern California; Zack, Screech, Lisa, and bumbling principal Mr. Belding (Dennis Haskins) remained in the cast, while Mills and the other teachers were out. The show, now focused entirely on the students, was retitled *Saved by the Bell*.

Result: It became a massive hit, running for four years (and endlessly in reruns ever since).

JUST THE FACTS

First attempt: The *Diff'rent Strokes* spin-off *The Facts of Life* debuted in fall 1979, transplanting housekeeper Mrs. Garrett (Charlotte Rae) to an upstate New York boarding school to work as a housemother. Episodes revolved around the growing pains of seven female students, as well as a headmaster and a few teachers. The show finished a dismal #74 in the ratings its first year.

Do-over: Producers thought that part of the show's problem was that it had too many characters. So four of the seven girls were dropped (one of them portrayed by future teen idol Molly Ringwald), as were the headmaster and teachers. To keep Mrs. Garrett close to the girls, her job changed to nutritionist, and a new student, a tough tomboy named Jo (Nancy McKeon), was added. Another change was the theme song: In the first season, Rae herself warbled it; in the second season, it was sung by pop singer Gloria Loring (wife of the song's composer, Alan Thicke).

Result: Everything worked—*The Facts of Life* became a top-30 hit, all the way until it was canceled in 1988.

DAY JOBS

First attempt: Doris Day was planning on retiring from show business in 1968...until her husband/manager, Martin Melcher, died. At that point, she learned two things: 1) Melcher had squandered her fortune and she was broke, and 2) he had contracted her to star in a sitcom that coming fall for CBS. *The Doris Day Show* was rushed into production, with Day playing a widowed mother of two little boys who had just moved from San Francisco to a Northern California ranch. Other characters included her father (Denver Pyle) and a ranch hand (James Hampton).

Do-over #1: The show finished in the top 30, but CBS didn't think it was the right fit for Day. The network was also in the process of removing rural-themed shows from its lineup (see page 77), so for its second season (1969–70), CBS made *The Doris Day Show* into a workplace sitcom: Day commuted into San Francisco to be a secretary for *Today's World* magazine, interacting with an editor (McLean Stevenson) and a sassy co-worker (Rose Marie). Day's family was still mentioned and seen, but rarely.

Do-over #2: In 1970—season three—Day's character and her sons moved into a San Francisco apartment. Pyle and Hampton were written out completely.

Do-over #3: CBS revamped the show for the third time in four years in 1971, in an effort to make *The Doris Day Show* more like its new hit, *The Mary Tyler Moore Show*. Day's character was now alone in San Francisco (the boys were never seen again, with the explanation that they'd "moved back to the farm") and the entire magazine staff was replaced. Day was promoted to staff writer and scripts referred to her long writing career, as if her years as a secretary had never happened.

Result: The final changes lasted the longest—two years—before the show, a top-30 hit throughout its run, was finally canceled in 1973.

ANOTHER CHANCE

First Attempt: *Sonny with a Chance* is basically a teenage version of *30 Rock*—a Disney Channel sitcom about the backstage world of a sketch comedy show for teens called *So Random!* In 2010 the show's star, Demi Lovato, checked into rehab.

Do-over: The folks at Disney didn't want to cancel a hit sitcom, so they retooled it: The show within the show became the show itself, and Lovato's character disappeared.

*　　*　　*

Random fact: When *Diff'rent Strokes* aired on Japanese TV in the 1980s, Arnold's catchphrase "What'chu talkin' 'bout?" was translated to, roughly, "Joke only about your face!"

NETWORK ORIGINS: FOX

In 1987 Fox became the first broadcast network that really gave ABC, CBS, and NBC a run for their money.

YOUNG FOX

In 1935 two Hollywood movie studios—Fox Pictures and 20th Century Pictures—merged to become one of the most dominant companies in show business, 20th Century Fox. Its finances grew rocky throughout the 1960s and '70s, but stabilized for good in 1977 when it produced what was to date the most profitable movie ever made: *Star Wars.*

With its finances in order, Fox put itself on the market, and was quickly purchased by two billionaire investors, Marvin Davis and Marc Rich. But while the studio was now stable, its owners were not. In 1985 Rich fled the U.S. when it was discovered that he had made illegal business deals with Iran during the 1980 hostage crisis, and also owed $100 million in taxes. (Famously, President Bill Clinton pardoned Rich hours before he left office in 2001.) Suddenly stuck with a giant movie studio and no business partner, Davis unloaded the company to News Corporation, owned by Australian publishing magnate Rupert Murdoch.

KILLER-DILLER

Murdoch hired former ABC vice president of development Barry Diller to run 20th Century Fox. Diller was a TV guy, having invented the made-for-TV-movie and later helped produce shows such as *Laverne & Shirley, Taxi,* and *Cheers.* And that abiding interest and experience in television is what drove his plans at 20th Century Fox. He didn't want to produce movies—he wanted to use the movie studio's resources to develop a new TV network.

Though apprehensive—"fourth" networks other than the Big Three had been proposed and fizzled out a dozen times since the 1950s—Murdoch gave Diller a green light. First order of business: buy some "seed" stations, or instant Fox TV affiliates, to attract advertisers. In 1985 Fox acquired Metromedia, a consortium of six independent stations. Diller then secured affiliate agreements with 90 unaffiliated local stations across the United States.

When John Lithgow won an Emmy for Showtime's *Dexter,* he accidentally thanked HBO.

STARTING SLOW

While News Corp. had plenty of money to spend on the new network, Murdoch didn't want to waste it by directly challenging the Big Three networks on prime time, their strongest turf. Instead, the Fox Broadcasting Network's first show was *The Late Show With Joan Rivers*, on October 9, 1986, at 11 p.m.

The Late Show was not a success (see page 283), but it put the network into the public consciousness. By spring, executives decided that Fox was ready to attempt prime time. They began conservatively: one night consisting of two shows, airing on Sunday, which, at the time, was the least-watched night of the week. On April 5, 1987, at 8 p.m., the first prime-time Fox show aired: *Married...With Children*. After that, at 8:30 p.m., came *The Tracey Ullman Show*, a modern variety show. Both were moderate hits—*Married* aired for 11 seasons; *Ullman* would stick around for four and spin off its cartoon segments into one of the most successful TV shows ever, *The Simpsons*.

DAYS OF THE WEEK

After that first night, Fox added a new show each Sunday until it had a three-hour Sunday-night lineup. First was the hour-long police drama *21 Jump Street* (starring Johnny Depp), then the comedy *Mr. President* (about the president's family life, starring George C. Scott), and then the romantic comedy *Duet*.

Programming for the rest of the week was also rolled out in a leisurely fashion. A Saturday lineup appeared three months later, in July 1987; Monday would be filled in 1989, Thursday and Friday in 1990. Full, seven-nights-a-week programming was finally in place by January 1993.

Although Fox had some popular shows, it still wasn't getting the respect accorded to the other networks. That would change when the new network outbid CBS in 1994 for the National Football League, which had been with CBS since 1952. After the shockwaves subsided, Fox was finally seen as a real network, more or less equal to the other three. In 2003, Fox became the most-watched network overall, on the strength of its top-rated talent show *American Idol*.

TV TIDBITS

Astound your friends with these AMAZING TV FACTS!

• For a week after the 1966 premiere of *It's the Great Pumpkin, Charlie Brown*—in which Charlie Brown goes trick-or-treating and gets only rocks—CBS received thousands of pieces of candy from viewers all over the U.S., addressed "To Charlie Brown."

• On *Desperate Housewives*, the Applewhites' gothic-style house is the same house that the Munsters lived in on their 1960s sitcom. It's located on "Colonial Street" on the Universal Studios backlot.

• During the 2007–08 writers' strike, *My Name is Earl* creator Greg Garcia worked at a Burger King to research a book he was writing on minimum-wage jobs.

• Michael Richards auditioned for Al Bundy on *Married...With Children* but wasn't right for the part. Two years later, the same casting director was auditioning actors for *Seinfeld*, remembered Richards, and invited him to read for Jerry's wacky neighbor, a part he *was* right for.

• April 26, 1989, was Carol Burnett's 56th birthday. That morning she received news that her friend Lucille Ball had died. That afternoon she received birthday flowers... from Lucille Ball.

• While filming *The Whole Nine Yards*, Bruce Willis lost a bet to Matthew Perry. Willis's payment: to guest-star on two *Friends* episodes...for free.

• In the 1952 film *Zombies of the Stratosphere*, 20-year-old Leonard Nimoy played an alien. Fifteen years later, he became famous for playing another alien, Mr. Spock.

• John Travolta's sister Ellen played Scott Baio's mother on three sitcoms: *Happy Days*, *Joanie Loves Chachi*, and *Charles in Charge*.

• When *Ugly Betty's* America Ferrera was a teenager, her parents sent her to law camp, where she saw the Joe Pesci movie *My Cousin Vinny*. That's when Ferrera realized, "I didn't want to *be* a lawyer, I just want to *act* like a lawyer."

What a way to go: Frank Sinatra's last TV appearance was on *Who's the Boss?*

- It was the late-1970s success of the *Mr. Bill* claymation shorts on *Saturday Night Live*, in which Vance DeGeneres played Mr. Hands, that inspired DeGeneres's younger sister, Ellen, to take up comedy.

- Ted Cassidy played two iconic roles on the same show, though he's known for only one of them—the butler Lurch on *The Addams Family*. But Cassidy (well, his hand) also played "Thing" on that show. He even signed separate contracts for the roles.

- In 1978 NBC hoped the Joe Namath sitcom, *The Waverly Wonders*, would end the network's ratings slump. But it was trounced by *Donny and Marie* on ABC and *Wonder Woman* on CBS, leading to an early exit. Luckily for NBC, *Waverly*'s midseason replacement, *Diff'rent Strokes*, fared much better.

- Dawn Wells's husband, also her agent, noticed that her *Gilligan's Island* contract gave her residuals for only the first five reruns of each episode. He renegotiated so Wells (Mary Ann) got paid for *every* rerun, making her the only cast member to make millions from the show.

- According to actor Max Wright, the most difficult actor he ever worked with was ALF. The hand puppet, controlled by show creator Paul Fusco, was a "technical nightmare" that not only caused every shoot to run hours long but also "got all the best lines." After shooting the final episode in 1990, Wright left the set without saying goodbye to Fusco, ALF, cast, or crew.

- To create *Law & Order's* "doink DOINK" sound effect, composer Mike Post combined several sounds, including a jail door closing and "500 Japanese monks stomping in unison." The two notes are designed to mimic a judge's gavel.

- Who wants to be on TV? Regis Philbin. He's been on TV more than anyone else. In 2004, he broke Hugh Downs's record with his 15,188th hour on the tube.

- When Jay Ward created *Rocky and Bullwinkle*, he gave both characters the middle initial J, after himself. Homer Simpson's middle name is Jay because *Simpsons* creator Matt Groening is a big Jay Ward fan.

That's a bunch: 464 children auditioned for the six kids' roles on *The Brady Bunch*.

"HOLY CATCHPHRASE, BATMAN!"

*Every TV show wants one, but few achieve it: a catchphrase.
The best ones not only propel their show into the limelight, but
eventually take on a life of their own, sometimes getting into
the dictionary, sometimes even electing a president.*

Catchphrase: "D'oh!"
From: *The Simpsons* (1989–)
Story: Dan Castellaneta, the voice of Homer Simpson,
came up with Homer's signature line himself. "It was written into
the script as a 'frustrated grunt,'" he explains, "And I thought of
that old Laurel and Hardy character who had a grunt like
'D'owww.' Matt Groening (*Simpsons* creator) said 'Great, but
shorten it.' ...No one thought it would become a catchphrase."
But it did—in a big way. The sitcom is seen by more than 60 million people in more than 60 countries. In 2001, "D'oh!" earned a
spot in the *Oxford English Dictionary*.

Catchphrase: "Holy _____, Batman!"
From: *Batman* (1966–68)
Story: Uttered by Robin (Burt Ward) whenever he was dumb-
founded, this silly phrase helped make the show a hit...and also
led to its demise. During the first season, which aired two nights a
week, *Batman* was fresh. ABC quickly realized that one of the
things viewers loved was Robin's quirky line, so they milked it for
all it was worth. But by the end of the second season, the plots
were all recycled and the "Holy [ ], Batman!" had lost its impact.
It didn't do much for Burt Ward's career either; he was never able
to get past the Boy Wonder image.

Catchphrase: "What'chu talkin' 'bout, Willis?"
From: *Diff'rent Strokes* (1978–86)
Story: Gary Coleman's snub-nosed delivery helped keep *Diff'rent
Strokes* going for eight years. After the show's demise, the strug-

gling Coleman began to use it at public appearances and in TV cameos to help keep his career afloat. But in later years he grew so sick of the line—and the TV business in general—that he vowed never to say it again.

Catchphrase: "Sock it to me!"
From: *Laugh-In* (1968–73)
Story: The phrase came from pop music (Aretha Franklin's "Respect"). But the popular variety show *Rowan and Martin's Laugh-In* turned it into a mindless slapstick sketch...and repeated it week after week. Here's how it worked: An unsuspecting person (usually Judy Carne) would be tricked into saying "Sock it to me!" Then he or she was either hit by pies, drenched with water, or dropped through a trap door. Viewers loved it; they knew what was coming every time, and they still loved it. It quickly became an "in" thing to get socked.

This catchphrase was more than popular—it may have altered history: On September 16, 1968, presidential candidate Richard Nixon appeared on the show. He was set up in the standard fashion but surprised everyone by changing the command into a question: "Sock it to ME?" It did wonders for Nixon's staid, humorless image, and may have helped propel him into the Oval Office.

Catchphrase: "Yabba-dabba-doo!"
From: *The Flintstones* (1960–66)
Story: Just like Homer's "D'oh!" this one came from the man who voiced the character—in this case, Alan Reed. *Flintstones* co-creator Joe Barbera tells the story: "In a recording session, Alan said, 'Hey, Joe, where it says "yahoo," can I say "yabba-dabba-doo?"' I said yeah. God knows where he got it, but it was one of those terrific phrases." Reed later said that it came from his mother, who used to say, "A little dab'll do ya."

Catchphrase: "Just the facts, Ma'am."
From: *Dragnet* (1952–59/1967–70)
Story: Sergeant Joe Friday's (Jack Webb) deadpan delivery made this statement famous...sort of. He actually never said it. Friday's line was "All we want are the facts, Ma'am." Satirist Stan Freberg

spoofed the popular show on a 1953 record called "St. George and the Dragonet," which featured the line: "I just want to get the facts, Ma'am." The record sold more than two million copies, and Freberg's line—not Webb's—became synonymous with the show. According to Freberg: "Jack Webb told me, 'Thanks for pushing us into the number one spot,' because after my record came out, within three weeks, he was number one."

Catchphrase: "De plane! De plane!"
From: *Fantasy Island* (1978–84)
Story: At the beginning of each episode, the vertically challenged Tattoo (Herve Villechaize) shouted this phrase to alert his boss, Mr. Roarke (Ricardo Montalban), that "de plane" was coming. The phrase did so much for *Fantasy Island* that in 1983 Villechaize asked for the same salary as Montalban. Instead, he was fired. Ratings dropped off dramatically and the show was canceled after the following season. In 1992 Villechaize turned up in a Dunkin' Donuts commercial asking for "De plain! De plain!" doughnuts.

Catchphrase: "Book 'em, Danno!"
From: *Hawaii Five-O* (1968–80)
Story: Even though *Hawaii Five-O* ran for 12 years, more people today remember this catchphrase than the show itself. When he caught the bad guy, detective Steve McGarrett (Jack Lord) would smugly utter this line to his assistant Danny "Danno" Williams (James MacArthur). To say the phrase is a part of pop culture is an understatement: a 2010 Internet search found more than 42,000 entries for "Book 'em, Danno!"

* * *

THE ORIGIN OF MISS PIGGY
Muppeteer Bonnie Erickson based the Miss Piggy puppet on singer Peggy Lee and originally named the character "Miss Piggy Lee." Jim Henson dropped "Lee" because he didn't want to offend the singer.

TREK STORY, PART II

In 1987 Star Trek made its return to the small screen, but the real drama was taking place behind the cameras. (Part I is on page 239.)

NUMBER ONE, THIS IS NUMBER TWO

As new producers, writers, and actors found their way, the first season of *Star Trek: The Next Generation* was uneven. Despite TNG's flaws, hardcore *Trek* fans kept tuning in, hoping it would get better. Few people, including the stars, expected the show to last. "We were all very nervous," said Levar Burton, who played Lt. Commander Geordi La Forge. "We felt that we were stepping into such big shoes that we took it, and perhaps ourselves, too seriously."

The entire concept of *Star Trek: TNG* was at odds with itself: It needed to have its own identity, but it also needed to piggyback on the legacy of the original series. Except for a brief cameo by DeForest Kelley as an elderly Dr. McCoy in the pilot, Roddenberry didn't allow any of the original actors to reprise their roles...but he did recycle plots and ideas from the old series.

KING LEAR IN SPACE

But Roddenberry was also nixing the edgier scripts. Head writer David Gerrold wrote an allegorical episode called "Blood and Fire," about the AIDS epidemic. Roddenberry rejected it. Gerrold and fellow writer D.C. Fontana quit after the first season because of office politics, and so did more than 30 other staffers, still a television record.

Roddenberry was increasingly suffering from heart trouble by the time the second season began, although he still held sway over the writers and actors. That gave Rick Berman an opportunity to take over. His first change was allowing actor Patrick Stewart to have more input on his character. Stewart, who'd trained with the Royal Shakespeare Company, had taken the role not because he was particularly interested in science fiction, but because he wanted to portray the inner struggles of a man whose duty was to protect hundreds of lives. As he put it, "I wanted to be King Lear in space."

First product sold on TV by Ron Popeil: Ronco Spray Gun hose nozzle (1964). 4 million sold

Then, against Roddenberry's wishes, Berman approved the script for "The Measure of a Man," in which Starfleet orders the android Data to be disassembled and studied, and Picard must defend Data's "humanity." The episode was the first time Stewart got to sink his teeth into the role. "I was very happy to finally have a chance to take on some serious issues," he said. Brent Spiner (Data) was happy, too—he'd had an equally difficult time with his one-note role and credits Berman with allowing him to "find Data." Things started to get easier for the cast and crew.

THE FINEST FLEET IN THE GALAXY
In 1991 two major events occurred in the *Star Trek* world: Gene Roddenberry died at age 70, and *The Next Generation* became one of the most popular shows on television. The show's stars reached celebrity status, too—especially Stewart, whom *People* magazine named the "sexiest man on TV."

Under Berman, *TNG* won 18 Emmy Awards. And in 1994, it became the only syndicated show ever to be nominated for Outstanding Drama Series (it lost to *Picket Fences*).

YAWN
As the series aged, however, the quality of the show occasionally suffered. Some critics and viewers felt that *Star Trek: TNG* had become a victim of its own formula: give a crew member a personal crisis to deal with, introduce an alien with a forehead prosthetic to reflect on a thinly veiled human folly (greed, racism, etc.), and then put the ship in danger. *TNG's* final two seasons revolved around stories like Commander Worf's young son not wanting to be a warrior, and Dr. Crusher falling for a man who turns out to be an alien who once seduced her grandmother.

Despite the formulaic plots, ratings for *TNG* remained high—so high, in fact, that Paramount executive Brandon Tartikoff ordered a new *Trek* spin-off in 1993. Tartikoff wanted a show about a father and son who travel through space helping people, but Berman and writing partner Michael Piller had other ideas. They kept the father-and-son angle (Avery Brooks as Captain Sisko and Cirroc Lofton as his boy, Jake) but put them on a remote outpost called Deep Space 9, located near a "wormhole" that very nasty aliens could get through.

Star Trek: Deep Space 9 went beyond *TNG* to deal with subjects that previous *Star Treks* had never explored in depth, including religious fanaticism, immigration and the franchise's first same-sex kiss. And unlike *The Next Generation*, most of the characters didn't get along, which heightened the drama. Like *TNG*, *DS9* lasted for seven seasons.

GENERATIONS GAP
After *Star Trek: The Next Generation* ended in 1994, Picard, Data, and company were promoted to the big screen. At first, fans were excited to hear that the movie, *Star Trek: Generations*, would include Kirk, Spock, and McCoy. But Rick Berman, who produced the film and co-wrote the story, soon angered many of them. How? He killed off Captain Kirk.

When word leaked out before the movie's release that Kirk was going to die, most fans assumed that he would go out in a blaze of glory, sacrificing himself for the ship. But his death, while it did help Picard defeat the bad guy (played by Malcolm McDowell), was, in a word, anticlimactic. What irked fans of the original series most was that, storywise, Kirk didn't *have* to die—the movie's plot included a "temporal nexus" that Kirk could have gone to and never aged. All Berman had to do was put Kirk in there at the end of the movie. Said Leonard Nimoy, "To end it with a fight scene between Kirk and Malcolm McDowell! What's the point?"

Generations made more than $75 million at the box office but received mixed reviews. "It is predictably flabby and impenetrable in places," wrote Janet Maslin of *The New York Times*. "But it has enough pomp, spectacle, and high-tech small talk to keep the franchise afloat."

CAPTAIN KATE
Maslin was right. The franchise stayed afloat, and Paramount called on Berman to create a fourth *Star Trek* TV series. The result was *Star Trek: Voyager*, the first *Trek* series with a female captain. The concept: Captain Janeway (Kate Mulgrew) and her crew become stranded on the other side of the galaxy and must find their way home. This gave Berman and writers Michael Piller and Jeri Taylor an opportunity to invent new

aliens and force the crew to survive without the help of "the mighty Federation."

Enough viewers tuned in to keep it going, but fewer than had watched *Deep Space 9*, and far fewer than for *The Next Generation*. And unlike the last two series, *Voyager* wasn't syndicated; It was the flagship show for the new United Paramount Network (UPN). To build an entire network around a single show—especially a sci-fi show—was a gamble, but it proved just how big *Star Trek* had become.

THE SEVEN OF NINE SHOW

Studio bosses had left Berman alone on *TNG* and *DS9*; this time he found himself at the mercy of network executives. When they complained that the show wasn't "sexy" enough, Berman was ordered to bring in curvy actress Jeri Ryan as Seven of Nine, a member of the Borg collective who is captured and rehabilitated by the *Voyager* crew. After the execs saw Ryan in her skin-tight Borg costume—she looked like a half-human/half-robot with gray skin—they sent Berman a memo complaining that she was *too* sexy. Mulgrew complained to Berman about the switch, and he agreed but told her that "orders are orders."

The tactic paid off, though, because *Voyager's* head writer, Brannon Braga, saw potential in the Seven of Nine character. Most *Trek* series had one nonhuman who helped the other characters learn about their own humanity. Spock filled that purpose in the first series; Data took that role in *TNG*. On *Voyager*, crew members—including the ship's holographic doctor (Robert Picardo)—ended up teaching the cyborg Seven of Nine how to be human.

If you realign the phasic warp array to emit a graviton pulse, that should be enough to get you to page 475 for the final chapter of our Star Trek saga.

TV MARKETING:
A TIMELINE

In the beginning, television manufacturers had to make Americans believe that they needed a television, even before there was anything to watch. Ever since then, they've had to sell the "next big thing" every step of the way.

1931: While there isn't any television on the airwaves beyond a handful of brief, experimental broadcasts in New York, the Western Television Corporation of Chicago is already trying to sell TV sets. It runs ads in newspapers and magazines promising consumers that they'll be "amazed to see and hear beautiful blues singers, studio boxing, and dancing girls" on its Visionette TVs. Cost: $150 (in today's dollars, about $2,000).

1933: In print ads, Scotland's Plew Television romantically dubs TV "the enchanted mirror," "the magic eye," and "the strangest dream that man has ever dreamed." They ask Brits to buy one of their sets in order to encourage the BBC to create some TV programming so there will be something to watch.

1936: In direct competition with the government-run BBC (which only airs a few hours of programs each day), the British television manufacturer Baird Television promotes its Televisor model—which has no audio—by airing weekly programs on its own network. Ads promise viewers that they might one day be able to watch an entire "talkie film" on a Televisor...while listening to the sound on an attached radio.

1938: General Electric promotes the immediacy of television, telling consumers they'll "see things at the very instant they happen!" Marketers also appeal to Depression-era Americans by pushing the possibility that TV would create jobs by opening up a whole new industry for artists, engineers, salespeople, and skilled workmen.

1939: TV is demonstrated at the New York World's Fair. The few thousand people who own a TV and live within a 50-mile radius of Manhattan can now watch two hours of experimental

Priorities: TV was adopted in the U.S. more quickly than indoor plumbing.

broadcasting each week. Bloomingdale's gives demonstrations of the device and promotes in-store viewings of the World's Fair broadcast.

- A 12-inch RCA television costs $1,000 ($15,400 in today's money), about the price of a new car. The company markets the sets as a luxury item to Americans. Magazine ads feature privileged-looking women and men lounging in formalwear, sipping champagne, and watching TV. Sample ad copy: "Newest scientific wonder clicks with world's most sophisticated public."

1943: Even though television manufacturing and broadcasts have halted completely due to World War II shortages, marketing continues to focus on TV's potential. General Electric predicts in a 1943 advertisement that "Everyone will enjoy television" and that TV will help Americans keep up with new dance crazes and recipes. It also touts TV as "the ultimate advertising medium."

1946: As regular broadcasting begins in the U.S., RCA follows the same model as Baird did in the U.K. In the 1920s and 1930s, it had established two radio networks, NBC Blue and NBC Red, to get people to buy the radios it manufactured. To sell more television sets, it creates the NBC television network. RCA tagline: "Telecasting Tomorrow–Today."

Late 1940s: Another early selling point for televisions sets is the surrounding cabinetry. TV consoles, considering their expense and size, have to contribute to the beauty of a room. Manufacturers hype the exotic woods and elegant styles of TV "furniture." There still isn't much on the screen, but a "hand-tooled French Provincial model" looks like an elegant sideboard.

1950: Nine percent of households have a television set.

1951: Networks are still broadcasting in black and white, but manufacturers are already producing and marketing color sets. One model promises "gay costumes and gorgeous setting in all their natural beauty and splendor." Price: $500 (about $4,300 today).

1954: Just over half of all American homes now have a TV set. By the end of the decade, 86 percent will.

Mid-1960s: Transistors replace vacuum tubes, and the era of portable television begins. Philco and Sony sell miniature sets for around $250 ($1,600 today). Ads promise the joy of watching these black-and-white wonders on the beach, in a boat, or in a car (if viewers have 10 D-cell batteries and can get a signal).

1970s: Most homes now have a color TV, so manufacturers switch tactics to encourage viewers to purchase a *second* TV for the home. A Motorola 16-inch model, advertised as "the best buy in color," sold for the equivalent of $1,400 and boasted that because its "works are in a drawer," it was easy to repair.

1980s: With the marketplace saturated, manufacturers have to get clever to convince consumers to trade up to a better TV. Zenith's System 3 offers "more sharpness" and "more color picture resolution." In 1984 RCA unveils "a giant-screen TV as big and bright as all outdoors" with "full spectrum" stereo audio. It boasts a 45-inch screen, the biggest available at the time.

2000: 99.95 percent of American homes have at least one TV set.

*　　*　　*

PAAR FOR THE COURSE

Jack Paar, host of *The Tonight Show* from 1957 to 1962, developed and solidified the format still used on most late-night shows today. But Paar had a temper—and didn't have much patience for being bossed around. In February 1960, NBC censors pulled one of his jokes for being too racy. (It involved a double entendre about the abbreviation "WC"—one person in the skit thinks it means "wayside chapel"; another takes it to mean "water closet.") Paar was livid, so the next night he delivered his monologue, went to his desk, and said, with tears in his eyes, "I am leaving *The Tonight Show*. There must be a better way of making a living than this." Then he walked off the set and out the door, leaving co-host Hugh Downs to finish the show. Paar returned three weeks later, quipping, "When I walked off, I said there must be a better way of making a living. I've looked, and there isn't." He eventually left the show for good in 1962.

First TV show with an electronic music theme: *Dr. Who* (1963).

ODD SPECIALS

*Some of the best moments on television have been TV specials:
Liza With a Z or A Charlie Brown Christmas, for example.
And then there are these TV "events": specials that are
memorable for their spectacular weirdness.*

The Paul Lynde Halloween Special (1976)
Paul Lynde was best known for being the longtime "center
square" on *Hollywood Squares* (see page 334), where he
gave campy, sarcastic answers to Peter Marshall's questions. ("Why
do Hell's Angels wear leather?" "Because chiffon wrinkles too easily.") In 1976 Lynde was tapped to host a Halloween-themed variety special. The razor-thin plot consisted of Lynde helping two
misunderstood witches (played by Margaret Hamilton, who'd portrayed one in *The Wizard of Oz*, and Billie Hayes, who was
Witchiepoo on *H.R. Pufnstuf*). This leads to a series of sketches
telling the tale of Lynde's adventures in overcoming prejudice.
Guest stars included Billy Barty, Donny and Marie Osmond, Florence Henderson, Betty White, and KISS.

Octomom: The Incredible Unseen Footage (2009)
Was Nadya Suleman—fertility-drug-taking single mother of six
who gave birth to octuplets (bringing the number of her offspring to a grand total of 14)—a generous, selfless, devoted
mother; a mental case; a publicity hound looking to become a
star; or some combination of all three? This special strung
together two hours of raw footage of Suleman berating medical
staff as she delivers her babies, Suleman "avoiding" paparazzi,
and Suleman talking to herself. One reviewer said that "a team
of monkeys could not have done worse" than the producers who
created it.

Conspiracy Theory: Did We Land on the Moon? (2001)
This hour-long "investigative report" was hosted by *X-Files* actor
Mitch Pileggi in what had to have been the lowest point in his
career. The show primarily consists of interviews with conspiracy
theorists and, in a particularly memorable moment of bad science,

cites the 1978 B-movie *Capricorn One*. The plot of that movie, in which NASA fakes a Mars expedition, somehow supports the idea that the 1969 moon landing was faked, too. Later, a conspiracy theorist named Bill Kaysing suggests that the *Apollo 1* fire that killed three astronauts in 1967 was deliberately set and then covered up by NASA because one of the astronauts was about to "go public" with a claim that the entire NASA moon launch program was a hoax.

The Kathie Lee Gifford Christmas Specials (1995–99)

These über-saccharine variety/musical shows featured talk-show host Kathie Lee Gifford, her husband Frank Gifford, and their toddler children. These specials were standard Christmastime fare for four years, but the most memorable thing about them may have been the unrepentant glee with which *Washington Post* TV critic Tom Shales skewered them. "What's the difference between the 24-hour flu and a Kathie Lee Gifford Christmas special? Twenty-three hours. This is the kind of television to be watched not from the couch, as it were, but while peering out from behind it and using it as a shield, as if perhaps an air raid or some other sort of massive bombing were in progress."

KISS Meets the Phantom of the Park (1978)

With all of their theatricality, one would think that KISS and television would be a match made in heaven. But this special/movie was so bad and embarrassing that reportedly no one was allowed to mention it again in front of band members and cast and crew left it off their resumes. The plot: At California's Magic Mountain theme park, a demented engineer named Devereaux (Anthony Zerbe) makes mind-control devices when he isn't designing rides. When the park's owner cuts Devereaux's budget to hire the rock n' roll group KISS to play on site, Devereaux goes mad and swears revenge on the band. The revenge? KISS robots destroy the park while the real band sits in an underground jail. The real KISS escapes just in time to battle robot KISS onstage. Bonus fact: Drummer Peter Criss's dialogue delivery was so garbled that his voice had to be (badly) dubbed over by another actor.

NEIL POSTMAN SAYS...

TV is entertaining, and TV news is informative, right? Not according to Neil Postman (1931–2003). One of the leading media critics of our time, he wrote extensively about how he thought TV and media were slowly destroying our culture. Here are some of this thoughts.

"Television is our culture's principal mode of knowing about itself. Therefore, how television stages the world becomes the model for how the world is properly to be staged."

"Television commercials promote the utopian and childish idea that all problems have fast, simple, and technological solutions."

"Television is altering the meaning of 'being informed' by creating a species of information that might properly be called disinformation. Disinformation does not mean false information. It means misleading information that creates the illusion of knowing something, but which in fact leads one away from knowing."

"Our politics, news, athletics, education, and commerce have been transformed by TV into congenial adjuncts of show business, largely without protest or even much popular notice."

"It is not that television is entertaining but that it has made entertainment itself the natural format for the representation of all experience." "Most of our daily news consists of information that gives us something to talk about but cannot lead to any meaningful action."

"To make the assumption that technology is always a friend to culture is stupidity, plain and simple."

"The message of television is not only that all the world is a stage, but that the stage is located in Las Vegas."

"When cultural life is redefined as a perpetual round of entertainments, when, a people become an audience, then a nation finds itself at risk."

"All the words uttered in an hour of news could be printed on a page of a newspaper. The world cannot be understood in one page."

A plasma TV uses about twice as much energy as an LCD set of the same size.

BANNED FROM SNL

*In its 35-year-run, Saturday Night Live has featured some of
the hottest stars and musical guests. But some got a little
too hot…and got banned from the show for life.*

ANDY KAUFMAN

Background: Quirky comedian Kaufman appeared on the first episode of *SNL* in 1975, lip-syncing to the "Mighty Mouse" song. He made several more appearances, but his offbeat humor sometimes put viewers off. So in November 1982, *SNL* held a poll to let viewers decide if he should return to the show or never appear again.

Banned! More than 360,000 people called in to vote: 169,186 in favor of Kaufman, 195,544 for the ban. Kaufman honored the final decision, although he made one final pre-taped appearance to thank those who had voted for him. (As it turned out, the poll was yet another unique idea thought up by Kaufman himself.)

LOUISE LASSER

Background: During the week of rehearsals before hosting the show in 1976, the *Mary Hartman, Mary Hartman* star was behaving erratically and seemed emotionally distant to cast and crew. She was nearly incoherent and was rumored to be drunk or extremely high when the show went on the air.

Banned! Lasser was told never to come back, and executive producer Lorne Michaels never allowed her episode to be rerun.

THE REPLACEMENTS

Background: The Minneapolis alternative-rock band was as well known in the music world for being boozehounds as they were for their songs—they frequently played gigs falling-down drunk. And just before the January 1986 episode on which they were the musical guest, they slammed beers with host Harry Dean Stanton.

Banned! The band managed to get through their two songs with no musical hitches, until singer Paul Westerberg began cursing during

"Bastards of Young." During the show-ending "good-nights," the Replacements jumped around the stage...while the cast ignored them. Later, the band got the news: they'd killed their chances of ever appearing on the show again.

ELVIS COSTELLO

Background: The Sex Pistols were scheduled to perform on a December 1977 *SNL* but couldn't get their visas in time. Elvis Costello filled in, and Lorne Michaels asked him specifically not to perform his current hit, "Radio, Radio," a vehement anti-mass-media song. So Costello went onstage and began playing "Less Than Zero." He then abruptly stopped, told the audience there was "no reason to perform it," and launched into "Radio, Radio."

Banned! For disobeying the order, Costello earned a ban from the show...until 1989, when he was invited back. Later, on the 1999 *SNL* 25th-anniversary special, Costello re-created his infamous moment, playing a few bars of one song and then launching into "Radio, Radio," with the Beastie Boys as his backing band.

ADRIEN BRODY

Background: Every moment on live television counts, so every episode of *SNL* is intricately mapped out beforehand. That's why, during a 2003 episode, Michaels grew furious when host Adrien Brody performed a 45-second-long impromptu monologue in a stereotypical Jamaican accent before introducing the musical guest, Jamaican singer Sean Paul, whom Brody called "Sean John."

Banned! Brody has not been invited back.

CYPRESS HILL

Background: There was speculation before an October 1993 episode regarding whether or not host Shannen Doherty would behave—she had an explosive temper and was well known for provoking on-set battles on *Beverly Hills, 90210*. But the real troublemakers turned out to be the musical guest, rap group Cypress Hill. One member lit a joint live on the air during their performance of "I Ain't Goin' Out Like That," and they ended the song by trashing their instruments.

Banned! Unhappy with the band's blatant drug use and violent performance, producers showed Cypress Hill the door. Musical guests usually perform twice in an episode; Cypress Hill didn't even get to do their second performance.

MARTIN LAWRENCE

Background: At the start of the February 1994 episode he hosted, the *Martin* star and stand-up comedian delivered an extremely graphic monologue about women with poor feminine-hygiene practices. Michaels and hundreds of viewers were so upset that on the West Coast broadcast and in reruns, NBC replaced Lawrence's routine with an explanatory text crawl and voiceover. A sample: "Martin's speech was a frank and lively presentation, and nearly cost us all our jobs."

Banned! Lawrence was never allowed back on *Saturday Night Live*...or any other NBC show, for that matter, until he appeared as a guest on *The Tonight Show* in 2001, seven years later.

FRANK ZAPPA

Background: Experimental rock musician Frank Zappa never took himself (or anything) all that seriously, so when asked to host *SNL* in October 1978, he tested the boundaries of the show. He purposely acted ill-prepared, repeatedly mugging at the camera and blatantly reading his lines off cue cards.

Banned! The cast and crew were enraged and stayed far away from him during the good-nights...except for John Belushi, who appreciated the stunt. Zappa never returned to the show.

FEAR

Background: Former cast member John Belushi returned to host the show's 1981 Halloween episode on the condition that he could invite the musical guest: the punk band FEAR. FEAR brought along a group of aggressive slam dancers, and the *SNL* crew allowed the punks to bump around the foot of the stage during FEAR's performance. But they regretted the decision when the dancers began stomping on and knocking over everything in sight, including cameras and lighting equipment. FEAR tried to speed through three songs in their allotted time, but were cut off after two.

Banned! Estimated damages to the *SNL* studios: $20,000. The band was the first—and last—hardcore punk group invited onto the show.

THE MINISERIES

*The sweeping saga and disastrous demise
of a once-grand television tradition.*

EPISODE ONE: THE ENGLISH INVASION

American television series have traditionally followed a standard formula: each week characters get a problem, solve it, and learn a valuable lesson. A series could go on like that for hundreds of episodes. British TV is different: dramatic series are serialized and can run for as few as six episodes. In the 1960s, this format was a very popular way to present adaptations of classic novels.

The first "novel for television" broadcast in the United States was 1967's English-made *The Forsyte Saga*. The 26-part series—a decades-spanning story of a prominent British family—was a big hit for the young, struggling National Educational Television network (later PBS) and led to one of PBS's signature shows, *Masterpiece Theatre*, a showcase for multiple-part literary adaptations, usually made in England.

It also led American commercial networks to test the idea of long-format television with made-for-TV movies broken up into shorter episodes. Examples: a seven-hour adaptation of the Leon Uris novel *QB VII* (ABC, 1974) and the six-hour biblical epic *Moses the Lawgiver* (CBS, 1975).

But the miniseries wouldn't become a TV force until CBS's vice president of programming, Fred Silverman, left to join rival network ABC in 1975. Silverman had a knack for predicting hit shows (he'd picked *All in the Family*, *The Waltons*, and *Scooby-Doo, Where Are You?*) and he thought the miniseries made great ratings sense. Unlike with other TV shows, Silverman reasoned, viewers would have to watch every episode. He also figured that if the network aired a miniseries during Sweeps Week (when networks set advertising rates and try to lure the most viewers with splashy programming), it could provide a huge ratings boost. Silverman called it "Event Television."

EPISODE TWO: THE SAGA BEGINS

Silverman and ABC produced the first American miniseries, *Rich*

Man, Poor Man, which aired in 1976. The 12-hour saga told the story of two brothers over a period of 30 years and featured Nick Nolte in his first lead role. Silverman's hunch paid off—*Rich Man, Poor Man* averaged a whopping 27 million viewers and was the second-most-watched show on TV for the year. Executives at all three broadcast networks (ABC, CBS, and NBC) noticed; "Event Television" meant big ratings.

EPISODE THREE: *ROOTS*

Silverman's next "event" would be the most popular miniseries of all time—and one of the most memorable TV shows ever—*Roots*. Based on Alex Haley's autobiographical novel, *Roots* traced the history of an African family through slavery to the present day. The all-star cast included Ben Vereen, Lou Gossett Jr., O. J. Simpson, Robert Reed, Todd Bridges, Edward Asner, Maya Angelou, John Amos, Richard Roundtree, and LeVar Burton.

Miniseries episodes were usually run in regular weekly time slots, but *Roots* aired on eight consecutive nights because ABC executives didn't think a program about African-American history could hold a broad audience over several weeks. They were wrong: more than 130 million viewers watched at least some of *Roots*. The final installment, airing on January 30, 1977, is still the fifth-highest rated broadcast in TV history.

EPISODE FOUR: AFTER *ROOTS*

From the late 1970s to the early 1980s, miniseries were common fare on television, though not all were as successful as *Roots*. The networks quickly learned what kinds of miniseries succeeded: stories about the Old West, the Bible, a powerful family, or a major war. Some of the most popular of the period include…

• *Holocaust* (1978). One of the first American productions to address Nazi atrocities, and also one of the first times schoolchildren were actually assigned TV viewing as homework.

• *Jesus of Nazareth* (1977). A reverent film that was so well received that it was expanded from four to six hours and still runs on cable TV every Easter.

• *Shogun* (1980). Based on James Clavell's novel, starring Richard

---

The French version of *The Simpsons* translates Homer's "D'oh" into "T'oh."

Chamberlain as an English captain shipwrecked in feudal Japan. A 2½-hour version was released theatrically in Japan.

- *The Thorn Birds* (1983). Spanning 60 years, the show featured Richard Chamberlain as a priest torn between his vow of celibacy and his love for a woman he raised from childhood.

- *V* (1983). Alien spaceships loom over U.S. cities, planning to devour humanity in this sci-fi allegory of Nazism.

EPISODE FIVE: THE END IS NOT THE END

Two World War II miniseries adapted from Herman Wouk novels ended the heyday of the miniseries. *The Winds of War* was a 14-hour, $40 million project that took nearly a decade to film...and it only covered the first two years of World War II. It was a hit in the spring of 1983, so ABC approved a sequel. *War and Remembrance* (1988) was even bigger, costing a record $110 million, but its lackluster ratings told their own story: audiences were no longer captivated by the miniseries.

By the late 1980s, broadcast TV networks were fighting for audiences against hundreds of new cable channels as well as home video. Result: very few major minis were produced after the *War* years. CBS and NBC aired a few small, four-hour miniseries, but nothing approaching a *Roots*. ABC, however, wasn't yet ready to let go of the high-profile mini. Filming budgets shrank considerably, but ABC continued to make miniseries thanks to a partnership with horror author Stephen King. He would be the creative force behind seven moderately successful ABC miniseries in the 1990s, including *It*, *The Tommyknockers*, and *The Stand*.

People don't gather for "Event Television" anymore. TV shows can be taped, TiVoed, or rented on DVD, but the miniseries didn't die—it still lives on cable. Since 2000, HBO, Showtime, and the Sci-Fi Channel have produced many acclaimed miniseries on par with *Roots*, including *Band of Brothers*, *From the Earth to the Moon*, and *Angels in America*. The secret to their success? Frequent re-airings.

MINI-DISASTERS

Not all miniseries attracted record-breaking audiences and truckloads of Emmys. Here are a few clunkers.

- *Beulah Land* (1980). Life on a pre–Civil War Southern planta-
tion, viewed through rose-colored glasses. Features many
extremely happy and satisfied slaves.

- *The Last Days of Pompeii* (1984). Ancient Rome meets *Peyton
Place*. People engage in lurid behavior of all kinds until the vol-
cano instantly kills them all. One of Sir Laurence Olivier's last
roles.

- *Amerika: It Can't Happen Here* (1987). Russian communists
take over the United States. Over the two years it took to film
Amerika, U.S.-Russia tensions had thawed so much that the
miniseries was irrelevant by the time it aired.

- *Fresno* (1986). A comic send-up of 1980s TV soaps like *Dallas*,
starring Carol Burnett and Dabney Coleman as the heads of two
rival, raisin-growing families in "America's 64th-largest city."

- *Sins* (1986). Joan Collins (*Dynasty*) produced it and played the
lead role, a woman separated from her family by death and war.
(Collins was twice her character's age.)

- *Scarlett* (1994). In this *Gone With the Wind* sequel, Timothy Dalton
and Joanne Whalley stand in for Clark Gable and Vivien Leigh.

- *The 10th Kingdom* (2000). A man and his daughter are trapped
in an alternate universe where trolls and giants threaten the king-
doms of Snow White, Cinderella, and Little Red Riding Hood.

*　　*　　*

BRETT UNDER FIRE

Comedian Brett Butler, who had survived an abusive relationship
with an alcoholic, landed an ABC sitcom in 1993, *Grace Under
Fire*. Butler herself also struggled with alcohol and an addiction to
painkillers, which led her to frequently lash out at co-workers, and
even fire writers, including creator Chuck Lorre. Butler's actions
and stays in rehabilitation centers caused filming delays for the
top-10 show, but the worst incident came when Butler reportedly
flashed her breasts at co-star Jon Paul Steuer…who was 12 years
old. His parents pulled him off of the series. In the middle of
Grace Under Fire's fifth season in 1998, ABC abruptly canceled
the series, citing Butler's unpredictability as the reason.

Alex Trebek claims to know "about half" of any given day's *Jeopardy!* answers (or questions).

WHERE EVERYBODY KNOWS YOU'RE DUMB

Every sitcom worth its laugh track has to have at least one stupid character.

Rebecca: So, did you get a chance to see Carla's babies? Who do they look like—Carla or Eddie?
Woody: Well, they're twins. They kinda look like each other.
—*Cheers*

"Here's a job I could do: 'Police seek third gunman.' Well, tomorrow I'm gonna march over to the police station and tell them that I'm the man they're looking for!"
—*Harry, 3rd Rock from the Sun*

"As a great Eastern religion says, it's all about striking a balance between the ping and the pong."
—*Kelly, Married... With Children*

Joey: If *Homo sapiens* were in fact "homo" sapiens, could that be why they're extinct?
Ross: Joey, *Homo sapiens* are people.
Joey: Hey! I'm not judging here!
—*Friends*

"I cheated wrong. I copied the Lisa name and used the Ralph answers.
—*Ralph, The Simpsons*

Lowell: Where are you going?
Helen: Well, if you must know, I'm going to see my OB/GYN.
Lowell: Fine, be that way. I'm having dinner with my m-o-m-m-y.
—*Wings*

Archie: Ask your mother. She believes in capital punishment.
Gloria: Do you, Ma?
Edith: Well, sure. As long as it ain't too severe.
—*All in the Family*

"I don't brush my teeth. I rinse my mouth out with soda after I eat. I was pretty sure Dr Pepper was a dentist."
—*Brittany, Glee*

"There is no *Star Wars* better than *Planet of the Apes*. I mean, those apes were really good actors."
—*Kelso, That '70s Show*

Fred Rogers once played a minister on a 1996 episode of *Dr. Quinn, Medicine Woman.*

OPRAH FACTS

The Oprah Winfrey Show is ending in 2011 so Winfrey can focus on her new cable network, OWN. Here's a look back at one of the most popular daytime talk shows of all time.

• In 1983 Winfrey left a news anchor job in Baltimore to host a Chicago talk show called *AM Chicago*. In a month, it was beating *Donahue* in the ratings. By 1986 it was renamed *The Oprah Winfrey Show* and was aired nationally.

• Topic of the first nationally aired episode: "How to Marry the Man or Woman of Your Choice."

• After a 1996 episode about the Mad Cow beef scare, a group of Texas ranchers sued Winfrey for libel. She moved to show to Texas for the duration of the month-long trial. (She was acquitted.) In Texas, she met jury consultant Dr. Phil McGraw, and later had him on *Oprah* more than 100 times to help viewers with their personal problems. McGraw got his own show in 2002.

• Winfrey's show is produced by her company Harpo—"Oprah" spelled backward. (Winfrey owns Harpo, and she's only the third woman in U.S. history to own a studio, after Mary Pickford's United Artists and Lucille Ball's DesiLu Productions.)

• Big *Oprah* moments: Liberace's final public appearance in 1986; Ellen DeGeneres announces she's a lesbian in 1997; Tom Cruise jumps on Winfrey's couch while professing his love for Katie Holmes in 2005.

• *The Oprah Winfrey Show* has been the most-watched daytime talk show on TV all 25 years of its run.

• *Oprah* has been aired in more than 140 countries, including Iraq, Vietnam, Libya, Denmark, and China.

• Highest-rated episode: 62 million watched a 1993 interview with Michael Jackson.

• By 1997 Winfrey had won seven Emmys for Best Talk Show Host, and the show had won nine awards for Best Talk Show. At that point, Winfrey took herself and the show out of Emmy consideration.

WHAT DID MAGNUM, P.I., DRIVE?

*On page 233 we asked, "What did Jim Rockford drive?"
Here are some more of our favorite TV cars.*

Series: *The A-Team* (1983–87)
Vehicle: 1983 GMC G-15 Van
Details: The van the government-fleeing mercenaries drove through all manner of gun battles and explosions was black and gunmetal gray, with diagonal red stripes on either side. The interior had white naugahyde bucket seats; and, of course, a custom gun case in the back. And it was owned by B. A. Baracus—the character played by Mr. T. (The Team drove everywhere because Baracus was afraid to fly.) Six vans in all were used for the show, and one still sits on a back lot at Universal Studios in Los Angeles. Another is in the Cars of the Stars Motor Museum in Keswick, England.

Series: *Starsky & Hutch* (1975–79)
Vehicle: Ford Gran Torino
Details: The trademark two-door, red Gran Torino with a white stripe down either side was actually two cars: a 1975 model for the first season, and a 1976 model for the rest of the show's run. The car's radio handle was Zebra-3, but it was nicknamed the Striped Tomato by Hutch. Starsky owned it; Hutch had his own car—a beat-up 1973 Ford Galaxie 500. To capitalize on the show's popularity, Ford produced a limited edition of 1,002 Starsky & Hutch Gran Torinos in 1976, complete with the red-and-white paint job. Many are still on the road today.

Series: *Magnum, P.I.* (1980–88)
Vehicle: Ferrari 308 GTS
Details: Thomas Magnum's (Tom Selleck) famous Ferrari was actually three different cars: a 1978 308 GTS for the first season, a 1980 308 GTSi for the second and third seasons, and a 1984 308 GTSi Quattrovalvole for the remainder of the series. All

three were convertibles, and almost always had the top off to accommodate Selleck's 6'4" frame, as well as to enable aerial shots. The producers originally wanted a Porsche 928, so they asked Porsche to make a custom model with an enlarged sunroof. But Porsche has a policy of not making special models for media purposes, so they refused—and the producers went with Porsche's competitor, Ferrari, instead. (Bonus: Magnum's Ferrari wasn't actually his—it belonged to his mysterious benefactor, Robin Masters.)

Series: *Mr. Bean* (1990–95)
Vehicle: British Leyland Mini 1000
Details: Originally, Mr. Bean (Rowan Atkinson) had an orange 1969 Morris Mini MK II, but it lasted just one episode—it was intentionally destroyed in a crash near the end of the show. For the rest of the series, Mr. Bean drove a 1977 British Leyland Mini 1000, "applejack green" except for the black hood. Like many of these famous TV cars, Mr. Bean's Mini was practically a character on the show and was used in a number of gags, including one in which Mr. Bean drove it while perched in an armchair mounted on the roof. This car's also in the Cars of the Stars Motor Museum.

Series: *Married...with Children* (1987–97)
Vehicle: Early 1970s Dodge...sort of
Details: Al Bundy loved to talk about his rust-colored Dodge with its eight-track player, screwdriver-controlled ignition, and nearly one million miles on the odometer. What year was it? Nobody knows for sure: On one occasion, Al says it's a 1971; on another, a 1974. But the best part: Al's Dodge wasn't a Dodge. Car-savvy fans quickly noticed from the few times the car appeared on the show that it was actually a 1971 or '72 Plymouth Duster.

Series: *The Fall Guy* (1981–86)
Vehicle: GMC Sierra 4x4 pickup
Details: Hollywood stuntman/bounty hunter Colt Seavers (Lee Majors) used his tough-looking truck to do spectacular stunts in nearly every episode, including improbable jumps that nearly

---

On *The Addams Family*, Morticia's maiden name was Frump.

made the truck look like it could fly. With all the wear and tear, producers therefore had to keep several on hand at all times. They were all two-tone (brown and tan) early 1980s Sierras, each with a roll bar behind the cab and an eagle and the phrase "Fall Guy Stuntman Association" painted on the hood. But they weren't exactly alike, and sometimes slightly different Sierras were used in the same episode. So if you look closely, you can see features—like headlight shape—vary from one scene to the next on what is supposed to be the same truck.

Series: *Miami Vice* (1984–89)
Vehicles: Fake Ferrari Spyder; real Ferrari Testarossa
Details: For the first two seasons, Detective Sonny Crockett (Don Johnson) drove a black Ferrari Daytona Spyder 365 GTS/4. But it wasn't real; it was a Chevrolet Corvette chassis with a Ferrari body kit built onto it. When Enzo Ferrari found out, he was enraged and sued the show. So in the third season, the fake is blown up and replaced by a brand-new white 1986 Ferrari Testarossa— donated by Ferrari himself (along with a second as a backup). He was so happy with the publicity from the show that he gave Don Johnson a 1989 silver Testarossa as a gift. (Johnson sold it at auction in 2003 for $88,560.)

MORE FAMOUS TV VEHICLES

• *My Name Is Earl* (2005–09) Earl (Jason Lee) drives a 1973 Chevrolet El Camino SS. It's red, with one blue door.

• *Baretta* (1975–78) Baretta (Robert Blake) drives a rusted-out blue Chevy Impala he calls "The Blue Ghost."

• *Get Smart!* (1965–70) Over the course of the show's five-year run, Maxwell Smart (Don Adams) drives a red 1965 Sunbeam Tiger, a blue 1967 Volkswagen Karmann Ghia, and an "Aztec gold" 1969 Opel GT.

• *The Monkees* (1966–68) The Monkeemobile is a 1966 Pontiac GTO customized by Dean Jeffries, who also worked on the Batmobile.

• *The Waltons* (1972–81) The family drives a 1929 Ford Model A pickup.

The computers on *The Office* are operational. Rainn Wilson (Dwight) blogs in character.

WACKY TV: THE WB AND UPN EDITION

Two new networks launched in January 1995: the United Paramount Network (UPN) and the Warner Bros. Network (The WB). Neither had the history, audience, or production money of the other four networks, so how did they differentiate themselves in a crowded TV landscape? By launching really nutty shows...almost all of which were quickly canceled.

CHAINS OF LOVE (UPN, 2001)
A game show in which a woman chooses which man she would most like to date...from five guys that she's literally chained to.

THE WATCHER (UPN, 1995)
Rapper Sir Mix-A-Lot ("Baby Got Back") portrays the chief of security at a Las Vegas hotel. Each week, viewers get a peek inside the lives of different characters, as revealed by security cameras.

BRITNEY & KEVIN: CHAOTIC (UPN, 2005)
Home-video footage of Britney Spears and her husband Kevin Federline, mostly flirting and goofing off.

HOMEBOYS IN OUTER SPACE (UPN, 1996–97)
In an odd combination of *Star Trek* and '90s hip-hop, this show follows two African-American astronauts (comedians Flex and Darryl Bell) who travel around the 23rd-century universe in an interstellar Cadillac called the "Space Hoopty."

MOVIE STARS (WB, 1999–2000)
Past-his-prime L.A. *Law* star Harry Hamlin plays a past-his-prime movie star living with his wife (Jennifer Grant) and brother (Mark Benninghoffen), an unsuccessful actor bitterly living in Hamlin's shadow. Most episodes featured a sequence with Benninghoffen's character playing poker with Joey Travolta, Don Swayze, and Frank Stallone—real-life less-successful brothers of movie stars, all playing themselves.

SUPERSTAR USA (WB, 2004)
In this reality-show parody of *American Idol*, aspiring singers compete for a recording contract. What they don't know is that viewers are actually voting on who is the *worst* singer. The supportive studio audience, meanwhile, is told by producers that the singers are terminal cancer patients, and participating in a TV talent show is their last wish.

KELLY KELLY (WB, 1998)
An English professor named Kelly (Shelley Long) marries a firefighter named Doug Kelly. So her name becomes Kelly Kelly. The *Boston Herald* called the show "a two-alarm failure."

THE OBLONGS (WB, 2001)
A very dark animated sitcom about a family who are all disabled or disfigured due to pollution and radiation from a local factory. The father (Will Ferrell) has no arms or legs; the mother (Jean Smart) is an alcoholic whose hair has fallen out; their twin sons are conjoined.

THE MULLETS (UPN, 2003–04)
In 2003 the "mullet" hairstyle from the early '80s became a minor fad. UPN jumped on the bandwagon with this sitcom about two mullet-wearing redneck brothers, Dwayne and Denny Mullet, who clash with their straight-laced stepfather, a game-show host played by actual game-show host John O'Hurley.

SECRET DIARY OF DESMOND PFEIFFER (UPN, 1998)
Chi McBride (*Pushing Daisies, Boston Public*) portrays Desmond Pfeiffer, a black English nobleman in the 1860s who gets kidnapped and put on a slave ship, where he lands a job as President Abraham Lincoln's personal valet. The show resembles *Benson* and *Mr. Belvedere*, in that the "help" is far smarter than the family he works for, and the title character frequently insults and looks down his nose at his employers (Lincoln was portrayed as a buffoon, Mary Todd Lincoln as a sex-crazed alcoholic). The show immediately stirred up controversy—the NAACP protested that it made light of slavery (even though Pfeiffer wasn't, technically, a slave). That, and poor ratings, led UPN to cancel it after four episodes.

"MAKE IT WORK"

Can you name the shows that spawned these familiar catchphrases? (Answers are on page 502.)

1. "Come on down!"
2. "Who loves ya, baby?"
3. "The tribe has spoken."
4. "Bam!"
5. "Mom always liked you best."
6. "Missed it by *that* much."
7. "Make it work."
8. "Kiss my grits!"
9. "Is that your final answer?"
10. "Sit on it!"
11. "I said *good day!*"
12. "I know nothing!"
13. "You rang?"
14. "Let's be careful out there."
15. "Up your nose with a rubber hose!"
16. "Now, cut that out!"
17. "And that's the way it is."
18. "Dyn-o-mite!"
19. "Say goodnight, Gracie."
20. "Nanu, nanu."
21. "Baby, you're the greatest."
22. "Good night, and good luck."
23. "We control the horizontal and the vertical."
24. "Danger, Will Robinson!"
25. "You eeeediot!"
26. "Are you havin' a laugh?"
27. "You just said the secret word."
28. "Homey don't play that."
29. "Hey now!"
30. "That's what *she* said."
31. "I'm ready!"
32. "Don't do the crime if you can't do the time."
33. "Clear eyes, full hearts."
34. "Make it so."
35. "Ah, blerg."
36. "Save the cheerleader, save the world."

First female nightly news anchor: Barbara Walters, on *The ABC Evening News* (1976).

THE COSBY SHOWS

Bill Cosby is one of the true icons of television, having starred in classic shows from the 1960s through the 1990s. He also used the medium for more than entertainment: He helped to change white America's perception of blacks.

CLASS CLOWN

By the time Bill Cosby reached high school in 1952, he'd discovered he had a talent for making people laugh. He was the class clown all through his childhood in Philadelphia, and that tendency to goof around led him to flunk out in the 10th grade. He found a job resoling shoes and then, when he didn't find it satisfying, joined the Navy and went to work in a military hospital caring for Korean War veterans.

Working in a hospital had two profound impacts on him: 1) he saw that laughter went a long way toward helping people feel better, and 2) he realized that if he wanted to do something with his life, he'd have to get an education. By the time he left the Navy at age 24 in 1961, Cosby had completed his GED and earned an athletic scholarship to Temple University.

COMEDY TONIGHT

To supplement his scholarship money, Cosby tended bar, where he learned once again that he liked to make people laugh. At the end of his sophomore year, he left college and headed for New York City to become part of its burgeoning stand-up comedy scene.

The Gaslight Café in Greenwich Village gave him a regular spot, and there he developed his comedic style: an easygoing narrative of funny stories rather than standard setup/punchline jokes. In contrast with other African-American comedians of the era, such as Dick Gregory and Redd Fox, Cosby used humor that was free of profanity and racial commentary.

Talent scouts from *The Tonight Show Starring Johnny Carson* discovered Cosby and tapped him to perform on the show in 1964—just a year after he started his comedy career. The national exposure made him a star overnight and landed him a recording contract. In 1965 *Bill Cosby Is a Very Funny Fellow—Right!* sold a

---

In the 1982 pilot episode of *Mama's Family*, Mama (Vicki Lawrence) dies.

million copies, and the follow-up, *I Started Out as a Child,* led to the first of his six straight Grammy wins for Best Comedy Album.

CULP FICTION

By mid-1965, Cosby was on top of the world. His albums were million-sellers, he packed clubs and concert halls all over the country, and he was one of Carson's permanent guest hosts on *The Tonight Show.* At 28, he was the most popular comedian in America.

All that publicity attracted the attention of legendary TV writer and producer Carl Reiner (*Your Show of Shows, The Dick Van Dyke Show*). Reiner saw Cosby's act in Pittsburgh and recommended him to producer Sheldon Leonard, who was casting a new TV spy show. Reiner thought Cosby would be perfect for it, even though he had no acting experience.

Cosby landed the role, and starred opposite Robert Culp in *I Spy* (1965–68). Culp played a secret agent, traveling under the guise of a tennis player, while Cosby played his "trainer." The series was notable for its tightly plotted scripts, exotic locations, and chemistry between its stars. It marked the first time a black actor had a starring role on a TV drama. Cosby won Emmys for Best Actor in a Drama for all three seasons of *I Spy.*

HEY HEY HEY

Although Cosby was loved by TV audiences, his next few projects—a string of specials, the sitcom *The Bill Cosby Show* (1969–71), and the variety show *The New Bill Cosby Show* (1972)—all had middling ratings. It wasn't as if Cosby faded into obscurity—he still brought in huge crowds as a touring comedian. But he also had larger ambitions: He returned to college to earn a doctorate in education.

Cosby's biggest TV triumph of the '70s was a Saturday-morning cartoon show he created and provided voices for: *Fat Albert and the Cosby Kids* (CBS, 1972–84). Loosely based on Cosby's upbringing in inner-city Philadelphia, it was one of the first kids' cartoons to portray African Americans, as well as one of the first to include a moral or lesson with each episode.

I HEART HUXTABLE

In the 1980s, Cosby parlayed his status as a producer of quality entertainment into one of the most highly regarded series of all time: *The Cosby Show* (1984–92). Cosby's show was a throwback to the gentle, warm sitcoms of the 1950s, such as *Leave It to Beaver* and *The Donna Reed Show*. *The Cosby Show* wasn't considered a "black" show—it appealed to everyone, and as such, it was the most-watched show on TV for five straight years. For a generation of Americans, "it wasn't Ward Cleaver who was the all-American dad," wrote journalist Alisa Valdes-Rodrigues, "it was Cliff Huxtable."

THE COSBY EFFECT

Cosby was very careful about how black American culture was portrayed on his show. He hired Harvard psychiatrist Dr. Alvin Poussaint as a consultant to screen scripts for stereotypes and to ensure that they, as Cosby said, "depicted blacks in a dignified light." The Huxtable parents were upper-middle-class professionals: Cosby portrayed a pediatrician; Phylicia Rashad co-starred as his wife, an attorney. They and their five children lived in a lush Brooklyn brownstone. In addition, musical icons like Stevie Wonder and Dizzy Gillespie were guest stars, works by black artists dressed the set, and when the Huxtable kids went off to college, they mostly went to historically all-black universities.

For the most part, NBC went along with whatever Cosby wanted. Not only had he brought in millions of dollars for NBC, but the success of *The Cosby Show* helped lift the network from third place to first. In a 1985 episode, however, when a script called for an antiapartheid sign to be hanging in a bedroom, the network balked—too controversial, they said. But Cosby stood his ground. In an interview with the *Toronto Star*, he recalled saying to the NBC brass, "There may be two sides to apartheid in Archie Bunker's house. But it's impossible that the Huxtables would be on any side but one. That sign will stay on that door." And it did.

Into his 70s, Cosby continues to tour to sell-out crowds across the country. Some social critics even think that his portrayal of blacks on TV aided the groundwork for the election of President Barack Obama. Cosby himself pooh-poohs this notion, but some see a link. Republican Party strategist Karl Rove, commenting on the historic impact of Obama's election, said, "We've had an African-American first family for many years in different forms. When *The Cosby Show* was on, that was America's family. It wasn't a black family. It was America's family."

...For his newscasts, Walter Cronkite trained himself to speak at a rate of 124.

PRIME-TIME PROVERBS

Still more reflections on life from some of TV's most popular shows.

ON DEATH
"Death is just nature's way of telling you, 'Hey, you're not alive anymore.'"
—Bull, *Night Court*

"If you really want to study police methods, do what I do: watch television."
—Officer Toody, *Car 54, Where Are You?*

ON AMBITION
Red: You been in bed all day?
Eric: Yeah, I've been reading the Jack Kerouac classic *On The Road*. Why get out of bed when you can read about people who got out of bed?
—*That '70s Show*

ON CULTURE
"Culture is like spinach. Once you forget it's good for you, you can relax and enjoy it."
—Uncle Martin, *My Favorite Martian*

ON TIMING
"I used to do a year in 365 days. Now they go by much faster."
—Dr. Graham, *Ben Casey*

"There are three things you don't get over in a hurry: losing a woman, eating bad possum, and eating good possum."
—Beau La Barre, *Welcome Back, Kotter*

ON LEARNING
"What a wonderful day we've had. You have learned something, and I have learned something. Too bad we didn't learn it sooner. We could have gone to the movies instead."
—Balki, *Perfect Strangers*

ON SEX
"Sex can screw things up. Why do you think the Three Stooges went through so many Curlys?"
—Veronica, *Better Off Ted*

ON CHARITY
"I'm not big on charities. Give a man a fish and you feed him for a day. Don't teach a man to fish, and you feed yourself. He's a grown man. Fishing's not that hard."
—Ron, *Parks and Recreation*

Angie Dickinson was the only honoree who ever refused to appear on *This Is Your Life.*

MOVIE OF THE WEEK

Remember the "made-for-network-TV" movie? In the 1970s, it was one of the schlockiest—and most popular—things on TV.

CHEAP AND EASY

One of the most popular TV genres of the 1950s was the anthology series. Over one to two hours, shows like *Playhouse 90* and *GE Theater* showed a complete dramatic presentation each week. Episodes weren't connected; each played like a mini-movie. But by the mid-1960s, audience tastes had evolved to favor series with regular characters and continuing storylines.

Old movies were often shown on TV in those days, mostly during the day and late at night. When the anthology died, the networks didn't drop the concept—they started showing Hollywood movies in prime time instead. One problem: Movies were expensive—the studios charged the networks about $700,000 for the rights to air a single movie.

NBC was broadcasting in color full-time by 1964 and didn't want to pay a fortune for black-and-white movies, even recent ones. So they decided to make their own: They could control the costs, and there'd be no hefty rights fees to cut into profits. *World Premiere Movies,* an anthology of stand-alone, two-hour films, premiered on October 7, 1964, with a crime thriller called *See How They Run* (starring John Forsythe and Leslie Nielsen). The plot: Hired killers follow three children who are unknowingly carrying evidence that could sink an international crime ring, which also just murdered the kids' father. It was a hit, landing in TV's top-20 shows of the week. Apparently audiences liked the novelty of seeing a brand-new movie, at home, for free.

UNIVERSAL THEMES

In 1966 NBC contracted with Universal Pictures to make movies for television. Universal had traditionally made B movies for drive-in theaters, but drive-ins were rapidly closing down all across the country. In NBC, Universal found a profitable outlet for its films, and made-for-TV movies could have higher production values. The first NBC/Universal project (today they're actually the

TV cop Dennis Farina (*Crime Story, Law and Order*) was a real Chicago cop for 18 years.

same company) aired on Thanksgiving weekend in 1966. Titled *Fame Is the Name of the Game*, it was about a magazine reporter using clues in a murdered prostitute's diary to find her killer. The movie was so popular that in 1968 it was turned into a regular TV series called *The Name of the Game*.

EASY AS ABC

Barry Diller, the 27-year-old head of primetime programming at ABC, noticed NBC's success and decided to make movies at his network. The difference: NBC aired only 6 to 10 movies a year; Diller wanted a new movie every week of the TV season—about 25 per year. So he hired independent film producers (including future superstar producer Aaron Spelling), set a $500,000 budget per 67-minute movie (90 minutes with commercials), and set out to make each and every movie feel like a television event. To make that happen, he told the producers to make the movies over-the-top: as titillating, violent—or sappy—as possible. In fall 1969, ABC's *Movie of the Week* premiered with *Seven in Darkness*, a plane-crash drama starring Milton Berle. It was a smash hit. For the 1970 TV season, *The Movie of the Week* was the #6 show on television.

SCHLOCK IT TO ME

The majority of TV movies were exactly what Diller had ordered: exploitative and sensationalistic.

Sarah T–Portrait of a Teenage Alcoholic (1975) Linda Blair (*The Exorcist*) plays a 15-year-old alcoholic who hits rock bottom, learns her lesson, and straightens up.

Dawn: Portrait of a Teenage Runaway (1976) A teenage girl (Eve Plumb—Jan from *The Brady Bunch*) runs away from home and turns to prostitution to support herself.

Alexander: The Other Side of Dawn (1977) In this sequel to *Dawn*, Dawn's friend Alexander runs away from home to become a movie star but turns to prostitution to support himself.

Trilogy of Terror (1975) Three horror vignettes, all starring Karen Black: "Julie" (a college student blackmails his teacher into dating him, until she kills him), "Millicent and Therese" (a disturbed woman claims to have killed her sister, but the two sisters turn out to be the same person), and "Amelia" (an African doll stalks and kills a woman).

Killdozer (1974) Construction workers uncover a magical meteorite that takes "possession" of their bulldozer. The bulldozer goes on a killing spree.

The People (1972) A teacher (Kim Darby) is sent to a school in an isolated rural community. But her students aren't hillbillies—they're aliens!

Bad Ronald (1974) A teenager accidentally kills a neighbor, so his panicked mother hides him in a secret room of their house. His mother dies a few years later and a new family moves in. Ronald's still there and he's gone crazy from the isolation.

The Desperate Miles (1975) A crippled Vietnam War vet makes an inspiring, 180-mile journey in a wheelchair. Heartwarming? No—along the way, a crazy truck driver keeps trying to kill him.

Someone I Touched (1975) Cloris Leachman plays a woman who contemplates divorce when she finds out her husband has been unfaithful and contracted a venereal disease. She also finds out that she's pregnant, especially surprising because she's 50 years old.

HEY, THAT WAS ACTUALLY PRETTY GOOD

The Movie of the Week also aired many well-regarded, critically acclaimed movies.

Brian's Song (1971) In this fact-based drama, NFL stars Gale Sayers (Billy Dee Williams) and Brian Piccolo (James Caan) are best friends having the time of their lives. Then Piccolo dies of cancer. *Brian's Song* won an Emmy for Outstanding Single Program (Caan and Williams were also both nominated but didn't win) and a Peabody Award.

The Boy in the Plastic Bubble (1976) John Travolta plays a teenager trying to explore the world and exert his independence, which is tough because he's confined to a plastic bubble because of an immune-deficiency disease.

Duel (1971) A businessman (Dennis Weaver) driving on desolate backroads is pursued by an evil, possessed semi truck. It was one of the first movies ever directed by Steven Spielberg. It was so well regarded that it played in movie theaters in Europe.

The Morning After (1974) Dick Van Dyke plays a man who's a successful public relations agent by day and an uncontrollable alcoholic at night. One of Van Dyke's first dramatic roles, it made headlines because around the same time, Van Dyke announced that he was also an alcoholic and had begun to seek treatment.

That Certain Summer (1972) A teenage boy (Scott Jacoby) tries to cope with his parents' divorce, as well as with the reason for it: his father (Hal Holbrook) is gay. This movie was one of TV's first-ever depictions of homosexuals. Jacoby won an Emmy, and the movie won the Golden Globe for Best TV Movie.

MOVING ON

All the networks (broadcast and cable) still air made-for-TV movies, but the ABC *Movie of the Week* showcase ended in 1976. Many of them were so popular that they lived on as regular ABC series, including *Wonder Woman, Fantasy Island, Kolchak: The Night Stalker, The Six Million Dollar Man, The Bionic Woman, The Young Lawyers, Starsky and Hutch,* and *Marcus Welby, M.D.* But there were also a few wannabes that didn't make it, such as the 1971 flop *The Feminist and the Fuzz,* in which a radical feminist (Barbara Eden) ends up sharing a house with a male-chauvinist cop (David Hartman).

*   *   *

A BANNED AD

At a Norwegian Cruise Line executive meeting in 1994, company president Adam Aron reportedly remarked that "all people want to do on a cruise is have sex." Then he commissioned an ad that would focus on that aspect of a cruise. The artsy black-and-white TV commercial depicted a nude couple sensually touching each other while on-screen copy read, "There is no law that says you can't make love at four in the afternoon on a Tuesday." NBC refused to air the commercial, so NCL recut it, obscuring the naked couple and fading to and from black screens. NBC aired the new ad…and NCL bookings increased by 20 percent.

Survey results: Democrats are 124% more likely to watch *Mad Men* than Republicans are.

SO LONG, NEIGHBOR

*One thing that nearly all Americans born after 1965 have in
common is that they grew up watching Mister Rogers. He was
one of the true pioneers of children's television. We hadn't
written much about him before, but when he passed
away, we decided it was time we did.*

HOME FOR THE HOLIDAYS

In 1951 a college senior named Fred McFeely Rogers finished school in Florida and went home to stay with his parents in Latrobe, Pennsylvania. He wasn't exactly sure what he wanted to do with his life. For a while he wanted to be a diplomat; then he decided to become a Presbyterian minister. He'd already made plans to enroll in a seminary after college, but as soon as he arrived home he changed his mind again.

Why? Because while he was away at school, his parents had bought their first TV set. Television was still very new in the early 1950s, and not many people had them yet. When Rogers got home he watched it for the very first time. He was fascinated by the new medium but also disturbed by some of the things he saw. One thing in particular offended him very deeply. It was "horrible," as he put it, so horrible that it altered the course of his life.

What was it that bothered him so much? "I saw people throwing pies in each other's faces," Rogers remembered. "Such demeaning behavior."

KID STUFF

You (and Uncle John) may like it when clowns throw pies and slap each other in the face, but Fred Rogers was appalled. He thought TV could have a lot more to offer than pie fights and other silliness, if only someone would try. "I thought, 'I'd really like to try my hand at that, and see what I could do,'" Rogers recalled. So he moved to New York and got a job at NBC, working first as an associate producer and later as a director.

Then in 1953, he learned about a new experimental TV station being created in Pittsburgh. Called WQED, it was the country's first community-sponsored "public television" station. WQED

The original form of the aliens on *3rd Rock from the Sun*: "gelatinous purple tubes."

wasn't even on the air yet, and there was no guarantee that an educational TV station that depended on donations from viewers to pay for programming would ever succeed. No matter—Rogers quit his secure job at NBC, moved to Pittsburgh with his wife, Joanne, and joined the station.

"I thought, 'What a wonderful institution to nourish people,'" Rogers recalled. "My friends thought I was nuts."

LOW-INCOME NEIGHBORHOOD

When Rogers arrived at WQED in 1953, the station had just four employees and only two of them, Rogers and a secretary named Josie Carey, were interested in children's programming. The two created their own hour-long show called *The Children's Corner* and paid for all of the staging, props, and scenery (mostly pictures painted on paper backdrops), out of their own meager $75-a-week salaries.

Because *The Children's Corner* had to be done on the cheap, Rogers and Carey decided that much of the show would have to revolve around showing educational films that they obtained for free. Rogers was in charge of hustling up the free films and playing the organ off camera during the broadcast; Carey would host the show, sing, and introduce the films.

LUCKY BREAK

That was how *The Children's Corner* was *supposed* to work, but the plan fell apart about two minutes into their very first broadcast. The problem wasn't that Rogers couldn't scrounge up any free films, it was that the films he *did* manage to get were so old and brittle that they were prone to breaking when played. Sure enough, on the first day of the show, on WQED's first day on the air, the first film broke.

Remember, this was before the invention of videotape, when television shows were broadcast live—so when the film broke, the entire show came to a screeching halt. *On the air.* In the broadcast industry this is known as "dead air"—the TV cameras are still on, and the folks at home are still watching, but there's nothing happening onscreen. Nothing at all.

PAPER TIGER

At that moment, Rogers happened to be standing behind a paper backdrop that had been painted to look like a clock. He quickly looked around and spotted "Daniel," a striped tiger puppet that the station's general manager, Dorothy Daniel, had given him the night before as a party favor at the station's launch party.

"When the first film broke, I just poked the puppet through the paper," Rogers remembered years later, "and it happened to be a clock where I poked him through. And he just said, 'It's 5:02 and Columbus discovered America in 1492.' And that was the first thing I ever said on the air. Necessity was the mother of that invention, because it hadn't been planned."

The puppet worked and the old films didn't, so *The Children's Corner* became an educational puppet show. Daniel Striped Tiger, who lives in a clock, remained a fixture on Rogers's shows for the rest of his broadcast career. Numerous other characters, including King Friday XIII, Lady Elaine Fairchilde, and X the Owl all made their debut on *The Children's Corner*.

NEIGHBORHOOD WATCH

The Children's Corner stayed on the air for seven years; then in 1963 Rogers accepted an offer from the Canadian Broadcasting Corporation to host a 15-minute show called *Misterogers*, the first show in which he actually appeared on camera. (That year he also became an ordained Presbyterian minister.)

By 1965 *Misterogers* was airing in Canada and in the eastern United States, but it had the same problem that *The Children's Corner* had—not enough money. *Misterogers* ran out of funds and was slated for cancellation...until parents found out: when they learned the show was going off the air, they raised such a stink that the Sears Roebuck Foundation and National Educational Television (now known as the Public Broadcasting Service, or PBS), kicked in $150,000 apiece to keep the show on the air.

Lengthened to a full half hour and renamed *Mister Rogers' Neighborhood*, the show was first broadcast nationwide on February 19, 1968.

INNER CHILD

Very early in his broadcasting career, Rogers drew up a list of things he wanted to encourage in the children who watched his show. Some of the items on that list: self-esteem, self-control, imagination, creativity, curiosity, appreciation of diversity, cooperation, tolerance for waiting, and persistence. *How* Rogers encouraged these things in his young viewers was heavily influenced by his own childhood experiences:

• **His grandfather.** Many of the most memorable things Rogers said to children were inspired by things his own grandfather, Fred Brooks McFeely, said to him. "I think it was when I was leaving one time to go home after our time together that my grandfather said to me, 'You know, you made this day a really special day. Just by being yourself. There's only one person in the world like you. And I happen to like you just the way you are,' " Rogers remembered. "That just went right into my heart. And it never budged." (Rogers named Mr. McFeely, the show's Speedy Delivery messenger character, after his grandfather.)

• **The neighborhood of make-believe.** Fred Rogers was a sickly kid who came down with just about every childhood disease imaginable from chicken pox to scarlet fever. He spent a lot of time in bed, quarantined on doctors' orders. To amuse himself, he played with puppets and invented imaginary worlds for them to live in. "I'm sure that was the beginning of a much later neighborhood of make-believe," Rogers said.

• **Explanations.** Like most children, when Rogers was very little, he was frightened by unfamiliar things—being alone, starting school, getting a haircut, visiting a doctor's office, etc. "I liked to be told about things before I had to do them," he remembered, so explaining new and unfamiliar things became a central part of the show. (On one episode he even brought on actress Margaret Hamilton, who played the Wicked Witch of the West in *The Wizard of Oz*, to explain that she was just pretending and that kids didn't need to be afraid.)

• **Sweaters.** Rogers got most of his sweaters from his mother, who knitted him a new one every year for Christmas. He wore them all on his show.

• **Sneakers.** Those date back to his days on *The Children's Corner*—"I had to run across the studio floor to get from the puppet set to the organ," Rogers explained. "I didn't want to make a lot of noise by running around in ordinary shoes."

GOODBYE, NEIGHBOR

Rogers taped nearly 900 episodes of Mr. *Rogers' Neighborhood* over its more than 30 years on the air. They're still broadcast by more than 300 public television stations around the United States as well as in Canada, the Philippines, Guam, and other countries around the world. Videotapes of the show are used to teach English to non-native speakers (singer Ricky Martin credits Mr. Rogers with teaching him to speak English).

Rogers retired from producing new episodes of the show in December 2000, and the last new episode aired in August 2001. He came out of retirement briefly in 2002 to record public service announcements advising parents on how to help children deal with the anniversary of the September 11 attacks. He made his last public appearance on January 1, 2003, when he served as Grand Marshal of the Tournament of Roses Parade and tossed the coin for the Rose Bowl Game. Mr. Rogers passed away from stomach cancer two months later.

THOUGHTS FROM MR. ROGERS

• "The world is not always a kind place. That's something children learn for themselves, whether we want them to or not, but it's something they really need our help to understand."

• "Anything we can do to help foster the intellect and spirit and emotional growth of our fellow human beings, that is our job. Those of us who have this particular vision must continue against all odds."

• "People don't come up to me to talk about the weather. I've even had a child come up to me and not even say hello, but instead say right out, 'Mr. Rogers, my grandmother's in the hospital.'"

• "So many people have grown up with the 'Neighborhood,' I'm just their dad coming along. You know, it's really fun to go through life with this face."

*   *   *

Magic numbers: Through his adult life, Fred Rogers made sure he always weighed 143 pounds. Why? As he told a reporter, "It means 'I love you.' It takes one letter to say 'I,' four to say 'love,' and three to say 'you.'"

THE MONKEES, PART II

Laugh-In, Arrested Development, 30 Rock, and other innovative comedies all owe a debt of thanks to The Monkees, *as do* American Idol, Glee, *and MTV. And after all the flak they took, the Monkees could use a little gratitude. (Part I is on page 197.)*

MONKEE FACTORY
On the set of *The Monkees*, the on-screen action was wacky and loose. But behind the scenes, NBC and Screen Gems had put so much into promoting the show that nothing was left to chance. During filming, any cast members who weren't in the scene being shot were kept in a room with black walls and a meat-locker door. They could be loud, smoke pot, and even entertain women without being seen. Each Monkee had a corner, and in each corner a light was installed. When a Monkee's light started blinking, that Monkee or Monkees would report to the set and perform. Then it was back to the black box.

During press interviews, they were given a list of topics they could not talk about, including politics, Vietnam, and drugs. "We were hired actors," said Nesmith. "We came in at seven in the morning and did what we were told until seven at night. We had almost no part in the creative process." And they often had to add vocals to their songs in recording sessions that went long after midnight.

DAYDREAM DECEIVERS
Screen Gems' head of music, Don Kirshner, was hired to develop the band's sound into something catchy and marketable. Kirshner tapped top songwriters of the day, including Neil Diamond, Tommy Boyce, Bobby Hart, and Carole King, who contributed to the band's hits, such as "Last Train to Clarksville," "I'm a Believer," and "Daydream Believer." Although Tork and Nesmith were both skilled guitarists and Jones was a decent drummer, the "band" wasn't allowed to play instruments on their first two albums, *The Monkees* and *More of the Monkees*.

As the first season came to a close, word had leaked out that the Monkees were a fabricated band, but their popularity had already skyrocketed—especially that of Davy Jones, who became a teen heartthrob. To capitalize on their fame, NBC sent them on a concert tour in early 1967 to perform their hits—which they hadn't even played in the first place. TV's first manufactured band was about to become a real band, and the task was daunting. "Putting us on tour was like making the cast of *Star Trek* fight real aliens," said Dolenz.

STEPPING STONES

The Monkees' early concerts didn't go well musically, but few noticed because their teenage fans didn't stop screaming long enough to even hear them. Jimi Hendrix got the job of being their opening act, against his wishes (his manager made him do it). "Jimi would amble out onto the stage," recalled Dolenz, "fire up the amps, and break into 'Purple Haze,' and the kids would drown him out with 'We want Daaavy!' God, was it embarrassing." Hendrix quit after seven shows.

The Monkees soon learned to actually play together, and got a big boost on the European leg of their '67 tour when the Beatles threw them a lavish party. John Lennon didn't see them as competitors or imitators, but contemporaries. He called the Monkees "the Marx Brothers of rock."

Meanwhile, back in the States, tension mounted between the Monkees and Kirshner, especially after he rejected songs Nesmith had written...because they weren't "Monkee enough." The final straw came when Kirshner released a Monkees song—the Neil Diamond-penned "A Little Bit Me, A Little Bit You"—without Screen Gems' or the Monkees' approval. Nesmith was so angry that he punched a hole in the wall of Rafelson's office. Kirshner was fired, which gave the group more control over their music but not over their image...or even their lives.

OF MONKEES AND MEN

By this time, the Monkees were widely resented by musicians who'd paid their dues for years, only to be upstaged by a fabricated band. Not even the 1967 album *Headquarters*, which the Monkees wrote and performed themselves, could save their reputations. Even when the Monkees were honored, they were dissed. After season one, the show won an Emmy for Outstanding Comedy and another for Jim Frawley's directing. In his acceptance speech, Frawley said, "I couldn't have done this without four very special guys—Harpo, Chico, Groucho, and Zeppo." The band took his remarks as a snub, not a compliment.

As the second season dragged on, the Monkees spent most of their waking hours working, and grew increasingly tired and jaded. How many episodes could be written about country clubs or haunted mansions the band gets lost in? The band agreed to come back for a third season only if the show switched formats to a variety program. (They got a taste of that toward the end of the second season when Frank Zappa, dressed up like Mike Nesmith, interviewed Mike Nesmith, who was dressed up like Frank Zappa.) NBC didn't want to change the format, so they canceled *The Monkees* in 1968 but signed a deal with them to make three specials a year.

HEADING TO THE BIG SCREEN

The Monkees as a band, however, remained intact. In the summer of 1968, Raybert began filming a Monkees feature film conceived of by their friend Jack Nicholson while he was tripping on LSD. *Head* was a stream-of-consciousness, psychedelic diatribe against Hollywood—TV in particular. It began with the Monkees chanting, not singing, a parody of their theme song: "Hey, hey, we are the Monkees, you know we love to please / A manufactured image, with no philosophies." *Head* only got weirder from there—and it confused its teeny-bopper audience. The film was panned and made only a fraction of its budget, squashing any plans for a sequel.

The band then made a few guest appearances on TV variety shows in 1969. Their last hurrah was a bizarre NBC special, *33 1/3 Revolutions Per Monkee*. In once scene, the guys were placed inside giant test tubes, a reference to being "grown in a lab." Later, Little Richard, Fats Domino, and Jerry Lee Lewis all played pianos stacked on top of each other. The program got such poor ratings (it had run opposite the Academy Awards) that NBC canceled the remaining contracted Monkees specials. Then, citing exhaustion, Tork quit the band. The special was the last time all four Monkees would appear together for 16 years.

THE SECOND COMING...AND GOING

Throughout the 1970s, Micky Dolenz, Mike Nesmith, and Davy Jones continued performing together occasionally while also pursuing solo careers. However, the money they had made from their TV series and album sales was poorly handled, so Jones and Tork ended up deep in debt. Nesmith never had to worry about money thanks to his mother's invention—Liquid Paper. In 1979 he inherited $25 million.

While the Monkees' success on vinyl faded, the popularity of their old TV show stayed strong. From 1969 to 1972, CBS aired reruns on Saturday mornings, and local stations aired it here and there. Then in 1986, MTV began airing the show, and it was a huge hit all over again. Now in their 40s, the Monkees reunited and recorded a new album, *Justus*, and followed it with a successful world tour.

Everything was rosy until the Monkees failed to show up at an MTV-thrown Super Bowl party in 1987. Though the band had missed the date because of a scheduling snafu by their manager, MTV execs saw it as an ungrateful snub and retaliated by banning the band's videos and reruns. Monkeemania 2.0 quickly died.

THE REFAB PREFAB FOUR

While the band was still selling out stadiums around the world back in 1986, Screen Gems producer had Steve Blauner thought that the Monkees revival could give way to a totally new incarnation of the band, with new members, and to reflect the music and sensibilities of the 1980s.

Following a casting process like the one conducted 20 years earlier, Blauner found four young musicians and cast them in *The New Monkees*, which began airing in fall 1987. Don't remember it? That's because it lasted only 12 episodes, it generated no hit songs, and the four guys never went on to much else.

Another *New Monkees* attempt was made in 2003 by *American Idol* creator and Spice Girls mastermind Simon Fuller. He hired *Simpsons* writers Bill Oakley and Josh Weinstein to write scripts. NBC passed.

WHERE ARE THEY NOW?

• Micky Dolenz has released several solo records and had a successful radio show on a New York oldies station. He's also produced children's shows and has lent his voice to cartoons, including *Scooby-Doo* and *The Tick*.

• Davy Jones has also recorded several albums. He continued to be a minor teen idol into the 1970s, which led to a memorable cameo on *The Brady Bunch* in 1971, when Marcia gets Jones to play at her school dance. A recent TV appearance: SpongeBob SquarePants is searching for the mythical "Davey Jones's Locker"...but finds the live-action Davy Jones using his locker to wash his dirty socks.

• Peter Tork has toured and recorded with his band Shoe Suede Blues. He battled throat cancer in 2009; at last report, it was in remission.

• Mike Nesmith moved into country rock and became the only ex-Monkee to score a Top 40 solo hit. When his song with the group the First National Band, "Joanne," hit #21 in 1970. From there, he moved into TV production for shows like the short-lived 1985 NBC sketch comedy series *Television Parts*.

*　　*　　*

GOODBYE DOODY

The final episode of *Howdy Doody* in 1960 was one of the first *planned* TV series finales, since most shows before that had simply been canceled during breaks between seasons. In this case, it was decided that, after 14 seasons, *Howdy Doody* would end—and the series finale would reveal a secret.

At the beginning of the final episode, the kids in the Peanut Gallery were told there was a big surprise coming. In the show's closing moments, Clarabell the Clown (Lew Anderson), who had never spoken a word on the show, mimed a secret to Buffalo Bob. Incredulous, Buffalo Bob said, "You mean...you can talk??" Clarabell nodded yes, and Bob replied, "Well, Clarabell, this is your last chance. If you really can talk, prove it. Let's hear you say something." The camera zoomed in on Clarabell's face, she looked into the camera, and she said, "Goodbye, kids." And after 13 years, that was the end of *Doody*.

CHIMP, CHIMP, HOORAY!

Believe it or not, primates used to be as common on prime-time TV as forensic investigators are today.

Chimp: Bingo
Show: *The Abbott and Costello Show* (1952–53)
Story: Lou Costello came up with a great sight gag: Get a chimpanzee, dress it up to look like him, and then train it to follow him around and imitate everything he did. Bingo was hired and became a regular cast member (she's the one who looks like Costello—only smaller and hairier). Between scenes, she ate as much as 50 pounds of bananas a week. Ultimately it didn't work out—Costello started to resent the fact that Bingo got more laughs than he did. The resentment seemed to be mutual: Bingo bit Costello's finger during a rehearsal, and Costello fired her. She never worked in TV again.

Chimp: J. Fred Muggs
Show: *Today* (1953–57)
Story: A year into its run, the NBC morning news magazine show *Today* was struggling to attract viewers. Acting on the advice of NBC chairman Pat Weaver, who said, "Get the kids watching; their parents will follow," producers brought in a co-host for anchor David Garroway: a chimpanzee named J. Fred Muggs. Ratings soared. Garroway, however, wasn't happy; he felt that his reputation as a serious newsman was suffering by having to share the screen with a chimp. Garroway was even rumored to have spiked a glass of Muggs's orange juice with amphetamines to make the monkey go ape on camera and get thrown off the show. It didn't work—Muggs and Garroway co-hosted for four years, and NBC earned more than $100 million from Muggs merchandise. Muggs is still alive today: He lives in a Florida home for retired animal performers with his girlfriend, a chimp named Phoebe B. Beebe (seriously).

Chimps: Candy, Charlie, and Enoch
Show: *The Hathaways* (1961–62)
Story: In the early 1950s, the Marquis Chimps, three trained chimpanzees, were making the rounds of the English theatrical circuit. Movie star Danny Kaye discovered them and booked them in a Broadway show, which led to appearances on *The Ed Sullivan Show*, and eventually, starring roles on a comedy called *The Hathaways*. The concept of the show: Peggy Cass and Jack Weston star as a Los Angeles couple who can't have children, so they adopt three chimps and raise them as kids. Candy, Charlie, and Enoch interacted so seamlessly with humans that it was easy to forget they were chimps. Once, off-camera, Weston barged into Candy's dressing room by mistake to find the chimp, petticoats and dress pulled up around her waist, sitting on a potty chair. The embarrassed Weston backed out quickly, mumbling apologies; the silliness of it didn't hit him until hours later. After *The Hathaways* was canceled, the Marquis Chimps remained in demand, guest-starring on *The Lucy Show* and appearing as a rock band in a series of ads for Red Rose Tea.

Chimp: Judy
Show: *Daktari* (1966–69)
Story: *Daktari* (Swahili for "doctor") was a TV version of the 1965 film *Clarence the Cross-Eyed Lion*, about an American veterinarian living in the African wilderness. Judy, a chimpanzee, was a comic-relief character who frequently annoyed cast members. Judy could understand 75 hand signals (a sizable vocabulary for a chimp). But, like a true diva, she refused to work without having first had her morning coffee and donut.

Chimps: Tonga and others
Show: *Lancelot Link: Secret Chimp* (1970–72)
Story: Two of the hottest shows of the late 1960s were the secret-agent parody *Get Smart* and the rock-band comedy *The Monkees*. *Lancelot Link: Secret Chimp* combined the two. A cast of apes played the good guys from the Agency to Prevent Evil (APE) and the bad guys from the Criminals Headquarters for Underworld Master Plan (CHUMP). The apes chewed bubble gum to make it

look like they were talking, and their lines were dubbed in later. When not engaging in international intrigue, APE's apes played in a band called the Evolution Revolution. The title role was played by a chimpanzee named Tonga, who answered phones, tackled bad guys, and even rode a motorcycle. One day, Tonga was sitting on the bike waiting for his cue when the studio gates opened. The chimp hit the gas and sped out onto the streets of Los Angeles. His trainer caught up with him about the same time the cops did.

Chimp: Sam
Show: *B.J. and the Bear* (1979–81)
Story: What do most chimp actors have in common? They enjoy performing and being on set. Well...almost all of them. Sam, the chimp on *B.J. and the Bear*, had no interest in acting or, for that matter, pleasing humans. He especially disliked men, and bit co-star Greg Evigan, handlers, and other cast and crew members more than 25 times. On the other hand, Sam adored the starlets who appeared weekly on the show, and would snuggle up to them and slyly pinch them when they weren't looking. Once he even grabbed an unsuspecting guest star and thrust his head up her blouse. (She was not amused.)

*   *   *

GET DUMB

In 1967 Steve Samwell sued Mel Brooks, creator of *Get Smart*, claiming Brooks got the idea for the series from Samwell's unpublished 1958 story about an inept spy. Brooks denied the claim but decided to settle out of court because it would be cheaper and faster. And that, says Samwell, started a trend of people filing frivolous lawsuits against TV shows. "I've been watching the progress of this for four decades, right up through the recent *Mrs. Mom* suit against Rainier Wolfcastle." (Samwell was referring not to a real case, but to a *Simpsons* episode in which Marge sues an actor for stealing her movie idea.) And so, in 2007, Samwell sued every individual who had ever sued a TV show. "They are totally infringing on my intellectual property," he explained. "And I need to get a piece of the action."

SMOTHERED BROTHERS

In 1967 CBS hired the Smothers Brothers to host a variety show that would attract a young, hip audience. The show did all that...but CBS didn't like it. Here's a look at the controversy behind The Smothers Brothers Comedy Hour.

FAMILY BAND

In the 1960s, musical comedy duo Tom and Dick Smothers, professionally known as the Smothers Brothers, were already veterans of the folk scene. They'd recorded several hit albums of their unique act: singing and playing folk songs before shifting into scripted sibling arguments and topical stand-up comedy bits.

After the brothers appeared on a string of talk and variety shows, CBS signed them to a contract in 1965 and created *The Smothers Brothers Show*. It was a forgettable sitcom—Dick's character was a playboy, Tom was the ghost of his dead brother—and the brothers felt it didn't play to their strengths. There was none of their usual bantering, and they got to perform music on only one episode. The show was canceled due to low ratings in 1966.

HOW TO BEAT A BONANZA

Meanwhile, the network was trying—and failing—to compete with NBC's hit *Bonanza*, the #1 show on television. Nothing could touch it in its Sunday night time slot, and it had even killed off former hits *Perry Mason* and *The Garry Moore Show*. When *Moore* was canceled at the end of 1966, CBS decided that the best way to compete with *Bonanza* was counter-programming. *Bonanza* attracted mostly viewers over 40. What if CBS put something on that appealed to people in their 20s and 30s? At some point, the network realized that it already had the ideal stars of this new show under contract: the Smothers Brothers.

Before agreeing to a new show, executive producer and star Tom Smothers insisted on full control. His reason: *The Smothers Brothers Show* had been so stressful for him that he'd developed an ulcer and gotten divorced. CBS agreed and the brothers got to work hiring writers and performers from the burgeoning Los

---

In 1997 David Lander (Squiggy on *Laverne & Shirley*) became a pro baseball talent scout.

Angeles comedy scene. Some of those unknowns: Steve Martin, Rob Reiner, Pat Paulsen, and Albert Brooks.

FOR WHAT IT'S WORTH

The Smothers Brothers Comedy Hour debuted on Sunday, February 5, 1967, at 9 p.m. The Smothers formula for bridging the generation gap was presenting edgy new comedians and musicians alongside beloved veteran performers. George Burns and Jack Benny guested on one episode. On another, comedy skits with Bette Davis gave way to Buffalo Springfield performing their anti-war song "For What It's Worth." A later episode offered a mod fashion show, a satirical anti-gun editorial from Paulsen, and a song from Jimmy Durante. And every episode included songs and comedy routines from the Smothers Brothers.

The show was a big hit. The brothers delivered the young demographic CBS was after, and by the end of the season, *The Smothers Brothers Comedy Hour* was routinely beating *Bonanza*. CBS was pleased with the ratings and the critical acclaim.

WAIST DEEP

But this was 1967, and the show's rise dovetailed with the growing influence that young, edgy, and angry Baby Boomers were having on American culture. The Smothers Brothers grew increasingly bold, using their *Comedy Hour* as a political soapbox and a platform for comment, social change, and exploration.

They gave rock bands like the Byrds and the Doors national TV exposure, and many performed songs that were either pro-drug or anti-Vietnam War. The Brothers themselves pushed the envelope with jokes and editorials criticizing the American presence in Vietnam. They also performed alongside black singers Harry Belafonte and Diahann Carroll in an era when integration was still not completely accepted. Sketches contained thinly veiled references to recreational drug use, particularly "hippie" Leigh French's regular segment, "Share a Little Tea with Goldie."

But just because CBS "gave" the Smotherses creative control, it didn't mean they actually got it. In the first season, for example, CBS edited out a performance of folk singer Pete Seeger at the request of network president William S. Paley, an outspoken supporter of the Vietnam War and good friend of President Lyndon

Johnson, who had asked Paley to ensure that the Smotherses would "go easy on him." Seeger's scathing, anti-war, government-critical song "Waist Deep in the Big Muddy" didn't air until more than a year later, after Johnson declined to run for reelection.

SEASONS CHANGE
The Smothers Brothers Comedy Hour finished its first season as the #12 show on TV. The second season continued the successful blend of young and old, but with more edge. Bette Davis returned for another episode, along with the Who. At the end of an especially loud (and pyrotechnics-enhanced) performance of "My Generation," the band destroyed their instruments, as per usual. But pyrotechnic charges exploded in the chaos, throwing drummer Keith Moon backward, igniting Pete Townshend's hair (and permanently damaging his hearing), and filling the studio with smoke. Tom Smothers was visibly shaken; Davis was so shocked that she collapsed backstage. Younger viewers loved it, but some of their parents weren't so thrilled; the ratings started to slip.

By late 1967, the Vietnam War was escalating, Georgia had just elected a segregationist governor, and anti-war demonstrations and race riots filled American streets. Material produced by the young *Comedy Hour* writers became less lighthearted and more topical, reflecting the liberal politics of their generation rather than the conservative views of mainstream television and its executives.

But CBS brass wanted the *Comedy Hour* to be more neutral. After network censors cut a December 1967 skit on censorship written by guest star Elaine May, the brothers saw red. In a subsequent show, while brandishing the banned script, a seething Tom and Dick explained to viewers that they were "being shut up by CBS." In early 1968, *Comedy Hour* got its revenge. The topic of Pat Paulsen's weekly editorial was censorship. His concluding line: "There is a place for censors. We only wish that we could tell you where it is."

CENSORS AND SENSIBILITIES
Unfortunately for the Brothers, the place of a censor was well-defined at CBS, and through 1968, they were kept busy:
• Comedian David Steinberg's sarcastically delivered religious "sermonettino" (a weekly parody of the devotionals aired by sta-

tions when they signed off the air each night) drew so much attention it was were banned outright, leading CBS to allow local affiliates to preview *Comedy Hour* episodes before airing them.

• Harry Belafonte's "Lord, Don't Stop the Carnival," performed in front of a backdrop of bloody police beatings at the 1968 Chicago Democratic Convention, was to be a highlight of the third-season premiere. CBS cut the entire number, leaving the show five minutes short. The network sold the time to the Republican Party for Richard Nixon's presidential campaign ads.

CBS had commissioned the *Comedy Hour* to attract young viewers, and those viewers wanted rock, suggestive comedy, drug references, and editorials about war, racism, and censorship...the very subjects that the network was determined to keep out of the show. During the third season, CBS demanded to preview each episode well in advance of its air date. On March 9, 1969, CBS broadcast a repeat instead of a new episode with activist and folk singer Joan Baez, claiming not to have received a review tape in time.

In June 1969, Paley personally canceled *Comedy Hour*. (Replacing it: *Hee Haw*.) But the show had already been renewed for a fourth season, so the Smotherses filed a breach-of-contract suit against CBS. The case was finally settled in 1973, with a judge finding in favor of the Smotherses: CBS owed them $916,300.

THE LEGACY

A little over a year later, the Smothers Brothers returned to TV, now on ABC. *The Smothers Brothers Summer Show*, debuting in June 1970, copied the bright sets and previous format but failed to recapture the energy, relevance, or audience of the edgy original, and was soon canceled. And so was the similarly lifeless *The Smothers Brothers Show* on NBC in 1975.

Both brothers guest-starred on TV shows and appeared in movies throughout the next two decades. In 1988, at the peak of a wave of '60s nostalgia, CBS aired a *Comedy Hour* retrospective. It got such good ratings that CBS asked the brothers to revive their show as a summer series in 1988 and '89. The new *Smothers Brothers Comedy Hour* mimicked the old show: Pat Paulsen gave whimsical editorials, Tom and Dick still argued over who "Mom liked best," and a handful of other series regulars returned. The only thing missing: the politics. Instead, Tom Smothers showed off yo-yo tricks.

THE ABCs OF PBS

Major moments in the history of the network your tax dollars help fund.

- **1952:** The Federal Communications Commission (FCC) sets aside the use of 242 individual television stations nationwide for use by noncommercial educational broadcasters—against the vehement opposition of commercial stations. But what programs would the new stations show? The Educational Television and Radio Center (ETRC) is founded to provide content. Bankrolled with $170 million from the Ford Foundation, the ETRC's job is to help educotional stations around the country to exchange local programming with each other.

- **1953:** On May 25, the University of Houston–owned KUHT begins broadcasting, making it the first publicly funded TV station in the country.

- **1954:** The ETRC begins producing programming rather than just distributing it. Technically, that makes it a broadcast network like CBS, NBC, and ABC. Its five-hour-a-day schedule (sent to stations on tapes, through the mail) is broadcast by educational stations around the U.S. The programs themselves are dry, adult-oriented, and long—mostly interviews with artists, scientists, and politicians.

  In contrast, member station WQED in Pittsburgh debuts *The Children's Corner*, a half-hour show for preschoolers. The host: Fred Rogers.

- **1963:** Deciding to focus entirely on TV (and drop radio), the ETRC changes its name to National Educational Television (NET). At this time, NET begins producing documentaries on cultural issues, such as *The Poor Pay More*, *Black Like Me*, *Appalachia*, and *Inside North Vietnam*, garnering a wider audience and critical acclaim.

  Julia Child's cooking show *The French Chef*, produced by WGBH in Boston, debuts.

- **1966:** Citing growing costs, the Ford Foundation begins withdrawing its financial backing of NET. Affiliates respond by lobby-

---

James Arness (Marhall Dillon on *Gunsmoke*) and Peter Graves...

ing the government about the importance of educational television, leading Congress to create the Corporation for Public Broadcasting (CPB). It's a private nonprofit organization charged with the sole purpose of promoting, and finding funding for, public television (and, once again, radio).

- **1968:** NET nationally debuts a WQED (Pittsburgh) production: *Mister Rogers' Neighborhood.*

- **1969:** When member stations complain to the CPB about edgy NET programming, CPB creates a new public television network called the Public Broadcasting Service (PBS). NET continues to provide some programming. One of their shows: *Sesame Street.*

- **1970:** The remains of NET merge with New York public station WNDT to become WNET, an affiliate of PBS, now the major public television provider in the U.S.

  Evening at Pops, a musical performance show featuring the Boston Pops, debuts on WGBH in Boston and is distributed nationally.

- **1971:** *Masterpiece Theatre* first airs. It consists mostly of filmed BBC adaptations of literature. In 1972 the *Masterpiece* presentation *Elizabeth R.* (a biographical drama about Queen Elizabeth I) wins an Emmy for Best Drama Series. A few years later, another miniseries, *Upstairs, Downstairs*, wins the award three times.

- **1974:** Ron Devillier of PBS station KERA in Dallas finds some tapes of a British series on a shelf at the station. He watches them, likes them, and starts airing them. The show: *Monty Python's Flying Circus.*

  The science anthology *Nova*, another WGBH production, debuts nationwide.

- **1975:** The first national public TV pledge drive takes place.

- **1983:** KAET in Phoenix airs *The Operation*, an open-heart surgery televised live via satellite.

  WGBH debuts the hard-hitting news and public affairs series *Frontline.*

- **1984:** The FCC makes the controversial decision to allow PBS to expand the acknowledgements of its underwriters, meaning it can now identify its corporate sponsors on the air, as long as it doesn't promote the sponsors or their products. At this time, corporate money provides roughly 15 percent of all PBS funding.

• **1986:** The Oklahoma Educational Television Authority acquires the rights to *The Lawrence Welk Show*, which had been canceled after 27 seasons in 1982, and sells it to PBS stations all over the country. Since then, the show has aired at 7 p.m. on Saturday on many affiliates, the same time slot it had in its original run on ABC. It's still one of PBS's most-watched regular series.

• **1990:** Ken Burns's epic 10-part documentary *The Civil War* airs, setting new PBS audience records. Burns follows with *Baseball* in 1994; *Jazz* in 2001; *The War* in 2007; *The National Parks: America's Best Idea* in 2009; and another baseball series, *The Tenth Inning,* in 2010.

• **1998:** PBS makes history with the first national, high-definition television broadcast: a documentary about glassmaker Dale Chihuly called *Chihuly Over Venice.*

• **1999:** PBS begins requiring all shows to be preceded by an announcement: "This program was made possible by contributions to your PBS station from viewers like you. Thank you." (The actor who reads it is Harlan Hogan, famous for voicing such commercial catchphrases as "Strong enough for a man, but made for a woman," and "Quaker Life: It's the cereal even Mikey likes.")

• **Today:** PBS has more than 360 member stations and is watched by roughly 115 million people every month.

*   *   *

THE 10 MOST-WATCHED COMEDY SERIES FINALES

1. M*A*S*H (1983)
2. *Cheers* (1993)
3. *Seinfeld* (1998)
4. *Friends* (2004)
5. *The Cosby Show* (1992)

6. *All in the Family* (1979)
7. *Family Ties* (1989)
8. *Home Improvement* (1999)
9. *Frasier* (2004)
10. *Everybody Loves Raymond* (2005)

Today prime-time TV begins at 8:00pm EST, but prior to 1970 it began at 7:30pm

"THE MOST TRUSTED MAN IN AMERICA"

Many TV viewers still remember Walter Cronkite. He was the most powerful news anchor in TV history, and some say he could end wars and even presidencies with the turn of a phrase. Here's Part III in our history of network news. (Part II is on page 228.)

GONE FISHIN'

When the *CBS Evening News with Walter Cronkite* pulled ahead of *The Huntley-Brinkley Report* in the ratings in the summer of 1967, no one at NBC was too worried. Their *Huntley-Brinkley* had been the top-rated network news broadcast for nearly a decade. Cronkite had briefly passed it in the ratings twice before, for a few weeks in the summer of 1965 and again in the summer of 1966. But both times, his ratings had slipped back, allowing *Huntley-Brinkley* to reclaim first place.

"Some NBC people had a rather smug explanation for this seasonal deviation," Gary Paul Gates writes in *Airtime: The Inside Story of CBS News.* "They contended that their nightly news audience, being brighter and more affluent, spent the summer sailing off Martha's Vineyard or attending music festivals in Europe, while Cronkite's viewers, presumably the dull and the indigent, estivated [the summer equivalent of "hibernated"] in front of their television sets because they had nothing better to do."

GONE FOR GOOD

The summer of 1967 would be different. This time, when *Huntley-Brinkley's* audience went away, it stayed away. The *CBS Evening News* moved into first place and remained there for as long as Cronkite anchored the broadcast.

Cronkite's position was strengthened three years later when Chet Huntley retired and NBC stumbled in its attempts to find a new co-host for David Brinkley. First they tried a rotating anchor team, matching Brinkley with co-anchors John Chancellor and Frank McGee, with only two of the three hosting the broadcast on any given night. When that didn't work, McGee was reassigned,

---

According to *The Simpsons*, Montgomery Burns' younger brother is George Burns.

leaving Chancellor and Brinkley as co-anchors. Then Brinkley stepped back from anchoring to become a commentator on the show in 1971; Chancellor became the sole anchor. The continuous changes did nothing for NBC's ratings, and allowed Cronkite to build his lead at CBS. (ABC's evening newscast was a perpetual, distant third-place finisher, and would be for years to come.)

UNCLE WALTER

The 1960s and '70s were turbulent decades in American history, and that, too, may have boosted Cronkite's career. Once viewers came to trust him as a steady, authoritative presence, it was that much tougher for NBC and ABC to lure viewers away. From the Cuban missile crisis of 1962, followed by the assassination of President John F. Kennedy a year later, through the Civil Rights movement, Vietnam, and Watergate, "Uncle Walter" was the person most viewers turned to for help in understanding the difficult times they lived in. In a 1972 poll, Cronkite was even voted "The Most Trusted Man in America," a title that stuck for the rest of his life.

MAKING HISTORY

As his stature grew, Cronkite became not just a presenter of major events but, on occasion, a shaper of them as well:

• After a visit to the front lines of the Vietnam War in 1968, Cronkite became skeptical about the U.S. prospects for victory. When he returned home he said so, in a rare editorial at the end of a special report. President Lyndon Johnson was watching and afterward told an aide, "If I've lost Cronkite, I've lost Middle America." The following month, Johnson ordered a halt to the bombing of North Vietnam, called for negotiations to end the war, and announced he would not run for another term as president.

• In the fall of 1972, Cronkite devoted more than half of a 30-minute evening news broadcast to a single story: the growing Watergate scandal. He gave it another eight minutes the following evening. Other than in *The Washington Post*, whose reporters Bob Woodward and Carl Bernstein had broken the story, Watergate had not received a lot of coverage. It might have faded away entirely, had Cronkite not called so much attention to it. *Washington Post* owner Katharine Graham credited him with "turning our local story into a national story," one that forced President Richard Nixon from office in 1974.

• When Egyptian president Anwar el Sadat told Cronkite in a 1977 interview that he wanted to go to Jerusalem to discuss peace and would go "within the week" if invited by the Israeli government, Cronkite set up an interview with Israeli Prime Minister Menachem Begin the same day and asked him about Sadat's comment. "Tell him he's got an invitation," Begin replied. Five days later, Sadat was in Israel. In 1978 he and Begin signed the Camp David Peace Accords, which was followed by the signing of a peace treaty between Egypt and Israel in 1979.

END OF AN ERA

Walter Cronkite was arguably the most influential journalist in American television history, and he may have been the luckiest as well. He certainly had excellent timing, taking the anchor's chair in 1962, just as TV was edging out newspapers as the place where most Americans got their news. His career spanned the entire era of unrivaled network news dominance. Then, just four months after he announced his retirement in February 1980, CNN—America's first 24-hour news network and first real challenge to network TV news—debuted on June 1, 1980.

As if CNN and the other cable news channels that followed weren't enough of a threat, by the mid-'80s, the Big Three networks were all entirely under corporate control—CBS was now owned by the Loews Corporation movie theater chain, NBC by General Electric, and ABC by the Capital Cities media group. The days of lavish network news budgets subsidized by profits from the entertainment side of the network were over. From now on, news would be expected to earn a profit, just like any other part of the business. And with growing competition from cable, those profits would be harder than ever to find.

PAY-B-C

Adding to that challenge was the fact that ABC News, long the distant third-place finisher in the ratings, roared to life in the early 1980s under the leadership of an executive named Roone Arledge and *World News Tonight* anchor Peter Jennings. Arledge launched a bidding war to lure top reporting talent away from

CBS and NBC. Where Walter Cronkite's salary had never reached $1 million a year, thanks to pressure from Arledge, CBS now had to pay his successor, Dan Rather, more than $2 million a year to keep him from defecting to ABC.

The huge raises were great for the anchors and star correspondents who got them, but they were terrible for everyone else—because in the early 1980s the combined viewing audience of the three network newscasts began a long, steady decline that continues to this day. Between 1980 and 2010, the number of people watching the three evening newscasts fell by more than half, dropping from 50 million viewers in 1980 to just over 20 million in 2009. As viewership has shrunk, so too have the advertising revenues and the news budgets that depend on them. Network managers who began their careers 30 years ago, when Cronkite was ending his, have spent their entire working lives closing foreign bureaus, laying off staff, and figuring out how to do more with less. They're still at it: In its latest brutal round of layoffs in April 2010, ABC News cut its staff by 28%, for a loss of more than 400 jobs.

THE CBS EVENING PODCAST?

Even more disturbing to the networks than the shrinking size of their audience is the increasing age of that audience: In 2009 the average age of an evening news viewer was 62.3 years. And while watching the evening news is an ingrained habit with many older Americans, it is clearly not a habit that their children and grandchildren have picked up, despite the desperate attempts of the networks to attract them. (CBS hired *Today* co-host Katie Couric in the hope that she'd be able to attract a younger demographic, but she hasn't even held onto the older folks.)

Older viewers came of age in an era when, if you wanted to watch the national news, you had to get it from the networks—when the networks wanted you to have it, and in the format that the networks wanted to present it to you. The Internet generation, of course, has never had such restrictions. They can get the news whenever they want it, organized in whatever way works for them. It remains to be seen whether they will ever watch the evening news shows in great numbers. It's possible that, as older viewers pass on, the network news audience will shrink to the point where the revenues generated simply won't support all three network news broadcasts, and one or more of them will have to close its doors.

A WORLD WITHOUT WALTER

Will we ever again live in an age when network news anchors have the authority, popularity, and power that Walter Cronkite had in the 1970s? It seems unlikely. Cable news anchors and pundits are giving the networks a serious run for their money, and there's no telling where the Internet will take the news business. Even the network anchors don't have the clout they used to—try imagine Brian Williams driving a president from office, or bringing peace to the Middle East.

That seems about as likely as a return to the days when Americans had only four or five TV channels to choose from, and when NBC ended its evening news broadcast with a live shot of a cigarette smoldering in an ashtray.

*   *   *

BOTCHED-CO

Steven Bochco is one of most successful TV creators of all time—he's responsible for *Hill Street Blues*, *L.A. Law*, and *NYPD Blue*. But he also came up with these ill-fated series:

• *The Gemini Man* (1976) A secret agent (Ben Murphy) is injured in a diving accident, which somehow makes him invisible. He uses his power to fight crime with the help of a special watch that can turn his invisibility on and off. But if he's invisible for more than 15 minutes a day, he'll die. It lasted six episodes.

• *Capitol Critters* (1992) This prime-time cartoon satirized politics by showing the literal underbelly of Washington, D.C.—what the rats, mice, and other vermin did in the sewers. *Critters* was exterminated by ABC after 13 episodes.

• *Cop Rock* (1990) At first glance, the show was a gritty, big-city police drama, similar to *Hill Street Blues*. But then everybody started singing and dancing. *Cop Rock* is universally regarded by TV critics as one of the worst shows ever made. It was canceled after 11 episodes.

IT WAS ALL A DREAM!?!?

When Roseanne *viewers learned the final season was a dream (see page 177), they were fuming mad. Why even tell a story if it never happened? More often than not, there's a real-world explanation for why shows pull this stunt.*

Show: *Dallas* (CBS, 1978–91)
Dream: In the final episode of the seventh season in May 1985, Bobby (Patrick Duffy) is run down by a car and killed. A year later in the eighth season finale, Bobby's wife Pam (Victoria Principal) wakes to the sound of running water. She goes into the bathroom...and there's Bobby, alive, taking a shower. His death—along with the *entire* eighth season—had been one long dream of Pam's.
Reality: Bobby was originally killed off because Duffy was bored with the role and wanted to leave the show. But he was also a big ratings draw, and *Dallas* dipped from #2 to #6 the following year, so producers begged Duffy to come back. Because he couldn't find any better work, he did. (Never mind that Bobby's return demolished logic—for example, several characters who left the show during the dream season, and who therefore didn't *really* leave, remained gone.)

Show: *Married...With Children* (Fox, 1987–97)
Dream: At the start of season 6, Peg (Katey Sagal) announces she's pregnant. A few episodes later, Al (Ed O'Neill) becomes a private detective, solves a murder, earns $50,000, romances a beautiful heiress...and then wakes up to his old humdrum life. The season thus far, pregnancy included, had merely been Al Bundy's crazy dream.
Reality: Sagal's character became pregnant only because Sagal did in real life. Sadly, she miscarried, so Peg's pregnancy was hastily written out of the series and never talked about again.

Show: *Life on Mars* (ABC, 2008–09)
Dream: This American remake of a British show ended much differently than the original. (Spoiler alert: In the British version, the main character was revealed to have been in a coma.) In the

---

updated version, a New York City cop named Sam (Jason O'Mara)
is hit by a car in 2008 and wakes up in 1973. He joins the NYPD
and tries to find a way home, but keeps seeing flashes of his 2008
life. Sam can also see tiny robotic vehicles scurrying about. In the
series finale, Sam learns that his 1973 world is a dream...and so
was his 2008 world. Sam isn't even a cop—he and the other characters are astronauts in the year 2035 on the first manned mission
to Mars. The events of the show took place in a collective dream
shared while they were all in an induced hibernative state to make
the months-long flight go by faster.
Reality: Why such a bizarre twist? The writers wanted a different
ending than the U.K. version (to keep a surprise at the end for
viewers who'd watched both series), and they wanted a finale that
would truly surprise, but would still make sense to viewers. It also
explained the cryptic title.

Show: *Newhart* (CBS, 1982–90)
Dream: In the final episode of the series, Dick Loudon (Bob
Newhart) gets whacked in the head by a golf ball. The screen goes
black, then a light turns on. Newhart is in bed. He says, "Honey,
you won't believe the dream I just had." His wife wakes up and
rolls over, and it's not Joanna (Mary Frann), it's Suzanne
Pleshette, in character as Emily from Newhart's previous series,
The Bob Newhart Show. He tells her that he dreamed he was as an
innkeeper in a small Vermont town, making all 184 episodes of
the surreal *Newhart*—and all its characters, including Larry, his
brother Darryl, and his other brother Darryl—nothing but a dream
in the mind of Dr. Robert Hartley from *The Bob Newhart Show*.
Reality: The dream idea came from Newhart's wife, Ginnie. He
liked it, saying it "really fit the show," but was apprehensive
because *St. Elsewhere's* twist ending had received harsh criticism
from viewers (see page 149). But Newhart decided to film the
ending just to see how it would play out. As the cameras began
rolling, a facade was removed to reveal the bedroom set from
Newhart's former show...and the studio audience broke out into
loud applause even before Pleshette's surprise appearance. Right
then, Newhart later said, he knew he'd made the right choice. *TV
Guide* later named it "the most unexpected moment in the history
of television."

TV TIDBITS

More scintillating bits of trivia to fascinate your friends.

• In 1983 Richard Moll shaved his head for a part in the movie *Metalstorm: The Destruction of Jared-Syn*. During filming, Moll auditioned for Bull on NBC's *Night Court*. The producers loved Moll—and his bald head—so he kept it shaved for the show's nine-year-run.

• When Tim Allen was a kid, he was too short to see over his fence, and could see his neighbor only from the nose up. That inspired Allen to create the barely seen Wilson character on *Home Improvement*.

• In 1990 Will Smith owed the IRS $2.8 million in back taxes. The rap star was broke...until NBC offered him a sitcom. To pay it back, 70 percent of Smith's wages were garnished for the first three years of the show.

• On M*A*S*H, Radar's real first name wasn't revealed until the show's 81st episode, after four years on the air—it's Walter. In Richard Hooker's source novel, it's mentioned in the very first sentence.

• When Dick Van Dyke received a star on the Hollywood Walk of Fame in 1992, his name was misspelled as "VANDYKE." So he took out a felt pen and drew an editor's "add a space here" slash mark between the two words. (The star was later fixed.)

• The sitcom *Mr. Belvedere*, based on a 1949 movie, was first pitched to CBS in 1956. CBS didn't pick it up. It was pitched again in the mid-1960s, again without success. Finally, in 1985, after three decades in development, *Mr. Belvedere* aired on ABC for five seasons.

• On Greg Garcia's NBC sitcom *My Name Is Earl*, Earl made a list of all the wrongs he wanted to right, but the show was canceled in 2009 before he had a chance to finish. In 2010, on the pilot episode of Garcia's next show, Fox's *Raising Hope*, a TV news reporter can be overheard saying, "...and a crook with a long list of wrongs he was making amends for has finally finished." Yay for Earl!

Actress Katey Sagal wore her own red bouffant wig to audition for *Married...With Children*.

• NBC programming chief Brandon Tartikoff came up with the sitcom name *Punky Brewster*. The name of the title character, played by Soleil Moon Frye, came from a childhood crush that Tartikoff had on a tomboy named...Punky Brewster. Before the show aired, Tartikoff tracked her down and got her approval for the name. Brandon, Punky's dog on the show, was named for...Brandon Tartikoff.

• The ABC Family network used to be the Fox Family Channel, and before that the CBN (Christian Broadcasting Network) Cable, founded by televangelist Pat Robertson in 1977. Robertson's show *The 700 Club* aired on CBN and still must air daily on ABC Family (or any future incarnation) according to an agreement Robertson made when he sold CBN to Fox in 1998.

• Dixie Carter hated the political rants her character had to deliver on *Designing Women* (1986–93), so she made a deal with producers: Every time she had to make a speech of indignation, she'd get to sing in a later episode.

• "A lot of people thought we named them after Ted Bundy, the serial killer," said *Married...With Children* creator Michael Moye about the show's Bundy family. They were actually named for King Kong Bundy, the professional wrestler. "You know, the good Bundy."

• The portrait of the Keaton family shown in the opening credits of *Family Ties* (1982–89) was painted by Michael Gross, who played the father on the show.

• Dinah Shore won Emmys five years in a row (1955–59) in four different categories. The 1958 trophy had the strangest title: "Best Continuing Performance (Female) in a Series by a Comedienne, Singer, Hostess, Dancer, MC, Announcer, Narrator, Panelist, or Any Person Who Essentially Plays Herself."

• On an episode of *Third Rock From the Sun*, the alien Dick (John Lithgow) emerges from the bathroom carrying a book. He wonders aloud about the nature of humor. The book he's holding: *Uncle John's Bathroom Reader*. (We're glad we could help.)

THE FIRST NETWORK

You may not remember when TV was black and white. You may not remember when there were no remotes and you had to get up to change channels or adjust the volume. Even if you do, you still probably don't remember the DuMont Network.

PIONEER
Like a lot of people involved with the early development of television, Allen B. DuMont started in radio. In 1924 he was in charge of tube production at Westinghouse, the country's largest radio manufacturer. But by 1928, after his innovations had increased daily tube production tenfold, DuMont got bored and wanted to try something new.

Companies like RCA and the radio networks (CBS and NBC) were already experimenting with television. DuMont proposed to his bosses at Westinghouse that they do the same. They weren't interested, so DuMont quit and set up his own TV lab in the basement of his house. Just two years later, he had perfected the *cathode ray tube*, the component that allows a TV set to convert the received broadcast signal into an image. In other words, the most vital part of a television. And unlike previous cathode ray prototypes, DuMont's lasted indefinitely, rather than burning out after a few days.

DuMont sold the patent to RCA and used the money to start a TV manufacturing business. In need of more cash, he sold 40% of the company to Paramount Pictures in 1939, giving him plenty of money to make TVs. One problem: In 1939 few people were buying TV sets—there weren't any TV shows to watch. CBS and NBC aired a few experimental broadcasts in the New York area in the early 1940s and were rapidly moving toward regular commercial broadcasts, but when World War II broke out, they halted all TV work. DuMont felt that to sell TVs, there'd have to be programming. And now it looked like he'd have to do it himself.

ON THE AIR
In 1944 DuMont got a broadcasting license and opened his first station in New York: WABD (for "Allen B. DuMont"). He opened

a second station, WTTG (after DuMont's vice president Thomas T. Goldsmith) in Washington, D.C., in 1945. Then, using more than 200 miles of coaxial cable, DuMont connected his lab in Passaic, New Jersey, to the two stations. On August 9, 1945, DuMont aired an announcement that the U.S. had just dropped an atomic bomb on Nagasaki, Japan. That brief message was seen on TV sets in New York, New Jersey, and Washington. The DuMont Network—and commercial TV—was born. The network began regular broadcasts a year later with its first show, *Serving Through Science*.

IT'S THE PITTS

The television industry was about to take off. NBC was on the air in several cities in late 1946, including New York City, Philadelphia, and Schenectady, New York. CBS and ABC, a new network, followed in 1948. That year, more than a million TV sets were sold in the United States, most of them made by DuMont Labs.

The third DuMont station went on the air in 1949—WDTV (for "DuMont Television") in Pittsburgh. It was a smart move: CBS and NBC weren't broadcasting in Pittsburgh yet, even though Pittsburgh was America's sixth largest city at the time. In cities where it competed with NBC and CBS, DuMont was a distant third in the ratings; advertising profits suffered. But the profits from the monopoly in Pittsburgh offset the losses and kept the network afloat.

STANDARD VIEWING

CBS and NBC moved a lot of talent from radio to TV (Jack Benny, Edward R. Murrow, Lucille Ball). But DuMont didn't have a built-in pool of entertainers from which to draw. So for onscreen talent, the network hired New York theater actors and comedians. (Jackie Gleason hosted a variety show called *Cavalcade of Stars*; *The Honeymooners* originated as a sketch on that show.) And unlike CBS and NBC's shows, which were produced in state-of-the-art TV studios, DuMont shows were produced in unused rooms at Wanamaker's, a department store on Broadway.

DuMont made up for its lack of funds by innovating and taking risks. The result: groundbreaking ideas that defined the standards of television, even to this day. Among DuMont's contributions:

- **The First TV Sitcom:** *Mary Kay and Johnny* (1947). Mary Kay and Johnny Stearns, married in real life, played "themselves." Most of the action took place in the couple's apartment.
- **The First TV Soap Opera:** *Faraway Hill* (1946). Widow moves to small town and falls in love with a man who's already engaged.
- **The First Religious TV Show:** *Life Is Worth Living* (1952). Hosted by Catholic bishop Fulton J. Sheen, who delivered lectures on moral issues. It was DuMont's top show.
- **The First Kids' Show:** *Your Television Babysitter* (1948)
- **Home Shopping:** On *Your Television Shopper*, a host presented items (cheap jewelry, small appliances) and viewers called in to have them shipped to their home (they paid for them COD).
- **Televised Sports:** DuMont was the first network to regularly air football and basketball games (and boxing and wrestling matches).
- **The First Science Fiction Show:** *Captain Video and His Video Rangers* (1949). A group of interstellar police keep Earth and its space colonies safe.
- **TV Advertising:** The other networks did with TV what they had done on radio: One company sponsored an entire show. But DuMont sold individual blocks of commercial time—thirty seconds to a minute each—to multiple sponsors. That's how TV advertising works today.

    DuMont's low-budget try-anything style produced a lot of really weird TV, too.

- *The Plainclothesman:* A private-eye filmed from the point of view of the main character, who's never seen.
- *Night Editor:* A newspaper editor acts out news stories.
- *Inside Detective:* A cop solves crimes without ever leaving his office.

THE SIGNAL FADES

DuMont finished in third or fourth place in the ratings every week (always behind CBS and NBC, and always jockeying with ABC for third). He had affiliates in just three cities—New York, Washington, and Pittsburgh—but independent TV stations around the country paid DuMont and ABC for the rights to broadcast their shows. Allen DuMont wanted to buy more stations in more cities to increase viewers. But he couldn't—an FCC rule allowed a company to own a maximum of five stations. DuMont already owned three; his partner, Paramount, owned two.

Then in 1953, United Paramount Theaters, a movie theater chain (not owned by Paramount Pictures), bought ABC and funnelled millions of dollars into the network to make it more competitive. It worked: By the end of 1954, ABC had pulled ahead of DuMont into a solid third place. Most of the independent stations that had been splitting their schedules between ABC and DuMont shows switched to ABC programming exclusively.

SIGNING OFF

As a last-ditch effort to save the company, DuMont sold his most profitable asset, WDTV in Pittsburgh, for $10 million. But the money wasn't enough—the network was still losing viewers and stations to ABC. In early 1955, he decided to pull the plug. *Life Is Worth Living* broadcast on DuMont for the last time on April 26 (the show moved to ABC). The network feed remained intact for occasional sports broadcasts until August 6, 1956. That night, after a boxing match, the DuMont Network went off the air for good.

DuMont sold the New York and Washington stations to media mogul John Kluge for $7 million, who used them as the basis of a consortium of TV stations called Metromedia. Allen DuMont became a philanthropist and donated much of his fortune to help fund National Educational Television, a nonprofit TV network that evolved into PBS. He died in 1965.

A NEW BROADCAST DAY

The DuMont Network still exists today...sort of. Australian businessman Rupert Murdoch, owner of the 20th Century Fox film studio, set out to start a fourth major network in 1986. To do it, he put together a loose affiliation of independent stations around the country—many of which were the same stations that ran DuMont programming in the 1950s. But his first step: He created the basic elements for a new network by acquiring Metromedia, including the two original DuMont Network stations in New York and Washington, D.C., and created the Fox Network.

First celebrity to sit in the center square on *Hollywood Squares*: Ernest Borgnine.

BIKE AND LOAFER

Ready for a puzzle? Guess the name of the titular TV duo based on the synonyms, descriptions, or clues given. Got it? Good. (Answers on page 502).

1. *The Crop Guardian and the Queen*

2. *The Governess and the Academic*

3. *The Elected Leader & Magpie Magpie*

4. *The Legal Code & Keeping Things Tidy*

5. *Bike and Loafer*

6. *Northern California City and the Male Adult*

7. *The Compression Release Brake and the Morbidly Obese Guy*

8. *The Stone Fortress and the Spice Merchant*

9. *The First Name of the Mean Judge from* American Idol *and The First Name of the Mean Judge from* American Idol

10. *Playgrounds and Leisure*

11. *One's Spouse and Offspring*

12. *Outcasts and Nerds*

13. *Steal and Large*

14. *Male Siblings and Female Siblings*

15. *Intercourse and the Metropolitan Area*

16. *Bequeath & Mercy*

17. *The Overbearing and the Pretty*

18. *Little Boy and Divvy Up*

In 1984 George Clooney starred a sitcom called E/R. In 1994 he starred on the drama ER.

THE CSI EFFECT

How real are the TV shows that focus on police and lawyers? A few go all out for accuracy, while others get laughed at by the professions they portray. But they've all had an impact on society...both positive and negative.

FAMILIAR FORMULA

If there were no cops, prosecutors, or defense attorneys, the television airwaves would probably be far less crowded. Over the past 60 years, these professions have dominated primetime schedules. Why? They all offer formulas ready-made for drama: A brand-new conflict is presented to the protagonists each week, promising to be full of mystery, intrigue, and...predictability. Viewers can rely on the fact that near the end of the viewing hour, one crucial piece of evidence will appear and lead to the capture of the elusive killer, or to the acquittal of the wrongly accused defendant. Then comes the philosophical musing that wraps everything up neatly, providing a clean slate for next week's episode.

Real life is rarely so cut-and-dried. And while some may argue that cop and lawyer shows are merely entertainment, actual cops and lawyers claim these shows can make their already-difficult jobs even harder.

JURORS' PRUDENCE

The "CSI effect" occurs primarily inside the courtroom. Its first incarnation was referred to as the *Perry Mason* effect, based on the popular fictional defense attorney's trademark ability to clear his client by coercing the guilty party into confessing on the witness stand. During Mason's TV heyday, from the 1950s to the '80s, many prosecutors complained that juries were hesitant to convict defendants without that "Perry Mason moment" of a confession on the stand—which in real life is very, very rare.

After *Perry Mason* went off the air, a new kind of law enforcement program appeared: the scientific police procedural (which started with *Quincy, M.E.*, a drama about a crime-solving medical examiner that aired from 1976 to '83). But few cop shows have

---

matched the success of *CSI: Crime Scene Investigation*, which debuted in 2000 and has spawned two successful spin-offs. A 2006 TV ratings study in 20 countries named *CSI* "the most watched show in the world."

MYTH-CONCEPTIONS

Along with similar shows such as *NCIS*, *Diagnosis: Murder*, and *Bones*, *CSI* focuses on forensic evidence and lab work as the primary means of catching killers. These dramas may be "ripped from the headlines," but when it comes to telling an entertaining story, certain liberties must be taken by the writers:

• Experts who perform scientific analyses are rarely the same people who do the detective work and make arrests, unlike TV where one team tackles every aspect of the investigation. (And few real forensic scientists ever drive a Hummer to a crime scene.)

• The almost instant turnaround of DNA tests is what TV writers refer to as a "time cheat," a trick necessary to get the story wrapped up. In reality, due to the screening, extraction, and replication processes (not to mention the backlog), DNA tests can take months. And the results are rarely, if ever, 100% conclusive.

• Just about every murder investigation on TV leads to an arrest and conviction. In the real world, less than half of these cases are solved.

"If you really portrayed what crime scene investigators do," said Jay Siegel, a professor of forensic science at Michigan State University, "the show would die after three episodes because it would be so boring."

SHOW ME THE SCIENCE

The main problem caused by the *CSI* effect: Juries now *expect* conclusive forensic evidence. According to Staff Sergeant Peter Abi-Rashed, a homicide detective from Hamilton, Ontario, "Juries are asking, 'Can we convict without DNA evidence?' Of course they can. It's called good, old-fashioned police work and overwhelming circumstantial evidence." In the worst-case scenarios, guilty people may be set free because a jury wasn't impressed with evidence that—as recently as the 1990s—would have led to a conviction. In fact, many forensic experts find themselves on the stand explaining to a jury why they *don't* have scientific evidence. Some

lawyers have even started asking potential jurors if they watch
CSI. If so, they may have to be reeducated.

Shellie Samuels, the lead prosecutor in the 2005 Robert Blake
murder trial, probably wishes that her jury had been asked beforehand if they were CSI fans. Samuels tried to convince them that
Blake, a former TV cop himself (on Baretta), shot and killed his
wife in 2001. Samuels illustrated Blake's motive; she presented 70
witnesses who testified against him, including two who stated—
under oath—that Blake had asked them to kill his wife. Seems
like a lock for a conviction, right? Wrong. "They couldn't put the
gun in his hand," said jury foreman Thomas Nicholson, who
along with his peers acquitted Blake. "There was no blood spat-
ter. They had nothing." The verdict sent a clear message
throughout the legal community: Juries will convict only on
solid forensic evidence.

This new trend affects cops, too. CSI-watching detectives tend
to put unrealistic pressure on crime scene investigators not only to
find solid evidence, but also to give them immediate results.
Henry Lee, chief emeritus of Connecticut's state crime lab (and
perhaps the world's most famous forensics scientist), says that,
much to the dismay of the police, his investigators can't provide
"miracle proof" just by scattering some "magic dust" on a crime
scene. And there is no machine—not even at the best-equipped
lab in the country—in which you can place a hair in at one end
and pull a picture of a suspect out of the other. "And our type of
work always has a backlog," laments Lee, who's witnessed the
amount of evidence turned in to his lab rise from about five pieces
per crime scene in the 1980s to anywhere from 50 to 400 today.

MIRANDA WRONGS

The CSI effect doesn't stop at science—the entire judicial
process is being presented in a misleading fashion. Mary Flood,
editor of a Web site called The Legal Pad, asked a dozen prominent criminal lawyers to rate the most popular shows. Her findings: "Generally, they hate it when Law & Order's Jack McCoy
extracts confessions in front of speechless defense lawyers. Not
real, they say. They go nuts over the CSI premise of the exceed-
ingly well-funded, glamorous lab techs who do a homicide detective's job. Even less real, they say. And they get annoyed when

The Closer's heroine ignores a suspect's requests for a lawyer.
Unconstitutional, they say."

DUMB CROOKS
In the real world, it's usually neither the crusading prosecutor nor
the headstrong cop who solves the case. Most criminals, cops
admit, are their own worst enemies. Either they don't cover their
tracks or they brag to friends about what they did, or both. People
tend not to think clearly when they commit crimes. But in the
past few years there has appeared a new kind of criminal: the kind
that watches CSI...and learns.

In December 2005, Jermaine "Maniac" McKinney, a 25-year-
old man from Ohio, broke into a house and killed two people.
He used bleach to clean his hands as well as the crime scene,
then carefully removed all of the evidence and placed blankets
in his car before transferring the bodies to an isolated lakeshore
at night, where he burned them along with his clothes and cigarette butts—making sure that none of his DNA could be connected to the victims. One thing remained: the murder weapon,
a crowbar. McKinney threw it into the lake...which was frozen.
He didn't want to risk walking out on the ice to get it, so he left
it behind. Big mistake: The weapon was later found—still on the
ice—and linked to McKinney, which led to his arrest. When
asked why he used bleach to clean his hands, McKinney said
that he'd learned that bleach destroys DNA. Where'd he learn
that? "On CSI."

Using bleach to clean a crime scene was almost unheard of
until CSI used it as a plot point. Now the practice is occurring
more and more often. "Sometimes I believe it may even encourage
criminals when they see how simple it is to get away with murder
on television," said Captain Ray Peavy, head of the homicide division at the Los Angeles Sheriff's Department. It's difficult enough
to investigate a crime scene with the "normal" amount of evidence left behind.

MAYBE DON'T SHOW THEM THE SCIENCE?
So should these shows be censored? Should they tone down
the science or, as some have argued, use *fake* science to throw
criminals a red herring? "The National District Attorneys

Association is deeply concerned about the effect of *CSI*," CBS News consultant and former prosecutor Wendy Murphy reported. "When *CSI* trumps common sense, then you have a systemic problem."

But not everyone agrees. "To argue that *CSI* and similar shows are actually raising the number of acquittals is a staggering claim," argues Simon Cole, professor of criminology at the University of California, Irvine. "And the remarkable thing is that, speaking forensically, there is not a shred of evidence to back it up."

And furthering the debate about whether criminals learn from *CSI*, Paul Wilson, the chair of criminology at Bond University in Australia, stated, "There is no doubt that criminals copy what they see on television. However, I don't believe these shows pose a major problem." Prison, Wilson maintains, is where most of these people learn the tricks of their trade. So while law enforcement officials may agree that cop and lawyer shows do have an effect on modern investigations and trials, the jury is still out on exactly *what* that effect is.

THE SILVER LINING

The shows do have their positive aspects. For one thing, they teach basic science, saving the courts time and money by not having to call in experts to explain such concepts as what DNA evidence actually is. Anthony E. Zuiker, creator of the *CSI* franchise, is quick to point this out. "Jurors can walk in with some preconceived notions of at least what *CSI* means. And even if there are false expectations, at least jurors aren't walking in blind."

Perhaps most significantly, though, ever since *CSI* became a hit in 2000, student admissions into the forensic field have skyrocketed. So even if Zuiker's show is confusing jurors, misinforming police, and helping to train criminals, at least it's proven to be an effective recruiting tool. "The *CSI* effect is, in my opinion, the most amazing thing that has ever come out of the series," he said. "For the first time in American history, you're not allowed to fool the jury anymore."

And finally, a message from Zuiker to anyone who walks up and points out his shows' inherent flaws: "Folks, it's television."

The award for the best TV commercials is called a Clio, named after the Greek muse of history.

CANCELED CLASSICS

People often complain that there's nothing good on TV.
Why didn't they watch these shows?

FREAKS AND GEEKS (NBC, 1999–2000)
Background: Paul Feig created this hour-long comedy drama about two groups at a suburban Detroit high school in 1980: the freaks (stoners and troublemakers) and the geeks (nerdy freshmen). *TIME* magazine called it a "rare, realistic depiction of small-town life, with its class divisions and dawning realizations that some kids' escape fantasies are more likely to come true than others'." It launched the careers of Jason Segel, James Franco, and Seth Rogen.

Canceled: *Freaks* debuted during the reality-show craze, a difficult time for scripted shows. It was also in the middle of a teen pop-culture boom. Shows like *Dawson's Creek* and movies like *She's All That* attracted teen audiences, but *Freaks* wasn't that kind of show—it focused on outcasts, not pretty and popular kids. Poor marketing and scheduling didn't help: NBC never figured out if *Freaks* was for kids or adults (Feig and executive producer Judd Apatow designed it for both), and aired it on Saturday night. After 18 episodes, NBC canceled *Freaks and Geeks* because of its low ratings (#93 for the season). Two years later, Apatow and several *Freaks* cast members reunited for Fox's *Undeclared*, a show about college freshmen. It, too, was hailed by critics, loved by fans, and canceled after a few episodes.

BUFFALO BILL (NBC, 1983–84)
Background: Many sitcoms have one mean character to serve as a comic foil (e.g., Frank Burns on M*A*S*H, or Dwight Schrute on *The Office*). Created by comedy writers Jay Tarses and Tom Patchett (*The Carol Burnett Show* and *The Bob Newhart Show*), *Buffalo Bill* took a big risk by making the mean character the main focus. Dabney Coleman portrayed Bill Bittinger, a cynical Buffalo talk-show host who takes out his frustrations on his guests and staff. (The supporting cast included Geena Davis, who also wrote for the show, and Joanna Cassidy, who won a Golden Globe for her role.) The show also garnered 11 Emmy nominations. According

---

to TV critic Richard T. Jameson, "*Buffalo Bill* was, if not the best sitcom ever, indisputably the most brilliant, outrageous, exquisitely detailed and nuanced."

Canceled: After a summer run, NBC's programming chief Brandon Tartikoff placed *Bill* in a plum Thursday night time slot between *Cheers* and *Hill Street Blues*. But the show couldn't match the popularity of the other two, and was pulled the following March after 26 episodes. It failed, according to some critics, because Bill was simply too mean—he was bigoted, paranoid, scheming, crude, and sexist. Perhaps if the show had lasted, Bill's human side—or at least his pain—would have been explored. Tartikoff later admitted that canceling *Buffalo Bill* is the biggest regret of his career.

WONDERFALLS (Fox, 2004)

Background: In this quirky, hourlong comedy, Niagara Falls gift shop clerk Jaye (Caroline Dhavernas) thinks she's going crazy when the figurines on the shelves start moving and delivering cryptic messages—that only she can hear—urging her to help people. The TV Critics Association nominated *Wonderfalls* for Outstanding New Program, and the Writers Guild of America nominated it for its writing. The show attracted a small but loyal fan base.

Canceled: *Wonderfalls* closed up shop after only four episodes. Fox did the series no favors—it ran the episodes out of order, sentenced it to a deadly Friday-night time slot, and promoted it as a romantic comedy. Viewers who did tune in saw a much darker and more intriguing show than promised—If Jaye failed to follow the knick-knacks' instructions, they'd annoy her relentlessly or even hurt someone she loved. Even more damning was that it seemed to have a similar premise to a show that debuted the same season: CBS's *Joan of Arcadia*, in which God speaks to a teenage girl. *Joan* was a hit; when *Wonderfalls* debuted midseason, it looked like a knockoff.

MY SO-CALLED LIFE (ABC, 1994–95)

Background: Created by Winnie Holzman (*The Wonder Years*) and produced by *thirtysomething*'s Edward Zwick and Marshall Herskovitz, this show addressed tough issues faced by teens. It starred 15-year-old Claire Danes as Angela, who narrates her struggles to

shed her popular veneer and join a seedier crowd, where she falls
for Jordan (Jared Leto), a quiet loner in a rock band. Danes won a
Golden Globe for a portrayal that IGN movies called "incredibly
genuine and believable."

Canceled: The series ended its first season on a cliffhanger, and
then it was canceled. In the summer of 1995, MTV re-ran the
episodes in the hopes that *Life* would be renewed by ABC or
picked up by another network. Neither happened, and fans never
got a resolution to the cliffhanger. While it was unlikely that *Life*
would have ever pulled in the numbers of the most popular teen
show at the time—*Beverly Hills 90210*—it didn't even come close.

EERIE, INDIANA (NBC, 1991–92)

Background: The success of David Lynch's *Twin Peaks* helped
pave the way for *Eerie, Indiana*, created by José Rivera and Karl
Schaefer. While it wasn't necessarily a kids' show, it starred 13-
year-old Omri Katz as a boy named Marshall Teller, who moves to
the titular town, "the center of weirdness in the universe." There
he encounters Bigfoot, Elvis, dogs bent on world domination, and
Tupperware that grants eternal life. JoBlo's Movie Emporium
wrote, "For anyone who enjoyed the quirky side of *Twin Peaks*, the
adventurous tone of *The Goonies*, the fantastical angle of *Amazing
Stories*, and the otherworldly *Twilight Zone* or *The X-Files*, strap
yourself in for a ride through one of television's more groundbreaking and surreal programs."

Canceled: *Eerie, Indiana* lasted 19 episodes. It was too weird for
adults and too scary for kids, even though it aired on Sunday
nights at 7:00, a family-friendly time slot. *Eerie* lived on, however,
as a successful series of young-adult novels, and reruns performed
so well in syndication that Fox greenlighted a Saturday morning,
kid-friendly remake in 1998 called *Eerie, Indiana: The Other
Dimension*. That show lasted only 15 episodes.

THE TICK (Fox, 2001–02)

Background: Based on a 1986 comic book, *The Tick* starred
Patrick Warburton (Puddy from *Seinfeld*) as a hulking, confused
man who believes he is a superhero charged with protecting "The
City." His sidekick: an ex-accountant named Arthur (David
Burke), who wants a more exciting life.

Canceled: Fox didn't own the show (Disney did) and didn't put much effort into promoting it. Instead of running it on Sunday night, where it would have fit perfectly with *The Simpsons*, Fox aired *The Tick* on Thursday night opposite NBC's *Friends* and CBS's *Survivor*. Plus, creator Ben Edlund wanted to keep the show tame enough for kids, while Fox wanted more vulgarity and sexual innuendo to play to their target audience of young men. What resulted was an uneven but often hilarious superhero show that drew dismal ratings and was squashed after only eight episodes. Said *Entertainment Weekly*'s Dalton Ross: "It was too smart. Too funny. Too weird. So, of course, it failed."

FIREFLY (Fox, 2002)

Background: A western set in space in the year 2517, *Firefly* was created by Joss Whedon (*Buffy the Vampire Slayer*). A bunch of outcasts on the losing side of a civil war travel in a spaceship to smuggle and run odd jobs while trying to avoid the authoritarian Alliance government. Critics loved *Firefly*: "A truly great series, better than most sci-fi movies in the theaters," wrote Robert Roten of Laramie Movie Scope.

Canceled: Accolades did not translate to good ratings. Less than five million viewers tuned in each Friday night, not enough to sustain a network show with a big budget, and *Firefly* lasted just 11 episodes. No other cancellation in Fox's history brought a bigger uproar than *Firefly*'s. Fans bought a full-page ad in *Variety* begging the network to keep it on—or for another one to pick it up. None did. Fans did get a *Firefly* movie, 2005's *Serenity*, but a 119-minute extension to a story that Whedon intended to last seven years was far less than they wanted.

*　　*　　*

"I just thought up a great idea for a reality show. You pull people over who have those 'honk if you love whatever' bumper stickers, and you make them do whatever the bumper sticker says they like to do."

—Lorelai, *Gilmore Girls*

...so that viewers wouldn't think the two women were lesbians.

OMG!

What do TV characters know about religion? Judging by these quotes, not much.

Barney: Lots of chicks think that architects are hot. Think about that, you create something out of nothing. You're like God. There is no one hotter than God.
Ted: I love it when you quote Scripture.
—*How I Met Your Mother*

"When I'm in charge of the bar, I know what God feels like. I'm in complete control of people's destinies. I can make their drinks too strong so they get sick. Or I can water them down so they're paying for nothing. Or, if I don't like their attitude, I can spit in it."
—Carla, *Cheers*

Booth: God doesn't make mistakes.
Angela: I don't know. Putting testicles on the outside didn't seem like such a good idea.
—*Bones*

"I love the way holding a gun feels. It makes me feel like God, the way he must feel when He holds a gun."
—Homer, *The Simpsons*

"If you talk to God, you're religious. If God talks to you, you're psychotic."
—Dr. House, *House*

Hawkeye: I just wanted to borrow your Bible, Frank.
Frank: Since when are you interested in the Bible?
Trapper: I peeked at the end, Frank. The Devil did it.
—*M*A*S*H*

"The Lord giveth, and the Lord taketh away. Sometimes the giveth seems a little disproportionate to the taketh. There seems to be a lot more taketh-ing going on, but there it is."
—Priest Maxi, *South Park*

"To me, religion is like Paul Rudd. I see the appeal, and I would never take it away from anyone, but I would also never stand in line for it."
—Jeff, *Community*

"Yes, I rather like this God fellow. He's very theatrical, you know—a pestilence here, a plague there. Omnipotence. Gotta get me some of that."
—Stewie, *Family Guy*

TREK STORY, PART III

By the year 2000, Star Trek had played a major role in American television for more than half TV's existence. Would Trek go boldly into the new century, or would its dilithium crystals finally peter out? (Part II is on page 398.)

AN ENTERPRISING IDEA
After *Voyager's* seven-year run ended in May 2001, Rick Berman begged Paramount to give *Star Trek* a one-year hiatus before launching another series. "It's oversaturated," he argued. "People are losing interest." They gave him until September.

The struggling UPN network needed viewers, and other than professional wrestling, *Star Trek* was its only bankable commodity. Berman and co-producer Brannon Braga, decided to go back in time in the *Trek* universe and base a series on how it all began.

By Berman and Braga's latest series, *Enterprise*, didn't look much like any of the other *Star Treks*. It took place a century before the original series, and there was no Federation, no Prime Directive, and no carpeted bridge. This starship *Enterprise* looked like a submarine on the inside. Another change: Instead of the typical symphonic theme that marked every other *Trek* incarnation, *Enterprise* opened with a rock ballad called "Where My Heart Will Take Me," sung by opera singer Russell Watson.

ARCHER'S GANG

Enterprise premiered on UPN less than two weeks after the 9/11 terrorist attacks. More than 12 million viewers tuned in looking for a diversion from all the bad news—UPN's biggest audience ever. And what they saw looked sort of like the familiar *Star Trek*—there was a Vulcan, played by supermodel Jolene Blalock, and there was a rugged Starfleet captain, Jonathan Archer (Scott Bakula).

Ratings dropped off for the second episode and continued to decline, but compared to other shows on UPN, *Enterprise* did fairly well. Some critics and die-hard *Trek* fans, though, weren't happy. What seemed to irritate them most was Berman's indifference to *Star Trek's* canon. For example: Trekkers know that the first captain of the *Enterprise* was Captain April, not Captain Archer. Plus, some of the familiar *Trek* villains, like the Cardassians, were missing.

BACK TO BASICS

Even UPN execs noticed the lack of continuity, and they told Berman that if he wanted the show to survive, he'd have to "*Trek* it up." Berman renamed the show *Star Trek: Enterprise* in its third season and introduced a time-travel plot about a "temporal cold war" and a decidedly dark turn of events involving a major attack by an alien race. Fans on Internet message boards skewered the contrivances. Berman paid attention and pulled out all the stops to turn the series around. He eased off the writing and renewed his efforts in overseeing the show as a producer.

By the fourth season (2004–05), *Enterprise* had finally become what fans were promised in the beginning: a direct prequel laying the foundation for what was to come. Berman wound plots around the franchise's two most popular villains—the Klingons and the Romulans—and provided detailed explanations to correct continuity issues, such as why the Klingons on later *Treks* had bumpy foreheads while the original Klingons didn't (a genetic mutation). Now the faithful could finally watch a real *Star Trek*! Well, they could have...if only they'd tuned in.

END OF THE LINE

Much to Berman's dismay, UPN put *Enterprise* in the infamous Friday-night "death slot," where no show on a broadcast network had attracted a decent audience in more than a decade. In February 2005, UPN gave it the ax. While the majority of TV viewers barely noticed that *Enterprise* had even been on, much less canceled, some die-hard Trekkers are to this day livid at UPN (which folded in 2006). According to the fanzine *Trekdom*, "UPN suits cringed at the thought of intellectually challenging their *Sweet Valley High*, *Moesha*, and *WWE Smackdown* viewers. A network that thrived on fluff didn't have a high tolerance level for provocative drama."

Braga, who went on to oversee Fox's *24*, also blamed the network. "I think UPN hurt *Voyager* and much more with *Enterprise*, to be on a constantly shifting fledgling network that in some places was on channel 92, if you could find it, and you needed the foil rabbit ears." Still, Berman says, "I have nothing to be ashamed about. We created 624 hours of television and four feature films and I think we did a hell of a job."

MEET FRED FLAGSTONE

Would these shows have been as successful
if they'd kept their original titles?

Original title: *Not the Cosby Show*
Became: *Married...With Children* (1987–97)
Story: "The show was sold on the premise that no one is
ever going to learn anything watching it," said series creator
Michael G. Moye, who, with partner Ron Leavitt (both writers on
The Jeffersons), found a willing network in the fledgling Fox after
the Big Three turned it down. The premise: A sitcom based on a
crass family with parents played by comedians Sam Kinison and
Roseanne Barr. While pitching it to Fox, Moye and Leavitt ham-
mered home the fact that this was "not *The Cosby Show*" so often
that the project took on the phrase for its title. When Fox bought
the show, they rechristened it *Married...with Children*. Kinison was
too controversial at the time, so Fox passed on him (he later guest-
starred as a guardian angel). Fox did want Barr, but her manager
advised her against it—he had something else in mind for her...

Original title: *Life and Stuff*
Became: *Roseanne* (1988–97)
Story: When ABC came up with a title for comedian Roseanne
Barr's sitcom, they were selling the concept (lower-middle-class
life), not the star. Barr reportedly loved the title *Life and Stuff*, but
in the few months after the show was picked up, she'd become so
famous that ABC renamed it *Roseanne*. The show started a trend
of sitcoms built around stand-up comedians, including *Home
Improvement* (Tim Allen), *Grace Under Fire* (Brett Butler), and
Seinfeld (Jerry Seinfeld).

Original titles: *Insomnia Café; Friends Like Us; Six of One*
Became: *Friends* (1994–2004)
Story: In early 1994, writers David Crane and Marta Kauffman
shopped their show about 20-something Manhattanites to NBC.
The network liked the concept for *Insomnia Café* but not the
title. So Kauffman changed it to *Friends Like Us*. NBC loved that

name, especially the word "friends"...until ABC debuted a comedy starring Ellen DeGeneres called *These Friends of Mine*. So the NBC show was renamed *Six of One*, and a pilot was filmed. After a tense few days of waiting, executive producer Kevin Bright received a call from NBC. Good news: The show had been picked up. Better news: It would air on Thursday nights in the plum time slot between hits *Mad About You* and *Seinfeld*. When the network executive asked Bright, "How about we just call the show *Friends*?" Bright was so elated that he replied, "You can call it *Kevorkian*, for all I care!" And there was no name conflict with *These Friends of Mine* after all—by fall 1994, that show had changed its name to *Ellen*.

Original title: *45 Minutes from Harlem*
Became: *Diff'rent Strokes* (1978–86)
Story: In 1976 producer Norman Lear saw a commercial starring eight-year-old Gary Coleman and knew he could make the kid a star, so he started grooming Coleman with guest spots on *The Jeffersons* and *Good Times*. NBC chief Fred Silverman then asked Lear to cast Coleman in a pilot called *45 Minutes from Harlem* with Canadian actor Conrad Bain (*Maude*). Bain would portray a rich white man from Westchester, New York, located about "45 minutes from Harlem," who adopts an African-American boy. The setting ultimately changed to a Park Avenue penthouse (Bain's idea), meaning that Lear had to come up with a new title. He borrowed a line from the 1968 Sly & The Family Stone song "Everyday People" about racial harmony—"different strokes for different folks."

Original title: *Teenage Wasteland*
Became: *That '70s Show* (1998–2006)
Story: Producers Marcy Carsey and Tom Werner (*Roseanne*, *The Cosby Show*), along with Bonnie and Terry Turner and writer Mark Brazill (*3rd Rock from the Sun*) wanted to tell stories about what they all had gone through as teenagers in the 1970s. Music was a big part of their lives—hence their original title, *Teenage Wasteland*, a reference to the Who's "Baba O'Riley." They were also toying with other song titles and lyrics, including *The Kids Are Alright* (another Who song) and *Reelin' in the Years* (a Steely

Dan song). Due to copyright concerns, they couldn't use the Who songs, and no one was thrilled about the Steely Dan option. Test audiences, however, loved the unnamed pilot for "that show about the '70s," or, as some were calling it, "that '70s show." So it became the working title until they could think of a better one. No one ever did.

Original title: *Please Stand By; Beyond Control*
Became: *The Outer Limits* (1963–65, 1995–2002)
Story: Inspired by *The Twilight Zone*, Joseph Stefano (who penned the screenplay to Hitchcock's *Psycho*) and Leslie Stevens (the playwright of Broadway's *The Marriage-Go-Round*) set out to create one-hour sci-fi morality tales. ABC liked the concept and the opening narration: "There is nothing wrong with your television set. Do not attempt to adjust the picture. We are controlling the transmission." But they were afraid the show's title, *Please Stand By*, might fool viewers into believing an actual emergency was occurring. This was during the height of the Cold War, shortly after the Cuban Missile Crisis, and two decades after the infamous Orson Welles "War of the Worlds" radio show that had caused a panic. The name *Beyond Control* was briefly considered before ABC changed it to *The Outer Limits*.

Original title: *Scenario 5*
Became: *Chuck* (2007–11)
Story: "In retrospect," said *Chuck* creator Chris Fedak, "*Scenario 5* would have been a terrible name." But Fedak was new to TV; his old college friend happened to be Josh Schwartz, who, at 26, became the youngest person ever to run the day-to-day production of a network show (*The O.C.*). On a whim, Fedak pitched Schwartz a show idea about a regular guy who gets swept up into espionage thanks to a microchip in his head. Fedak thought it should be a thriller, but Schwartz saw a lot of comedic potential. He didn't like the title *Scenario 5*, though. What to call it? Schwartz noticed a book by music critic Chuck Klosterman. "What if we named the main character Chuck and called the show *Chuck*?" Fedak hated it, but his wife loved it and thought "Chuck" was the perfect "regular guy" kind of name. *Chuck* stuck.

Original title: *The Beast*
Became: *The Honeymooners* (1955–56)
Story: This show about a bitter Brooklyn bus driver and his jaded wife began in 1950 as a series of sketches on the DuMont Network's *Cavalcade of Stars*, hosted by and starring Jackie Gleason. The working title of the sketches was "The Beast," but Gleason didn't like it: "That makes it sound like it's the husband who's doing all the fighting." One of the writers asked, "How about 'The Lovers'?" "No," said Gleason, "Folks will think we're not married." Another writer suggested "The Couple Next Door," but Gleason found that bland. "We need something that will keep going and going, like…'The Honeymooners.'" Gleason was the boss, so the name change was made. The sketches became the most popular part of *Cavalcade*, and even more so on CBS's *The Jackie Gleason Show*. They became a standalone sitcom in 1955, which lasted for 39 episodes.

Original title: *The Flagstones; The Gladstones*
Became: *The Flintstones* (1960–66)
Story: William Hanna and Joe Barbera modeled the first prime-time cartoon after *The Honeymooners* (they even hired two *Honeymooners* writers) but had no idea where, or when, to put their Ralph and Alice clones. "We tried making Fred and Wilma pilgrims and Indians and Romans and hillbillies," Barbera recalled. "Then one of the fellows came up with a sketch of a man and a woman in animal skins, and we instantly knew that was it." After ABC announced that their new fall show would be called *The Flagstones*, the network received a cease-and-desist letter from Mort Walker, co-creator of the comic strip *Hi and Lois*, a married couple whose last name is Flagston. The cartoon was briefly changed to *The Gladstones* (a Los Angeles telephone exchange), before Hanna-Barbera finally settled on *The Flintstones*.

* * *

Worst name ever: The "real" name of Comic Book Guy on *The Simpsons*: Jeff Albertson. A staff writer named him that when show creator Matt Groening wasn't around. Groening had wanted to give him a more comic-book-inspired name: Louis Lane.

VIDEO PIRATES

*Imagine you're watching TV when suddenly...the screen scrambles
and some strange person appears, hijacking the signal. Despite
the technological sophistication of TV broadcasting, it's
actually happened quite a few times.*

CAPTAIN MIDNIGHT

The Crime: On April 27, 1986, HBO was showing the
movie *The Falcon and the Snowman* on the East Coast.
Suddenly, the movie disappeared, replaced by a color bar test pattern. Over the color bars was a message in white text that read:

"Good Evening HBO from Captain Midnight, $12.95/month?
No way! Showtime/Movie Channel Beware!"

The message remained on-screen for four minutes. Then, just as
suddenly as it had appeared, the message went away and *The
Falcon and the Snowman* returned. HBO (and the government) had
no idea how it could have happened—every person and every
piece of equipment in its operations were accounted for—until an
anonymous caller contacted the FBI a few weeks later.

The Aftermath: The tipster was calling from a phone booth in
Gainesville, Florida, where he'd met a guy named John MacDougall in a local bar and heard him brag about breaking into
HBO's feed. MacDougall was promptly arrested...and he confessed.
Why'd he do it? MacDougall was a satellite dish salesman frustrated
that HBO required satellite owners to buy extra equipment to
access its channel, which, along with high subscription fees, hurt
his business. So, while working his second job as a satellite uplink
supervisor at Central Florida Teleport, he intercepted the HBO signal and broadcast his message. MacDougall was fined $5,000 and
sentenced to a year of probation. (He still sells satellite dishes.)

BOOB TUBE

The Crime: East Coast viewers who tuned in to the Playboy
Channel on the night of September 6, 1987, didn't get the movie
they'd paid for—they got a guilt trip instead. For six minutes, the
broadcast was replaced by a black screen with a message in white
text that said simply, "Repent your sins."

The gold chains worn by Mr. T on *The A-Team* weighed between 35 and 40 pounds.

The Aftermath: Within just a few days of the signal's being hijacked, the FBI determined that the message text was produced with a Knox K50 Character Generator, of which only five were in use in the United States. One of those was located at the Virginia headquarters of the Christian Broadcasting Network, the religious television company that produces *The 700 Club*. Confronted by the FBI, a CBN employee named Thomas Haynie proudly admitted that he was the hijacker. Haynie had access to CBN's satellite, which he used to intercept the Playboy Channel's transmission with the intent to "instill morality." Haynie was fired by CBN, paid a $1,000 fine, and received three years of probation. (When his sentence was up, CBN re-hired him.)

VRILLON OF THE ASHTAR GALACTIC COMMAND

The Crime: On November 26, 1977, the Independent Television News was airing its daily report in southern England when the audio feed suddenly dropped out. Although the image of the news-caster remained intact, what viewers heard was the buzzing, highly distorted voice of someone calling himself "Vrillon of the Ashtar Galactic Command." Vrillon went on to explain that he was from a distant planet and was hijacking the news to warn people that nuclear war was inevitable unless humanity could "learn to live together in peace and goodwill." Vrillon rambled on about peace and understanding for five minutes; then the news returned to normal.

The Aftermath: The identity of the signal hacker was never discovered. But because the highly distorted voice had a clear British accent, authorities are fairly sure that "Vrillon" was not a real alien.

MAX HEADROOM

The Crime: Fifteen minutes into a November 22, 1987, late-night airing of *Doctor Who* on Chicago's PBS affiliate WTTW, the image changed to a shot of a man in a Max Headroom mask (Max Headroom was a character from a short-lived science-fiction TV show). In an electronically distorted voice, "Headroom" went on a three-minute, seemingly nonsensical rant. Among his statements: "he's a freaky nerd," "this guy's better than Chuck Swirsky" (a Chicago sportscaster), "they're coming to get me," and "I just made a giant masterpiece printed all over the greatest world news-paper nerds." The man then dropped his pants and mooned the camera as a masked woman slapped his buttocks with a flyswatter. Then the picture turned to static and *Doctor Who* reappeared.

The Aftermath: A joint FBI/ FCC investigation determined that the pirate had extensive knowledge of electronics and broadcast-ing, because he hijacked the *Doctor Who* broadcast by overpower-ing it with a more powerful signal. This was no small feat, considering that the WTTW antenna was on top of the Sears Tower. According to the FCC, a suitcase-sized device capable of overtaking the WTTW signal could be produced for about $25,000. Agents believe that's what the pirate used, and he beamed his message from a nearby rooftop. But searches of build-ings adjacent to the Sears Tower turned up nothing. What was the reason for the signal interruption? It may have been a grudge against Chicago TV station WGN. The same night as the *Doctor Who* interception, the Max Headroom guy also cut into WGN's nightly news for a few seconds, and his comment about the "great-est world newspaper nerds" could have been a reference to WGN's call letters, which stand for "world's greatest newspaper" (the sta-tion was owned by the *Chicago Tribune*). But whoever the pirate was, and exactly why he did it, have never been discovered.

*   *   *

THE TONIGHT SHOW...WITH MIKE DOUGLAS?

On a 1965 episode of *The Tonight Show*, host Johnny Carson quipped that his show was so entertaining—and distracting—to late-night viewers that it had done more for birth control than the birth control pill. Then, a few weeks later, guest Ray Milland told a story on the show about accidentally urinating while filming a love scene in a swimming pool. These two incidents so angered Federal Communications Commission chief E. William Henry that he began an investigation into *The Tonight Show*, "lest the industry degenerate into indecency." No fines were levied, but NBC executives were so spooked by Henry that they nearly fired Carson and replaced him with daytime TV host Mike Douglas.

TV'S FATHER: PHILO T. FARNSWORTH

*On a spring day in 1920 near Rigby, Idaho, a farm boy named
Philo took a break from his plowing and invented television.
Then his amazing invention was stolen from him.*

ALONE IN HIS FIELD

Electricity and radio in 1920 were like computers in the 1970s: exciting new innovations into which the technologically minded put their dreams, mental energy, and considerable spare time. Fourteen-year-old Philo Taylor Farnsworth—tall, skinny, and full of ideas—was already showing promise as an electricity prodigy. Two years earlier, shortly after he'd seen an electric light for the first time, he'd rewired a burned-out motor and presented his family with its first automatic washing machine.

Living on a farm in Idaho meant lots of tedious chores, which gave Philo plenty of time to think. As he was plowing a field one day, he started wondering if it was possible for radios to broadcast moving pictures as well as sound.

SPINNING THE WHEELS

Philo certainly wasn't the first person to come up with the idea of sending images over the air. He'd found a stack of science magazines in the attic (they were there when his family moved in), with articles about European experimenters trying to do just that. One of the more promising attempts: German inventor Paul Nipkow had rigged a spinning wheel mounted on a lit picture, dotted with tiny pinholes. As the hand-cranked wheel spun rapidly in front of a brightly lit scene, the first pinhole let in a thin strip of light from the top of the scene, the next let in another thin strip, and so on—thus the entire scene was rapidly scanned from top to bottom over and over again.

How did that make TV? The thin strips of light landed on photosensitive material that generated a little surge of electricity when the light hit it. The brighter the light, the more juice was produced; connected electrically to that wheel was another wheel spinning at exactly the same rate of speed while transforming the electric signals back into light again. Demonstrations showed promise: Images, while ill-defined, could be recognized and transmitted.

PLOWING AHEAD

Philo thought about the spinning-wheel device as he plowed. He felt it was a great idea but knew it would never lead to broadcasting images. First of all, the two wheels would have to spin at the same rate all the time, or the image would be lost. That can easily be managed if the wheels are a few feet apart in a laboratory, but how do you maintain the same speed if the wheels are hundreds of miles apart, the transmitter in one place and the receiver in a home? And if it was used in large-scale broadcasting, *every wheel* on *every receiver* would have to be synchronized—a near-impossible feat.

Philo knew there had to be a better approach, one that wouldn't require wheels or mass synchronization. That's when, according to legend, he stopped plowing and looked around—his plow had created equally spaced parallel lines over the entire field. He'd read that scientists could manipulate the motion of an electron thousands of times per second in a vacuum tube, so he looked at the field and saw a large vacuum tube acting as a screen. And "plowing" that field was a thin ray of light, pulled by alternating magnetic fields, moving across the screen in superfast "furrows" while lighting up selected pieces along each furrow. Philo realized that if this were done in a fraction of a second and repeated, the human eye would perceive motion.

Over the next few months, Philo thought about his vision some more and realized that if he scanned the picture electronically instead of mechanically, he could add more speed and more high-definition scan lines (the "furrows")—maybe 30 frames a second at 500 lines or more—instead of the 20 frames and 50 lines that European researchers like Nipkow had obtained.

SHOW ME THE MONEY

Farnsworth continued to research and refine his ideas in his spare time, eventually enrolling in Brigham Young University at age 17. He had access to laboratories and like-minded students, but the problem was funding. Nobody wanted to blow money on the fantastical invention of a self-taught farmboy trying to outdo some of the greatest scientists in Europe.

His luck changed when he joined the Community Chest, a charity group at BYU. A couple of the organization's directors were philanthropists from California, and one of Farnsworth's friends told them about his ideas. To his surprise, they agreed to provide modest funding to set him up in California. Farnsworth moved west and rented a 30-by-30-foot lab in San Francisco. He had just turned 19 years old.

Farnsworth and a small staff diligently experimented with electricity, vacuum tubes, and electrons in the lab for three years. His backers became impatient, having yet to receive a return on the $1,000 a month it cost to keep the research afloat. Finally, in late 1927, Farnsworth's team projected a line of light into a camera behind a photographic slide, and sent it to a screen. Seven months later, in May 1928, Farnsworth presented more than a line of light—he transmitted an image. Fittingly enough, it was a dollar sign.

SMEAR TACTICS

When word got out that a guy working on his own in San Francisco had accomplished a system for broadcasting and receiving moving images with electric signals, one man saw red: David Sarnoff, an executive with the Radio Corporation of America (RCA), in charge of NBC Radio, the company's emerging radio network and TV development. Sarnoff had been trying the same thing, spending years and millions of dollars on a staff of 60, headed by inventor Vladimir Zworykin. While working with RCA, Zworykin had applied for a patent in 1923 for a rudimentary electronic television system but had been turned down by the patent office because there was no evidence that he could produce a workable device. He tried again in 1925 with some changes, including a way of producing color, and was eventually awarded a patent in 1928 for the technology, even though it didn't actually work. It was at that time that Farnsworth's developments went public.

Under Sarnoff's direction, RCA amassed a busy staff of patent lawyers who sued anybody stepping on what they considered their turf. They had hounded and financially ruined several inventors who wouldn't sell out to them; they figured they could make similar short work of young Farnsworth.

BATTLE OF THE STARS

When Farnsworth was granted a patent on *his* television system in 1928, Sarnoff declared war. RCA launched a publicity campaign lauding Zworykin as the "true father" of the coming television age and sent employees to harass Farnsworth when he made public appearances. It worked—potential licensors of the technology were confused about who actually held the rights.

Eventually, RCA's actions goaded Farnsworth into filing a patent clarification suit, an expensive proposition in which he would have to prove to a judge that his inventions (and the documentation of them) had come first. RCA also sued Farnsworth for patent infringement based on the application Zworykin had made in 1923 for his own original, unworkable system.

PHILO'S DOUGH

Farnsworth fought back—he hired excellent patent attorneys that he couldn't afford, hoping to recoup his losses from licensing when his patent was cleared. To raise money, he went overseas and sold the rights to his patents in England and Germany, where RCA couldn't easily interfere. (Cameras developed by Farnsworth broadcast the 1936 Olympics in Berlin.) Farnsworth's lawyers tracked down witnesses to back up his claims, including the science teacher he had run his ideas past in high school.

The testimony of science teacher Justin Tolman was enough to demolish RCA's patent infringement claim. After describing his conversation with the teenage Farnsworth, he pulled a rumpled, yellowed sheet of paper out of his coat pocket and explained: "This was made for me by Philo in early 1922." The drawing showed Farnsworth's idea for his "Image Dissector" camera, drawn more than a year before Zworykin had applied for his patent.

The court ruled for Farnsworth. He now had six clear patents and licensing rights to collect payment from any company—including RCA—that wanted to make television equipment based on them.

PLAYING DIRTY

RCA was determined to exact vengeance. While quietly negotiating the rights to use Farnsworth's patents, eventually agreeing to pay a million dollars up front and a royalty on every RCA receiver sold, the company embarked on a publicity blitz. Most notably, President Franklin Roosevelt appeared at their pavilion at the 1939 World's Fair in New York City. The event was aired to the handful of TV sets in existence at the time—one of the first-ever widespread broadcasts. Sarnoff gave a bold speech announcing RCA's intention to begin broadcasting regular TV programming, and claiming the company had developed the technology itself.

The press took him at his word and trumpeted RCA's "breakthrough" across the land. It was the first step in a long campaign to erase Farnsworth's name from the history of television, successfully replacing it with the names of Sarnoff and Zworykin. It worked so well that even now, with the record finally set straight even a postage stamp honoring Farnsworth, some sources still mistakenly list Zworykin as the "inventor of television."

By the time Farnsworth had definitively established his claims to his patents, it was 1939. However, the patents had been granted in 1928 and, since patents lasted for only 17 years at that point, his time to profit from his invention was more than half over. He was still deep in debt and ready to make some money. Television manufacturers were lining up to make deals. In a few more years, he expected that he would be not just solvent but fabulously wealthy.

BLITZKRIEG FLOP

Then something happened that was even bigger and even more financially disastrous than RCA's campaign: World War II. In 1941—year 13 of Farnsworth's 17-year patents—the Japanese bombed Pearl Harbor. When the United States entered the war, the government shut down the manufacture of "nonessential" products, especially those whose components and engineers were needed for the war effort. Like televisions.

As it sunk in to Farnsworth that his invention could never pay out, he went into a deep depression—he drank, stopped eating, and shrank to 100 pounds. It didn't help that Sarnoff convinced the Radio Television Manufacturers Association to honor *him* as "the "Father of Television," and instructed his employees to always add "Inventor of Television" to any public mention of Zworykin.

"If it weren't for Philo T. Farnsworth, we'd still be eating frozen radio dinners." —Johnny Carson

MOVING FORWARD

The war ended in 1945, and TV manufacturing and development resumed, but Farnsworth's patents had expired. Adding insult to injury was what he saw being broadcast. Farnsworth had cherished a belief that his invention would lead to widespread education, culture, and understanding of other people. Instead it featured commercials for cars, headache remedies, and beer, sandwiched between soap operas, game shows, and wrestling matches.

With the help of his family and new ideas for inventions, Farnsworth eventually regained his emotional equilibrium. He went on to hold almost 300 patents on products as diverse as a baby incubator, a gastroscope, an electron microscope, and even a small nuclear fusion device.

INTO THE FUTURE

Finally, two years before he died, Farnsworth was able to experience a father's pride as his ne'er-do-well child lived up to everything he had hoped. On July 20, 1969, the inventor joined much of the world in watching the live broadcast as astronauts stepped onto the moon for the very first time. When it was over, he turned to his wife and said, "This has made it all worthwhile."

Years of disappointment had soured Farnsworth on television, and he rarely watched it before his death in 1971. However, he did appear on TV twice. Once was for an interview at the local station in Rigby, Idaho, near where he had invented TV as a boy. The other was as the mystery guest "Dr. X" on *I've Got a Secret*, in which celebrity contestants attempted to guess his accomplishment using only yes-and-no questions. When the panel couldn't guess his secret, he won $80 and a carton of Winston cigarettes.

*   *   *

MUNCH TIME!

While filming a scene in Baltimore for *Homicide: Life on the Street*, Richard Belzer, who played Detective Munch, was standing on a street in police costume when a real-life shoplifter turned the corner and happened upon him. The robber dropped his loot and said, "Oh no, it's Munch!" Security officers quickly apprehended the man.

Smallville was originally conceived as a Batman series—*Gotham*, about young Bruce Wayne.

POLITICAL TV TIMELINE

On April 30, 1939, Franklin Roosevelt became the first U.S. president to appear on TV, as part of a test broadcast from the New York World's Fair. It was probably the last time a politician would show up on television without slamming an opponent or praising himself.

1948: A few months before the November presidential election, Republican challenger Thomas Dewey was comfortably leading incumbent Harry Truman. Dewey's advisor, advertising veteran Rosser Reeves, urged Dewey to record campaign commercials to air on television in the competitive districts that had TV service—he could reach thousands of voters for relatively little cost. Dewey rejected the idea as "undignified" and chose to sit on his lead. Meanwhile, Truman went on a whistle-stop campaign train tour. Dewey's lead eroded and he lost the election.

1950: The first politician to truly recognize the persuasive power of filmed advertisements was, not surprisingly, a former ad executive. Running for a Senate seat in 1950, William Benton of Connecticut set up kiosks with rear-projection screens in shopping centers and on street corners to play his campaign commercials. It was even more practical than buying time on broadcast television, since even voters who didn't have a TV would see his ado while shopping. Benton was elected, narrowly defeating Prescott Bush (father of future president George H.W. Bush).

1952: While Democrats were riding a wave of postwar prosperity to congressional power, so Republicans hired Rosser Reeves to counter their slogan, "You never had it so good." Reeves came up with a television advertising blitz called "Eisenhower Answers America," featuring former general and presidential candidate Dwight Eisenhower taking "off-the-cuff" questions from everyday Americans (the questions were actually scripted). These were the first-ever presidential campaign ads to air in the United States. Eisenhower's opponent, Adlai Stevenson, hit television, too—with 30-minute-long speeches. They were so long and difficult to schedule that they aired far less often than Eisenhower's brief spots.

That same year, another politician forever altered the relationship between politics and television. Eisenhower's running mate, Richard Nixon, was accused of accepting illegal campaign contributions, so he went on TV to appeal directly to the public, saying that the only gift he'd received was a black-and-white dog named Checkers, for his children. The "Checkers Speech" was seen on TV and heard on radio by an estimated 60 million people, and elicited an outpouring of sympathy that historians say helped lock up the election for Eisenhower and Nixon.

1960: By this time, 90 percent of American households owned a TV set. Historians say that may have made the difference in the debate between presidential candidates John F. Kennedy and Richard Nixon. Kennedy was more media savvy than Nixon—he knew enough to wear makeup before appearing on TV during the first-ever presidential debate, for example. Nixon, recovering from an illness at the time, didn't—and he appeared haggard compared to the confident, youthful-looking Kennedy (who was actually only four years younger than Nixon). Polls indicated that people who watched the debate on TV thought Kennedy won; those who listened on the radio—a much smaller audience—declared Nixon the victor. Kennedy ultimately won the election by a hair.

1964: Although it ran only once—on NBC on September 7, 1964—the infamous "Daisy Ad," created by the Doyle Dane Bernbach agency, helped propel Lyndon Johnson to a landslide victory over Barry Goldwater in that year's presidential race. The commercial featured a little girl standing in a field plucking petals off a daisy, and culminated with a countdown and nuclear mushroom cloud, implying that Goldwater couldn't be trusted with his finger on the button of U.S. atomic weapons. ABC and CBS never aired the ad officially, but did show it in news programs—at no cost to the Johnson campaign—while reporting on the controversy.

1968: A turning point in American politics, the 1968 presidential election was the first time that the politicians themselves became highly polished products. Roger Ailes, a media consultant to three presidents and future president of Fox News, said at the time, "This is the beginning of a whole new concept. This is it. This is the way they'll be elected forevermore. The next guys up will have to be performers." Ted Rogers, media consultant for returning presidential candidate Richard Nixon, heard the message loud and clear. He recommended a full-on image makeover for Nixon—by fattening him up with "milkshakes, eggs, and butter" and ensuring plenty of rest to make Nixon look healthier. Nixon also realized the power of TV, so in addition to Rogers and Ailes, he hired a team of TV consultants, who devised a series of weekly televised sessions between Nixon and a hand-picked panel of sympathetic Republican citizens asking scripted questions. They were designed to make Nixon—who could come off as grumpy or aloof—look more informal (and, just to be safe, no close-ups of Nixon were allowed). Nixon was elected president that fall.

1976: Following the Watergate scandal that ended Nixon's presidency in 1974, conventional wisdom said that Americans were in no mood for another career politician as president. Result: The birth of the "regular guy" political advertisement. Democratic candidate Jimmy Carter, a peanut farmer and former Georgia governor, starred in his ads wearing jeans and a work shirt, standing out in the fields. Carter won the election.

1980: By 1980 Ailes's prediction regarding the power of TV had come true—the winning presidential candidate was a former actor. Former B-movie star and California governor Ronald Reagan was elected, and television had played an important role. Reagan's folksy, relentlessly optimistic ads declared it "morning in America" and asked voters if they were "better off now than they were four years ago."

1988: With Republican vice president George H.W. Bush facing an uphill battle against the insurgent candidacy of Democratic Massachusetts governor Michael Dukakis, it was Ailes, then Bush's media consultant, who came to the rescue. Ailes approved an ad that painted Dukakis as soft on crime. It featured convicted murderer Willie Horton, who, while serving a life sentence in Massachusetts, was released on the weekend-pass program Dukakis approved—and then stabbed a man and raped his fiancée. "The only question," Ailes reportedly told Bush staffers, "is whether we depict Willie Horton with a knife in his hand or without it."

1992: For the first time in decades, the presidential race featured a viable third-party candidate: billionaire Texas businessman H. Ross Perot, running as an independent against incumbent Republican president George H. W. Bush and Democratic governor Bill Clinton. Rather than pay for 30-second commercials, Perot harkened back to Adlai Stevenson's long-form approach and bought 30-minute chunks of network time to air infomercial-style programs that mapped out his plans to improve the economy. Drawing as many as 10.5 million viewers in prime time, Perot even pulled ahead of Bush and Clinton in the polls at one point. He ultimately garnered 20 percent of the vote.

2010: Pundits predicted that the era of political advertising on television was coming to a close, and that the new consensus-building medium would be the Internet, via sites like Facebook and YouTube. In fact, presidential candidate Barack Obama won the 2008 election in part by using social-networking sites to attract and organize young, tech-savvy voters. But television in politics is hardly dead. Spending on political ads in the 2010 midterm elections topped $4 billion—crushing the $2.8 billion record set two years earlier. Two-thirds of that $4 billion went to television airtime.

*   *   *

LITTLE BUDDY

In the first season of *Gilligan's Island*, the theme song's lyrics listed five of the show's seven characters and ended with "...and the rest, here on *Gilligan's Island*." Dawn Wells and Russell Johnson, who played Mary Ann and the Professor, complained to studio executives that their characters should be included in the song too. The studio refused, explaining that changing the song would be too costly. But when the second season premiered, the last line was changed to "...the Professor and Mary Ann, here on *Gilligan's Island*." So why did the execs change their minds? Because Bob Denver (Gilligan) had threatened to have his own name moved to the end of the credits, diminishing his draw as the show's star, if the studio didn't give in to Wells and Johnson. The rest of the cast didn't find out about Denver's bold move until 20 years after the series went off the air.

LET'S GET *LOST*, PART III

According to Lost's producers, the series' two main themes are science versus faith, and fate versus free will. With that in mind, here's our third and final chapter in explaining just what the heck was going on on Lost (2004–10). (Part II is on page 312.)

QUE SERA SERA
When the time-traveling island strands Sayid in 1977 (during season 5), he's captured by Dharma, which thinks he's a Hostile. Young Ben (about 12 years old) goes to visit Sayid, and Sayid convinces Ben to free him. Once safely away, Sayid shoots Ben in an attempt to keep him from growing up and causing trouble. But Kate thinks it's wrong to let a little boy die—even a potentially evil one—so she takes Ben to the only people on the island who can save him: the Hostiles/Others, led by Richard.

Meanwhile, Jack figures out a way to send everybody back to the future: Blow up that abandoned nuclear bomb. Faraday does some math and determines that it *might* work. Jack is convinced it *will* work, even though it could blow up the entire island. So Juliet sacrifices her life by blowing up the bomb. (Why Juliet? Elizabeth Mitchell had to leave the show because she had a role in ABC's remake of *V*.) This, then, becomes the "incident" Desmond once explained that requires Swan personnel to repeatedly enter the Numbers and keep that electromagnetic pocket at bay. The *past* that the Lostaways learned about in their *present* was actually caused by their *future* actions in the *past*!

TORN BETWEEN TWO TIMELINES
Season 6 begins with Jack Shephard...on board Oceanic Flight 815 traveling from Sydney to Los Angeles on September 22, 2004. The plane hits turbulence...but this time the plane *doesn't* crash. And the Lostaways appear to have no knowledge of the island events that seemingly never happened. Did Jack's nuclear-bomb trick work? It appears so. In this new reality, the island lies on the ocean floor.

After the new Flight 815 lands in L.A., the Lostaways are the same people, but their pasts are different: Jack has a son he is try-

---

The Dharma Initiative's logo (on *Lost*) is actually a Taoist symbol called a *bagua*.

ing to reconnect with. Juliet is alive...and is Jack's ex-wife. Hurley still won the lottery, but he's happy this time around and owns the Mr. Cluck's Chicken Shack chain. Even Ben is different—he's a history teacher and, *gasp*, a nice guy! The storytelling is also different. Whereas the first three seasons featured "flashbacks" to the characters' pasts, and seasons 4 and 5 featured "flash-forwards," season 6 includes "flash-sideways" between this newly created, non-plane-crash universe of 2004 and the previous seasons' timeline, continuing in parallel, to chronicle the endgame between Jack and *Lost*'s final villain, the Smoke Monster.

THE SMOKE MONSTER

Well, it *is* the Smoke Monster, but it's also *not* the Smoke Monster. When the Ajira Airlines plane landed on the island in season 5, Locke's corpse was resurrected. Only he was different. More confident. *Badder*. It turns out that this is *not* John Locke, but the Smoke Monster, nicknamed the Man in Black (MIB) on the island, or "UnLocke" by *Lost* fans. MIB is a shapeshifting entity (played in his "human" form by Titus Welliver) that has appeared on the island in many forms, including as Ben's dead mother and Jack's dead father. While MIB can take on many forms, he can't leave the island.

MIB is the brother of another mysterious figure (this one has a name): Jacob. Their mother was shipwrecked on the island many centuries ago, but when Jacob and MIB were babies, a strange woman killed their mother and raised them as her own. The boys eventually grew estranged, and when MIB found out that the woman who raised them wasn't their mother, he killed her. Jacob then attacked MIB (a biblical allusion to Jacob wrestling an immortal deity) and threw him into a glowing stream (the same glowing body of water near the time-travel wheel, and called "the Light of the Island") that apparently provides the island with its magical powers.

It's also what gives MIB *his* magical powers. MIB's body was dead, but his consciousness inhabited a shapeshifting Smoke Monster. The "Adam and Eve" skeletons that Jack finds in the first season? Mother and MIB. Jacob later gives everlasting life to Richard, who came to the island in the 1800s as a slave on the ship the *Black Rock*. In return, Richard agrees to help Jacob protect all subsequent island inhabitants from MIB, no matter what form he might take.

THE LIGHT

After the nuke blows up in 1977, Jack, Kate, Sawyer, Hurley, Sayid, Jin, and Juliet (among others) wind up on the island in 2007, shortly after Ajira 316 crashed. Juliet soon dies from her nuclear-bomb injuries. Then they discover that Jacob brought them all there as "candidates" to replace him as the island's protector. He gave each Lostaway a secret nudge here and a push there, placing them all onto the paths that would eventually put them on Oceanic Flight 815. Jacob's plan unravels when MIB, now taking the form of Locke (UnLocke) coerces Ben into killing Jacob. According to their mother's rules, Jacob and MIB cannot kill each other—Ben was the loophole that MIB had been looking for for so many centuries. With Jacob dead, MIB would finally be able to take control of and destroy the island, then rule the world.

UnLocke offers each of the Lostaways what they've always desired...in return for helping him get off the island. But as Jacob once explained to Richard, the island is like a cork: "It is the only thing keeping the darkness where it belongs. If the Light goes out here, it goes out everywhere." In short, if that cork is removed, MIB—the darkness—will wreak hell on Earth.

THE FINAL SHOWDOWN

After the Lostaways learn they are the candidates, they find out that each of them was assigned a number by Jacob. You guessed it: 4, 8, 15, 16, 23, and 42. For Jack, though, the point is no longer to find answers, but to finally accept that they actually *were* brought there for a reason. However, Jack realizes that his destiny is not to become the island's leader, but its savior. It's his job to keep the cork on tight. He throws UnLocke into the Heart of the Island, the same place where, centuries earlier, MIB was turned into the Smoke Monster. Now MIB is finally *really* dead, but Jack is mortally wounded. He tells Hurley that it is now *his* job to protect the island. Hurley becomes the new Jacob, and Ben, having repented, becomes Hurley's second in command.

Back in the sideways universe, Desmond and Charlie find each of the Lostaways and place them in some kind of life-changing situation, causing each one to figure "it" out. Figure what out? That the Lostaways are—or *were*—the most important people in each other's lives. In the show's final moments, which take place in an interfaith church where the Lostaways have gathered, Christian tells Jack that they are all dead. Everything that happened on the island really happened; the sideways universe was just a place for them to meet up in the afterlife so they could all move on.

THE END

The final flash-sideways finds the real Jack stumbling through the island's jungle. Jack lies down to die in the same patch of grass where we first met him in season 1. He smiles, knowing his friends have escaped and that the Light of the Island still shines. He accomplished what Jacob began and what the Others and Dharma continued—he changed the equation and saved the world.

* * *

IT'S BACK!

After three little-watched seasons, Fox canceled the animated series *Family Guy* in 2002. But reruns on Cartoon Network brought in so many viewers and so many DVD sales that the network revived the show in 2005. The first episode of the revived series opened with a fourth-wall-breaking scene in which the main character, Pete Griffin, tells his family that "*Family Guy* has been canceled," and that the only way for the show to return would be if Fox cut some of its other series. Peter then lists *every* show that came—and went—on Fox during *Family Guy*'s three-year absence. "We've just got to accept the fact that Fox has to make room for terrific shows like *Dark Angel*, *Titus*, *Undeclared*, *Action*, *That '80s Show*, *Wonderfalls*, *Fastlane*, *Andy Richter Controls the Universe*, *Skin*, *Girls Club*, *Cracking Up*, *The Pitts*, *Firefly*, *Get Real*, *Freaky Links*, *Wanda at Large*, *Costello*, *The Lone Gunmen*, *A Minute with Stan Hooper*, *Normal Ohio*, *Pasadena*, *Harsh Realm*, *Keen Eddie*, *The Street*, *American Embassy*, *Cedric the Entertainer*, *The Tick*, *Louie*, and *Greg the Bunny*." His wife Lois remarks, "Is there no hope?" Peter: "Well, I suppose if *all* those shows go down the tubes, we might have a shot."

On *The Partridge Family*, the band played their first concert at Caesar's Palace.

ANSWER PAGES

FIRST LINES QUIZ
(Answers for page 36)

1. *The Brady Bunch*
2. *South Park*
3. *Star Trek: The Next Generation*
4. *Lost*
5. *Futurama*
6. *Sesame Street*
7. *Charlie's Angels*
8. *All in the Family*
9. *The Dick Van Dyke Show*
10. *ALF*
11. *Twin Peaks*
12. *Scrubs*
13. *The Cosby Show*

UNUSUAL TV PETS QUIZ
(Answers for page 100)

1. q) pp), 2. e) bb), 3. j) oo), 4. m) ee), 5. o) aa), 6. i) jj), 7. a) mm), 8. t) dd), 9. p) ii), 10. r) ss)—Jub-Jub is Selma Bouvier's pet, 11. k) nn), 12. f) tt), 13. s) gg), 14. b) kk), 15. c) ff), 16. h) cc), 17. g) rr)—On *Dinosaurs*, the humanlike characters watched a show called *Mr. Ugh*, a parody of *Mister Ed*, in which a dinosaur kept a primitive human as a pet, who one day shockingly discovers that it could talk, 18. d) ll), 19. n) hh) 20. d) ll), 21. o) hh), 22. l) qq)

THEME SONG SINGERS
(Answers for page 108)

1. h; 2. m; 3. n; 4. l; 5. i; 6. r; 7. a; 8. e; 9. j; 10. c; 11. f; 12. q; 13. o; 14. b; 15. s; 16. g; 17. p; 18. d; 19. k; 20. t

TV PORTMANTEAU QUIZ
(Answers for page 161)

1) *The OC* + *CSI Miami* = *The OCSI: Miami*

Q: Who provided the original voice of the Geico Gecko? **A:** Kelsey Grammer.

2) *You Bet Your Life* + *Life Goes On* = *You Bet Your Life Goes On*

3) *How I Met Your Mother* + *My Mother the Car* = *How I Met Your Mother the Car*

4) *CSI: NY* + *NYPD Blue* = *CSI: NYPD Blue*

5) *Playboy After Dark* + *Dark Shadows* = *Playboy After Dark Shadows*

6) *Gentle Ben* + *Ben Casey* = *Gentle Ben Casey*

7) *Newhart* + *Hart to Hart* = *Newhart to Hart*

8) *Kate and Allie* + *Ally McBeal* = *Kate and Allie McBeal*

9) *Mary Hartman, Mary Hartman* + *Manimal* = *Mary Hartman, Mary Hartmanimal*

10) *Room 222* + *24* = *Room 224*

11) *Samantha Who?* + *Who's the Boss?* = *Samantha Who's the Boss?*

12) *Futurama* + *Mama's Family* = *Futuramama's Family*

A COMMON QUIZ
(Answers for page 232)

1) They all guest-starred on *Friends*.

2) They are the only four shows in history that, at different points in their runs, finished the weekly ratings in both first and last place.

3) Each show made its debut immediately after the Super Bowl (1985, 1988, 1987, 1984).

4) Former child and sitcom star Ron Howard directed each of these eight actors in Oscar-nominated performances. The two who won: Ameche (Best Supporting Actor for *Cocoon* in 1985) and Connelly (Best Supporting Actress for *A Beautiful Mind* in 2001).

5) Each bowled a perfect game.

6) They played Pete, Berg, and Sharon—the two guys and a girl on *Two Guys, a Girl and a Pizza Place* (ABC, 1998–2001). The pizza place was played by Stage 20 at 20th Century Fox Studios.

7) It's unclear exactly where these shows take place. Judging by the weather, *Hill Street Blues* is set in a northeastern city somewhere between Baltimore and Buffalo. *Malcolm* appears to take place in California, but for some reason, they're only three hours away from Alabama. The *Scrubs* hospital is somewhere in

California—the cast and crew said they were in "San DiFrangeles." And *The Tick* solemnly protects The City, wherever that is.

8) All were canceled by the broadcast network where they first aired (*Baywatch* and *Punky Brewster* by NBC; *Charles in Charge* and *Hee Haw* by CBS). But they lived on, because all continued in first-run syndication, sold directly to local stations.

9) Actors from all of these shows dated co-stars who played their family members. Don Johnson dated his *Nash Bridges* on-screen daughter, Jodi Lyn O'Keefe. Joely Richardson dated her *Nip/Tuck* son John Hensley. Barry Williams was linked to both his *Brady* mom Florence Henderson and *Brady* sister Maureen McCormick. And *Dexter* foster siblings Michael C. Hall and Jennifer Carpenter were married in 2008.

10) Paul McCartney, Ringo Starr, and George Harrison all guest-starred on *The Simpsons*...on separate occasions.

11) None of them ever won an Emmy Award for acting.

THE NICKNAME QUIZ
(Answers for page 295)

1. d), 2. m), 3. p), 4. c), 5. i), 6. o), 7. b), 8. k), 9. j), 10. n), 11. l), 12. a), 13. q), 14. f), 15. t), 16. h), 17. e), 18. r), 19. s), 20. g)

TV QUIZ: THE NAME GAME
(Answers for page 360)

HIGH SCHOOLS
1. e; 2. a; 3. b; 4. f; 5. g; 6. c; 7. d; 8. i; 9. h

WORKPLACE
10. c) Darrin Stevens reports to Larry Tate at the McMann/Tate Advertising Company. (Don Draper works for Sterling Cooper Advertising; Michael Steadman works for an ad agency known only as DAA.)

11. a) On *Sex and the City*, Carrie Bradshaw writes a weekly column for the *New York Star*. (Oscar Madison of *The Odd Couple*

works at the *New York Herald*; the *New York Ledger* is a fictional
newspaper in the *Law & Order* franchise.)

12. b) On *Gilmore Girls*, Lorelai Gilmore co-owns the Dragonfly
Inn bed & breakfast with chef Sookie St. James. (Dick Loudon
runs the Stratford Inn in Vermont; Julia Sugarbaker manages Sugarbaker Designs from a Southern mansion that looks like an inn.)

13. a) Betty works at *Mode*. (*Blush* is the fictional fashion magazine where *Just Shoot Me* is set; *Waif* is a satire of a '90s fashion
magazine on the cartoon series *Daria*.)

14. b) Laverne and Shirley work as bottle-cappers at the Shotz
Brewery in Milwaukee. (Assembling plastic toys at Wellman Plastics is one of many jobs held by Roseanne on *Roseanne*; Mel's is
the diner from *Alice*.)

HANGOUTS

15. The Regal Beagle
16. MacLaren's
17. Central Perk
18. Café Nervosa
19. Monk's Café
20. Gary's Old Towne Tavern

DOCTORS AND HOSPITALS

21. h; **22.** c; **23.** g; **24.** a; **25.** d; **26.** e; **27.** f; **28.** b

FIRST LINES QUIZ #2

(Answers for page 387)

1. *Buffy the Vampire Slayer*
2. *Cheers*
3. *The Office*
4. *How I Met
Your Mother*
5. *King of the Hill*
6. *Nip/Tuck*
7. *Desperate Housewives*
8. *Sex and the City*

9. *The Big Bang Theory*
10. *Home Improvement*
11. *Little House on the Prairie*
12. *The Wonder Years*
13. *Friends*
14. *My Three Sons*
15. *24*
16. *The Mary Tyler Moore
Show*

First American TV ads ever aired in Russia: Michael Jackson's 1988 Pepsi commercials.

"MAKE IT WORK"
(Answers for page 422)

1. The Price Is Right
2. Kojak
3. Survivor
4. Emeril Live
5. The Smothers Brothers Comedy Hour
6. Get Smart
7. Project Runway
8. Alice
9. Who Wants to Be a Millionaire?
10. Happy Days
11. That '70s Show
12. Hogan's Heroes
13. The Addams Family
14. Hill Street Blues
15. Welcome Back, Kotter
16. The Jack Benny Program
17. The CBS Evening News
18. Good Times
19. The Burns and Allen Show
20. Mork and Mindy
21. The Honeymooners
22. See It Now
23. The Outer Limits
24. Lost in Space
25. Ren and Stimpy
26. Extras
27. You Bet Your Life
28. In Living Color
29. The Larry Sanders Show
30. The Office
31. SpongeBob SquarePants
32. Baretta
33. Friday Night Lights
34. Star Trek: The Next Generation
35. 30 Rock
36. Heroes

BIKE AND LOAFER
(Answers for page 464)

1. Scarecrow and Mrs. King
2. Nanny and the Professor
3. The Governor & J.J.
4. Law & Order
5. Tenspeed and Brown Shoe
6. Chico and the Man
7. Jake and the Fatman
8. Hardcastle and McCormick
9. Simon & Simon
10. Parks and Recreation
11. My Wife and Kids
12. Freaks and Geeks
13. Rob & Big
14. Brothers and Sisters
15. Sex and the City
16. Will & Grace
17. The Bold and the Beautiful
18. Sonny and Cher

Actor Tony Dow (Wally on *Leave it to Beaver*) became a sculptor. He has a piece in the Louvre

UNCLE JOHN'S
BATHROOM READER
CLASSIC SERIES

Find these and other great titles from the *Uncle John's Bathroom Reader* Classic Series online at **www.bathroomreader.com**. Or contact us at:

Bathroom Readers' Institute
P.O. Box 1117
Ashland, OR 97520
(888) 488-4642

THE LAST PAGE

FELLOW BATHROOM READERS:
The fight for good bathroom reading should never be taken loosely—we must do our duty and sit firmly for what we believe in, even while the rest of the world is taking potshots at us.

We'll be brief. Now that we've proven we're not simply a flush-in-the-pan, we invite you to take the plunge: Sit Down and Be Counted! Log on to *www.bathroomreader.com* and earn a permanent spot on the BRI honor roll!

If you like reading our books...
VISIT THE BRI'S WEBSITE!
www.bathroomreader.com

- Visit "The Throne Room"—a great place to read!
- Receive our irregular newsletters via e-mail
- Order additional *Bathroom Readers*
- Face us on Facebook
- Tweet us on Twitter
- Blog us on our blog

Go with the Flow...

Well, we're out of space, and when you've gotta go, you've gotta go. Tanks for all your support. Hope to hear from you soon. Meanwhile, remember...

Keep on flushin'!